Nothing Like a Dame

ALSO BY THORA HIRD:

Thora Hird's Book of Home Truths
Thora Hird's Book of Bygones

Nothing Like a Dame

Scene and Hird
Is It Thora?

Thora Hird
with Liz Barr

GRAND RAPIDS, MICHIGAN 49530 USA

ZONDERVAN™

Nothing Like a Dame

Scene and Hird
First published in Great Britain in 1976 by W. H. Allen.
First published in Fount paperbacks in 1995.

Is It Thora?
First published in Great Britain in 1996 by HaperCollins*Publishers*
First published in Fount paperbacks in 1997.

Requests for information should be addressed to:

Zondervan, *Grand Rapids, Michigan 49530*

A catalogue record for this book is available from the British Library.

ISBN 0 00 710766 8

Printed and bound in the United Kingdom

05 06 07 08 /OMN/ 10 9 8 7 6 5

Contents

Preface

It always amazes me how fast time disappears, and as I look back over my eighty years or so, I'm grateful for the time that I have been given. Of course, we can't control time – I've found that even taking the battery out of my wall clock doesn't stop each precious moment ticking away! Maybe it's only when you reach my time of life, though, that you realize just how precious each moment really is. Who would have thought that my first theatrical debut at the age of six weeks would be the beginning of such a long career! I am lucky, aren't I?

The Bible says that there is a time for mourning and a time for dancing, a time to laugh and a time to cry. I've had my share of tears, but I've had a lot of laughter too. I really do believe that laughter is God's greatest medicine. There's nothing I like better than having a good laugh, apart from making other people laugh with me. The sound of hilarity still brings me out in goose bumps. I suppose it's one of the things I've devoted my life to.

I've had many precious moments that I hold close. Times with my wonderful American grandchildren, Daisy Ann and James Scott Torme, and the day I hid the fairy shoes in their back garden in Beverly Hills as a surprise. Moments with my own daughter, Janette, and in particular the wonderful feelings of great pride when I saw how much time and energy she devoted to helping others. These are the memories that have helped me through even the most difficult of times.

Of course it's Scottie who was always the closest to my heart. My darling husband died in 1994, but he's still here in many ways. Well, you can't forget fifty-eight years of marriage that quickly, can you? There are so many memories swishing around in my head that it's sometimes difficult to believe he's actually gone. He was my business partner, and my driver, and always helped me make decisions about work. He was my nurse, chief cook, bottle-washer and butler when my arthritis started to frustrate me and my fingers wouldn't work properly first thing in the morning. I simply could not have done what I did without him, and for a time I wondered how I would be able to carry on at all.

Yet life did carry on without Scottie. I was determined not too feel sorry for myself and spend the rest of my days cleaning my nice copper kettle that sits on the mantelpiece. The garden we shared needed tending too, but an actress never retires until she's not wanted any more. Fortunately for me, the telephone has never stopped ringing.

All manner of jobs are offered, and I accept the ones that I feel are 'me'. I don't have Scottie to ask advice from any more, but I seem surrounded by friends in the business who are very supportive. When I really can't arrive at a decision I phone Janette who is always able to give me some straightforward help in deciding.

As time moves on like the waves on the seashore that I love to watch, I realize that there's no going back – what's done is done. I'm just hoping that the good Lord is pleased with how I have used the talents he invested in me all those years ago. When I meet him face to face I shall say, 'Hello, Lord, it's me, Thora. Did I do all right then?'

Thora Hird
March 2001

SCENE AND HIRD

Dedication

I have written this book, basically, for my dear American grandchildren, Daisy Ann and James Scott Tormé, so that when they are older they can read it and learn all about *me* . . . from *me*.

I would also like to use the book to show my sincere gratitude for having been blessed with a wonderful mother and father, who not only taught me most of what I know about the precarious business known as the theatrical profession but who between 'em bestowed upon me a sense of humour that has sustained me sufficiently to remain in it!

For a super brother and a good man, Neville, who could make me laugh more than anyone I've ever known.

It's also for Scottie . . . my husband, who escorted me out of the Wesleyan Chapel, my arm firmly through his (to make sure he didn't get away) thirty-eight years ago . . . for better or worse. Poor soul! It's been an endurance test but he says he's getting used to it now.

For my daughter, Janette, the most loving and charitable person I have ever met, who apart from being a splendid wife and mother manages to be an excellent Sunday School teacher, works for the blind babies, helps to save the mustangs and the whales, supports the Schools for Red Cloud Indian children, works for free spaying for animals, teenagers with emotional problems, is on the board of the Haemophilia Foundation and helps to save the Wilderness mountain regions and wildlife and uses white toilet rolls in each of her six toilets because, apparently, coloured paper poisons the fish! Dearest Jan . . . don't ever change!

Phew! And that's the first page done.

Contents

1

Overture and beginners, please!

I was born on a Sunday, when the church bells were ringing. My brother Neville was born on a Sunday, when the church bells were ringing. He was born just before Morning Service and I was born just before Evening Service – not on the same Sunday of course. He appeared one year and nine months prior to my arrival.

Knowing him as I do I think he was born twenty-one months before me so that he could look the world over, approve of it and make sure it was 'safe' for 'Our Kid', 'George' or 'Horace'. These are the names he always called me – I can't think why, as I am very proud of being extremely feminine!

I remember the love and devotion that shone in my mother's eyes when she recalled the church bells; it was such that, as a little girl, I liked to feel that they had rung *because* Neville and I had been born. There was no feeling of conceit about this, and if there had been it would have been daft because we were *chapel* not *church*.

I used to swank at school about the church bells bit, not in a 'clever clogs' way, but in a rather grateful way. I know I used to feel privately sorry for any of my school chums who'd had the misfortune to be born at five-to-one on a Tuesday or twenty minutes past three on a Saturday.

There was something else I rather enjoyed swanking about at school – it was that my mother's birthday was in April, my own in May, my dad's in June, my sister Olga's in July and my brother Neville's in August!

That statement was always received with open-mouthed amazement, and many times I was requested to 'Go on, Hirdie, and tell So-and-So about the birthdays at your house!' Whereupon I would oblige, with pleasure. Encouraged sufficiently I would tell 'em about the church bells as an encore!

My childhood, my home life, and my parents can sincerely be headed or entitled The Happiest in the World – and that *is* swanking, so I'll settle for *one* of The Happiest in the World. But I adamantly stick to that!

My mother, Mary Jane Mayor, was the daughter of a fisherman. He had a trawler and, along with my uncles, trawled for shrimps in Morecambe Bay.

My mother was born in Morecambe so comes under the heading of a 'Sandgrown 'un' – and because I was born in Morecambe, so do I.

She had a really beautiful mezzo-soprano voice and always sang the solo 'I know that my Redeemer Liveth' when *The Messiah* was performed at the Green Street Wesleyan Chapel.

When she was seventeen, she bravely left the Milliners and Drapers where she was employed and 'went into the business', as the theatrical profession is so often called (*another* profession has been called 'the business' but thank heavens they now refer to that activity as being 'on the job'!).

However, as I was saying, my mother went into the theatrical profession with the good wishes of all and the blessing of the Wesleyan Minister.

The choir presented her with a really lovely wooden trunk, decorated with embossed leather. In addition, the Minister presented her with some advice; he also assured her that if ever, during the precarious life she was about to embark on, she was in any trouble, she could always return home – and sing in the choir! I am happy to report that when she did return to Morecambe to live, it was neither because she was in trouble nor because she had led a precarious life. It was because in the years between leaving and returning she had met, fallen in love with and married James Henry Hird.

James Henry Hird was born in Todmorden, the town which boasted that half of its Town Hall is in Lancashire, the other half in Yorkshire. My father's personal boast was that he was born on the Lancashire side.

I am like my father in many ways, one in particular being my true love of Lancashire. I, too, am proud of being a Lancastrian – yes, even prouder of that than the church bells incident!

Although James Henry was born in Lancashire his forbears came from Fifeshire, and as my mother's family were believed to have descended from Viking stock, I'm not sure what that makes me and my brother Neville. But I don't wonder the church bells rang – perhaps they were sounding the alarm!

Prior to Miss Marie Mayor and James Henry Hird marrying, they had met in a touring company. In those days, artistes performed 'one night stands', and were on tour for many months. When I think of the work involved during these touring seasons, I feel I can never grumble about my own work.

I don't think there was a county in the British Isles in which my parents had not 'played'. As my brother and I grew older in school years, we would sit around the fire with our school chums, drinking cocoa and eating my mother's apple pie or currant pasty, while Marie Mayor would relate witty, pathetic and interesting stores of when she and Dad were 'on tour'.

We never wearied of these tales, which my mother told so well – about the business manager 'doing a bunk' and leaving them stranded without money; or about the young dandies who would crowd the stage door waiting for the girls, with bouquets of flowers. In fact, my mother swore that my father would never have proposed had it not been for the fact that one young gentleman waited for her at the stage door for four nights in succession, *avec* flowers!

I used to love the expression on her dear face as she came out with the 'curtain line' – 'so, on the fifth day, your father took me on a picnic and during our meal, he *proposed*.'

Good old James Henry, he showed 'em. You don't compete with a lad from Todmorden and get away with it, especially if he's born on the Lancashire side of the Town Hall!

2

Playing for real

I wasn't born in a trunk, a theatrical skip or hamper, I was born comfortably and snugly in bed. However, I did make my first appearance 'on the boards', 'on the green' or in everyday parlance 'on the stage', at the tender age of eight weeks old!

My mother was appearing in a drama at the Royalty Theatre as the young heroine who had been 'done wrong' by the Squire's son, I played the 'unfortunate result!' My father was the director. I had no audition. I was cast as the result of three short words which were directed at my mother by my father, 'Take *HER* on!' The *HER* was me – my first and only engagement I ever got through influence! According to records I didn't overplay, cry, or wet myself – I slept during the entire proceedings!

But eventually my parents decided to stay put, and made a permanent home for themselves in Morecambe. My father always had a fair share of initiative and was never afraid of hard work. Consequently, he was able to get a job which enabled him and mother to start a home of their own instead of the continual 'digs' they had lived in on tour.

Being a splendid swimmer, when offered the job of

manager and swimming instructor at the appropriately named Bare Bathing Pool he 'dived in at the deep end' as you might say!

Determined to better himself, his next job was stage manager on the West End Pier, and then with a foot on the next step of the ladder, he ascended one rung higher still when he became stage manager at the Alhambra, which in those days presented most of the biggest variety turns outside London.

From the Alhambra he moved onwards and upwards again to become stage manager of the Royalty Theatre. As stage manager of the Royalty, the house next door at Number 6, Cheapside, went in with his wage. Of course, up to this juncture I wasn't even a gleam in his eye.

I still smile when I recall my mother telling me how, after six years of marriage, they were *delighted* to discover a baby was on the way. That was Olga. And how, fifteen months after Olga was born, they were *delirious* to discover that another baby was on the way. That was Neville. And how, twelve months after Neville was born, they were *demented* to discover there was yet another baby on the way. Yes, that was *ME*!

3

Just Cheapside

Thora Hird, 6 Cheapside, Morecambe, Lancashire, England, Europe, The World. That is what I would write on my very own very personal possessions – such as the flyleaf of my Schoolgirl's Diary, my Sunday School prizes which were always books, the inside flap of my leather school bag, the bottom of my varnished wood pencil box and on many other very private and very personal possessions too numerous to mention.

Mind you, I grew out of the 'Europe' and 'The World' bit by the time I was about nine, but I'm quite sure it was only because I would have been satisfied – no, more than that, *proud* to have gone through life with the one word after my name. *Cheapside*!

I enjoyed the sound of the word. In fact, I was so proud of it, I swanked about it, defended it, scrubbed half of it (which I'll come to in a minute) and sincerely loved every inch of it, even the warm coloured *Yorkshire* stone flags that were used as a pavement – and that's praise indeed from a Lancashire woman!

Cheapside. Not Cheapside Street or Road or Avenue or Drive or Crescent – just Cheapside.

The word needed no embellishment to me. I always felt that there was a great sound of authority about it –

added to which there was the number of our house. Six.

Now you must admit that Six, Cheapside, has a bit of a musical ring to it – well, what I mean about Number Six is, it *goes* with the word Cheapside better than any other number.

For instance I would have been deprived of a lot of private pleasure had I been born at, let us say Number Two or Eleven or Twenty-eight or Thirty-one.

Our side of Cheapside – get that bit, *our side*; anyone would think reading this that we owned the whole of one side of Cheapside. Please don't misunderstand; the side of Cheapside we lived on was the one with even numbers – but more than that, our side was the three front steps and bay window side. The residents of the other side, the odd numbers, poor unfortunate souls, had only one small step and a flat ordinary window.

Now at this point, in fairness to readers, I must be my age and admit that it *was* a street. That's all, just a street. But a street that housed many, many wonderful, good and kind people.

We all knew and cared about each other in this street; and one of my greatest pleasures, even now at Christmas time, is receiving cards from dear elderly neighbours who knew me from my birth and who I knew as young women. The sad but inevitable thing is that each Christmas I receive fewer cards because the young women I knew have grown into old women and have passed on to an even more important place than Cheapside.

Running across the top of Cheapside was Market Street – so named, of course, because there was a red and yellow brick covered market in it.

Market Street also boasted the front entrance of The Royalty Theatre.

Turning into Cheapside, the side of the Royalty ran down the left hand side (our side) for about 50 yards. There were the exit doors of the Gods, then the exit doors of the balcony. Next, there was a little stretch of lovely stone wall, then the Pit exit doors and the Orchestra Stalls exit doors. Then came the exciting bit, the Stage Door – or Doors. They were double doors, but of course everyone always says 'the stage *door*', singular, don't they?

After the Stage Door there were the Scenery Doors, the bottom of which were about five feet above the pavement over some dressing room windows – and these afforded us untold – and I really mean untold, until now – pleasure. When all of us kids were 'playing out' in the street after tea, the dressing room lights would be on, and the windows slightly open to allow the artistes a little fresh air. They couldn't see us peeping in, but we could see *them* – changing or making up, and well, er! – other things.

Talk about the Permissive Society – crumbs! – I recall one week there was a very good looking actor (well, *we* thought he was, we were very young y'know – all of us) using the dressing room with the window which had the best view through the slit where it was open, and it didn't seem quite normal to we very unsophisticated young Lancastrians that he walked about the dressing room without clothes on – or as we called it, bare. What a week! We never played hop scotch, or rounders or marbles once! It was 'Window on the World Week'.

We started off by taking turns to peer in at his assets, but before long we were shoving and pushing each other out of the way. Add to this the fact that we had to keep dead quiet or he would have heard us and – tragedy – he would have shut the window, or worse still put some clothes on!

I remember what agony it was not to titter when he displayed his manly form, so the drill was that if we couldn't keep our titters in, we had to creep quietly away with our hand over our mouth and let our titter burst forth when we were out of earshot of the window.

It's amazing when one thinks back, that most of the peepers, including myself, had brothers. We'd all seen them on bath nights and knew how they were made – but this good-looking actor wasn't the brother of any of us – and a free look at a non-relative's piece of equipment was not to be missed. Anyhow he sang 'Roses are blooming in Picardy' whilst he was walking about nude and that was an added attraction. According to the dictionary the word 'equipment' is described as: 'Soldiers accoutrements' – well in this case it was 'Actor's accoutrements!'

To this day – and it's a long time since then – I can remember feeling guilty when I went indoors for my supper each night and I had no answer when my mother enquired, 'What have you been doing – your nose and forehead are all covered in black dust?' But however young you are you can *think* – and I was thinking, Why don't they wash the dressing room windows at the Royalty?

So much for the week of Abandoned Excitement. It never happened again. The following week the room was occupied by a very respectable character actor, and when he was off stage all he did was sit in the dressing room, smoke a pipe and read. Although we had all taken our positions and reminded each other to keep our titters in, it wasn't worth bothering about to get our noses and foreheads black. So we played hop scotch under the street lamp on the opposite side to our house until one of my friends exclaimed, 'Hey, there's some more dressing room windows up that passage next to your house, Hirdie.'

The Charge of the Light Brigade had nothing on us. Phfft! We were across the road quicker than I've written it – but our bunch halted at the entrance to the passage – or ginnel – and then quietly tip-toed the rest of the way only to discover no less than eight windows.

Pshaw! None of 'em open and on top of that they'd been painted all over with whitening! Each face registered disapproval and then we all let our titters burst forth. That's the great thing about being young – a disappointment doesn't last long.

Speaking of the passage, it was the next bit of the Theatre and also next to our front door. It hadn't always been so; from the time I was born to the time I was about five years old, there had been another house, Number Four.

Well, I say a house, but that isn't quite correct. The front of it was exactly like ours but only the ground floor was lived in. The first and the top floors were used as dressing rooms for the Theatre, so although the entire front of Number Four was in harmony with the rest of the houses on 'our side' it was really only habitable on the ground floor because it had no staircase.

The front bedrooms were approached by a staircase from the back of the theatre stage.

This was something that afforded my brother and me great fun – I'll tell you how.

When my mother was playing at the theatre or maybe visiting someone in one of those dressing rooms and we were in bed, she could literally be in the next room. My bed was next to the wall, and Neville's a bit further along, also next to the wall. We would lie in bed and wait for the exciting bit. It always came.

Suddenly, right next to either my head or Nev's, we would hear it – Pom tiddly-om-pom, *pom, pom* banged on the wall. Scuttling out of the bedclothes we would kneel up and reply with our Pom-tiddly-om-pom, *pom, pom* – I can remember even now how it hurt my knuckles. Then, clear as a bell, mother would say, 'Aren't you two asleep yet?' and we would chorus 'No-o-o'; and then she would say, 'Well, settle down, I'll be home in a few minutes!' and we would shout 'All right – good night and God Bless' and mother would reply 'God Bless.' And that was the end of the exciting bit!

Not a moment to be recorded in history perhaps, but all the same, I don't suppose I shall meet more than a hundred people tomorrow whose mother spoke to them through a wall, when *she* was in a Theatre and *they* were in bed?

Not long afterwards, Number Four became part of the Theatre building, so the passage or ginnel that had been on the other side of Number Four was then moved up next to us. This didn't alter the top of Number Four; the dressing rooms were still on a level with our bedrooms.

It was quite a few years after that that they scrapped those dressing rooms to make the back of the stage into a scene dock, so the hurt wasn't so bad. Nev's room was at the back of the house by then and although I had the big front bedroom to myself we were both in our teens and too 'grown up' to play at knocking on walls.

Or were we? Neither of us was madly sophisticated – of course, we *thought* we were – but I know now we weren't. Even though it wasn't long after that time that I was wearing my long hair plaited and coiled into two flat saucers called 'earphones', and I endured the agony of plucking my eyebrows into a thin take-all-the-expression-away line. My father caught me in the painful act, as I 'oo'd and ah'd'; and instead of reprimanding me, he enquired as only James Henry could, 'What are you doing?' 'Plucking my eyebrows,' I replied. 'It's the fashion.' '*Plucking* your eyebrows!' he echoed. There was a slight stage pause whilst he looked at me – it was a pathetic look – and then he said, 'And we bother to bloody well send missionaries abroad!'

I have already done the 'swank bit' about our side of Cheapside having three front steps to the front door, but there's more to those steps than that. There were the steps, the window sills and the large slab of Yorkshire stone at the bottom of the steps which was really a frame for the 'coal 'ole'.

And it really was a frame. There it lay, the slab, in all its scrubbed glory, with a circle cut out of the middle in which a disc of cast iron about a foot in diameter was set like a jewel, and if it was blackleaded successfully, it shone like a black pearl.

Now I want to stress something at this point – from about the age of six, I was taught to help in the house. Not forced. Not whipped. Just given little jobs.

For instance, like every other child in those days – and I only say 'in those days' because I am talking about a long time ago; things have altered so very much during my lifetime – like every other child, I had a little rolling pin and baking board, and when my mother was baking I was given a small piece of 'paste' as we called it, and I would make something like a jam tart, or with a few currants, it would become a teacake.

I loved doing this sort of thing. My pastry probably was a light shade of grey by the time I'd finished messing about with it – but at least it was always eaten by one of my parents and loving remarks were passed as they nearly broke their teeth on it.

I was taught housework in the same way and I hereby declare that whatever people may think of my acting endeavours, I'll take anyone on in the cleaning stakes. That's not boasting – it's a fact, and it brings me back to our front steps.

The scrubbing, rubbing-stoning and blackleading that was required came under the lovely northern heading of 'Doing the Front'.

I know that we use a lot of expressions that sound grammatically incorrect or clumsy, but at least these are expressive, and 'Doing the Front' is one of them.

I started 'Doing the Front' (when I come to think of it – it sounds a bit suggestive really) when I was about six and a half or seven. The full production was this: sweep the steps and the pavement in front of the house and then shoot indoors for two brushes and the blacklead.

We used Zebo. (If I'd been born a few years earlier I'd have had to mix a lump of blacklead with water in an old saucer or tin.)

Right, Zebo on and brush it well in until the dullness had gone and then a brisk polish with the polishing brush. I always did the round coal hole lid first, then moved on to the big grate under the (ahem!) bay window. This grate was a devil to do; it was iron and the pattern was like lattice work. Never mind, it got done and with the grates shining like black diamonds I'd shoot indoors for a bucket of hot water, floor cloth and scrubbing brush, the maula soap (which was brown and looked as though it was a piece of fudge with chopped nuts in it and smelt of lovely disinfectant) *and* the yellow rubbing-stone and its brush.

Now I must describe the rubbing-stone brush. It was really a circumcised scrubbing brush, or, in other words, a scrubbing brush whose bristles were so worn away that it was ready for the dustbin. Only then did it become a perfect rubbing-stone brush, the reason being that not only could you hold the wood, but the bristles were so short that after rubbing the yellow stone on the front of the steps you could smooth it over for a perfect finish.

I'll tell you this much – the front steps of the houses in Cheapside radiated the personalities of every householder. Ours were yellow stoned on the front face of the step as well as the sides; Number Eight had white stone along the edges of their steps, Number Ten had white at the sides, and so on. By jove, it was worth walking down Cheapside on a Friday or Saturday morning.

Of course one felt deeply distressed that our

neighbours on the opposite side of the street couldn't show off their artistic ability as much as we could, because, you'll recall, they only had one step each.

However, there I am one morning, doing the front, on my kness, my bottom on view to all 'The One Steppers' on the other side. Well, no – not my bottom; my knickers I should have said. Whether, in my imagination I was being 'Little Emmie, the poor Orphan Cleaner' or whether I was at school or dancing class, I always wore little white knickers with either pale pink or pale blue baby ribbons threaded through the embroidery round the minute legs.

I would wear a cleaning apron which in those days were of dark grey material. Mine came down to my ankles but my dress just covered the cheeks of my bottom, so you've got the picture – kneeling mat, cleaning apron and white 'knicks' with pink or blue ribbon.

A neighbour opposite came to her front door to look up and down the street – this was a habit most of them had, not out of noseyness, in fact, it was the only pleasure some of them had. She looked across and saw me – I didn't see her – but I heard her as she called laughingly, 'Thora! I can see your arse.'

Now on my word of honour, I had never heard that word before in my life. For one thing, although we were a great family for funny stories, and although I grew up to have a sense of humour as great, I hope, as my parents, my dad, who was not unknown to swear, had such a respect for women that he never used words like 'arse'. And, if he did, it was never in front of us. Hearing the neighbour call out this new word, I jumped up, ran indoors and asked my mother, 'What's my arse?'

Honest to God, she nearly jumped through the ceiling, '*What* did you say?' she asked.

'What's my arse?' I repeated in all innocence, '. . . because Mrs Mayton can see it – she's just told me so.'

It was my dear mother's expression in cases like this that I remember so well. I can see her now – she drew herself up to her full height (which was about 5 ft 1 in) and with flour all over her hands, a half-peeled apple in one hand and the peeling knife in the other, she said, 'Oh – *did* she! Well, I shall *have a word* with Mrs Mayton.'

This was an expression, this 'have a word', that was only used on occasions such as this; as we stood there, Mother with the apple and knife and me with the scrubbing brush and maula soap, she added quietly, 'Off you go, love, and finish the front and – it's your botty!'

I well remember another such occasion – I was down on my knees 'worshipping Allah' and scrubbing away when a man we knew very well – he had a business at the top of Cheapside – was coming along the pavement just as I plunged my hands into the bucket of water. 'Good morning, Thora!' he said. 'Oh, good morning Mr So and So,' I replied – you see, that was one great thing about 'doing the front', it was a kind of social reception centre. Quite a lot of people used Cheapside. Well, as I took the cloth out of the bucket to wring it out, he paused and looked down at me. He stood sort of posed – hands behind his back and I really thought he was admiring my craft as a step scrubber, but no, taking a deep breath – just like an actor about to deliver the big speech at the end of a play, he said, 'I take it your mother doesn't object to you putting your hands in a bucket of diluted dog shit!'

As I didn't know what he meant, I just laughed and said, 'Oh no, Mr So and So.' Really I laughed because he had used the word 'shit' – why do we always laugh at forbidden words when we are kids?

That's all he said and then walked off, but it was enough to make me laugh even more because he walked with a little tilt, like Jacques Tati in *Monsieur Hulot's Holiday*.

Up I got and shot into the house. 'Mam, what does diluted mean?' 'Diluted?' said my mother, who was hanging some sheets to air on the clothes rack. 'Well, love, diluted means to thin out, like – when we get the lime to do the yard we – what do you want to know for?' 'I only wondered,' I said, 'because Mr So and So just said he takes it you don't object to my putting my hands in a bucket of diluted dog shit!'

Now those readers who are *au fait* with a clothes rack know that it consists of long thin pieces of wood and is hoisted up and down with a rope anchored by a hook on the wall. The most popular place for a rack is obviously on the ceiling in front of the fire place.

Well, talk about perfect comedy timing! My mother, who was about to hoist the rack to its safe and warm harbour as I uttered Mr So and So's famous statement, pulled on the rope with such surprise, the rack nearly shot through into the back bedroom above. As she wound the rope, figure eight-wise, round the cleat hook, she once again drew herself to her full height and said quietly, 'Oh – did he! Well, I shall *have a word* with Mr So and So!'

She never did, of course, but it was nice to think she was protecting my youthful ears. The amazing thing was that it never dawned on her I was only enquiring about the word 'diluted' – I knew what the other word meant.

I should hate you to get the impression that the adventures of doing the front were all on the dog excretions and botty lines – they weren't. I recall that on one occasion when I was about nine years old (and this was a madly romantic period of my life), the leading man from the visiting company at the Theatre that week was coming up Cheapside, maybe to call for his mail or, as it was a Friday perhaps 'The Ghost was Walking' which in theatrical jargon means that it was pay day.

Just as he passed our door my father came out, and after very civil salutations the handsome leading man put his hand into his inside pocket and brought out a really lovely gold cigarette case with diamond initials on it!

My first reaction was that he must be a millionaire. Oh, cripes! not only good looking, but the owner of a gold and diamond fag case as well.

He offered my father a cigarette, helped himself to one, snapped the case shut, accepted a light from my dad and they set off up Cheapside chatting.

Now you may think that story unworthy of recording, but I am here to tell you that at that very moment I made up my mind for the umpteenth time that not only would I be an actress when I grew up but that I would also be the proud owner of a gold cigarette case with diamond initials on it. It never entered my dreamlike mind that I might not smoke. It was the case, and the elegant way he flipped it open and snapped it shut, that was the bit that impressed me.

It's amazing how one can get through work if you imagine lovely, almost impossible things. I was always doing that, and I really enjoyed my day dreams. As I smoothed the yellow rubbing stone along the front of the steps I was practically opening 'my' gold case and the diamonds shone in the reflection of the highly blackleaded coal 'ole.

Little did I realize as I knelt there that one day I *would* own a gold cigarette case with my initials on it in diamonds. In reality, that cigarette case was to be a loving gift from my husband and daughter – one of the many dreams of mine that came true.

There always seems to be a spot of humour attached to the memorable moments of my life, and the day Scottie – my husband – and Janette, our daughter, presented me with the gold case can still bring a smile to our faces. I suppose every happy wife and mother feels the same way about an expensive present and even a sixpenny present is expensive if the donor has had to save up for it. Why do we nearly always say 'Oh, you shouldn't have' or 'Oh dear – spending all that money on me!' We don't really mean that 'they shouldn't have', we are wildly happy that they *did* – in fact, we are so damned happy we are crying as we embrace them.

Amongst my very important treasures are many little homemade gift cards that read 'To my Mummy with all my love, Jan – and it was very expensive.'

However, back to the presentation of the 'fag case'. After we had gone through the tears and running nose routine, I was informed that the present wasn't complete, and that if I went to the jewellers he would show me various designs and letters which I could choose and which he would then execute in diamonds and attach them to the case. In spite of the tears and nose blowing, I didn't need telling twice and off I went. Now although my stage name is Thora Hird – which is, of course, my maiden name – I'm really Thora Scott. So on arrival at the jewellers it was quite understandable that I should be asked 'Oh Miss Hird – do you wish for the initials T.H. or T.S.?'

The jeweller was a little love, but he didn't help much when he said, 'Well, pardon me suggesting "T.S.", but it *is* from your husband and daughter.'

He was right, so I made a quick decision and my gold cigarette case sports a beautiful bit of craftsmanship which reads T.H.S. The reason we smile about that day is that, after all the tears and nose blowing and expostulation of Oh, you shouldn't have etc., etc., I'd managed to get *three* diamond initials on my case instead of the intended *two*!

When I appear to 'go on a bit' about the kindness, warmth and loving gestures of the Lancastrians, I beg to be forgiven. I am quite sure the same sort of wonderful people are all over England, Ireland, Scotland and Wales – in fact, I know they are – but you will understand that as I spent the early years of my life in Lancashire, they are the people I knew the best and who impressed me the most.

Thinking quickly, I hope my husband forgives and understands too, because I have been married for 38 years to the best advert for Scotland imaginable. The early years, the tender years, the impressionable years are always the ones we remember best, tend to forget for a while, then suddenly, with the passage of years, remember more clearly than ever.

I know this is how both my husband and I are. Sometimes when we are sitting over a cup of tea or coffee, one of us will suddenly say, 'Do you remember gas mantles?' or 'Did your mother scrape the paper the butter or lard was wrapped in, so as not to waste any?' I adore these conversations we have because from a little remark stems a really interesting conversation that can last an hour. Nostalgia? Yes, but always loving and warm – *and* this is a great way of reminding oneself how much better off we are than those dear, wonderful women who cleaned, baked, washed and ironed; who went without things so that we could have 'em. And who *never complained*. O.K. – they didn't get the British Empire Medal, but they happily worked themselves nearly to death, content with a title given to them by us – Mother.

Before I finish about 'our front steps' and the kindness of our Lancastrian Lot, I would state here and now that sometimes it was carried a bit too far. At least, when you're six or seven or even eight or nine years old it can seem so.

What I mean when I say 'carried a bit too far' is this. One morning after I had finished doing the front, I was just emptying the dirty water out of my bucket down the grate in our back yard, when my mother said, 'Will you be a good girl and do the front next door? Mrs Houghton's in bed, poorly.'

Assuring my big-hearted mother I would, I put the big iron kettle on the fire for some more hot water. Meanwhile I went and swept next door's steps and front, and blackleaded the coal 'ole lid and lattice-designed grate under their bay window. The entire procedure was the same as I had already executed at the front of number six. (I was already preparing myself for twice nightly performances in the theatre in the years to come!) Knocking gently on their front door, I requested their white rubbing stone, which we didn't have, being 'yellow stoners'. Everything else I had provided – bucket of water, floor cloth, maula soap, etc., from my own personal equipment, rather like the adverts one sees in *The Stage* where it reads 'So and So unexpectedly free for Pantomime Season due to misunderstanding; cat or goose, own skin provided.' In my case it was 'Thora Hird, unexpectedly free for step scrubbing, bucket and necessary equipment provided!'

Right, so next door looked clean and cared for, and once again I was in our back yard emptying the bucket of diluted 'you know what' down the grate. I got as far as rinsing out the bucket when I *felt* my mother watching me; as I turned the bucket upside down to drain, she appealed – there's no other word for it – appealed to me thus.

'Would it be asking too much of you to do Mrs Baines at Number Ten? Her husband is off work ill and she has such a lot of extra work?'

Hecky plonk! What colour stone did *they* use? Right

you are then . . . as it was in the beginning! Kettle on, more hot water. But I didn't mind really because this was all part of life in Cheapside.

I *must* be honest though – as I finished Number Ten I can remember thinking, 'And if Mrs Rhodes is ill at Number Twelve her son Percy can scrub her blooming steps. I've washed and blackleaded half way down Cheapside as it is!'

Well – I *was* only eight years old!

I have already said that my mother's heart was too big for her body; she was always helping people, but I must add that this was the general attitude and way of going on of most folks in 'our street'. If anyone was ill, it was all hands to the pump – every neighbour would help in some way. One would do the shopping (so that the patient and family didn't starve) or one would do extra baking. All our mothers baked bread, fruit pies, meat pies, and teacakes – you only had 'shop stuff' at the last gasp! One would do the housework one day and another would do it the next – it was always done willingly without thought of reward. In fact, they were all so damned proud that you offered reward at the risk of offending.

I remember vividly that I would run errands for neighbours and my mother's last words as I left the house were always the same. 'And remember, love, *don't* take anything for going!' What a training – great! Oh, the times I have refused those pennies – don't think I didn't WANT to take them, I did, but it was a sort of 'on your honour' thing, so that was that.

Another lovable, neighbourly thing about being part of a street was new babies. Now that's another expression that we always used, new babies. I suppose it's silly really, because there aren't any old or second-hand babies. But that's what we called the latest arrivals – NEW babies.

Between the ages of six and sixteen, I think I saw every *new* baby in Cheapside. Oh, the pleasure I've had, just looking at *new* babies – only to be surpassed by those moments of indescribable joy when the mother would say, 'Would you like to hold it?'

Oh, mate! that lovely warm smell of baby and scented soap, that infinite trust the little soul has in you. (I mean, how do they know you are not going to drop them, or throw them up in the air and catch them, or *not* catch them – coming down.) Yet they seem just to lie there all crumpled and pink with their little fists clenched ready to knock their way through life fully aware of the character of the person whose arms enfold them.

I'm still barmy about *new* babies, but I suppose when I was holding the Cheapside ones I was too young to realize *how* barmy I would be when I held my own *new* baby – and that I would be barmier still when my own 'new baby-that-was held her own new baby-that-is'.

And if that isn't an original way of saying I'm a grandmother, I don't know what is!

We had tram lines in Cheapside, not those for electric trams but for horse trams. They started from the front of the Royalty Theatre in Market Street and trundled down Cheapside on the first part of their journey to Lancaster, four miles away.

The two horses were changed at the Tram Stables –

always an exciting incident in the journey – and changed again at Cross Hill on the return trip. I loved the trams and can remember how sorry I was when progress demanded they must finish.

I was sorry about something else, too. Now we had an orange box full of soil in our back yard and faithfully every year a green plant bloomed in profusion. The something else I was sorry about was that not only had the trams and horses gone, but so had most of the horse manure. Year by year, our plant had been fed on as much horse manure as would cover a two-acre field, but it never did as well after the trams finished. It seemed to 'cock a snoot' at milk-float horse manure or green-grocer cart horse manure, or fishman cart horse manure. Come to think of it, my parents were cocking a snoot at the amount of manure I used. I was a faithful believer in it, but I suppose it was overplaying a bit to put a whole bucketful on a window box when there was only a penny packet of Virginia stock seeds planted in it! Only one Virginia stock came up! I couldn't understand it – the poor little object had a very long thin pale stem – I think it was trying to get as far away from the smell of the manure as possible!

When our daughter Janette bought her first country house the grounds were delightful but a certain weed had taken such a hold that it was literally pushing the paths up – it was called *polygonum cuspidatum*, alias *reynoutria japonica*. It took two gardeners and a builder four months to stem its enthusiasm, and then the gardeners had to work for another year before it was finally ousted.

Have you guessed? Yes, it was the same as our green plant in the back yard at Morecambe, which my mother used to admire and say, 'Well, it's a lovely bit of green and it's not hurting anybody!'

When I was about five or six I went into business. When I say I went into business it was more a kind of barter, a sort of exchange and mart. I would take a bucket of peelings and exchange it for a cut apple or an over-ripe banana.

Right, now I'll explain. The drill was, first to persuade mother to put all the veg or fruit peelings into a clean enamel bucket. Then I would go up to Houghtons.

Houghtons was two shops, a butcher's and a greengrocer's, next to the front entrance of the Royalty Theatre – and the bucket of peelings was carried through the greengrocer's shop and emptied into a bin in their yard, to feed the pigs being reared for the butcher's shop. When the empty bucket was returned, you were given a cut apple.

A cut apple is an apple that has seen better days. Patchy brown bruise marks had been scooped out with a potato peeler and the remains, when presented to you along with thanks for the bucket of peelings, were rather like a piece of modern art. There wasn't much apple left, although, to be fair, we were offered the choice of either a cut apple or two very over-ripe black-as-night bananas.

In the middle of our living-room table there was always a bowl of fruit, oranges, apples, polished and shining, pears or whatever else was in season, and bananas – yellow, not black! So why in Heaven's name I should have gone to the trouble of trading the bucket of peelings is a mystery. I suppose it was because my friends in Cheapside took their offerings for a cut apple, and what was good enough for them was good enough for me.

Besides, I liked Billy Hadwen, who served in Houghton's. He wore a cap and a shirt with his brass collar stud showing, and was a very nice, kind young man.

Many years later, I was guest star at the Royalty Theatre – being invited there often. I certainly enjoyed going home, for the Royalty occupied a very special place in my heart. With a Royalty performance, I was obliging the Theatre management *and* myself! And, as I usually played there August Bank Holiday week, I was obliging the tax man too!

On this occasion I travelled to Morecambe to appear in one of the plays I had done in the West End. There was the usual press party held in the Dress Circle Bar, scheduled for the night of my arrival because I was going to rehearse for a week before opening night.

During the chit-chat I saw a man having a quiet drink on the far side of the bar, and I found myself unable to concentrate on what I was saying because I kept thinking – I know that man's face. Whenever I visited Morecambe there were lots of people and faces I knew and recognized by sight. I very rarely forget a face though I often forget the name that goes with it. On this occasion, my mind worked overtime trying to put a name to the face. Eventually, the man made his way to the side of the bar where I was standing and very shyly said, 'Hullo, Thora, love – what are you having?' I looked into the kind, good face – and – bingo! – I remembered.

'A cut apple, please, Mr Hadwen!' I said.

4

There's no place like . . .

At the top of our three front steps was, of course, our front door. It was quite a solid job, opened by a large door knob about midway down on the right; to the left, on a level with the knob, was a letter box, horizontally placed and informing anyone who cared to look that it was there for the postman to push letters through. It had 'LETTERS' embossed quite clearly on its flap.

Of course, other things were pushed through – little envelopes inviting you to deposit a few copper coins inside for the Self Denial Week, bills announcing Great Jumble Sale, the daily and Sunday newspapers, *Comic Cuts*, *Chips*, *Rainbow*, *Children's Newspaper*, and so on.

It was quite a busy letter box. It was also used to pull the key through. By inserting the first and middle fingers of the right hand – left hand if you wished – the fingers could grope until they fastened on a piece of string that hung down for about two feet. The front door key was tied to the end of it.

Hung is the right word because our front door key was about five inches long and heavy; its appearance from the inside passage was rather like a body swinging on the gallows. I can literally *feel* the weight of that key, as I write this, and remember how embarrassed I used to be during my flapper days, when I was allowed to detach the key for late home-coming. The times I have had a Romeo escort me home after a dance and, as we said our good nights at our front door, I hoped he'd hop it before I opened my evening bag to expose the key. It was so large that it was about all I could get *into* my evening bag! Why couldn't we have a Yale key and lock? Something modern! I was going through a modern stage at that point – it didn't last long fortunately.

These days we spend hours at antique markets looking for things like our front door key. Why the heck I should have been ashamed of it I don't know – I *do* know I'm ashamed now of having been ashamed of it. Daft bitch!

Our front door opened on to a not-too-narrow passage that led to the middle door or living-kitchen door. This passage was covered with oilcloth (linoleum we called it), then with carpet, purposely narrow so as to leave a margin of oilcloth about ten inches wide at each side of the passage. Where the 'lino' and carpet started – at the top front step – there was a strip of brass which held the oilcloth together with the carpet, firmly in place. This strip of brass was polished, of course. The margins of oilcloth on each side of the passage were also polished and shone like glass. They were referred to as 'the sides'. The strip of brass, the boundary between outdoors and indoors, was referred to as 'the brass'. Hence, in cleaning jargon, one would be questioned thus: 'Have you done the brass and polished the sides?'

Along the passage, on the right, was the door to the

front room or sitting-room – it was referred to as both, depending on the mood you were in – and a little further along on the right were the stairs.

The first flight consisted of fourteen treads. These were carpeted with a bordered stair carpet which was held firmly in place by brass stair rods – which, each week, Nev or I faithfully unanchored from their harbour and polished. Again, the carpet was narrower in width than the stair treads – which meant that after brushing the carpet well with a stiff carpet brush (using a dust pan to receive the dust) there were still the sides to do! There were two sides to each tread, and the procedure was to wipe each side with a soft cloth wrung out in hot water, to which a drop of Izal had been added, wring the cloth out again, wipe as dry as possible, and then polish! The top of the stair sides were always conveniently dry by the time you'd wiped the bottom (excuse that remark) and one was able to start waxing. So it was continuous movement really.

What a performance! But, what a result! Smashing! But one can get just the same result today in about an eighth of the time.

At the top of the first flight of stairs was a small oblong landing with a door on the right leading into the front bedroom which was my mother's and father's room. On the left of the landing, facing the front bedroom door, was the door leading into the back bedroom. Making a rapid U-turn at the top of the first flight there was the second flight of fourteen stairs, at the top of which the landing was identical to the lower one, only the top front bedroom door was on the left and the top back bedroom door was on the right!

In retrospect, I realize now that my mother must have been a 'with-it' person, because she always had the bedrooms and staircase decorated in delicate shades of colour wash, which of course was the forerunner of your modern distemper and synthetic paint. She used to say that the curtains and bedspreads and furniture made the rooms fussy enough and that plain walls always looked so fresh and clean! They always did! The only drawback was, it wasn't washable like today's miracle products, so consequently a bucket of colour wash was often to be seen in our house.

I wasn't expected to assist in the colourwashing until I was in my teens. Even then I was never any good at it! Mind you – I always fancied myself as a dab hand at the painting – I don't mean portraits or landscapes, but skirting boards and doors and window frames. So fair-do's, I always pulled my weight. If I had any paint left I would wander around the house looking for something that needed the odd dab.

In my mind's eye I can still see the back of the door in my parents' bedroom. Whoever had lived in the house prior to us must have been very artistic – well, I suppose you'd call it artistic! The door was composed of four panels and in each panel an individual painting had been executed in oils. In the top left hand panel there were bullrushes in a pond and a bird hovering (a winged bird I mean); the top right panel had irises with leaves and buds; the two bottom panels sported flowers – I think they were geraniums and buttercups and poppies and cornflowers but I can't quite remember. What I *can* remember is that I thought they were *beautiful*!

Each time we decorated, I faithfully painted the woodwork white but left the panels untouched apart from a wash down. The end product gave the effect of a door with four narrow oblong oil paintings hanging on it! Every year when we started cleaning and decorating my mother would say, 'I think we'll paint over those this time, love!'

What? Sacrilege! I loved 'em! I can recall that I always used my little Orphan Annie or Ora Pro Nobis expression as I would plead, 'Let's leave them – just until next time we do the room – please?'

She would look at me ever so lovingly and say, 'All right then, love, leave them – some poor soul went to a lot of trouble.' Some poor soul! You see, there she was, my mother, conjuring up the idea of some poor soul on their knees for days, weeks or months painting away – never getting recognition for their talent. She saw my point – she always did – but I know why she agreed to leave the paintings on the panels. It was to give me pleasure.

When sitting in a theatre have you ever looked at a garden backcloth of a stage set and imagined what the rest of the garden round the corner would look like? I have, often. Neville and I knew every detail of the backcloths at the Royalty Theatre, knew them intimately and individually. They didn't stop at the edges for us – we imagined all sorts of extensions. The bullrushes and the irises, the geraniums and buttercups had the same effect on me – I made up a mental picture of the place where the bullrush pond was. As my mother would have said, 'Well – you're not hurting anybody!' Lovely expression that, isn't it? It condones so many things.

When we were little, the back bedroom was shared by Nev and me. He had a double bed and I had a single one.

I *loved* this room for three reasons. One, it had a small door on the left of the window. This door opened into a little room – about the same size as our back kitchen, which was below it – and it was the toy room.

This sounds as though we lived in a mansion where the governess would insist we put our toys neatly away in the special toy room each night. Oh, no! it was much more thrilling and exciting than that.

The toy room housed the greatest assortment of things imaginable. There were skips, or theatrical hampers, full of uniforms, dress swords, plumed hats. There was a leather hat box lined with cerise satin with a 'tall shiny' of Dad's in it. There were musical instruments we could have a go on, banjos, a harp, a euphonium, violins, a balalaika and a mandolin.

There was a tea gown of purple velvet with bishop's sleeves, satin slippers to match with little purple beads woven into a pattern all over the tiny pointed toes, and purple openwork stockings, an evening dress with an off the shoulder top all smothered in violets made of voile. There were various wigs – bald-headed ones, grey ones, a chinaman's pigtail. Oh, there was everything and it was all *to play with*! No holds barred! Can you imagine the glorious fun Nev and I had?

In our toy room, there was also my sister Olga's dolls' pram, which was a source of delight to me, though each time my mother looked at it her expression was heartbreaking, for Olga was knocked down by a motor bike on Morecambe Promenade and killed.

She was buried on her sixth birthday. I won't dwell on the heartbreak this caused.

My brother Neville was one of the funniest people I have ever met, and to have a brother older than oneself – and one you love dearly – is one of life's blessings. I have often wished I'd been clever enough to produce an older brother for our daughter Jan, but – what's the saying – it wasn't to be.

Our Nev could get some sort of a tune out of any musical instrument. I was always satisfied to dress up, especially in one of the tea gowns. I was never very mobile because most of the gown trailed on the floor, but what did it matter? I wish I could do full justice in words to our happiness in the toy room.

Reason number two for loving the back bedroom was what we called 'the corner'. It was nothing of the sort really, more like a miniature cave, an area about five feet wide and four feet deep that extended right back beneath the top flight of stairs – with only the opening on view. Great fun – there was an oil painting of Grandad Hird in there, still wrapped up with brown paper and string. It had been there since my father had come by it after my Grandmother Hird's funeral – it had been willed to him.

We were always about to hang it somewhere but never seemed to be able to find a suitable place, so there Grandad remained in the cave under the top stairs.

I write, with pride, that Grandad Hird – official title Captain Hird – owned his own schooner which was used for carrying cargo. He was a colourful, dashing character, with red curly hair and beard, and from the stories my father told us about him, we gathered he was a bit of a lad.

Sadly, there came a time when he *didn't* return from one of his voyages. Years later, a sailing ship took refuge from a storm in the mouth of a cave somewhere in the South Seas.

In that cave there was a wrecked schooner. They found the skeletons of the crew on board and locked in a chest, they found the log book of Captain Hird's ship. God Rest Grandad – the pirate!

The final attraction of the back bedroom was the toilet set. It was *lovely*. It had belonged to my Grandma Mayor. It was white with a two-inch band in the most wonderful, clear turquoise blue, all complete – bowl and jug, soap dish, tooth brush container and two 'gozunders' – and if anyone *hasn't* heard that old pantomime gag they've missed nothing. 'What's a gozunder? It *goes under* the bed!'

I was very fond of that toilet set. I don't know what happened to it but I do know that only a year or two ago I bought an old-fashioned toilet jug to hold flowers and bullrushes. Jan was visiting us from California. She went into raptures over it. It's in Beverly Hills now, gracing one of the loveliest homes in Coldwater Canyon. I hope it gives Jan as much pleasure as Grandma Mayor's gave me!

Perhaps it was the memory of Grandma Mayor's toilet set that inspired me to acquire a gozunder as a link with the past (also, a gozunder filled with sand makes a very useful large ashtray when you're having a party for friends on the lawn). But it's not as nice as those in our bottom back bedroom.

Right, Ladies and Gentlemen, if you will follow me down the twenty-eight stairs (and watch your step, they are rather steep and there is no light!) we will move into Happiness Hall – our living-room, I'd better explain that this room could go under the title of middle-room, living-room or living-kitchen, but that would be overplaying it a bit because it *was* the living-room and the back kitchen was, of course, a kitchen at the back! Well, it stands to reason it would be at the *back* if it was the *back* kitchen doesn't it?

As a child, I used to wonder why it was called the *back* kitchen, when we hadn't a *front* kitchen! Unless, of course, where we ate, laughed, entertained, played the piano and everything else, was called the *living-kitchen*. However, from now on I will refer to it as the living-room, which will be less confusing for anyone who intends to read on.

The floor of the living-room was of red and black tiles about nine inches square. I don't mean present day PVC adhesive ones, I mean quarry tiles, which were scrubbed with a hard scrubbing brush and plenty of maula soap. But this was only the first act of the domestic play – the second act opened with Thora on her knees with a saucer of sour milk (sounds as though I was doing a 'cat act' doesn't it?), which was rubbed over the tiles to leave a shine on them as the final curtain fell! Do you wonder I now use modern PVC adhesive ones on every possible occasion?

Mind you, our tiles looked jolly nice after they were done – that is, until they had been walked on. Half an hour later, I used to think – why did I bother to do those?

The same feeling applies now as it did then with regard to housework – the effect doesn't last long, does it?

The living-room fireplace was, of course, the focal point of the room. It had a fairly high mantelpiece that was always skirted with a cornish frill made of the same material as the curtains and cushion covers. My mother was Champion of the Northern Union with a fourpenny Drummer Dye, and many a time I have gone to school leaving a mauve cornish frill, curtains and cushion covers and returned home to find them rose pink! The moment she had seen us out of the house the drill was – all down, all washed, all dyed, all dried, all ironed – all up! Fab!

The fireplace itself was a typical kitchen range of iron with an oven on the right-hand side. It was never used for roasting the meat or making the Yorkshire Pudding in my day because there was a crack in it somewhere, but it served honourably as a receptacle for our pyjamas and bed slippers which were popped in there about an hour before bedtime.

As kids, we undressed in front of the fire, opened the oven door, pyjamas out – quick, and there you were, in hot pyjamas, hotter bedroom slippers, drinking even hotter cocoa! All as a preliminary to going upstairs into the frozen north! Br-r-r-r, it was cold in those bedrooms. We rushed upstairs into bed, and moved the stone hot water bottles, which mother had placed just where our little bottoms would nestle, down to the bottom of the bed to warm our feet.

What a carry on! Of course we didn't think anything of it – our bedrooms were always cold, weren't they?

Unless we had measles or chicken pox, when the big firegrate in the bedroom would come to life with a blazing fire!

I never did like the cold, and I am sure a lot of elderly people don't like it either but have to suffer it. I think that Parliament should bring in a law that all old age pensioners on reaching retirement should be presented with a very safe electric blanket along with their pension book! Or – if they are nervous of electricity – a couple of bags of coal!

On the left of our living-room fireplace was a boiler with a brass tap on it, which never worked either, because of some deep internal crack. But, sitting on top of the boiler was a huge iron kettle and since this was next to the fire itself we claimed constant hot water.

Above the boiler, the fire, and the oven, was an iron rack with a polished steel edge, very useful for keeping toast or muffins or crumpets warm or for airing or warming pieces of underwear. We also used to air the handkerchiefs on it. As they were ironed and folded into what looked like square sandwiches, they were placed on a dinner plate on the rack. I wonder why we aired hankies?

The firegrate proper had bars in front of it, and the top three could be let down into a horizontal position for use as a hob. To the side of where the fire actually burned was another set of three bars. These could either be flush against the side or, like the hob piece, let down into a horizontal position which laid them actually over the burning fire. I don't know if there is another name for them and if there is I apologize to them because we always referred to them as bars – put the bar up, or put the bar down. Poor things, they had no separate identity because the same instructions applied either to the one over the fire or the hob piece in front of the fire.

Our fire! That's worth a couple of lines! My mother used to say, 'Come on, now, put some more coal on and let's have a royal standback!' That's just what it was. You *did* stand back, it was always such a beauty.

The fireplace I have described was blackleaded to high heaven, with the exception of the polished steel edge on the rack, which was rubbed frenziedly with emery paper. That and the top of the steel fender. The surround of the fender was blackleaded but that top! Oh mate! It shone like silver! Nev and I took it in turns to emery-paper the fender on alternate Fridays, because it really did need some elbow grease.

The hearth was of stone and that came under the scrubbing department. After cleaning with metal polish the brass tap (on the boiler that didn't work) one was only left with the pegged rug to shake.

How many of you have ever shaken one of these rugs? Some sort of mask would have been a help. The dust and dirt that would shake out of our rug was fantastic considering it was shaken vigorously twice a week! Talk about a foggy day in London Town! It was a foggy day in our back yard each time we shook ours.

In those days, people sat for hours during the winter months pegging small strips of material into a piece of sacking or canvas to make a rug. Any worn-out trousers or jackets were washed and cut into strips three inches by one and pegged into a pattern. They looked cosy and comfy – until someone put one foot on the thing and left a flat imprint. They were veritable dust catchers, and just about the most unhygienic piece of furnishing ever thought of.

(Phew! I'm tired out after describing all that cleaning of the fireplace! Or perhaps it was shaking the pegged rug that did it!)

A horsehair couch, not to be confused with a sofa, stood beneath the living-room window. Ours had two curled ends, very useful when Nev and I played cowboys – we each had a faithful steed.

We called ourselves Tom and Mary Whitfield – don't ask me why! There is no offence meant and none taken I hope, by any Tom or Mary Whitfield who may read this. We were very respectable cowhands and none came any better than Tom and Mary of Cheapside Ranch! By the time we were becoming too heavy for our horsehair horses, I had assumed the name of Pearl White – it was more exciting than being Mary Whitfield, the cowgirl.

The piano faced the horsehair sofa. There it stood, with its naked top. My father didn't approve of things being put on top of the piano, but with time a few artistic bits found their way there and stayed.

The piano was in the living-room because my mother felt Nev and I should do our piano practice, one hour a day each, where it was warm. I recall her saying that she thought it was inhuman to make children go into a cold front room, where most pianos were kept, to practise. We agreed. Unfortunately *we* thought it was inhuman to have to do one hour's practice a day each whether a room was warm or cold!

A lot of pleasure was derived from the piano being

on the spot. When my mother was ironing or sitting mending our clothes or socks, one of us would sit at the piano and accompany her while she sang. My favourite songs were 'Oh, where is my boy tonight?', 'Robin Adair', 'Sweet Violets', and 'Sweet and Low'. This was because they were in two sharps! Actually, I was passable in three flats, not too bad in four sharps, pathetic in four flats and damned awful in anything else. But in two sharps I was confident – I might even put a few twiddly bits in or a few runs. Oh yes, I was very fond of two sharps. Good old F and C! The sad end to this part is that I'm still only any good in two sharps, and not very good at that.

Nev had a violin, a guitar, a musical saw, a swannee whistle and, joy of joys, he bought a flexatone. It was great fun. My father had at one time forty pupils studying the banjo with him. He had learnt to play the banjo when he was with 'Moore and Burgesses Minstrels'. That was long before the church bells rang for me, but it will explain to you that he was a very good banjo player. My mother played a zither banjo.

Happy Days! Dad on the banjo, Nev on the violin, Mother singing and Thora obliging on the pianoforte, in two sharps! All the old Moore and Burgesses Minstrel numbers. Oh! I forgot to tell you that at fifteen years of age, my dad joined Moore and Burgesses as a boy soprano. I'm glad I remembered I'd forgotten to tell you that! So, we were able to provide our own entertainment! Many friends came to the house uninvited, and they were all made welcome. Mother preferred to know how many folks would call in, but nevertheless, a huge meat and potato pie would be sizzling in the oven, puffing out a mouth-watering smell, and the seven-pound jars of homemade pickled red cabbage and onions were always standing at the ready.

I don't wonder my generous parents never became rich, our house was like Dr Barnardo's. I once remarked to my mother in later years, 'Oh, love, you are always giving, you'll never be rich, will you?' 'But we *are* rich,' she said. 'We've got you and Neville, and your dad and I have got each other, and look at all the friends we have!' She was right, of course. She usually was!

One night, I was obliging by accompanying Neville on his violin. We were rendering 'Poet and Peasant' and Nev was proudly using a new bow he had just acquired for his birthday.

There is one passage where the pianist *can* add a few trills, but *shouldn't*, and when we arrived at it, I was really doing my lot. Nev stopped and informed me, 'If you are not going to play what's written, our kid, I'm not going to play any more; stop putting your own fancy bits in!' We started again and I faithfully played as per copy until we got to another passage where I again embroidered it a bit. The music stopped and he landed me one over the head with his new bow! What a shame! It looked so sad broken in two! I was sad, I was really, and sorry. Never mind, another lesson learnt, I didn't execute my own twiddly bits after that.

When I was invited years and years later to be a guest on 'Woman's Hour', they kindly asked me what music I would like to play me in – I requested 'Poet and Peasant' and then told the listeners why. It was the least I could do as a rather belated gesture to Neville for upsetting him so much, and for owning the head he smashed his birthday gift bow over!

Just a couple of words about the back yard. It was white-washed twice or three times a year, swilled and brushed every week, window sills scrubbed and yellow stoned. The toilet, which was in the covered wash house, sported what had been a varnished seat, wall to wall. This was scrubbed and scrubbed until only a memory of varnish remained at each end. The floor was scrubbed with disinfectant and then yellow stoned. The toilet paper was pieces of neatly cut news-papers, about eight inches by six, threaded on a piece of string. It hung on the wall to the left of the occupant and provided a little light reading if you were going to be in residence for long – a comfortable retreat to avoid washing up the dishes or for a secret smoke. Just the place to sit and meditate!

And that, Ladies and Gentlemen, concludes the tour of this ancient and historic building – will you kindly mind the three steps as you go out. I hope you have enjoyed your visit – your guide will be grateful for any little acknowledgement! Your charabanc will leave almost immediately!

Late note. Since writing the above I have acquired another rather artistic 'gozunder'. But here's the good bit! That is, if you are interested. Going through some boxes that had been untouched by human hand for many years, I found . . . yes . . . a 'gozunder' from Grandma Mayor's famous toilet set!! Thought you might like to know!

5

We never closed

'Are you there, Mrs Hird?'

This enquiry always followed a quick knock on our front door, which was always open, that is from about eight o'clock in a morning until eleven or later at night, when my mother would say, very dramatically, 'Have you locked the front door, Jim?'

I must admit there was no need to lock the front door because we really had nothing of great value to pinch! Well, no, that's not quite fair of me really. There were things like the piano, my dad's various banjos, our Nev's many musical instruments, my mother's very tiny diamond earrings and silver coffee set, which an aunt had left to her when she had passed away.

Apart from those, everything else was only of great sentimental value, although, really, those *are* the most valuable of all one's possessions I think! But, 'Have you locked the front door, Jim?' was always said with such dramatic feeling that after my mother had been assured, we were able to go to our beds and sleep peacefully and safely (even though the back kitchen door was never locked because it couldn't be as there was never a lock on it!)

So, our front door was open, eight to eleven. I'd like

to think the Windmill Theatre derived its slogan 'We Never Closed' from us. But it didn't.

Rat-tat!

'Are you there, Mrs Hird?' If I had a shilling for every time I had heard that, or, 'Can I come in for a minute, Mrs Hird?' or 'Are you in, Mrs Hird?', I'd be well off.

There's no doubt my mother was a Living Wonder – her great big heart seemed to beat solely for the purpose of helping people, and I sometimes try to comfort myself by thinking it was not surprising that she died when she was only sixty-two, of heart trouble, because she had used her loving heart so very much – it was tired out.

When she did die, there was a hush of respect and loss in the whole district and it is with the same feeling and great pride that I pen this next bit. 'Are you there, Mrs Hird?' As I say, there would be a quick 'Rat-tat' on the front door, the enquiry as to whether my mother was in (which in itself was a laugh as she hardly ever went out!) and then there would be one of the following various requests, 'Can you lend my mother an eggcupful of tea please?' or 'Please, Mrs Hird, can you lend me two candles?' or, offering the teacup they held in their hand 'Can you lend me a drop of vinegar?' or, a frequent request, 'Mrs Hird, me mother says have you please got a piece of brown paper and some string, she wants to send a parcel?'

My memories of these daily requests are very warm and loving ones and I can still remember my mother's soft smile as she would say, 'Yes, of course, love,' to the tea, candles or vinegar type of requests and 'Just a minute, love, I'll have a look,' to the brown paper and string appeal. (I still carefully fold a piece of good brown paper and I have a biscuit tin painted red that houses good pieces of string – not that it's likely anyone is going to knock on our door and request either, but I suppose old habits die hard, and even in this Sellotape age it's amazing how often one uses brown paper and string – and it would be great if one of my splendid neighbours were ever in need and I could oblige. I don't think they ever *will* be – because I'll bet *they* save nice big pieces of brown paper and good lengths of string. Who doesn't?)

I recall one afternoon when there was the usual rat-tat on the door and a voice called, 'Oh, can you come a minute, Mrs Hird, the baby's had a fit!'

Off went my mother. She wasn't a nurse or anything – the frightened mother of the baby knew this – but the fact that my mother was *there* until the Doctor arrived was all the young mother wanted.

Another type of 'non-paying customer' – and there were dozens of these, bless 'em – would knock on the door without calling out to see if my mother was 'There' or 'In' or anything else. This type would remain at the open front door until my mother answered the knock by joining them. 'Oh hello, So and So,' my mother would say and then after an answering, 'Hello, Mrs Hird' the dialogue would usually run something like this:

'Er – sorry to trouble you, Mrs Hird, but I'm going to a Fancy Dress Ball as a gypsy on Friday at the Ambulance Hall (or "The Albert Hall" – oh, yes, we had an Albert Hall in Morecambe – or "The Tower" – we'd one of those as well!) and will you make my face up please?'

There was never any hesitation on my mother's part. 'Of course I will, love, what time does it start?'

'Eight o'clock,' the would-be gypsy would reply.

'All right, you'd better come here about seven and – oh – have you got plenty of beads and some brass curtain rings for earrings?' 'Well, no,' would be the doleful reply. 'Oh well, don't worry. I'll get out the bead box and you can choose which you would like after I've made you up, love!'

I must add at this point that the 'Fancy Dress Ballers' who called weren't always going to the Ball as gypsies. Oh no, we were perruquiers and make-up artists to Grecians, Italians, Romans, Red Indians, clowns and . . . all for love! Never mind about 'We Never Closed!' We Never *Charged* either!

That was my mother's principle and, as she would say to my dad, 'Well, Jim, if it's giving them a bit of pleasure!' To which James Henry would reply, 'You'll kill yourself doing for other people. You never stop, you're so soft, you'll run when the dog won't!'

I never knew the meaning of that remark but one thing I *did* know, he wouldn't have had my mother any different!

The prizewinning request for help came one Sunday. There was the usual rat-tat and, 'Are you there, Mrs Hird?' followed by a tearful young neighbour coming along the passage into our living-kitchen.

'Now then,' said my mother, her own face looking as sad and troubled as the young neighbour's, 'whatever's the matter, love?'

The young woman wiped her eyes and blew her running nose and amidst sobs informed us that her young husband's father and mother had turned up unexpectedly. (I can vouch for the unexpected bit – if you live at the seaside you are expected to run a free boarding house for relatives and always have enough food in to feed 'em!) However, her in-laws had turned up for the day and she and her husband had had their dinner, two chops, half an hour ago, and as it was the in-laws' first visit since she'd married their loving son, she wanted to impress them.

Stopping to have another nose blow and wipe the tears away she said, 'I – er – feel awful asking you this, Mrs Hird – but have you done a roast?'

Isn't the Lancashire idiom lovely? 'Have you *done* a roast?' *not* 'Have you roasted a joint?' My mother looked at the young wife. 'Yes,' she said, 'as a matter of fact I was just going to carve – why?' 'Well – er,' and the tears flowed again. 'Could you lend it to me – I do want to create a good impression – I'll bring it back after!'

My mother's eyes did a quick side glance at my father – he was sitting by the fire reading the Sunday paper. He was no help – he didn't even look up, he knew what the result would be, and he wasn't reading either – I could see that – he was thinking!

'Now don't upset yourself like that,' my mother comforted as she darted into the back kitchen. She immediately produced a large black japanned tray from down by the side of the old fashioned kitchen dresser. Placing the tray on the top of the dresser, the part of the dresser she baked or cut bread on etc., the next move was to the gas stove against the opposite wall. Quick as a flash, the still-sizzling joint of sirloin beef on its meat plate was transferred to the tray.

Plonk! I can still hear that meat plate landing on the tray as I write this – and I can still remember my dad's expression as he very carefully and deliberately folded the *Sunday Chronicle* and put it down.

'You'd better take the vegetables as well,' my mother was saying, as vegetable dishes of steaming goodness were lifted off the plate rack on the stove where thay had been keeping warm. The next item was the gravy – which my mother always made in the meat roasting tin, using all the lovely succulent juices of the roasted meat as a base. By this time my dear father was in a state of trance or at least that's what he looked like. Next item on the menu? A large apple pie and a glass jug of custard waltzed their way onto the tray, as my mother was advising, 'And you'd better go out the back way, love, then nobody will see you!'

During that bit of the drama the dresser drawer was opened and a spotless white towel whisked out and laid over the large trayful of food. Amid sniffs of gratitude and thanks, the lucky winner was saying, 'Ooo, you are good, Mrs Hird. I don't know what we'd all do without you – ooo, you are that kind,' etc., etc. And out she went, the back way.

Now you know the sort of silence that hits you? We experience it at our little country place at night – one can almost 'hear the silence'. Right, that was the atmosphere in our house after the sizzling sirloin, roasted potatoes, cauliflower, peas, roasted parsnips, carrots and light-as-fluff Yorkshire puds, not to mention the apple pie and custard, had made their exit, the back way! Neville and I had never uttered a sound during the entire pantomime – we knew better. We also knew this was typical of our mother, and we also knew from experience the expression on Dad's face!

There was a deathly hush. In fact Nev and I were nearly at our tittering stage, because James Henry Hird was standing 'looking at nothing', chin in air; he looked as though he was contemplating the narrow border of wallpaper that divided the paper on the wall from the two foot frieze. He was what is known as 'containing himself'. After what seemed about two days, but was actually about half a minute, my mother, who was still in the back kitchen, started to sing a few bars of 'Oh, where is my boy tonight?' – very softly, of course, and then, just as though nothing unusual had happened or as though it was the normal routine to go to all that trouble to cook a big dinner for your loved ones and then give it away before they'd even sampled it, she called out, 'Can you eat *two* fried eggs with your bacon, Jim, love?'

By now, my father was viewing the table, almost as though he'd never seen it before – the white linen cloth, places set for four people, Victorian silver cruet (cleaned by yours truly every Friday!), linen serviettes in our individual rings.

'Can you eat two fried eggs with your bacon, Jim, love?'

'Yes, please,' replied James Henry, in the voice he used when playing kings or Roman emperors – while still contemplating the table. 'They'll be very nice with horseradish sauce!'

6
Salute to the Royalty

The Royalty Theatre – a lovely old building, a wonderful theatre, acoustically perfect!

The few surviving records in existence report that it was 'a compact comfortable and well-appointed place of entertainment, a handsome stone structure, designed by Frank Matcham in the classic style, first opened April 4, 1898, with the W. Green production of *The Sign of the Cross*. Capable of seating 1,400 people with the stalls and pit on the ground floor, the dress and upper circles on the first floor, and the balcony and gallery above.' A contemporary chronicled, 'The entrance is in Market Street with the pit and gallery entrance in Cheapside. The Royalty Theatre and Opera House is lavishly decorated throughout, and is one of the most comfortable outside London.'

All the above (with the exception of *The Sign of the Cross* bit!) was to be a great big happy and wonderful portion of my life – some folks have all the luck! My dad was Stage Manager – beg your pardon, Stage *Director* cum-Front-of-House-Manager-cum-general-dogsbody! Great! He would often put on a dress suit and deputize for the Manager (on the nights when the manager preferred playing snooker in the Conservative Club!).

The theatre was not only part of our lives, it was part of our home, too, because many was the time when most of our furniture was on the stage! It's a fact – my mother came in from shopping one day, walked into the living-room and thought she had walked into an empty house – the table we ate off, the chairs, cushions, curtains, hearthrug, fender and fire irons – all gone! She knew where they had disappeared to – the Royalty stage! Not so much a kitchen more a way of life!

Neville and I would be sent off to play on the stage if my mother wanted us from under her feet. This was wonderful because we let our histrionic ability rip to an imaginary audience.

At a very tender age Nev and I knew quite a bit about stage management – when I say we knew about stage management, I mean we knew what the words brace, weight, backcloth, wings, borders, cleating and iron sheet meant – it was all part of our education, part of life and growing up among these things.

Mind you, there were one or two occasions when we let it rip at the wrong time! The following episode occurred when I was about four and a half and Neville was six. There was a visiting drama company appearing at the time and we were standing on the 'Opposite Prompt' side of the stage – we should have been in bed, but we weren't – and we saw our mother on the opposite side, near the prompt corner. Being aware that if we tip-toed very quietly behind the back-cloth we could go over to mum, we set off. Nev was wearing a sailor suit in navy blue, complete with bell-bottomed trousers, lanyard, sailor collar and a sailor hat informing all who were interested that he was a member of the crew of HMS IRON DUKE. The hat, incidentally, showed his ears off to a disadvantage.

As for me, I was wearing a white needlework dress with what can only be described as a low waistline, very short, my hair in curls (of course! Cloth rags every night!!) and a crêpe-de-chine mob cap! We weren't dressed up *as* anything, these were our normal clothes, and forgive my mentioning this, we were always considered 'very well dressed'!

Anyway, as I said, we saw our mother on the other side of the stage, so Neville took my hand and we proceeded to tip-toe behind the backcloth. When we got half-way across we stopped dead – the backcloth had a centre opening, and there we were, *in full view of the audience!*

The drama was in full progress, the audience gripped in silence! Until it saw us! Cripes! A howl of laughter greeted our appearance and the poor actors and actresses who were acting their socks off wondered what they'd done!

I suppose the correct thing would have been for us to continue on our way, but, you see, we were pros' kids, and we thought that the audience might accept that we were part of the play if we performed. So we started to dance the military two-step.

There was a louder gale of laughter accompanied by a round of applause. Well, need I describe what a round does to an artist? There we were, me doing the curtsey and Admiral Hird doing the salute, and when we came to the end part of the military two-step we made our exit waltzing off!

I shall never forget my poor mother's face as we

more or less waltzed into her arms; she was trembling all over and hurriedly pleaded with one of the stage hands, 'Get them out of sight, Harold, before Mr Hird sees them!'

Harold did, and whisked us out of the stage door and into 6, Cheapside – pffpt! He was a wonderful man, was Harold, NCOIC of pulling the curtain up and down, right up to the time of my returning to the Royalty Theatre as guest star years later.

There was one person who had *not* laughed at our execution of the military two-step! James Henry! He was in the dress circle bar (just socially of course!) when the first howl of laughter broke the silence. He rushed out of the bar, wondering what the audience were laughing at – it was a gripping drama, don't forget – and as he arrived at the back of the Dress Circle, he was just in time to see Nev saluting and yours truly doing a curtsey! He rushed down the stairs, down by the side of the stalls and through the pass door on to the side of the stage, by which time Harold was sitting by the curtain rope as though nothing untoward had happened, and my mother had stopped trembling enough to follow us home. 'Where are they?' he hissed at Harold, but – and here's where the devil looks after his own – Harold heard the curtain cue and, hands above his head, he grabbed the rope of the curtain and got on with his job. End of Act I! I know it all upset my dad that much, he had to go back to the bar for another drink!

We were seriously reprimanded – and rightly so – and we behaved ourselves . . . well, for a fortnight anyway.

My mother used to provide accommodation for some of the pro's to 'help get the rates together'. Because my parents had been in so many 'digs' themselves, they understood how important it was to make a week's digs like home, and actors and actresses used to fall over backwards to return to my mother's wonderful cooking and kindness.

Needless to say, Nev and I would get to know our paying guests very well, and about two weeks after the last little 'cantata', we had the leading man from the visiting company staying with us. By the middle of the week we had become very pally with him – he was really a very nice person, and was to become quite a famous actor. There we were, standing on the O.P. side, quiet as mice.

It was the first time we had been allowed on the side of the stage since our military two-step episode – so we were relishing it; a drama again – drama was very popular and was played very successfully at the Royalty in those days. The scene was a churchyard and the 'grave drop' was in use that week with the property headstone pushed back flat on the prop grass. Standing at the side of the newly dug prop gravedrop was our friend, attired in seventeenth-century clothes and wig and performing a very heartbreaking soliloquy. It was all very, very sad.

Suddenly, Nev nudged me gently, and putting his mouth to my ear he whispered, 'That's so and so who's staying at our house!'

'No, it's not,' I whispered back.

'Yes, it is,' whispered Nev.

You know what brothers and sisters are like – the

'No, it's not,' 'Yes, it is,' went on for a bit. I couldn't recognize our friend who played 'Snakes and Ladders' and 'Ludo' with us, in his old-fashioned get-up. 'Yes – it – is!' stated the Admiral and without more ado, walked onto the stage, tugged at the grief-stricken actor's long jacket and enquired,

'*I* know *you* – don't I?'

That did it! Big howls of laughter! I only stood in the wings, weakly pleading, 'Hey, come off, our Nev!'

When I grew old enough to understand what a terrible experience we had put the leading man through, the part that struck me as funniest was the actor *ignoring* Nev and carrying on with the very, very sad soliloquy, while trying to brush Nev's tugging hand off his coat!

Poor Harold was standing by to do his whisking!

The Iron Sheet (the name for the asbestos curtain) is the fire curtain that must be lowered once during every performance, to prove that the stage can be cut off from the audience in case of fire. The curtain at the Royalty was covered with advertisements. Not everyone bothered to read then, but the tradespeople who had paid to advertise on the curtain hoped the audience would! The adverts were very instructional and enlightening – you were *informed* that Dr Williamson manufactured 'Pink pills for Pale People'; you were *instructed* 'Don't wear a Truss – see us!' and the name of the firm who were 'Us' was there in its glory; you were *told* that you needn't suffer a cough if you tried 'Veno's Lightning Cough Cure'; and you were *shown* the figure you could achieve by wearing 'Spirella Corsets for Ladies'. (If you weren't a lady it was no use trying them, I suppose!) You were *advised* to use 'Ven-yusa Vanishing Cream'. Oh, it was an education in itself was that curtain! It was always lowered and raised very slowly because of its weight, being guided into position by a series of rings attached to its sides, which moved with the curtain up and down a strong wire. It's amazing the feeling of anticipation one could get when, after the interval, it started to go up! The noise of chattering would subside and by the time the iron sheet had slowly disappeared, the auditorium was usually quiet.

After the *I*-know-*You* episode, Nev and I were forbidden the stage during a performance, though we were allowed on the side of it during the interval. The iron sheet was down and the coffee and biscuits were being served. It was a play with the same set all night – so there wasn't even the excitement of a scenery change. I can only think that Jolly Jack Tar got a bit bored – whatever the reason, he suddenly thought he would have a 'look through' at the audience. Why not? – there might have been someone in front we knew!

Pushing his head, with the sailor cap on, between the guide wire and the iron sheet, he surveyed the house. This was great! He faithfully reported anything of interest to me, and then the first bar bell rang at the side of the stage – the signal to start to raise the iron sheet!

Immediately the first bell rang Nev started to withdraw his head, complete with cap; as he did so, the guide wire of the iron sheet put a brake on the proceedings – it wedged behind his ear!

It's all right saying that if he had gone forward again he could have backed out sideways, but you don't think of such technicalities when you are six! The more he backed the more the guide wire stuck in the back of his ear where it was attached to his head. He gave a piercing howl – the chatter stopped, the coffee cups rattled – and the entire audience looked round about them in wonderment trying to discover where the howls were coming from. Suddenly, someone spotted the sailor cap anchored in between the side of the curtain and the wire and shouted, 'Eee, it's little Neville Hird!'

By now, the brave sailor was not only in pain but frightened to death! The audience laughed, of course, it must have looked rather comic. James Henry was in the bar, but like a flash, same route as usual, he reached the stage and released his son in time to prevent any serious damage. That little episode made us behave ourselves for a long time afterwards.

And, of course, it didn't do our Neville's ears much good!

As far as I can remember, we were never allowed to stand at the side again, but we were allowed under the stage or in the 'prop' room and for the benefit of those who have never been in a prop room, I hereby declare they have missed a lot! Magic! Pure magic! Gold painted goblets, cushions, curtains, photographs in 'solid gold' painted frames, artificial flowers, thrones, suits of armour, swords, lances, Roman soldiers' helmets. You name it – it's in the 'prop' room.

We could even play 'house' there, for there were always stacks of pots and pans, cups and saucers; and we could be a Chinese Mandarin and his wife if we wanted – the prop headdresses were there; or a Zulu warrior and his wife, if we felt in that mood, since the horsehair, feathered headdresses and spears were there for the picking up.

Our vivid imaginations carried us into a world of make believe in this veritable Aladdin's Cave. Fantastic! Who wanted to stand at the side of the stage and watch the acting when there was this wonderland?

And talk about being lucky, it wasn't the only 'prop' room of which we were to be given the free run, because when my father left the Royalty to work on the Central Pier, we discovered to our indescribable joy that the Pier Pavilion and Concert Hall boasted a smashing prop room as well. But that will have to wait until I get to the 'Pier Period', later on!

7

'All that glitters'

It has always been the little seemingly unimportant things in life that have been important and given me the most pleasure. Take for instance, the stage door or doors of the Royalty, they were double doors but were always referred to as the stage door. If you wanted to get in you put your index finger into a hole at the joining of the two doors, a hole that had grown bigger with wear over the years because of the thousands of index fingers that had attacked it. If you were coming out, you pushed the crush bar up and made a hell of a noise by doing so, which you were warned, could be heard on the stage. The notice on the back of the door read, 'Please use care when using the stage door during a performance,' and another one read, 'Please close door quietly whilst the play is in progress.'

The doors of the dress circle were magnificent (I thought) and when I was very small I used to pretend that they were the doors to my Mansion, with solid gold handles! Solid gold, they weren't really of course, they were brass, but the cleaners would clean and polish them until they looked like solid gold, well, they did to me anyway, and when you are a very little girl with a vivid imagination, who would want a Mansion with brass handles? And once again, to quote my mother, 'I wasn't hurting anybody.' Little did I think that years afterwards I would be asked if there was any small piece of the Royalty I would like as a keepsake. I don't need to tell you what I requested, do I? That's it! Of course I chose the dress circle door handles.

Psychiatrists say that events in one's childhood affect life later on. Well I'm not clever enough to spout about that, but I do know that in our Mews House in London, we pull open the inner door with one of the brass handles from the late lamented St James's Theatre dress circle doors and another one opens the house door that gives access to the garage. The door to the stairs pulls too beautifully with the brass handle from the Pass Door from the late Exeter Theatre Royal. I clean all these – I love 'em! And although it may sound unbelievable and boring when I say that my husband and I have never had what you would describe as 'a real row', I hereby declare that I nearly hit him with the tin of metal polish when he suggested having the handles lacquered.

8
Walloping

It was a great advantage having a dad who, entertainmentwise, was as professional as mine. Everything, but everything, had to be rehearsed and rehearsed, timed and timed again, until the end product appeared to be done with complete ease. At the tender age of three I was taught my first 'break', or step, towards becoming a 'walloper'. Walloping was like clog-dancing, which later became step dancing, which later became tap dancing. I was very lucky in that respect, too. I had five cousins – Madge, Nellie, Queenie, Gwen and Alys (that was short for Alice), of whom Nellie and Alys were 'wonderful wallopers'. They were all in the theatrical business, with the exception of Gwen.

Alys taught me my first steps in walloping. Our living-kitchen floor's being red and black tiles was most accommodating (not because the tiles were red and black but because I could hear the taps of each break I made: 123, 123, 1234567). As we entered our living-kitchen from the passage from the front door there was a grained and varnished wooden partition from floor to ceiling, I suppose it was there to keep the draught out, but to me and our Nev it was always, 'the wings'. It was great, one could stand behind it and then make an entrance 'on cue' or make an equally convincing exit behind it!

I can remember as clearly as though it was yesterday, and I couldn't have been more than three and a half or four at the time, how I requested my audience (Mum, Dad and Neville) to 'Please watch me do this break!' Off I went behind the partition, made an entrance, did my break and made an exit! Don't think I got a lot of hand-clapping and praise, because I didn't. As I remember it, my mother said something loving and encouraging, but James Henry's contribution was constructive criticism and remarks such as, 'Smile!' and 'Don't stick your tongue out!' (This is a habit of mine while concentrating – in fact, I am doing it as I type this.)

Little did I know then that he would always criticize my work – but never destructively – and that I would only be able to repay his patience and teaching by trying my best to become a professional . . . and by loving and admiring him as much as any daughter possibly could.

During a visit to London, Neville told me how very well measured the tongue and grooved wood of the partition in our living-room was. He explained to me that there was not a nail or a spot of glue in its entire construction and that it stood perfectly between the living-room floor and ceiling, like the Trojan Wall! We had a very small wall built in our London home quite recently, and it was six inches out of plumb from floor to ceiling. You can't help laughing, can you?

9
The little urchin

As a little girl I attended a dancing class at Miss Nelson's School. Well, the school would often receive requests for children to entertain at church garden fêtes or bazaars or suchlike. The following little 'cantata' in my life happened when I was about eight years old.

One morning a gentleman called at the school and, after the usual amount of flattery, asked Miss Nelson if twelve of her 'very clever little girls' could appear at 'George Hall's Benefit'. Now George Hall was a very popular figure in Morecambe. He was a good-looking man and a splendid entertainer. He presented a concert party each summer season in a wooden structure on the promenade, and they revelled under the name of 'The Merry Japs'. I have no intention of underestimating anyone's intelligence by explaining that the artists were dressed in Japanese costume, but this was only for the first half of the programme. After the interval, it was concert party tradition for the gentlemen to wear tail suits and the ladies evening gowns. But I mustn't allow myself to get carried away about concert parties at this juncture because I shall endeavour to do full justice to them later on, because concert parties were responsible for a very happy portion of my life.

So now, where was I? Oh, I know. As I said, this gentleman came to the school and requested the artistry, talents, free services or whatever else you like to call it, of twelve little girls. I was one of the chosen few and off we went accompanied by Miss Merci Nelson, on a horsetram along the promenade.

When we arrived at the 'Merry Japs' we were received as though we were late, which of course we weren't, but isn't it strange that, quite often, if you are giving your services free of charge, you are treated like some amateur who is 'dying to go on the stage'? And the culprit is always someone who is being paid!

We were ushered into the empty auditorium – empty, that is, apart from the lone cleaner and 'The Not-so-Merry Japs'. Miss Merci instructed us to take off our coats and fold them and place them neatly over the backs of the empty stalls and then to change into our dancing pumps, 'as quickly as you can, girls, please.' We were then called on stage and asked to stand in a semicircle around the light comedian. We did this and then we were given a few moves and actions by the nice stage director, who I shall refer to from now on as the NSD.

The light comedian, who appeared to me to be 'so very good looking' (and was a bit bored as I remember it), started to sing a song, a little number that went something like this:

> When Rastas Brown goes to town
> You bet a dollar he's down
> Every night soon after dark
> He wends his way to the park

Children all run off to bed
They've seen a bogey 'tis said
Can't you hear him shuffling along
The bo-oh-gee man.

Now during these lines we talented little girls had to do what can only be described as, and was indeed called, the bobbing step, which was executed thus: step to the right with the right foot (of course), bend both knees and 'bob', step to the left with the left foot (of course), bend both knees and 'bob'. Now if you sing the first four lines – although you are not familiar with the tune – and you 'bob' on 'Rastas', 'Town', 'bet a', 'down', 'night', 'dark', 'wends', and 'park', you'll find that it fits. When he sang 'children all run off to bed', we got a greater opportunity to show our ability, for on this line we ran 'Pluto fashion' down right of stage. Then, on 'They've seen a bogey 'tis said', we ran back to our original semicircle, but at the same time we had to raise our hands in horror and fear and call out '*Ohhh!*' Now then, hold on a minute, because here comes the clever stuff. On the next line we had to really act and speak!!! As the light comedian sang, 'can't you hear him shuffling along?' we had to put our right hand cupwise at the side of our mouth and call out 'Whose dat?' and 'his nibs' very obligingly answered our question in song with, 'The BO-OH-GEE Man.' I should add that on 'the night' the very good-looking light comedian was blacked up with burnt cork for this memorable production number.

The lone cleaner and the 'Not-so-Merry Japs' all seemed extremely satisfied with our rehearsal efforts and whilst we were sitting resting in the newly dusted stalls the NSD came down from the stage, by the three little steps that were painted the same colour as the proscenium and imparted the news that the following week they were holding a 'Go-as-You-Please Talent Competition'. Now for the sake of any reader who doesn't know what a GAYPC is, may I explain that it is really a '*Do*-as-you-please competition', meaning that the contestants may sing, dance, recite, juggle, play spoons, do acrobatics, play the piano or any other musical instrument, yodel or anything – well, er, nearly anything. Talent and entertainment value are judged by the volume of applause afforded each entrant. At the end of the competition all the contestants stand on the stage in a row and then the master of ceremonies or the compere holds his hand over each hopeful's head and either the audience applaud, or, in unfortunate cases, they don't.

Right, the NSD went on to say that 'it would be a very good idea if you extremely clever and talented little girls were to come along and enter the contest.' I laugh now when I think of the NSD's performance . . . 'extremely clever and talented little girls', aged eight and nine!! What he really meant was, that he was making sure of plenty of contestants. Bless him, it's the same the whole world over – a bit of flattery from the opposite sex goes a long way, even if you are only eight years old.

Well, anyway, we were quite excited and the NSD was very nice and kind really. The moment he gathered we were very enthusiastic, he struck whilst the iron was hot and asked us all what we each had in mind as a competition piece. My form mate Phyllis said she would do a bit from *The Merchant of Venice* (which wasn't surprising, as her brother was a very good amateur Shakespearean actor). Maudie was going to sing 'Men of Harlech' (which was only natural when you come to think of it, her parents being Welsh). I can't remember what Vera was going to do, and I can't remember what Madge or Mabel were going to do, but I vaguely remember that Ada, well I think it was Ada, when asked what she would be doing replied without hesitation, 'The Valeta'. 'Oh yes,' said the NSD 'who with?' 'By myself!' replied Ada. Well, as I say, I think it was Ada. But whoever it was or wasn't I can clearly remember thinking 'By herself! – I wonder how that's going to look!' The above named were all my *best friends*, so whatever they chose to attempt I knew it would be all right.

'And what are you going to do?' the NSD asked me. 'Does the pianist know, "Ours Is a Nice House, Ours Is"?' I enquired. 'Does the . . . yes, I'm sure he does,' he replied, slightly surprised at my unexpectedly forthright request. 'Look, dear, go up those three little steps at the side of the stage and ask him!' So I did! The pianist was sitting at an upright piano having a cigarette after his patient efforts in the 'Rastus Brown' number. I stepped on to the stage and approached the piano. 'Excuse me,' I said, 'can you play "Ours Is a Nice House, Ours Is"?' His reply was to do so immediately, whereupon I politely stopped him carrying on by saying, 'Excuse me but will you give me four bars in please?' Honestly, he nearly fell off the piano stool. 'Will I give you four bars in . . . and how do you know about four bars in?' he asked, laughing (although I couldn't see anything very funny in what I'd said).

'Well,' I explained, 'I need four bars to make an entrance . . . please.' 'Certainly,' he replied, still laughing, and into the four bars he went. Bless him!

Now I must explain, four bars in, an orchestra tuning up, curtain music or anything in that line has the same effect on me as the 'Stripper' music had on the stripper who always started to strip when she heard it – wherever she might be! I don't mean I started to strip off . . . I was only eight . . . but remembering my dad's tuition, 'You must always make a polished entrance and exit,' and hearing the music, like a flash I was in the wings and then 'Making an entrance!' I sang one chorus of 'Ours Is a Nice House', and, as I was getting near the end of it I called out, 'One more chorus please!' On went the pianist, this time an octave higher, and into my 'wallop routine' I went. It's a great tune to wallop to and luckily I knew enough 'breaks' to last a chorus – well, just about. When the music arrived at the last line of the chorus I did what was to be my first 'big finish', the shoe wipe! Eeee, hecky plonk! The shoe wipe! Right heel forward, left heel forward, step back with right foot, step back with left foot, bend down and pretend to wipe toes of shoes from left to right and from right to left. The whole thing is so elementary it's difficult to describe, but it looks rather effective when you are only eight! I thanked the pianist (rather like a variety artist thanks the orchestra in the band pit) and tripping down the three little steps I returned to my seat in the stalls to as much applause as about twenty people can muster.

The NSD and some of the now 'Very Merry Japs' clustered round me bombarding me with questions such as 'Where did you learn to do that?' and 'Who taught you all about making an entrance and an exit?' and 'How old are you?' (What a question to ask an actress!) and 'What's your name?' I only answered the last question. 'Thora Hird,' I said. 'Hird?' said the NSD. 'You're not Jimmy Hird's little girl are you?' 'Yes, I am!' I replied. 'Aw, well then,' added the NSD, 'I don't bloody wonder!'

As we sat in the horse tram going back to school, I didn't bother to think what it was that he didn't bloody well wonder at, because I was too busy bloody wondering how I could enter that 'Go-as-you-please competition' without my parents knowing. Should I ask their permission and risk being refused? Or should I confide in my hero, our Nev? Yes, that would be the best thing, tell our Nev, he would advise me, he always did, and in any case he was the only person I could think of who would lend me the penny to pay my fare on the horse tram that was to carry me to George Hall's. I could pay my own fare back.

Well, and I say this modestly, I won, but first things first.

We all appeared at the benefit as arranged, Rastus Brown strode to town, we did the bobbing step magnificently, and that was that. Oh, and I think and really hope that George Hall really benefited from his benefit.

When the day of the GAYPC arrived, the following week, I went to school as usual. I'm going to describe what I was wearing, as it is quite important to the story. I had on a white knitted jumper with a pale blue crocheted edge round the neck through which was slotted a chainstitch cord with a little pom-pom on each end. When the neck was drawn up the woollen cord tied in a bow, leaving the pom-poms at chest level. Right? Now with this I wore a pale blue pleated skirt (mini length) made of silk morocaine, very short white socks and white buckskin strap shoes. Add to this rather innocent and charming sight . . . my curls! These were the result of my sitting each night before I went to bed, having my curl rags put in. Any reader who has suffered this form of torture will be aware of the procedure but for the benefit of all those lucky people who have been blessed with naturally curly hair and know not of what I speak, allow me to explain.

Curl rags are to encourage ringlets. The straight-haired victim such as I was (and still am) assumes a sitting position, whilst her loving mother, who is standing (and therefore at an advantage to lop you one with the hair brush if you don't keep still), with gentle care brushes out a strand of hair; one end of a curl rag, which varies in length according to the length of the victim's hair, is then passed over the head of the would be curly top and that same end is held tightly in the childish fist, whilst the other end of the rag is held equally tightly by the loving mother who then proceeds to wrap the strand of hair round her half of the rag. The victim's half of the rag is folded over the wrapped round hair and tied in a bow at the bottom of the now prepared ringlet. This process is repeated as many times as the thickness of hair allows, and the result is that the victim is reminiscent of the wonderful invention that landed on the moon! I will admit that when my curl rags were taken out in the morning, and the corkscrews of hair brushed round my mother's finger, it was worth all the agony – well, for a couple of hours, anyway. My being blessed with the straightest hair conceivable, and our living at the seaside, where the air is always a bit damp, meant that by lunchtime my curls were rather pathetic. Anyway, you've got the picture of me on the day of the GAYPC.

I'm sure you must be wondering why all the secrecy and the 'not telling my parents' bit. Well, you see, as I have already told you, my dad was a perfectionist and very professional, and even at that tender age I knew that he would not let me enter the competition until my simple little effort had been rehearsed and rehearsed – even if he had allowed me to enter at all, which was doubtful. Neither he nor my mother wanted Nev or me to be bitten by the acting bug: 'It's too precarious a business,' they would insist, hence the big secret with Nev. I can honestly say that it was the first time I had ever deceived my parents. Mind you, at eight years old I should hope it was!

I'm not making excuses, but everything fitted in perfectly, and that alone encouraged me. My dad was on the pier and my mother was 'doing the make-up' for the Amateur Shakespearean Company who were playing next door at the Royalty and having a go at *The Tempest*, so each of my parents would be leaving the house around five-thirty or six. I can't remember what time Nev and I set off for George Hall's and 'The Merry Japs', but I know Nev put me safely on the horsetram and I paid my fare with a penny of my own, saving the penny Nev had lent me to return home, which I did flushed with success and the proud recipient of a gold bracelet. It wasn't late when I returned home, and my parents were still out, so after a cup of cocoa (which didn't seem to go with winning a gold bracelet!) Nev and I went to bed where I kept looking at the little gold bracelet round my wrist. Surely my parents would be delighted? Or would they? Anyway, I didn't risk anything. I carefully took my prize off my wrist and tucked it under the pillow (for secrecy or safety, I can't remember which).

The following morning we got up for school as usual. I had to have my hair well brushed and plaited because, my mother having been at the theatre the night before, hadn't been able to put my famous curl rags in, and my hair looked like weary golden seaweed. Whilst my mother was plaiting my hair, I kept looking at Nev who really couldn't have cared less about my guilty secret.

I would like to mention something at this point. I suppose we have all had little daft habits when we were children – well, if we didn't we were very peculiar children, weren't we? If Nev and I had a secret or a bit of information that was very private to us alone, I would only have to look at him and I would start to titter. He would look at me with a Groucho Marx expression, and I would titter more than ever. After a while he would start tittering at me tittering – well, you know how it is with kids? Sometimes, when we were having a meal Nev would do things like nudging me ever so gently, and I would turn to look at him to find he was pointing his finger at the side of my head, and so his finger end would go in my ear 'ole. It would make me jump, and then I would explode with laughing and 'have to leave the table' – to return only when I could 'behave properly'. When I come to think of it, it was worth it because nobody has ever made me laugh more than my brother Nev. So who better than he to write some of my funniest and most successful stage comedies, many, many years after we'd tittered at the table? And although all this sounds as though we were the Barretts of Wimpole Street, with James Henry as Mr Barrett, please scrub that idea immediately, my parents were only making sure that we were obedient and observed our table manners. This they achieved. Hey, listen, I know this may sound rather old fashioned, and I don't care if it does, but I can honestly say that I get quite a lot of pleasure out of watching a child who has good table manners. I can say, just as honestly, that I get equal pleasure out of watching a scruffy, uncared-for child (who doesn't know any better) wolfing a large bread and jam sandwich!

What I'm not too fond of is the 'couldn't care less' middle attitude. But, of course, that's only my opinion.

However, back to the morning after my first act of deceit. Nev and I finished our breakfasts and I felt that that could have been the moment to confess all. But I didn't and after a quick nip upstairs and another admiring look at my gold bracelet, I wrapped it in my clean hanky and tucked it in the small pocket on the right hand leg of my knickers. I came downstairs, kissed my mother 'goodbye' (which I always did when I left the house, as though I were off on a world tour instead of only going to school), and Nev and I tittered our way out of the door and into Cheapside.

During that morning my mother was at the front door, sweeping the steps, when a lady we knew very well happened to pass our house. As she approached my mother she cheerfully said, 'Good morning, Mrs Hird, how are you?' 'Very well, thank you, Mrs Richardson . . . are you all right?' my mother replied. 'Yes thank you,' said Mrs R. 'Eeee, I say, your Thora at George Hall's last night . . . wasn't she grand?' There was a slight pause while my mother assured herself that she had heard right. Then she said, 'I think you have made a mistake Mrs Richardson, it was the last week she was at George Hall's, with some other pupils from Miss Nelson's. They were helping at the benefit you know.' And my mother continued with the job she was doing. 'I've made no mistake, love', stressed our friend. 'I was there myself last night and *saw* her. She sang "Ours Is a Nice House, Ours Is" and did a little step dance and won the Go-as-you-please competition. She didn't half get some applause and she won a gold bracelet!'

It's writing about moments like the ones that followed Mrs R's declaration that prove to me, more than ever, what a wonderfully faithful and loving mother I had. You see, there was no point in arguing with Mrs R because she had *seen* me with her own eyes and she knew me very well, so it required some rather nifty thinking on the part of my mother . . . Marie Mayor, Actress! 'Oh yes, of course,' said Marie, 'what am I thinking about! Jim was on the pier and I was making the amateurs up last night, so we couldn't go!' I think she said this because she was such a good mother that she wouldn't let me down, or show me up, and I'm sure she couldn't have borne anyone thinking that we, her children, didn't confide in her. I realize now, that she must have been wondering why I hadn't told her I was going. 'Oh, what a shame you couldn't go . . .' – Mrs Richardson was off again – '. . .what a little artist! and what a good idea to dress her up as a little urchin . . . hee, hee, that dirty face, mucky white shoes, one sock up and one down, and her hair . . . eeeeeeee, no curl in it . . . ooo, the detail, I'll bet all that was her dad's idea, wasn't it?' *Her dad's idea!!!* It was nobody's idea! It was the result of a day at school, dressed in pale blue and white, and due to the fact that Miss Trilby Hird and her personal manager Mr Svengali Hird had stayed out after school was over, getting increasingly dirtier, the curls dropping straighter, the white socks and buckskin shoes attaining a somewhat 'french-grey' appearance and the white woollen jumper losing what had been that clean, crisp, fresh look! In fact, I must have resembled a somewhat shop-soiled, eight-year-old edition of one of those grubby looking with-it pop singers we see today. (The only defence I can put up is, that *they* are old enough to know that cleanliness is next to godliness. I wasn't!)

As my mother turned back into the house (she told me all this afterwards), her first reaction was, how dare anyone accuse one of her children of looking like an urchin! That was overshadowed, however, by her sense of humour as she saw the funny side of the remark, 'I'll bet that was her dad's idea!' For she knew full well that Dad would go mad when he heard I had entered the competition, especially as I had done so on the sly, though at the same time he would be secretly proud I had won it!

When I came in from school at dinner-time, I sensed a doom-laden atmosphere as my mother said quietly, 'Sit down a moment please.' I did as I was told. 'Now, what's all this I hear about you being at George Hall's last night?' That gentle, loving face, those grey eyes so full of humour, looked straight at me. Now I can honestly say that I was never afraid of my mother, nor did she ever frighten me in any way, but when she added, 'Well, I don't know what your father's going to say I'm sure.' I can remember the ache that gripped my throat as I tried not to cry. I knew I had no cause to cry, my understanding mother was not scolding me, but even at eight years old you can feel guilty and wonder why you bothered to have a secret you needn't have.

It was at that moment we heard firm footsteps approaching along the passage from the front door. 'Here's your father,' my mother breathed . . . as if I didn't know! It's funny how my dad was always referred to as 'father' when the incident was serious enough to warrant it. Otherwise he was always 'dad'.

I put my hand in my knicker-leg pocket and clutched the bracelet as if it were a charm to ward off evil spirits! As my dad entered the living-room we both looked at his face. There was no need for Mum to explain anything, it was obvious he had already heard!

He looked at me then went straight into the back kitchen to wash his hands (I don't mean he went to wash his hands because he'd looked at me, I mean, I'm just explaining what he did). I heard the tap water running, then I heard the piece of carbolic soap thud gently back into the enamel soap tray and the little tinkle as the loose top of the soap tray settled back comfortably into position. My hand was like a clutching claw over the bracelet. Dad came back into the living-room drying his hands with great precision

. . . he often did this when he had an important announcement to make, then he looked straight at me. When I was old enough to understand 'that look', I realized it was the same look of determination that the fifteen-year-old boy who had run away from Todmorden (the Lancashire side) had had when he joined Moore and Burgesses Nigger Minstrels. But of course I wasn't realizing anything that day other than that I was going to cop it in a minute!

'And what's all this I hear about you entering a "Go-as-you-please competition" at George Hall's last night?' This was asked as he carefully folded up the towel he had been using, which was unnecessary, really, as it always hung behind the back kitchen door. I looked up at *my* dad – the man who was to teach me so very much in the ensuing years – and the pain in my throat burst into sound as the tears flowed. 'But I won, Dad! I'll won a gold bracelet!' I sobbed as I fumbled in my knicker pocket to prove it. As I did so my mother said to James Henry. 'Did you meet Mrs Richa . . .?' He decided that it was the moment to present her with the folded towel. He did this without taking his eyes off me. 'All right,' he said sternly, but not too sternly. 'All right. I'll forgive you *this* time, but don't ever dare . . . are you listening? . . . don't ever *dare* to enter a competition or anything else without first asking either your mother or me if you may and until whatever it is you are going to do is properly rehearsed and presented . . . (pause) . . . understand?' I nodded, with a sob. He offered me the clean hanky from his breast pocket (which was a beautiful gesture, really, because that particular handkerchief was the one 'for show and not for blow'). He did this because I was fumbling for my clean hanky, which as you know was in my knicker pocket, wrapped around my prizewinning gold bracelet, and not too easy to free. As he approached his chair at the dinner table he turned and said, 'And if there ever is a next time, for God's sake remember to have a *wash*! Little Urchin! . . . Bloody cheek!' The last part of the remark was obviously directed at someone who wasn't with us at that particular moment, so it seemed pretty certain that Mrs R had nobbled him as well as Mum. Pulling his chair out with great dignity he sat down. It was all beautifully done and the timing was perfect!

I wiped my eyes and blew my nose (on his handkerchief). I can't quite remember if I promised anything, but if I did I shouldn't have, because the following week Nev and I were on the sands and we heard the comedian in the pierrot show shouting, 'Now are there any little boys or girls in the audience who can dance, sing or recite? Come along and win a solid gold clock (this was said with a wink) or a cash prize!'

I'd like to think I weakened because I owed Nev a penny – not that he had asked me for it outright, but I had had a few brotherly reminders. However, whatever the reason, I found myself on that little wooden platform which was erected on wooden trestles about a foot above the sand, politely asking the pianist, 'Excuse me please, but can you play "Ours Is a Nice House, Ours Is"? And will you give me four bars in, please? Thank you!'

He could. He did. I did. And I won the cash prize . . . one shilling!!!

10

The monied lot

The prize – one shilling. When I think of the pleasure Nev and I had out of that shilling it seems unbelievable. Just wait whilst I describe what we did.

On the foreshore of the Central Pier were all sorts of automatic machines; so first of all we decided to be weighed, not on an automatic machine, though, on the jockey scales.

How lovely these particular scales always looked, all the brass shining like pure gold, the red plush upholstered hanging chair and the excitement of going up and down as weights were put on or taken off the brass plate that formed the other end of the scale. I used to love that. We each got a little paper ticket with our weight written on it in pencil, and all that only cost us one penny each, so we still had tenpence left between us.

Our next move was to put a penny each into an automatic machine. I got a little pink cardboard box of cough pastilles and Nev got a little green box which contained one Richmond Gem cigarette and a match. (He was nearly eleven and was already experimenting with a sly drag in the lavatory in our back yard.)

Now we had eightpence so we each had a go on another automatic machine.

This machine was very interesting. The top of it was like a big clock face but, instead of numerals only, it sported the letters of the alphabet as well. You inserted a penny and then proceeded to move the large iron pointer, which was similar to the big finger on a clock, round to the letter of the alphabet you required, pulling a lever after each letter had been duly pointed to. Then – this was the wonderful moment – you pressed a button and the end result was that out shot a strip of metal with your name pressed or impressed on it! On each end of the strip a hole was conveniently punched, so of course if you so desired you could nail it on a door, a box or anything you fancied.

On mine I had recorded the words THORA HIRD – ACTRESS, well, I had just won another competition, hadn't I? I think Nev only recorded his name on his strip, although I suppose he would have been eligible to have added, MONEYLENDER!

So we had sixpence now. Talk about blow the expense! We went to Anthony's Ice Cream Stall and each of us bought a halfpenny cornet. These were miniatures of the present day cones, but even so, Mr Anthony, a big, kind-hearted Italian, who knew us through Dad, to whom he paid his rent, gave us a lovely big top on our little cones.

We took our time over the ices because, well, we were getting a bit low on funds after our mad spending spree. Our method of ice cream cone eating enabled us to make them last longer: it was, lick the ice cream until it was a smooth point and then nibble a bit of the biscuit cone all round, repeat this procedure until you had a perfect miniature cone about half an inch long containing ice cream.

Right, what did the plutocrats do next? We went to Mr Bradley's pitch and had our photographs taken. This always fascinated me. I don't mean having my photograph taken, I've never enjoyed that – I mean the particular way it was done at this particular stall.

The subject sat on a wooden stool, was requested to 'smile please' and then, click, the photographer (pardon the expression) seemed to snatch something from the back of the camera, dip it furtively into an adjacent biscuit tin that held some mysterious fluid and then, the quickness of the hand deceiving the eye, plunged his hand into a bucket of water that was conveniently placed on the ground next to the legs of the camera, swish his hand about, one, two, three, four, and hey presto! the customer or subject – yes, I think 'subject' would be the better word – was presented with a tin disc about the size of a shilling, all wet! A little pin was attached to the back of the disc and on the front – hecky plonk – there was a picture of yourself, with a very wet grin, all for a penny!

One small copper coin! I confess that during my childhood I had dozens of these executed, but here's the sad bit. By the time one got home, however near one lived to the photographer's pitch, the recorded image had always grown so faint that it could have been a photograph of anybody – or anything! But who cared? Talk about your modern high speed Polaroid cameras – it will have to be damned quick to beat Mr Bradley!

We suddenly realized we only had three pence left! It

was at this juncture that my loving brother reminded me that, if I would excuse him mentioning it, I did still owe him a penny. It's amazing, the extraordinary shareholders' meeting that can take place when the final item on the agenda is what to spend the remaining capital of twopence on, something that can be shared equally between the only two shareholders in the company. Quite a lot of thought went into that, as Nev pinned my very wet photograph onto my cotton dress.

It was unanimously agreed that a penny bar of Cadbury's Nut Milk Chocolate each would be quite satisfactory. What a wonderful afternoon! I have often wondered how much I would need to win today, to do and to enjoy all the things that the shilling prize afforded us. And, please bear in mind, I was out of debt as well!

On my dressing table at the moment, I have a favourite picture of Jan as a little girl. It was taken by a visiting school photographer and had the school's brick wall as a backing. It cost ninepence. I mention this because, although it is in a Victorian silver frame, at the bottom of the photograph, wedged behind the glass, is a precious gift from our nine-year-old daughter that was. It's a strip of metal and pressed or impressed on it are the words, 'To my Mummy from Janette.'

When I was playing at the Palladium in 1966 Lawrie Kingsley and Michael Craig, the scriptwriters, called to see me and saw the above framed photograph on my dressing table – a week later I received their offering, a metal strip which read THORA HIRD – ACTRESS. They'd discovered an automatic machine in the north, still working! Aren't we all barmy? And isn't it lovely?

11

The Central Pier

There is no doubt at all that the Central Pier was responsible for a very long and happy portion of my life, in fact, during the period that my father was Manager there, I will go as far as to say it *was* our life.

Marvellous, indescribable! The hours Nev and I spent on the Pier were enjoyed to the fullest. The antics we got up to, the excitement we experienced, the jobs we had – all these things were handed to us on a plate during the period in which we grew from very small children to teenagers.

Central Pier! According to Research: 'In November 1867, public notice was given by local businessmen of their intention to form a company with the aim of providing the increasingly popular little resort with a pier. By March, 1868, the Central Pier Company had been formed, and in 1869, the Central Pier opened, apparently using some of the basic structure of a pier which had been bought for £2,500 from, apparently, Liverpool.

'The Central Pier cost £10,000 to erect altogether and was enlarged in the 1870s at a cost of a further £5,000. Architecturally, it resembled the Taj Mahal and its appearance in Morecambe Bay was certainly striking.

It featured an aquarium, baths, saloons, catering and refreshment rooms, and an observatory with a large telescope, in addition to sun decks and promenades. Later, accommodation was provided for dancing and roller-skating.

'The Pier was also used as an anchorage for ships in the late nineteenth and early twentieth century; these vessels were primarily pleasure steamers.'

Little did that English Taj Mahal know that during its chequered career it was to be invaded, cared for, enjoyed and loved by the Hird Family!

Where shall I start? That's the difficulty. I think I had better tell you about the Skating Rink first.

For those of you who roller skate, don't bother to read the next few lines – but for those of you who don't and never have – oh mates, you've missed a lot! The uninhibited freedom, the speed, the turning round and going backwards, you couldn't see where you were going but you could see where you'd been! Great!

Right, then (new readers start here), my dad had a pair of 'King of the Rink' skates made specially for me – size O. In those days the roller skates were slightly different from present-day ones. There was a leather strap attached to the back of the skate, which came round the front of the foot, just above the instep, and buckled at the side; but the front part of the skate held a sort of vice-like clip each side, which the skating rink attendant screwed tightly and savagely to the shoe sole, with a special key.

After the 'skating fiend' had collected a pair of skates (sixpence), the next bit of the procedure was to sit down, taking your turn in a row of anxious would-be champions, and when it was your turn, one foot was placed on a wooden rest – similar to the ones that are used in shoe shops these days – and then the other foot, while the attendant tightened the clips with his special key.

However, there was a bit of a drawback to this method, because, if you were a keen attender of the rink, eventually your shoe soles began to part company from your uppers! Hence the reason for most 'regulars' leaving a pair of old boots in the 'skates department'. Ooo, that room did smell awful! As the wheels of the skates had ball bearings in them, that meant they required oiling, so what with the smell of oil mixed with the smell of feet and old boots (because no regular skated in shoes) – blimey! I don't know how the attendant stood it without a gas mask!

I *loved* it all, especially the little stage at the far end of the rink. There was usually an orchestra there on a Wednesday and Saturday, not that anyone could hear the music, but you could hear the skates! It was during the 'Hird Dynasty' that a new, modern, breathtaking composition floor was laid. It was wonderful for us, we were able to skate at twice the speed we had managed on its predecessor, the wooden one. The only drawback was the *noise* – it was deafening! But we didn't care. Nev and I would waltz! Yes, *waltz*! We'd skate side by side and execute the 'Two-Step' with our arms round each other's waist, then Nev would skate backwards and I would skate forwards – we held hands for this bit – then a quick turn – whoops – and yours truly would go backwards and Nev forwards. Oh, all good stuff – no rubbish!

There was one regular called Rosie. Hecky plonk! What a wonderful skater! I used to admire her so much! *Not* her skating, her skating *boots*. She had painted them *gold* and instead of ordinary laces she used red ribbon! To my childish eyes they were smashing! I know I asked my mother if she would gild my skating boots if I brought them home, and her reply was quick and to the point, with a definite finality which informed me that I hadn't a hope of red ribbon laces either!

It was great fun for about ten skaters to form a chain, similar to a conga chain, and pretend to be a train. Unfortunately it was considered dangerous, as the speed attained by the back end of 'the train' as it whipped round corners, was terrific, and rightly, it was forbidden. So, while we might get once round the rink in that formation, we were always halted by the referee's whistle the attendant. used to blow! The attendant rather enjoyed blowing his whistle. It gave him an authoritative feeling of power, and it made him feel superior. One couldn't begrudge him it really, as he didn't get much chance of feeling superior in the Skate Department, amongst the smell of sweaty boots and oil! I often wondered if he came out and blew his whistle just to exhale and get away from the smell!

Actually, blowing his whistle was not to be compared with his performance at closing time, because for the ceremony he used a big brass handbell which he used like a fiendish Town Crier. He must have been fairly strong because that bell was a helluva weight. I once tried to pick it up and nearly fell on my face. Of course, I was only a child and never massive at that, but his handling of it, as he rang it, seemed to be child's play. What a row – I'll bet they could hear it across the Bay at Grange-over-Sands.

Sometimes he would 'build his part up' by hollering 'All off! Clear the Rink! Closing Time!' and with a final 'two-step' or 'waltz' we would make our way to the grained and varnished forms that ran along the wall of the rink, and sit in line while he performed the task of unscrewing our skates. If nobody was looking we would undo the ankle strap and kick the two back wheels of our skates against the six inch high surround of the rink, thereby releasing the skate from the boot sole. We never did that if my Dad was there, but one thing we always did was to put our own skates away, instead of passing them through the pigeonhole to the attendant.

We suffered the smell only long enough to put our skates in their own 'hole', and why not? In half a tick, we would be out on the Pier deck inhaling the healthy and invigorating sea breeze which on dozens of occasions when it was behind our backs nearly blew us down the pier!

It's funny that I have just referred to coming off the Pier, as *down* the Pier. I'll tell you why. I do know that grammatically I should say 'on the pier and off the pier', but when I was little we always used to say, 'I'm going *up* the pier' or 'I'm going *down* the pier'. The dozens of times Miss Elizabeth Nelson, my headmistress at school, corrected me about my grammatical error. She used to correct me by putting her arm straight up above her head, pointing heavenwards and saying,

'Does the pier stand on end and go upwards, Thora?' and I would reply 'No, Miss Nelson, I'm sorry, I meant to say "*on* the pier".' She was a wonderful person – God rest her – well, she must have been, because I loved school so much.

I left school when I was fourteen, prior to the Whitsuntide holidays and I didn't *want* to leave a bit. The 'Whit' holiday was always a short one, a week or ten days, and although I loved school holidays like any other normal schoolgirl, that particular holiday was rather marred by the fact that I wouldn't be returning to school after it.

The day arrived when school started again – I was miserable. Quite a few of my friends used Cheapside en route for Union Street, where the 'Preparatory School, Morecambe' was situated, so I went and stood at our front room window, to watch them enviously on their journey back.

When I got up on that particular morning, I had dressed in my gym slip, clean white blouse and school tie. Wishful thinking I suppose.

I heard my mother call out, 'Where are you, love?' when she couldn't see me in the living-kitchen.

'In here,' I replied on a dull note. That was all. In a couple of minutes I heard my mother coming along the passage and then entering the front room (or sitting-room), I didn't turn round, well, not immediately, but I did a couple of seconds later as I heard her say, 'Here you are!' With these words she handed me my leather school bag.

'Go on,' she said smiling, 'and see if Miss Nelson will let you start another term.' The hug I gave my understanding mother nearly broke her neck. Pffft! Grabbing my school hat, I was out of the house and had caught my pals up before they'd reached the top of 'our street'.

As we all filed into school Miss Nelson was performing her usual ritual of Good morning, Madge – Good morning, Una, Good morning, Ada, Good morning Mabel – between each of these greetings there was a 'Good morning, Miss Nelson' from each pupil. On she went, 'Good morning, Maud – Good morning, Lilian, Good morning, Thora – Good morn —' By then I had walked past with the rest. However, she caught up with me, and very kindly asked, 'What are you doing here, Thora? You're supposed to have left school, aren't you?'

I looked into her face, and started to say, 'Yes, I have left school *really*, Miss Nelson, but I saw the girls coming back this morning and I wondered if . . .'

I didn't get any further, I didn't need to; she looked at me steadily – d'you know, she was quite moved? It was with a very soft and gentle voice she assured me, 'Of course – I'm proud to have you back – now, come along, girls!'

This last bit was in her normal Headmistress's voice, and, clapping her hands, she instructed us all to get in line. Quite honestly, I don't think I have ever sung 'Holy, holy, holy' better, or with more gusto!

So, I was back at school – good egg! Back with Ada Lob, Mabel Bagshaw, Una Yates, Kathy Mortimer, Lilian Cross, Maudie Poles, Vera Muff, Madge Peel and Uncle Tom Cobley and all – *my lot! My friends!*

Now, you've just read that last sentence and you are thinking I've made up those wonderful names, aren't you? Oh yes you are! Well, I haven't! And I'll tell you this, when our register was called at school and the surname of the pupil was called out first, it was like a funny story because it sounded like this: Lob Ada, Muff Vera, Cross Lilian, Hird Thora, Stretch Billy, Peel Madge, etc. etc., Cross Lilian heard Thora stretch Billy peel Madge!

It is with the greatest affection and respect I tell you these names, and it is with happy remembrances that I mention them whenever I play a summer season anywhere. I'm not taking the mickey out of them, it's because I don't want to forget them. They were all part of the time when we were all preparing to become decent citizens of the future. God bless 'em!

I must think of some way to get my train of thought back to the Central Pier – I *do* go off the subject a bit – don't I?

Actually, it was only shortly after I had made my 'return visit' to school that I got a job – on the Pier. But all that I will tell you later on.

The Central Pier Pavilion was a really magnificent structure. The wooden steps that were the approach to its front doors were very wide. I can't recall how many there were but I do remember that just ascending them gave you the feeling that you were going to be entertained to a really first-class evening of enjoyment. You weren't disappointed either. It *was* first class entertainment. No doubt about that!

The theatre part had a most imposing stage, splendid electrical equipment, gantries, the flies – oh, everything. The boxes in the auditorium were each supported by three nude women, my 'Vestal Virgins'.

Well, I say they were nude, they were nude to the

part just below their navels, beyond which they were swathed in plaster ninon drapes. Their arms were behind their heads and their beautiful faces with blank eyes were crowned with wavy plaster hair, parted in the middle and kept in place by a soft-looking plaster turban.

They each sported a beautiful pair of wonderfully moulded breasts. I was very fond of these shameless ladies and I really cannot understand why we are supposed to 'tut, tut' at a permissive society when we have always been allowed to gaze freely at statues. Even undraped statues!

As young as I was then, I thought my 'Ladies of the Boxes' were really beautiful, and they didn't shock me in any way. I had my own 'Temple of the Vestal Virgins' right there.

As a point of interest, although I adore Greece and have visited it several times, I cannot honestly say that standing in front of the remains of the authentic 'Temple of the Vestal Virgins' gave me as much pleasure as my plaster friends who appeared to support the Central Pier Pavilion boxes did!

There was a great advantage to the structure of the Northern Taj Mahal – in front of each of the two smaller domes gracing the roof was a small balcony. Yes, very advantageous were those two balconies. Nev and I grew mustard and cress on one, and kept doves on the other! I'll tell you about the Market Gardening first.

Having acquired four shallow wooden boxes, we pestered my mother until she gave us small pieces of a woollen blanket. These were wrung out in cold water and placed in the boxes, and then we diligently sprinkled mustard seed in two of the boxes and cress seed in the remaining two. You see, the idea was, to present my mother with not only 'mustard and cress' but mustard *or* cress. How about that, then?

It grew like mad and we looked after it with loving care. As soon as one crop had been gathered in we planted another lot. The balconies were real suntraps – we had access to them through two doors high up in the balcony of the Pavilion (we were only allowed through either of these doors and on to the balcony outside when Dad was with us!). The aforementioned doves were really Neville's concern and in the winter, when the weather was not really suitable for human beings to be out in, never mind gentle doves, he kept them indoors in Dad's room at the side of the stage.

During the summer season on the Central Pier, there would be various Concert Parties in the Pavilion. These were really first-class productions, with excellent artistes who were always beautifully dressed. 'The Superbs', 'The Emeralds', 'Frills and Flounces', 'The Ideals', 'The Seven Nobody's', 'The Mountebanks' and 'The Pelicans'.

They always opened the first half of the show in the traditional pierrot costumes, wearing ruffles and pierrot hats, and clothes as well of course. How I used to admire the ladies' short, full and frilly skirts, and the net and sequin ruffles.

You see, each Concert Party had a different colour scheme for costumes and the drapes on the stage, and I could get quite excited with the anticipation of wondering what 'Next week will be like!'

Nev and I 'lived' in the Prompt Corner. We were now a bit older and more aware of behaving ourselves than we had been during the Royalty Theatre days. Something else was great fun, too. On 'thin' matinee days, when the weather was fine Nev and I would sit in front and help to swell the laughs and applause, or, stand in the Prompt Corner and hope to be taken on stage during one of the sketches! This was what we really preferred.

The first half of the show always finished with a sketch. When I say we took part in some of the sketches, I don't mean we ever had speaking parts – oh no, we would oblige by being part of a funeral procession, or members of a jury, that kind of thing. We were, you will gather, very versatile! I mean, we were only young children. And I might quickly add, we only ever appeared on 'thin' matinee days! It was 'just a bit of fun!'

Many of you will know what I mean, when I say, we only appeared on the occasions when the artistes would remark, before the curtains went up, 'Mr and Mrs Wood and family are in front' or 'I see Rosa is in front!' Both sarcastic remarks mean, 'rows of empty seats!'

There was 'your bit of culture' on the pier as well, you know. Herr Von Beck, the 'cellist, and his orchestra were employed by the Pier Company and often performed for the Sunday Night Concerts in the Pavilion.

But before I forget to tell you about the Iron Sheet or

Safety Curtain in the Pavilion, I'll do it now. It was lovely! John Birkett, a Morecambe chemist, and a gentleman if ever I met one, distilled his own perfume; it was called 'AMO-DEL' and it was very fragrant and pleasant. He hired the entire safety curtain and advertised 'AMO-DEL' on it. It was very artistically and attractively done. The picture was of an Indian canoe full of flowers floating down a wide river with an Indian, complete with feathers, 'paddling his own canoe' as you might say. The background was mountains in hazy mauves and blues, and the only lettering on the curtain was 'AMO-DEL', in a half hoop in the sky portion of the picture, and underneath it stated 'THE GATHERED FRAGRANCE OF INDIAN DALES'.

Now I've no doubt a lot of people will feel like laughing at that! I hope they don't, because compared to some of the present day advertising and some of the words that are used, the AMO-DEL idea is very ahead!

The programmes of the performances which took place in the Pavilion were all dipped at one end in 'AMO-DEL', so you don't wonder that I used to love selling programmes! I can see that line of print now, as I think of it: 'THIS PROGRAMME HAS BEEN PERFUMED WITH AMO-DEL'. The programmes were threepence each, and on the occasions I was employed as 'a seller of same' my salary was threepence for every dozen I sold. Not bad money, was it? Apart from that, one went home 'smelling gorgeous!'

By the way, next to handbags and shoes I'm mad about perfume, and I am wearing a perfume at the moment that is really – Ooooo, smashing! When I first acquired this particular perfume I remarked to Scottie

'Oh, that's nice, isn't it? – go on – have a smell!' He agreed it was eligible to go on the list of 'driving him up the wall' or 'attacking the first female he saw' (I don't mean *me*, we've been married 38 years!) and so on. All that day I kept on saying, 'Oh, it *does* remind me of something and somewhere!' In fact, during the first week I used it I nearly drove myself barmy trying to think what it reminded me of and where I'd smelt it before. Ladies, *please*, if anything 'dawns on you suddenly' don't do what I did. One morning, after my bath, I was in my room dabbing half a pint of the 'madly expensive elixir' here and there, when it dawned on me what it reminded me of – I flew into the bathroom, flung my arms round Scottie exploding as I did so, 'It's *Amo-del*, darling, *Amo-del*!' As he withdrew his shaving brush from his mouth and started to spit the lather out, he blubbered, 'What is?'

Sorry, Scottie!

We all know that most theatres sell 'goodies' during the interval – ices, soft drinks, chocolates and so forth – but the Pier had a very original little offering: jellies! They were made in 'little tiny pudding basins'. Just like my mother's white basins in the kitchen at home but in miniature! It was the basins that first attracted me to the jellies. Each jelly – various flavours, strawberry, raspberry, orange or lemon – was turned out on to a small saucer and then surrounded with ice cream. Threepence!

On the left-hand side of the stalls next to the orchestra pit was the 'Pass Door' (No Admittance) and on the right-hand side was a corresponding door, with a small hatch in the top half of it. Through this hatch were passed the trays of jellies! If trade was brisk, the drill was: the attendant, with empty tray, approached the 'jelly door' rapped briskly on it twice and demanded, 'More jellies please!' Or perhaps she might be even more explicit and say, '*Two* more jellies please' or '*Five* more jellies please!' or, and the next request was a more descriptive one, 'Two more jellies please, a red and a yellow!'

Right then. The occasion arose when – and I can't think why it was – Nev and I were asked whether we would 'Assist with the jelly sales'. Certainly, we were very happy to oblige – same contract as before – threepence for every dozen sold – *and* – a bonus. The bonus was, if there were less than four left over we could eat them! I mean to say, what about that! Mind you, I had never known when there *were* any left over – but the sporting chance appealed to us.

So round the auditorium we went 'plying our trembling jellies' and we did very well. I was in my element when I was able to go to the hatch and knock twice and ask for 'More jellies please!' It had a sound of authority!

As the safety curtain and the advert for 'AMO-DEL' slowly began to disappear upwards towards the Indian Dales, it was accompanied by the sound of spoons being rested in saucers and smacking of lips. Of course, there were none of your plastic spoons in those days – oh no, every piece was genuine 'hotel ware'. Nev and I made an exit through the door with the hatch, to discover that the charge hand who had been pushing the jellies through had gone – well, at least she wasn't there. On the bench that ran along the side of the wall was a tray, and sitting on it, dithering away – two jellies! One red, one yellow – I've already told you – some folks have all the luck! Right, get stuck in, one each!

Bear in mind, if you will please, they were only small jellies and by the time I had scooped a good teaspoonful out of mine, you could say it was half gone.

Oh yes, this is the life, very nice I must say, I thought as I next helped myself to a spoonful of Anthony's Italian Ice Cream. Nev had progressed about as far as I had when, knock, knock, 'One more jelly please!' sounded through the hatch! We stopped dead just as though we were playing 'statues!' We each had our mouths full and as soon as we'd swallowed the contents we looked at each other and the 'great idea' seemed to dawn on us both at the same moment.

'We'll have to stick both halves together on one saucer, won't we?'

'But they're different colours!'

We decided that couldn't be helped, and stick 'em together we did! Thank the Lord we hadn't eaten more than we had. Gently, putting the remaining half of my jelly on Nev's saucer, I sort of stuck the two halves together with my fingers, with gentle pressure – no sculptor used more care – then, putting my remaining ice cream into his saucer we arranged it rather neatly over the join of the jellies.

'One more jelly, *please*!' the urgent request came from the other side of the hatch.

'They are bound to notice it's two colours,' I said.

'No they won't,' comforted Nev, 'the house lights have just gone down!'

And the multi-coloured jelly trembled its way through the hatch!

'When I appeared in Opera!' I throw that line away. No, wait a minute, I won't throw it away. I'll tell you about it! If you insist!

'John Riddings Opera Company'. Oh yes, they used to arrive for a six weeks' season on the Pier. What an education! Fabulous! Year after year they came. *Maritane, Il Trovatore, Faust, Martha, The Bohemian Girl, Rigoletto, La Traviata, Daughter of the Regiment*, and *Lily of Killarney.*

All these, for the pleasure and delight of the public, and Thora and Neville Hird. I reckon, considering we were only children, Nev and I knew as many opera and operetta scores backwards as the next one.

It was in *The Bohemian Girl* that I made my 'debut'. As is well known, the young daughter of wealthy parents is stolen during the first act by Devilshoof, the gipsy king. The dramatic bit, or so I thought, was where the gipsy king carries the child over the property rocks at the back of the stage set, whilst the child's parents and their faithful retainers are kneeling at prayer down at the front of the stage. Actually, they are praying on behalf of their stolen chee-ild! I played the stolen child! On my left forearm was a birthmark, which had been put there by applying a stick of carmine No. 3 grease-paint and running it along my forearm for about four or five inches. The size and length of the fake birthmark had to be large enough for the audience to see from the back of the auditorium!

If you are not familiar with the story of *The Bohemian*

Girl I'd better explain that the birthmark is put on the arm of whoever plays the child because in Act II the leading lady takes over, indicating that the child has, by then, grown up into a beautiful gipsy maiden! So, of course, she has the carmine birthmark, too, otherwise you wouldn't know who she is, would you? I mean it wouldn't matter how much she waved her arms about when she sang 'I Dreamt That I Dwelt in Marble Halls' if she hadn't the carmine on her arm, would it?

Well, as I say, there I was, appearing in Opera. I had no script to learn because I had nothing to say, so it was just pure acting! When we got to the part where the gipsy king carried me across the rocks – I *did* put on a frightened look, as a matter of fact, because 'Devilshoof' looked enough to frighten anybody – he'd gone a bit mad with his make-up!

There knelt my heartbroken father (John Riddings himself – no less) and my stage mother, and all the servants – eyes closed (but of course, otherwise they would have seen Devilshoof carrying me across the prop rocks!), hands together in prayer and singing really beautifully, very softly. As the gipsy king and I approached our exit, I can vividly remember thinking, 'Well, I haven't done much!' so, before we disappeared out of sight, I assumed a heartbroken voice, and stretching my arms towards the praying family I wailed, 'Daddy! Daddy!'

I must have 'moved' Devilshoof with my performance because he nearly dropped me on the prop rocks! Oh dear, I thought everyone would be pleased, but I didn't realize of course that I'd shouted 'Daddy' so loudly that even allowing for stage licence Daddy and

Mummy must have appeared stone deaf not to have heard me! Of course they *did* hear me, which made John Riddings do a startled twitch, but they went on praying as though they hadn't. Good job, too, otherwise there would have been no reason to continue with the rest of the Opera!

My salary for that piece of histrionic ability was a bottle of Lime Juice and Soda per performance, it was one of those exciting bottles with a glass alley in the neck. They are collector's pieces now. I am lucky enough to own three.

Faust was one of my favourite operas – I loved the music and still do. However, it's not the music that I wish to tell you about. I don't know whether you will believe it, but I assure you, it did happen. The leading lady in the John Riddings Opera Company was called Miss June.

She was 'a really fine looking young woman' – well, I say 'young', I reckon she would be thirty something or other, and that's young enough, isn't it? Well, *I* think it is, at my age, but of course when one is only round about the tender age of eight or nine or ten, anyone who is over twenty-one seems rather old, don't they?

Back to the subject. Miss June was 'a fine figure of a woman', and she was also a very fine singer, which of course came in useful as she was in an Opera Company!

It was on a matinee day that the following happened. I saw Miss June coming 'up' the pier looking very smart. She was wearing a navy blue serge costume; you'll notice I say 'costume' – that's because when I was young I can't remember anyone referring to that type of feminine wear as a 'suit'. Ladies always wore 'costumes' and only men wore 'suits'. Even on the beach the feminine gender wore 'a bathing costume'.

However, as I say, she was coming 'up' the pier in this smart navy blue costume. The skirt reached just below her calves – rather like today's fashion, really – the jacket was well in at the waist, and the entire cut displayed her figure to advantage. Her hat was a white panama, rather on the Breton sailor lines, with a broad black ribbon round the crown of it. She presented me with a dazzling smile and accompanied the smile with a rich-voiced, 'Hello, my dear.'

When 'half an hour please' was called at each dressing room door the well mannered artistes all acknowledged it with musical voiced 'Thank you's'. I give full marks to opera artistes, they are all very professional, serious with it – and by and large a happy and laughing lot. There wasn't much to laugh at on that particular matinee afternoon. The audience numbered seventeen! After the 'quarter of an hour, please', had been called, Miss June came down from her star dressing room and on to the stage. 'How's the house?' she enquired in her rich musical voice. Without waiting for an answer she proceeded to have a look for herself. This was going to be quite an achievement, really, because at this juncture of the proceedings the iron sheet or safety curtain was down, informing the seventeen avid opera fans sitting in front that AMO-DEL was the gathered fragrance of Indian dales, and the velvet swish curtain was down hanging behind it. The usual procedure was for the Safety Curtain to start to rise as the orchestra took their positions in the pit prior to the overture.

Actually, it's considered 'not done' to go peeping at the audience before 'curtain up', but everybody does it. I know I do, providing there is the 'wherewithal' to do so.

Miss June approached the swish curtain and, inserting both her thumbs in the centre part, where they swished together, opened them minutely and gazed with one eye through the little hole that someone had conveniently made in the Indian's canoe on the Safety Curtain. It was only a tiny hole, so there was no fear of the canoe sinking into the Indian River! She peered through, and (it's amazing how much one can see with one eye through a little hole, isn't it?) she then stepped back, drew a deep breath through her nose, which raised her ample bosom, exhaled through her nose, which lowered her ample bosom, and declared to the empty stage, as she made her exit, 'I shan't bother to change!' And she didn't!

Have you ever seen Marguerite in *Faust* played wearing a navy blue serge costume and a white panama hat? I have! I saw it at that matinee. I don't think it mattered so much until she got to the Jewel Song. There she was, kneeling on the stage, golden-handled mirror in one hand, the other hand taking ropes of 'prop' pearls and glass diamonds out of the jewel box and putting them round her neck (which is no mean feat when you're wearing a panama hat) and singing, 'Oh, no, this is not I! Oh, no, this – is – not I!' I'd gone 'in front' to swell the audience to eighteen, and I felt like calling out 'No, you're right, it isn't you,

Marguerite – it's Miss June in her navy blue costume and panama hat!'

The incredible thing was that, although it had nearly reduced me to 'my tittering habit', the remaining seventeen opera lovers didn't seem to notice or mind! They'd only come for the singing or a rest! Dear Miss June, perhaps you were the instigator of playing Shakespeare in modern dress!

12

Firm as a rock

Neville didn't get the chance to display his histrionic ability by 'appearing' in any of the Operas, but he did get a chance to 'save the sinking ship' as you might put it, and who better than Admiral Hird to do so?

I can't remember which Opera it was but I remember that there was a 'rock' made of scenery that was involved in the story, behind which one of the players had to hide.

During the setting of the scene, the stagehands couldn't find a short enough 'brace' to hold the 'rock' in position. Bear in mind, it was really only a flat piece of scenery, but the scenic artist had painted it so realistically that it would have fooled anyone, even if they were sitting on the front row of the stalls!

When the 'quarter of an hour' was called the stage hands still hadn't found a short enough 'brace' *and* they still hadn't told my dad that they couldn't find one. At the 'Five minutes please!' my dad was informed and 'a bit of quick thinking' took place. The 'rock' had to be held as firm as the Rock of Gibraltar – Dad wouldn't endure any 'trembling or waving' rocks, I can tell you! So he said to Neville, 'Will you lie down behind that rock and hold it still and firm?' Would he?

You bet he would – and he did – for a whole Act!

Poor little blighter. In the first place, it's not easy to hold a piece of scenery by the wooden frame even if there is a cross-piece, and in the second place, he took his life in his hands each time the actor darted behind the rock! However, cramped but victorious he crept from the back of the rock as the curtain dropped on Act I.

Nev was kept on to assist with the properties (or in case the rock was needed again) and on the Saturday when my dad made up the wages for the stage staff, an additional wage packet was prepared, marked 'N. HIRD, ASSISTANT PROPERTY MASTER', and it contained half a crown. You see however you looked at it I suppose Neville was 'indispensable' – especially if the 'rock' was needed on the set, and that was more than I was, because any little girl could have played the stolen child in *The Bohemian Girl* but *anybody* couldn't hold a 'prop rock' still and firm for a whole ACT! My brother could – I was at his feet in admiration. Neville presented his wages to my mother with as much aplomb as Clive Jenkins orders twenty-five hand made shirts!

The halfcrown was quite yellow, even though it was still in the packet, when we found it in my mother's Jewel Box after she died. There was something else in the Jewel Box as well – but I haven't told you about that yet.

I was rather partial to the Ladies' Lavatory that was situated on the left-hand side of the Pavilion and was for the 'convenience' of outdoor patrons. What I mean is, it was not a Pavilion toilet, the Pavilion had its own, indoors. It wasn't the Skating Rink Ladies' Toilet either, the Rink also boasted its own 'Ladies' and its own 'Gents'. No, it was a Ladies' Toilet that went entirely under its own title – it wasn't in partnership with any other part of the pier. A 'Ladies' Toilet' was all it was and all it intended to be.

The charm of it was the decor, the furnishings, and the equipment therein. It had obviously been there since 1869, and if it hadn't, it had certainly taken up residence no later than 1870 when the Pier Company had splashed out and spent another Five Thousand Pounds. The joy was, during the winter months it was hardly ever used, and ten to one if it was it was only by the woman who cleaned it, and I didn't begrudge her!

The washbasins were of pale grey marble, quite large really, and there were two large brass taps gracing each bowl. Even the plug was brass on a brass chain.

Under each basin was a wooden cupboard with a brass knob on it. The cupboards weren't there merely to hide the plumbing, because each contained a small shelf. Even the panels on the cupboards were graceful and feminine. But the thing that impressed me so greatly was – it was all spotless!

The taps and plugs and knobs gleamed, the marble was washed regularly, as was the white paintwork. It was really due to my dad. I don't mean he cleaned it, I mean he was very particular about the entire pier being kept clean. The toilets themselves were more on the 'throne lines' than mere pedestals, and even the brass chain and handle that brought forth 'The Handle Water Music' (sorry, Mr Handel!) were cleaned with metal polish, and to prove it there was quite a deposit of dried polish left in the links of the chain.

Yet much as I loved all the above, the one thing beyond price in all that luxury, as far as I was concerned, was a small round mirror about the size of a pudding plate. Printed on it, the letters going round like numerals on a clock face, were the words, MENE TOWELS FOR LADIES, and I loved it. Never mind the large mirrors above the marble basins, they were very nice but not to be compared with my little round one that declared there were 'many towels for ladies'. Of course, I didn't know what the mirror was advertising until I was of an age when I might need to know. I made so many computations of those letters it isn't true. Let's remember I was only young, and not a child genius. One of my favourite arrangements of the letters was 'MEN ET OWELS' which to me sounded like 'Men ate owls'.

Of course, 'The Ladies' was also a great place in which to play house, with all its little cupboards and running water, and often I would share my 'private residence' with a few of my friends when we had gone on to the pier to play after school, when it was too cold to play on the sands.

Summing things up, I realize the big advantage was – and I speak about during the winter months – it was private! The Boys weren't allowed in there! And that was another rule of my dad's!!

13

Madame Rosa Vere

At the far end of the pier, over the steamer landing stage but constructed on the deck of the pier itself, was a high diving board. Now there's nothing exciting about that, I know, but if you add Madame Rosa Vere, in bright red satin bathing costume, trimmed with sequins, and legs encased in red tights, the entire ensemble hidden tantalizingly under a red cape, you must admit it's not a sight you will see every day. Yes, that sight was something else the pier offered.

Madame Rosa's long black hair flowed down to her waist, and she would execute the high dive mornings and afternoons according to when the tide was high. To avoid disappointment, there was a board nailed on to the diving structure which displayed not only a photograph of Madame Rosa Vere in tights and sequins but also the times at which she would 'take the plunge'.

I loved the entire performance and stood holding my breath hundreds of times. She would mount the diving platform and stand there with her hair blowing about and the sequins on her cape sparkling, and announce, 'Ladies and gentlemen, I crave your indulgence . . . I shall do a high dive from this board into the open sea.'

At this point she discarded her long cape and revealed all. A gasp of admiration would escape from the crowd of holiday makers, who all thought they were about to witness not only a breathtaking spectacle but a free one. They were soon enlightened, however, as Madame continued, 'I receive no salary from the Pier Company, so if you will kindly show your appreciation in the usual way, my assistant will pass amongst you. Thank you!'

Her assistant was her mother, and who better to do the bottling? If you don't know what bottling means, it's going round with a small black bag on a little wooden handle as a rule, like the Punch and Judy man does. So round her mother would go whilst Rosa stood poised on view, keeping an eye on the amount of coppers flopping into the little bag. When the bottling was over, Madame prepared to take off. Hands and arms high in the air, she would hesitate long enough for all the crowd to get the full effect and then, whoops, off she went. As she entered the sea to a round of applause, I used to think to myself, 'Oooo, how brave!' She would then swim to the pier iron steamer landing, pull herself out of the mighty sea and then disappear into the rope hut, out of sight. And that was the end of the performance. Not bad for a copper coin, eh?

If ever I said to Dad, 'I'm going to watch Madame Rosa Vere' he always gave me a few coppers to drop in the little bag. In fact, I was often the first of the amazed audience to show my appreciation in the usual way!

When the decision had been arrived at to change the Pavilion from a concert hall into a ballroom – and here I must add that my father not only suggested it, but worked every hour God sent to achieve it – the first job was to remove the rows and rows of seats. This was quite a mammoth job and during the achievement of it I kept thinking, 'I see "Rosa" is in front!' or 'Mr and Mrs Wood are in front!' as piles and piles of seats were transported down the pier. I was remembering the remarks made by the performing artistes when it was a small audience. Some of the seats were saved and put round the sides of the ballroom – but they weren't 'The Wood Family' or 'Rosa' because in their new positions they were always full.

My father lived in a pair of overalls at work and helped manually all that winter. He worked like a slave which, happily, encouraged the workmen employed to do the same thing.

Nev and I would go on the pier after school, out of sheer interest in 'the great change' but before long we went there for sheer fun and took our school friends with us! I'll tell you why.

When, eventually, the maple floor was finally laid, we borrowed about a dozen 'kneeling mats' from the pier char-women (Cleaning Ladies would be a better title). I haven't seen a 'kneeling mat' for donkey's years so I wonder if you know what I'm talking about? A kneeling mat is made of coarse coconut fibre, half moon shaped, with about a six-inch-high gallery round the semi-circular part of it, leaving the front entrance without a gallery, for the knees to go in!

They are marvellous really, because if you are in a kneeling position to scrub or wash or polish, you don't need to get up to move your mat – you simply push your knees against the gallery bit and 'Shuffle off to Buffalo!' Anyway . . . that is a kneeling mat, and as I've already said, I haven't seen one for years! I suppose there's no call for them in these days of long mops, vacuum cleaners and so on.

Well, we borrowed the kneeling mats and fastened a long piece of rope to the front of each one. The idea was for the girls to assume a charwoman kneeling position on the mats, and the boys (after removing their boots or shoes) to pull us round the shiny and highly polished floor! Chariot races took place, we would have heats and then the grand final. It was great! Some kind of powdered polish, French chalk and wax I think, had been scattered over the new floor and we were helping to polish the wood! Get the idea?

My dad willingly allowed this, providing we didn't scratch or harm the floor, because we really were helping to achieve a mirrorlike finish. We also achieved a few holes in our socks or stockings because the girls had to take their shoes off as well. We had more school friends during that period than 'soft mick' (and I don't know what *that* saying means either!).

The 'Big Night' arrived. Grand Opening of the Central Pier Ballroom! Dad had arranged for two dance bands so there would be non-stop dancing – this was quite an innovation, I can tell you.

The stage with its commanding proscenium had been left in its original form apart from the fact that the stage area had been 'boxed in' to make a more appropriate size to accommodate a dance band. At the opposite end of the ballroom a new band stand had been erected, so that as the music finished at one end, the opposing band struck up at the other! Fab! A large fountain, surrounded with fresh flowers and ferns, played non-stop in the centre of the floor. Different coloured lights were directed on to the fountain by using lime lights (today they would be called spot lights) from the lime perches, which were rigged up in the stage boxes and manipulated expertly by Neville Hird Esq in one box and Jack Carr Esq in the opposite box. My 'Vestal Virgins' displayed their figures with pride as they held the boxes up and I was very content that they played their parts in the exciting and successful evening!

The new ballroom had a full capacity opening night! There were even a lot of people there who had paid!

I must just digress for a moment, having written that last line. My dad had a sensible, clear idea about 'Free Pier Passes' or 'complimentary tickets'. A lot of Morecambe business men – councillors and suchlike – used the bars on the pier as a kind of rendezvous. They spent a lot of money as well, so my dad felt it was unfair to ask them to pay pier toll (3d). To be quite honest, the free pass holders thought it would be unfair as well – hence, as Dad put it: 'It pays to give them yearly free passes because of what they spend in the bars – summer *and* winter!' And it did!

It sounds a bit silly when I say I had every intention of being 'the first on the new dance floor' – but bear in mind that it was my dad's brainchild – and I *had* helped to polish it! So that was excuse enough.

The usual hubbub of laughing and chattering and excitement filled the atmosphere when Benny Bolton and his band took their positions on the band stand.

Miss Mercy Nelson – better known as 'Merce' – and I stood at the side of the floor, at the ready. So did dozens of other couples, but I record with pride that without cheating or 'jumping the gun' – *we made it!* And we did a nifty foxtrot to 'Oh, Horsey! Keep Your Tail Up!' with victorious abandon!

I was so enthusiastic that, even though 'being first on the new dance floor' had been achieved, when the opposition band struck up for the first time I was 'first on' again.

14

My bosom friends

'Open air dancing at the Pier Head, mornings and afternoons.' That's what it said on the bills.

And that was good fun if you like! It was quite a large dance floor and there was a solid, well constructed band stand – none of your rickety make-shift things – well built to stand there for ever, so one hoped! In fairness, I should say that it had a proper stage and proscenium, wings, backcloth and a couple of dressing rooms.

When my father first went to work on the pier, the pierrots used to perform on there, but when dancing became so popular they were promoted – or demoted – to the big stage in the Pavilion, where they performed until it was decided to change even that into a ballroom.

On the left-hand side of the dance floor was quite a big cafe where you could get ices, mineral waters, afternoon teas – at popular prices – and on the right-hand side was the deck chair house where all the deck chairs slept at night and therefore were kept clean, with no fear of soiling your summer frock! This was another of my Dad's ideas. He said, 'People don't want to pay 3d for a dirty deck chair!'

If the weather was warm and sunny, there would be an evening dancing session, and I used to love that. Coloured lights would be festooned round the dance floor and although it sounds so simple, it really was quite romantic. When my friends and I were about fifteen, we would often 'click' or 'get off' (they were popular expressions in those days) with boys who were on holiday in Morecambe, and a spot of dancing under the coloured lights never did hurt anybody, did it? I think probably the sexiest thing we ever did was to look into each other's eyes over a cup of hot Horlicks – but it was living!

My pals and I rarely let on we were locals – we'd decide beforehand where we were supposed to have come from, but we never told our dancing partners until they told us where *they* came from, just in case we'd decided on their hometown. It was a bit difficult if they asked us to go out during the day-time, but we usually got over that by saying we had made arrangements for the day (indeed we had – we were at work!) and we would meet them on the pier the following night.

My friends were well in, anyway, because I took them on the pier for nothing and we were usually entertained to a Horlicks or a cream soda! Sophistication! Yes sir! That was us – flat chests and the lot!

I could go on for ever about incidents that involved the pier, but I won't although Carnival Week is worth a mention, I think. All right, perhaps we couldn't compete with a continental 'Mardi Gras' but all the same it used to be a great week in our lives, and of course the pier entered into the spirit of carnival one hundred per cent!

When I recall that people walked about in carnival costumes throwing streamers and confetti at each other and blowing 'tommy talkers' it seems as though I have imagined it! But it's a fact!

We always had a sack of confetti at 6, Cheapside, so that we could fill and refill a large bag to take with us as we went out! None of your small twopenny packets – a sack! One year everybody sported the 'Morecambe Carnival Colours' – rock pink and pale blue – lovely ordinary people walked about in an original costume they had enthusiastically 'run up' in pink and blue sateen, which was about 9½d a yard! A carnival song was composed and published and the happy carnival-minded population and visitors sang it lustily. It was a little number that went something like this:

> It's carnival time once more, it's carnival time once more.
> Young and old come from near and from far
> To join in the fun and say 'Well, here we are –
> Hey Willie, why, lad it's you – I thought I had seen you before!'
> Cheerio! Toodle-oo! It's a right champion do
> It's carnival time once more!

The above may not be word perfect and I apologize if the song-writer is still alive – but I can vouch for all the lyrics except 'Cheerio and Toodle-oo!'

A year or so later, another carnival anthem was born, incorporating an advert for the town, and that one went as follows:

Dear old Morecambe – more come to Morecambe
by the sea,
There's good fresh air – from Heysham up to Bare,
Jollity everywhere. So, throw away your care
And come to dear old Morecambe
Here's to its prosperity
Folks don't die and that's the reason why
More come to Morecambe by the sea!

What about that, then? Rows of revellers would walk along the promenade, arm in arm, singing away, the illuminations would sparkle from lamp post to lamp post, while the flower beds in the promenade gardens were a mass of twinkling lights! This effect was achieved by placing thousands of night lights in little coloured glass containers. They were replaced and lighted each evening by hordes of volunteers armed with tapers and matches! How they used to pray for a calm evening! It's amazing how people always state the obvious – as you walked along the prom, you would hear this remark dozens of times: 'Oh, look – there's one there gone out!' or 'Oh look! There's one there not in!' Never mind all the others that were twinkling away – it was the ones that had given up the ghost that were noticed the most!

Oh, yes, they were wonderful times, the carnival procession; the ox roasting (and the excitement of watching the brick enclosure, which housed the revolving spit, being built on the previous night, to the ox's cremation); the firework display on the Friday night; the prayer of all the locals, 'I *do* hope it doesn't rain for the firework display!' (It nearly always did!) It was all marvellous, I thought, and I am sincerely grateful for having experienced those times.

Isn't it sad that in this modern age things have become so sophisticated and commercial that the 'Carnival Spirit' and the 'Hail Fellow well met' seems so old fashioned and out of place. May the Lord preserve me from ever trying to 'spout' or appearing to be a 'do-gooder', but when one reads about, or sees on television, the evil vandalization that takes place at a football match and the way the 'rotten sports' of supporters slash the railway carriages for the 'fun' of it, I think I shall stick to my opinion that the hosts of unsophisticated ordinary people who enjoyed Morecambe Carnival were to be admired! All right – so perhaps they did knock back a few beers but they didn't knock the railway carriage to hell on their way home! And as my mother would have said, 'they weren't hurting anybody!'

15

Watch it!

It was bang in the middle of James Hargreaves', Jewellers, shop window! It was unbelievable! I'd never seen anything like it before! It was so small, yet perfect! It hypnotised me! Just imagine being the proud owner of it! It was only as big as a plum stone! I knew it would be dear.

It was a watch! No, not *a* watch, *the* watch! All this was years ago, I had just entered my 'teens'.

Without any hesitation, I darted into the shop. We knew Mr Hargreaves very well, he was 'our' jeweller. When I say 'our' I don't mean he was a jeweller exclusively on our behalf – I mean he was in the same category as 'our' grocer, 'our' fishmonger, 'our' coalman and 'our' insurance man!

It was a good job he knew me, otherwise he might have taken offence at my first remark.

'That little watch in the middle of the window, Mr Hargreaves, does it go?'

He assured me it did, and enquired with a smile, 'Do you want it?'

Did-I-want-it? At that moment I wanted it more than anything else in the world!

'Oh, *no*!' I answered quickly, thinking he meant did

I wish to buy it. 'No, it's just that, isn't it lovely?'

He was a very nice man and, as I say, he knew our family well.

'Would you like to look at it?' he enquired in a very understanding way. I said, 'Yes, *please*!' before he'd finished his enquiry.

He took it out of the window, and the moment he laid it with reverence on the piece of black velvet on the top of the glass counter, I can remember thinking, 'Fancy anyone *owning* that!'

I'd like to explain something at this point, if I may, and I find it a bit difficult to put into words. I stood there, full of admiration for the watch and although, as I have just told you, I wanted it more than anything in the world, never, for one moment, did I think 'I must have that!' and I wasn't in any way envious of the person who would eventually own it. I know this sounds a bit argumentative, but do you understand what I mean?

In the first place, I *knew* I couldn't have it and in the second place I was getting so much pleasure out of just looking at it that I was quite satisfied to stand there and admire it! Does that all sound a bit daft? If it does, I'm sorry, but that is how I am. It's amazing the pleasure one can derive from just looking at something beautiful, isn't it?

I thanked Mr Hargreaves for having gone to the trouble of disrupting his window, and came out of the shop in a very happy mood and feeling better off for having looked at something which in my opinion was very lovely. I was only thirteen, and, don't forget, a tiny oval watch was a bit unusual in those days.

When I arrived home, I related the incident to my mother, with a few embellishments of course!

From that day forward, part of my daily routine was to go and have a look at that watch in the centre of Hargreaves' window. The shop was on Market Street, one minute from Number Six, Cheapside, and therefore conveniently situated for viewing purposes. The 'peak viewing time' was usually after tea. I'd nip up our street, stand looking in the window, with all its bright lights making everything glitter, and pay homage to *the* watch! It deserved it! The bonny little thing!

There it reclined, centre stage, holding the fort, as you might say. As a matter of fact, I went to pay homage so often that I had almost reached the stage of saying 'Hello' to it, as I arrived faithfully each late afternoon to pay my respects.

I was having my tea one day, and bear in mind, tea in the North is a knife and fork affair, usually something a 'bit tasty', and not cucumber sandwiches and sponge cake. The weather was dreadful, it was blowing a gale and the rain was pelting down. (And that remark was unnecessary, because nobody ever saw the rain pelt UP! Did they?)

I had to go to the post office for some stamps or something, I can't remember, so as soon as I had finished whatever it was I was eating, I put my oilskins and sou'wester on (oh yes, I wore this type of sexy and smart rainwear) and left the house looking like an advert for Skipper Sardines!

As I came out of the post office, which was in Market Street at the top of Cheapside, I thought, I'll just go and have a look at my friend, the watch. I walked along Market Street – correction – I was *blown* along Market Street, but it didn't worry me, we were used to this kind of weather and thought nothing of it. The rain lashed down and by the time I had taken my position at Hargreaves' window I was sopping wet – well, no, *I* wasn't but my oilskins were. The rain was streaming down the plate glass window making it practically opaque, but that didn't matter because as a 'constant viewer' I knew the exact position of the watch. I peered through the rivulets of rain that were racing down the window and – *Tragedy! Panic Stations!* The watch had gone! Without even waiting to think that probably the window had been redressed, I flew into the shop like a rocket!

Mr Hargreaves came out of his little office.

'Hello, Thora,' he said as he moved to behind the counter. 'What a dreadful night, isn't it?'

He could say that again! It certainly *was* a dreadful night for me if *the* watch had disappeared from sight forever!

'Excuse me, Mr Hargreaves, but – er – have you sold that little watch?' I enquired painfully.

I stood there whilst the rain ran off my oilskins and proceeded to make a pool on his very clean shop floor!

'Yes, as a matter of fact, I have – why, did *you* want it?' he replied quite brightly.

By now, the rain that covered my glasses (I've worn specs since I was eleven) was plopping on to my face and dripping off my nose end.

'Oh, no!' I informed him. 'No, it's – er – just that I enjoyed looking at it, that's all!' I added rather lamely.

As I had used the word 'no' twice, and accompanied it with a shake of my head, the rain on my sou'wester had shaken free and added its contribution to the steadily increasing pool round my feet.

'Oh well, that's all right them,' he assured me. 'As a matter of fact, I sold it this morning.'

I stood there, in my own personal pool of rain! So that was that! It had gone!

I was grateful for the remaining rain on my glasses. Even with all those bright lights it was impossible to distinguish tears from raindrops, and with a much too brittle brightness I said, 'Oh well, thank you, Mr Hargreaves – good night!'

Leaving my personal pool of rain on his clean floor to prove I had been there, I retraced my steps and forlornly left the shop, without even a passing glance at the brilliantly lit window.

16

A pinch of cinnamon

The fashionable colour that autumn was cinnamon, and the 'with-it' material was velour cloth embossed with endless curly lines running all over it. Like the wavy lines of a jigsaw puzzle. It sounds awful, doesn't it? But I can assure you, it was very smart, the wavy lines weren't really noticeable until you handled the cloth. One of my best friends had acquired a coat in cinnamon complete with beaver rolled collar. Although by today's standards we were unsophisticated at that age, we were all a little bit fashion conscious and all of us managed to be quite smart. It was usually in the autumn we got our new winter coats (for best!) and the comparing and admiring of each friend's new outfit afforded us quite a lot of pleasure. Here again I go quoting my mother, 'And we weren't hurting anybody!'

At the beginning of October, I had voiced 'my desire' for a cinnamon-coloured coat, with a rolled squirrel fur collar. The coat was to be my Christmas present. We duly ordered it through a shop that we dealt with, therefore the shop came under the heading of '*our* Drapers and Outfitters'. Miss Jowett, who was responsible for the ordering was 'as nice a person as you would meet on a day's march'. (And it took years to work out what *that* Northern expression meant!) She assured us that it would arrive in about a month's time.

Owing to the fact that it was 'a special order' we felt that was quite a reasonable period to wait, and in any case, as I had no intention of wearing it before Christmas Day, I was grateful for 'the waiting period' of the delivery, because it meant by the time it arrived at the beginning of November, we should be so much nearer Christmas Day and 'the wearing o' the cinnamon!'

By the end of October I was excited at the thought of the coat with its squirrel collar, and why not? I revelled in the anticipation of folding the wrapover front about me and snuggling into the soft fur as it embraced my throat and neck on Christmas Day. You are probably thinking, 'Why wait until Christmas Day?' Well, you see, it was to be a *Christmas present*, so, of course, I couldn't dream of wearing it until – the day! Yes, I would quite enjoy waiting to put it on, I'd be able to *look* at it, wouldn't I? The lovely warm cinnamon colour on a dull day, the pale grey of the squirrel collar – I'd be able to blow gently on the soft fur and it would be reminiscent of a miniature field of grain in the wind. There's no doubt, it would all be worth waiting for! Oh, to be thirteen! Wonderful! Events impress you so deeply when you are thirteen!

The coat hadn't arrived by the end of the first week in November, but who was worrying? Plenty of time yet before Christmas!

By the end of the second week, I was calling at Miss Jowett's daily – no coat! From then on I almost lived at

Miss Jowett's. It was no fault of hers that it hadn't arrived, in fact, by the first week in December, she had written so many letters to the firm who were supplying the coat that she nearly had writer's cramp!

Second week in December – no coat. One evening I even went down to Euston Road Station (now defunct) and enquired at the Parcels Office if a large parcel had got pushed behind something and been forgotten – still no coat.

On December 23rd, Miss Jowett received a very apologetic letter from the firm in Manchester, informing her that due to the extensive orders for cinnamon-coloured velour cloth with wiggly lines on, they regretted they would be unable to execute the order until early March. They also assured her of their *prompt* attention at all times!

Early March! Early Blooming March! That was next year! Early March, well they could stick it, that's what they could do, and their prompt attention with it! Oh God! Was life always going to be full of tragedies? It was just one disaster after another. Mr Hargreaves had sold the watch, and Miss Jowett couldn't get the coat!

17

The velvet hand in the bright red glove

'Never mind, love, don't be too disappointed, we'll go up to the West End (in Morecambe, not London) tomorrow, and see if there's a coat like you want in one of the shops!' My loving mother tried to comfort me with these words. It was Christmas Eve.

Now just hang on a minute, will you? Before I go any further, I am going to admit, here and now, that I am ashamed to write the next few paragraphs. What I mean is – I am ashamed of my attitude and behaviour on that never-to-be-forgotten Christmas Eve. My dear patient mother should either have 'given me a fourpenny one' or taken my pants down and tanned my behind in the middle of Regent Road. She *didn't* – but she should have done!

Get the picture, if you will, please. It was pouring down in bucketfuls – the wind was howling and blowing from the sea, it was cold and ready to snow any minute. Well, that's a good backing for a drama anyway. We pushed our way along the promenade, leaning against the wind, we couldn't talk much because the wind almost took our breath. After we had been in about four shops we practically gave up hope of my appearing on Christmas Day in a cinnamon velour cloth coat!

All the assistants knew us and assured us they could order a coat for me for the New Year, but that's not the point, is it? If for weeks you have dreamed of wearing said coat on Christmas Day?

During our entering and leaving shops, my mother was in full sympathy with me and although, as I have admitted, I was ashamed of my behaviour, I don't mean I was cheeky or rude to anyone, I mean that I kept on 'moaning'. Moan, moan, moan, 'Oh, I did want it for Christmas Day!' 'Oh, I wish Miss Jowett could have got one!' 'Why couldn't the firm in Manchester have let us know earlier' – all that sort of thing. 'Niggling', non-stop! Never once did my patient mother reprimand me. We exhausted all the shops in Regent Road and after catching a bus to the Central we got off at Euston Road and made our wet and weary way to Queen's Street.

Even the brightly dressed Christmas display windows failed to cheer me up.

Edgar Bell, Gents' Outfitters, was situated a little way down on the right. The window was dressed in a Christmassy way, quietly, because it was what we call in Lancashire 'a classy shop'. The gents' ties bore small, holly-decorated tickets informing the world at large that they were 'A Suitable Gift!' The tickets on the shirts were 'Wishing you a Merry Christmas!' and the tickets on the pyjamas were appropriately decorated with mistletoe and proclaimed that they were 'A Seasonable Gift!' which struck me, because of the mood I was in, as though Christmas was the only time men wore pyjamas!

One side of the window displayed ladies' gloves.

They draped themselves in a ladylike way, one hand placed delicately over the other and instructing you in the fact that they were 'Real Nappa'. I was standing there in the rain and wind thinking that when gloves are displayed in that way it looks as though there should be a pair of legs underneath them, one leg crossed over the other and the hands of the gloves crossed and resting on the knee, when my mother asked, 'Do you like those?' As she asked me this she was pointing to a pair of ladies' *red* gloves! *Red!* Are you listening? Quite honestly, I had never seen a pair of coloured leather gloves before. I'd seen coloured leather gloves in Costume plays in the theatre and I'd seen them in the Opera Company on the pier, but never had I seen coloured leather gloves for ordinary outdoor wear.

The gloves in the window were a lovely holly berry red, beautifully made. One glove had the wrist part turned back to prove to all and sundry that they were lined in wool knitted in a Fair Isle pattern! I couldn't believe it! They must have been the first pair of coloured leather gloves in Morecambe.

'Those are unusual, aren't they? Would you like them?' I heard my mother ask. 'They would help to take away a bit of the disappointment over your coat!' she added.

Would I? I would! We went into the shop, Mr Bell took them out of the window and I tried them on. *They fitted!* I felt like Cinderella at the end of the pantomime when she tries on the glass slipper and the entire company shouts, 'It fits – it fits!'

How marvellous! Oh, how lovely they were! Oh, what

a wonderful mother mine was! Oh, how happy a time Christmas is! Oh, how lovely all the world is! (You'll gather I was rather pleased!) Wishing Mr Bell a Merry Christmas we came out of the shop – my mother walked, I floated. Did I say it was pouring down and blowing a gale? *I* didn't notice it! *Red gloves!* Bluddy 'ell!

Christmas Eve was always magic at 6 Cheapside. The door was open for anyone to pop in and be wished a Merry Christmas whilst they drank a glass of you-name-it-we-had-it!

Jobs were done during the evening before to lighten the burdens of Christmas Day. The vegetables for dinner were washed and prepared, sage and onion stuffing and apple sauce was made, six dozen mince pies were baked, fresh fruit was arranged artistically in a rustic basket and decorated with sprigs of holly, dishes of nuts and raisins and boxes of dates and figs, Turkish delight and crystallized fruits were allowed on top of the piano, and a large fruit dish was ready to receive the contents of the box of tangerines and the fresh pineapple that Dad used to bring home along with twelve new gramophone records every Christmas Eve, without fail!

The 'Royal Standback' fire would be blazing brightly and the emery-papered and blackleaded grate reflected the flames as its contribution to the warm welcome extended at Number 6. The aroma of mince-meat, pastry, apple sauce, etc., from the back kitchen was mouthwatering. Add to all this the smell of ever-greens arranged behind each picture above the big old clock on the wall and along the mantelpiece, and the slight whiffs of alcohol and cigars as different friends popped in and lifted their elbows to wish you 'all you wished yourselves' and the only word you have to describe our living-kitchen on these occasions is *Magic!*

18

'Hail, Smiling Morn'

Well, back to the 'Cinnamon coat replaced by the Red Gloves Christmas!' I was telling you about.

On Christmas morn, we were awakened as usual by the Salvation Army Band, who were standing in the middle of the road in Cheapside and musically demanding that 'Christians Awake! Salute this Happy Morn!'

Whether we were Christians or not we awoke, and as Cheapside was such a happy street, we saluted the happy morn without any trouble. The band always arrived fairly early, invariably catching the Christians *out* by catching them *in* – bed! The Salvationist who carried the wooden collecting box would knock on each door. Bedroom windows would be pushed up and offerings were thrown down.

Mind you, lots of the Cheapsiders were up and about, in which case they would come and stand at their front doors and enjoy the seasonable carols and hymns. When your own personal knock sounded on your front door, it was really the beginning of your Christmas Day! I was NCOIC of carrying coins to box and wishing the Salvation Soldier a Merry Christmas! About half an hour after the Salvation Army had gone the Morecambe Borough Band arrived to play. Their opening number was usually 'While Shepherds Watched Their Flocks By Night', and then there was the same ritual as previously, only there weren't as many bedroom windows opened because most of the people in the street were up and about by the time 'The Boro' started to perform.

On the particular Christmas morning I am telling you about, by the time the Sally Army had gone I had begun to open my presents.

It was a lovely old-fashioned custom of ours always to hang up a stocking – we usually borrowed one each from my mother. Small-sized gifts were put in the stocking and larger-sized gifts were laid at the foot of our beds. In the stocking, without fail, there was always an apple, an orange, some nuts and a new penny, which all helped to fill the foot part. In my case there was always a tablet or tablets of scented soap – glycerine and cucumber for preference! The annual Christmas joke and always a 'sure laugh' was when our father unpacked his stocking and feigned surprise when, after pretending to expect an apple and an orange etc., he discovered an onion, a potato and a carrot! Big laugh that! Poor old Dad!

I started to empty my stocking – handkerchiefs, a little manicure set – I say a *manicure* set, it comprised a small piece of sandpaper stuck on cardboard, a piece of red wax nail polish the shape of a lipstick and a small buffer, all of these being in a miniature red oilcloth envelope-type case that fastened with a red-domed press stud. I thought it was lovely! And it *was*! It was from one of my best friends and it had cost her tenpence.

There was a little bottle of 'Sweet Pea' scent (just what I wanted – honestly), a box of miniature Christmas Crackers made of gold paper, and the little label on the box they were in assured me that each cracker contained a gift, a paper hat and a motto – smashing!

Next out of the bran tub was a packet of sugared almonds, after which came the orange, the apple, the nuts and the new penny.

In the toe of the stocking and extending about a third of the foot was an oblong packet the size of a glycerine and cucumber tablet of soap. But as I drew the box out into view I saw it was a little white jeweller's box. I was quite excited wondering what could be in it, and pressed the little catch on the front of the box and opened it.

I gasped – I couldn't believe it – it was lying on a white velvet pad – it was looking up at me! It was the watch! I was holding it in its bed of velvet – in my hand! THE WATCH!

I literally flew into my parents' bedroom and flung myself on my mother, who was still in bed. I was trying to say, and not doing it very coherently, because I was crying with joy – and *shame* – I was trying to say, 'Thank you and I couldn't believe it was mine and I was sorry I had moaned last night about the coat and she shouldn't have because she'd bought me the red gloves and –' . . . once again I was nearly breaking her neck as I smothered her with kisses and tears.

She kissed me in return and then gave me her handkerchief from under her pillow. As I wiped my eyes and blew my nose she said, 'I nearly told you about the watch a dozen times last night, when we weren't able to get you the coat, but I didn't want to spoil my own pleasure of seeing your face this morning!'

I put the watch on to convince myself it was mine and after 'showing it everybody' (my mother, my father and Nev) I took the little box back into my room. In my excitement I had not noticed a visiting card of my mother's that must have fluttered down on to my bed. I picked it up, saw what it was and turned it over. On the back was written: 'Just to fulfil one desire, I wish I could fulfil them all! Mother.'

Out in Cheapside the Boro' Band were playing 'How Beautiful Upon the Mountain', double forte.

It's understandable that as soon as the shops opened again after their Christmas holidays, I went in to see Mr Hargreaves. He told me that on the morning of the day I had stood in a pool of rain in his shop and he had broken the news to me that the watch was sold, my mother had gone in to ask him to put the watch 'on one side' and had left a deposit on it. Apparently, when my mother had 'made someone up' for a Fancy Dress Ball for which she would never charge, quite often out of gratitude, people would insist she should 'have a drink or some chocolates' and had left two shillings or half-a-crown. Every time, she had put the money away, and then taken it to the jewellers towards the watch. She added the balance when Christmas came.

I shall always remember Jim Hargreaves' face as he told me how my mother had saved for it, just as I shall always remember something he said, 'So treasure that watch, Thora, your mother denied herself a lot of things so that you could have it!'

I *have* treasured it, Mr Hargreaves, I promise you. A few years ago I did a television show called 'The Magic Box'. The idea of the programme was, if you had a magic box, what would you keep in it and why? I told Margery Baker, the Director, about the little watch and said I would like to keep it in my magic box and bring it out and look at it if ever I felt like 'moaning' or 'niggling' because it had really taught me a lesson when I was young. She's a very imaginative director and an understanding one, and agreed immediately that I should use the 'watch story'. I did. As I held it up (it was given a 'full frame to itself') I said to Kenneth Robinson who was interviewing me: 'Of course, it doesn't look very small compared with today's little watches', and I showed him the watch I was wearing, which has a dial no bigger than a piece of confetti. We laughed because I have to take my glasses off to see the time by it! Scottie gave me the tiny watch on my opening night at the London Palladium. I also told Kenneth, 'Of course, this treasure my mother saved up to buy me doesn't "go" any more, but I wouldn't part with it for anything.'

The following week I received a most charming letter from a jeweller in Dumfries. He said he had seen the 'Magic Box' programme and would I trust him with the watch because he felt sure he could do something with it. He did, too, bless him. He returned it to me, all clean and bright, in full working order, and apologized that he had been unable to replace the black moire silk strap and would I suffer a black nylon one. This was all done with his compliments.

Aren't there some nice people in the world? And aren't I lucky, because I'm always coming across them? I wore the watch for my BBC television series *The First Lady* – I felt the title of the series fitted my mother.

19

Now being played

You will recall I returned to school after I was supposed to have left. Right! Well my return visit only lasted two and a half weeks because, one morning, much to my surprise, my father called at the school and after a short conversation at the school door with Miss Nelson, I was brought out of the class to join them.

Apparently, Arthur Hickman-Smith who ran the music shop on the Central Pier required an assistant for the season and had asked my father if I would be interested. I was *very* interested! Miss Nelson agreed this would be 'a very nice kind of occupation' and when my dad asked her if it would be convenient for me to go along with him then, she said 'certainly' and added her blessing!

I went to the cloakroom to collect my coat and it dawned on me that I was leaving school for the second time in a few weeks, but this time I didn't mind.

'Hicky' Smith was a friend of my father's of many years' standing. I could not have wished to work for a kinder or more thoughtful employer – he was a dear man.

My duties were simple, when I say I worked at 'The Music Shop' that is precisely what it was – a shop that sold music. You'll appreciate that when I was fourteen, people on holiday always bought copies of popular songs, they were sixpence! It was quite an advantage having a jazz band playing on the outdoor bandstand on the pier too, because they would play all the up-to-the-minute numbers and in turn we would sell the music in the shop, which was situated on the side of the Pavilion that was about twenty or thirty yards from the Open-Air Dance Floor! Couldn't be better, you see!

During the band interval we made hay while the sun shone. There was an upright piano practically in the shop doorway and on the top of the piano was a little easel, just big enough to display a copy of music. I would play the popular number on the piano and as I did so Hicky Smith, in his splendid voice would announce to the crowd of holiday makers, 'This week's popular number now being played! Sixpence a copy!'

After I had played a couple of choruses, I would get off the piano stool like lightning and help 'to wrap'. It was great fun, really, and I loved it.

There is only one thing about that period I didn't love. I was developing a bust! Now just hold on a minute, before you say 'And what's wrong with that?'

I agree there is nothing wrong with that and indeed I would hate to be without half an inch of my present day thirty eight inches! *BUT*, when I was on my way to fifteen years old we were going through the flat-chested period! The dress fashion was on the tubular lines, the length was above the knee and as I was fashion conscious, I was wondering what the heck I could do with my bust. I'm laughing whilst I'm writing this because I've made it sound as though I was the owner of a forty-two inch bust! Not at all – it was only about thirty inches, but it was big enough to *show* I had one! Or two!

One morning, I had put on a favourite dress; it was pale mushroom coloured fine woollen stockinette. Well, every woman reading this knows how stockinette *clings*! I looked at myself in the mirror and thought, 'Oh crumbs it's all sticking out worse than ever!' Not to be beaten, I slipped the dress off and tied a piece of ribbon round my womanly assets, pulling the points of my feminine trademark flat! 'Good, that would do it,' I thought. I nipped back into my dress and set off for the Music Shop, flat chested and full of confidence.

Perhaps it was playing the piano, perhaps it was rolling the copies of music up, perhaps it was the heat, I don't know, and I never will know. It wasn't until I saw a customer giving me a rather quizzical look that I took a quick look at myself in the shop mirror. The ribbon must have rolled in to the width of a piece of string because to my horror and embarassment the reflection revealed that I had not only two breasts, but four! I looked like that advert for Michelin Tyres!

Bust or not, I enjoyed every second of that musical, double breasted summer season!

When 'The Music Shop' closed at the end of the season and I was 'at liberty' as you might say, I didn't waste my time.

I attended night school four nights a week during the winter. The subjects I decided on were Monday, French and cookery – Tuesday, book keeping and accounts and English Grammar – Wednesday, shorthand and

Thursday, typing. You'll gather I had decided to accumulate a little knowledge that might assist me to get a job if I didn't enter the precarious business called 'The Theatrical Profession!'

But wait . . . during that period between finishing in the Music Shop and going to work in my dad's office the following season, I entered into a very precarious bit of business. And all because of a pair of shoes. I must have wanted my brains washing!

20

A life on the instantaneous wave, or, It's enough to make your hair curl!

I grumbled when I had no shoes
Until I met a man who had no feet

Isn't that a wonderful saying to read daily? We have it framed and cannot avoid seeing it as we approach our front door. I wouldn't *want* to avoid it – I think it's a great mind jogger!

This episode is about shoes. They were in the middle of 'Tyler's' window, real patent leather in black – no toe caps – tie-ups – a little heel – *and* – (this was the detail that took my eye) narrow black ribbon instead of laces.

Fourteen shillings and elevenpence they were. Oh, there was no doubt about it, they lived up to Tyler's slogan – *North, South, East or West – Tyler's Boots Are The Best!* Suddenly I knew, they were the only pair of shoes in the world for me! Bear in mind I wasn't yet fifteen!

I've always had a lot of imagination and I've always got a lot of pleasure out of life by imagining and anticipating things. There I stood and, as I looked at the shoes, I was imagining them on my feet the following Sunday. I was also anticipating how, each time I took them off, I would faithfully stuff newspaper into the toes and rub them with Vaseline so that they wouldn't crack across the instep – yes, I would certainly have to put Vaseline on them, especially as they had no toe caps. Thinking back, this Vaseline procedure was a lot of old codswallop, because patent shoes *always* crack where your foot finishes and your toes start! But never mind that – they were lovely, fourteen and eleven-pence! Dirt cheap really! Well, no, they were quite expensive to tell the truth and the sad thing was, I didn't really need them.

I debated with myself whether to tell my mother about the shoes, but bearing in mind that I'd left school (for the second time!) and I wasn't earning anything at that moment, I didn't! It was no great shakes to forget them – it didn't bother me! Much!

Anyway, in a few months the summer would be with us, so I would be wearing sandshoes a lot of the time. Sandshoes or ropesoles, which, of course, are referred to as Espadrilles nowadays, were our usual footwear during the summer. They were in natural, or, to be more precise, oatmeal coloured canvas, with a good thick plaited ropesole. They tied on with a piece of white tape which threaded through the front and then through two holes in the sides. They cost the large amount of fourpence! We would wear them until the soles looked like Grandad's Whiskers and then throw them away and get another four pennyworth!

It's a joke when one thinks of the price of a pair these days, isn't it? Of course, nowadays they are made in every colour under the sun and perhaps dye is expensive.

However, 'the real patent leather jokers' were to

remind me of their existence within a week of the day I had knelt in worship 'at their feet'. It was thus.

On the following Wednesday I saw an advert in our local paper, which goes under the splendid title of *The Visitor* (good name for a holiday resort paper, isn't it?). The advert informed me: 'Girl required to assist at stall at Trades Exhibition, Winter Gardens, *must have long hair*. Apply – stall 47, Wednesday, twelve noon.'

Very interesting! I had a plait of auburn hair to my waist – I was 'at liberty' at the moment, and the real patent shoes were in Tyler's window! I might just stroll along there about twelve o'clock – no harm done. And as my mother would have said, 'I wasn't hurting anybody!' Well, it would be more to the point if I said, 'I didn't *intend* to hurt anybody!'

When I arrived at the Winter Gardens I thought there was a fire or an accident, there were so many women round the stall, but I soon discovered they were all applicants for the job! I stood at the back of the crowd. I couldn't *see* anything because everybody was taller than me.

Have you ever noticed that if you 'stand still' in a crowd and you don't push or 'shuv' you automatically and magically move? I did – I suddenly discovered I was in a position to peep through a four inch slit between two bodies! I listened and discovered the stall was for demonstrating and selling 'haircurlers' – the stall wasn't 'in business' at that moment, of course, but would be later in the day.

The gentleman who had requested us to be at the Winter Gardens complete with our long hair, at twelve noon, was explaining why we had been invited. He wore a white overall, but a white overall with a difference – well, I'd never seen one like it before. It had a polo neck and buttoned down the side, I remember thinking as I looked at 'our host's' overall, 'Oh, yes, very smart.' It impressed me very much.

The would-be employer was talking in a cockney voice explaining what the job involved. Suddenly he pointed and called out,

'Hey! You – you, the young lady with the glasses on!'

Well, I'm only five feet one inch tall *now* so you'll appreciate I wasn't very tall then! I didn't think for one moment that he was pointing to me, so I just stood there. When nobody moved, I turned round to see who it was he was pointing to – and found I had been pushed to the back row again and there was nobody behind me!

'You – you at the back there! Come along, come forward please!' I realized it *was* me he was referring to, so with a few 'excuse me please-es' I joined him.

He invited me to sit on a stool – which I did. He asked me to undo my plait – which I did. Although I had left school (for the second time, you'll remember), I still wore my panama school hat, minus the school badge, because, to tell you the truth I rather felt it suited me! I often wore my gymslip with a white crêpe-de-chine blouse as well, for the same reason. When I had removed my panama school hat, 'my auburn tresses covered my shoulders like a cape' (writers always used that description about the heroine's hair, in magazines), but he broke the spell by starting to look through my hair with a comb! How dare he! The indignity of it!

I whipped round on the stool – as a matter of fact, I whipped round so quickly I nearly fell on to the floor (this got a laugh of course). Anyway, firmly back on the stool, I demanded 'Excuse me, but what are you doing? I've nothing in MY head!'

This expression was one we used at school when referring to our unfortunate play mates whose mothers didn't use a 'small tooth comb' as often as they should, and we would remark in the 'charitable' way kids have, 'oo-heck . . she's got things in her head!' I was furious! He ignored my remark and like lightning enquired, 'Can you go 'ome, wash your 'air and be back here by 2.30?' Like lightning I replied, 'I can be back here at 1.30 if I've got the job!' There was no impudence in the way I said this, it was just a statement of fact, and I was a bit on the defensive because he'd dared to look through my hair.

'You've got it!' he stated. 'Fifteen shillings for the four days, afternoons and evenings!'

Fifteen bob! FIFTEEN BOB! And the real patent leather shoes were fourteen and elevenpence!

I quickly plaited my hair, banged my panama hat on and shot out of the Winter Gardens like a dose of salts!

I ran all the way along Northumberland Street – whizzed round De Lacy's Corner and along Victoria Street, crossed Market Street and pelted down Cheapside at the rate of knots!

I was home, putting the kettle on for some hot water to wash my hair, when it suddenly dawned on me – my mother and father would 'go mad' if they knew what I had taken on!

Try to understand, there wasn't an atom of snobbery

in either of my parents (thank God!) but what they lacked in snobbery they made up for in pride! I *knew* – and I freely admit this – I knew that they would not approve of my taking on a job of this sort, and quite honestly, I didn't know myself why I had! Just as I didn't know why I didn't tell them about it – perhaps the real patent leather shoes had something to do with it, perhaps I wanted to show my independence. Anyway, I didn't tell them.

After all, they had 'made me' between them so I suppose each of them had inbred a chunk of pride in me! I vividly remember thinking that I would be able to buy and pay for the shoes myself, without bothering them. At least, I comforted myself with that thought and it eased my conscience a bit!

By the time the water in the kettle was boiling I had decided to 'go it alone!' (That's what Pearl White would have done!) I was running some cold water into the enamel bowl in the kitchen sink when my mother came into the kitchen.

'What are you doing, love?' she asked

'I thought I would just wash my hair,' I replied in a nonchalant manner. I was grateful for the steam that rose from the boiling water as I added it to the cold water in the enamel bowl, it covered the guilty expression on my face a bit! 'Wash your hair – at dinner-time – on a Wednesday?' my mother said, as though she couldn't believe it.

May I explain why washing my hair at dinner-time on a Wednesday seemed such an unusual occurrence? It was because I always washed my hair on a Friday night with carbolic soap and a pinch of borax in the final rinsing water to make it shine – so why the heck was I washing it on a Wednesday, at dinner-time? Cripes! What would Pearl have done?

'Well, I thought as it is such a lovely day I would dry it in the sun, in the back yard!' I explained feebly.

Isn't it amazing how the romance goes out of anything if you use the word 'back yard', 'back street' or 'wash house'? However, my explanation appeared to be accepted (which made me feel more guilty than ever!), and a very worried 'Thora the Cheapside Mermaid' sat in the back yard in the sun amid the aroma of carbolic soap – 'codgertating! (And they can't touch you for it!)', as Ken Dodd would say!

When my 'cape of hair' was passably dry, I went indoors and started to plait it. There's an advantage about a single plait – it's difficult to see whether the hair is perfectly dry or not.

I guzzled my lunch, pretending I wasn't doing so at all – and gazing at the big kitchen clock, I saw it was by now 2 o'clock. Great, I had time to have some apple pie and custard, which I did. Well done – if I ran I could easily be at the Winter Gardens with ten minutes to spare. I did and I was.

His nibs was there, preparing the stall and arranging pyramids of little oblong pink boxes, which, I discovered later, housed three curlers each. On the demonstration table was a small appliance, the sort of thing hairdressers used to push curling tongs into to heat them, and a couple of tortoiseshell combs. However, it was none of the aforementioned that my eyes had riveted themselves on – it was a wig block and wig.

I say wig, for want of a better word. It was pathetic –

there's really no other way of describing it. There were a few tufts of hair, dead straight, gallantly holding on to the wig lace, and, as wig blocks in those days were usually made of wood and not at all like the polystyrene five-bob jobs one can buy today complete with a face, you can imagine the picture. I'm glad really that it hadn't a face because if it had had one I would have imagined it saying, 'Don't blame me – *you* try having your hair curled day after day, year after year, with those damned curlers!'

There was another small surprise for me. A young lady was there who had also been engaged by 'his nibs'. She was much older than fourteen and informed me that she was receiving the princely wage of thirty bob! Oh, so that was the way things went, was it? All right then, a bit of competition never hurt anyone (said Pearl White in an undertone).

We were both given an overall to wear, and don't think for one moment that 'Pearl slipped the overall on and it fitted her perfectly.' Honest to God, I think the one 'his nibs' handed to me had been made for a woman six feet tall and sixteen stone in weight. Never mind the wig and block looking pathetic – I looked tragic or barmy – both, I should think.

However, as there wasn't another overall available and the other woman looked as though hers had been made for her, there was nothing for me to do but roll up my sleeves, which I did. Then I took off my gym slip girdle, which was navy blue plaited cotton, put it outside the overall and took the overall in to my own waist size. The overall result (that's not meant as a pun) was disastrous! I looked rather as though I was entering a carnival competition with the massive rolls of sleeves round my little biceps, my little waist and then a sort of white starched crinoline effect. Never mind, in for a penny, in for fifteen bob! My instructions were to loosen my plait and sit on the stool. His nibs would do the 'spiel' and demonstration, using my 'auburn cape of hair' instead of the wig block.

All right then, and why not? The shoes in Tyler's *were* 'real patent leather'.

The doors of the Hall opened and in came the public. Quite a few people approached the stall – well, they had no choice really – because we were in the middle of a long row of stalls running down right of the Hall, opposite the entrance.

Quick as a flash his nibs started the spiel.

'Now just a moment, ladies, this instrument is known (he was holding a curler in the air with great pride) as the Ideal Instantaneous Hairwaver, and with it I guarantee to give you as good a wave in two minutes as any hairdresser will give you all day.' He took a breath here.

'All you have to do is take a piece of hair' – at this point he took a strand of my hair, running his comb point along the crown of my bonce – 'as you will observe, the Ideal Instantaneous Hairwaver is comprised of a small hollow tube, a small double-ended pin and a clip which embraces the tube and holds the waver firmly in place.' Another breath. 'All you have to do is to place the tube as near the head as you can reasonably get it and wind the hair round in the same manner as I am doing, and I ask you to notice there is no trickery in the winding!'

No trickery! Perhaps not, but blimey, he had wound my hair so tightly round the little tube that I thought it was coming out by the roots!

'Now, here we have the small double-ended iron or pin which I shall place in this heating contraption on the table – kindly lent to me by the Morecambe Gas Company who are exhibiting at Stall 93 on the balcony. Place the pin in the heater and when you think it is sufficiently heated place the pin into the tube – you cannot injure or harm the hair in any way.' Another breath.

'Leave the curler to do its work for two minutes only.' (Dramatic look).

Now at this point, he really started to act and informed the interested onlookers, 'With a Hine's waver or curler, what do you do? You sleep in them or you walk about in them all day – but with an Ideal Instantaneous Hairwaver you can be invited to a Ball or Banquet . . .'

This made me laugh – Ball or Banquet in Morecambe! – and he caught me a quick flick on my head with his hand, without even looking my way!

'Yes, ladies – invited to a Ball or Banquet and within ten minutes your hair can look as I am about to show you in a few minutes.'

In a few minutes? He'd just told them *two* minutes and anyway the tube was burning my scalp! I put my hand up to my head, to sort of ease what felt like a red hot metal tube from my scalp – and, quick as a flash, another quick flick of his hand, this time on my fingers and a hissed, 'keep your 'ands down.' Just for a second, but only a second, I felt the tears sting my eyes and I remember thinking, all in the same second, 'Oh I wish I was at home – my mother doesn't flick me across the head like that!' He then repeated the waver procedure and put two more curlers or wavers in. By now he was explaining to the crowd that 'I shall now take out the waver and show you the breathtaking result – release the clasp – remove the tube – and allow the hair to be free.'

He took out the Instantaneous Hairwaver then carelessly cast it on to the table and it just caught the side of the wig block where its face would have been had it had one, and I suddenly felt so sorry for it – it really looked sad with its awful bits of hair. In fact I became devoted to it there and then. We had something in common – His Nibs had flicked me twice, and had thrown a curler at 'poor old wiggy!' Never mind, the shoes were real patent leather. Oh God, off he was going again, 'I shall now run my comb through this piece of waved hair' (he did) with great experience and then with a sort of sigh of incredulity, he breathed, 'A more symmetrical or more even wave – is it possible? Now, if you go to your hairdresser's for a Marcel wave he will charge you at least 1s 6d, but the Ideal Instantaneous Hairwaver is *not* 1s 6d, ladies. This week, as a special Exhibition Concession, we are offering you not *one* waver, not *two* wavers *but three* in the small pink box for – 1/-! Now, who will be the first – we have only a limited supply.'

Talk about a rush! Purses were being opened at express speed, and pockets were being fumbled around for shillings. His nibs and the young lady in an overall that fitted her were passing the pink boxes across the front of the stall like hot soup to the starving. Success – for his nibs. Meanwhile I sat there on my little stool looking like God-knows-what in my comic overall, my hair hanging limp over my shoulders, with the exception of one thin strand that was waved and the two remaining curlers. I was too disheartened to think of 'the auburn tresses like a cape' bit. I looked at my friend – 'old wiggy' and I'm damned sure it said, 'See what I mean?'

Closing time – thank heavens – and after what seemed thousands of demonstrations, it was time to go home. Actually his nibs was quite grateful for the way we had assisted him to have a very good day financially, and as I got to know him better he turned out to be quite a decent sort. The fact that he had flicked me was, I suppose, because I had rather let him down as regards the 'cannot injure or harm the hair in any way' bit by putting my hand up to the hot curler precisely as he said that. All the same I had a little blister on my scalp to prove that the blooming Instantaneous Hairwaver had instantaneously burnt me!

Now, if I was a clever writer, I would be able to give a credible description as to how I looked when I left the Trades Exhibition. *Please* try to visualize the picture. His nibs had given demonstration after demonstration and as each demonstration required a strand of my 'auburn cape' to be wrapped round the tube of the waver – you can imagine by knocking-off time I looked like a Fiji Islander or a modern 'frizzed out' hippie. I couldn't plait my hair and I couldn't get my hat on!

As I left the Winter Gardens, I really felt guilty, not only guilty but embarrassed, and I knew if I walked into our house, looking as I did, it might frighten my mother to death.

I ambled home with my hands behind my head, rather as though I was lounging on the beach – only standing up to do it instead of lying down. I had a lot of school friends who lived quite near, and it dawned on me that I might pay one of them a social call. I did. Talk about 'the devil looks after his own' – my friend herself answered the door and, after nearly jumping through the ceiling of their vestibule at the sight of me, she burst out laughing and couldn't stop!

I endured that – I deserved it! As she wiped her eyes with the back of her hand, she tittered, 'Aye, Hirdie, what have you done to your hair?'

'Can I come in a minute?' I asked.

As we walked into their kitchen she was still laughing as she said, 'Me mother's gone out – ee, I wish she could have seen you!'

Well *I* didn't wish her mother could have seen me! I then gave birth to an idea – I would take my friend into my confidence. I told all.

'Oo, heck, what will your mother and father say?' she asked.

'They won't say anything if they *don't know, will they*?' I said with firmness. 'And they won't know if *you don't tell them – will they*?' I added.

She thought it was great fun, the two of us 'having a secret', so she showed no surprise when I said, 'Can I wash my hair to take this frizz out and dry it in front of your fire?' She said I could . . . so for the second time that day I washed my hair, half dried it, plaited it, pulled my panama hat on. I thanked her profusely and set off home.

'Is that you, Thora?' my mother called out as I

entered our open front door. 'Yes, it's me, Mam!' I answered.

'Wherever have you been 'til now – I was getting quite worried,' she said as I entered the kitchen.

Now I would have defied anyone – *anyone* – to lie to my mother if they were looking into her eyes. I could never lie to her – in any case, I never wanted to or needed to – but I didn't want to tell her about my fifteen bob job – yet!

Quite truthfully, I answered, 'I've just *come from* Dolly's!' This was true, and although I hadn't answered her as to where I'd been I had told her where I'd come from.

'Oh, well that's all right then, love – would you like a cup of cocoa?'

Would I like a cup of cocoa? And I hadn't really told her where I'd been – I could have cried. I was rotten, that's what I was, *rotten*! I'd been sitting on that stool, in a stall, at a Trades Exhibition. I'd called at a friend's and washed the frizz out of my hair and she, my lovely wonderful mother, knew none of this and was mixing a teaspoonful of Bournville Cocoa with some sugar and a drop of milk (so it would form a paste) to which she would add the hot milk – for *me*! *Rotten*, secretive old Thora!

As I went up the 'fourteen treads' to bed, I really was very unhappy. I had my own room by now and as I undressed and put on my (get this bit) crêpe-de-chine nightdress, I thought, 'How am I going to be able to go to the Trades Exhibition tomorrow without telling them?'

When I was in bed, my mother came in the room to

'kiss me good night and God Bless' – she always did this – until she was bedridden, and then we always kissed her good night and God Bless.

As she bent down to kiss me, I threw my arms round her neck and nearly strangeld her. 'Oooo, I *do* love you!' I said.

'Yes – I know you do,' she said, 'and I love *you*!'

When she had gone downstairs, I lay there thinking for a time – but I was so tired I could hardly keep my eyes open. I remember, though, I wasn't too tired to decide that the deceitful life I was living wasn't worth a pair of real patent leather shoes! It's funny how out of proportion things could look when you are young.

When I was having my lunch the following day, my mother asked me, 'And what are you going to do this afternoon?' It was asked very pleasantly.

'Can I go to the Trades Exhibition?' I asked, and added, 'If you don't mind.'

'Yes – if you want to, love,' and that was that. 'Don't worry, I'll have a cup of tea there,' I said, and went.

When I arrived at the stall I immediately felt there was 'something up'. His nibs was building the pyramids of pink boxes and the 30/- assistant was putting her well fitting overall on.

'Good afternoon,' I said.

'Oh, good afternoon, Thora,' he replied. Well I say he *replied* – he *croaked*!

'Am I in a mess?' he went on. 'That this should happen to me and such marvellous business – my bladdy (he pronounced bloody, "bladdy") voice has gone!'

'Oh, what a shame!' I said, well, I couldn't think of anything else to say that sounded comforting.

'I don't know *what* I'm going to do!' he said, in a croaking whisper – he paused, contemplated the pyramids – he looked so sad – I really did feel sorry for him and I suddenly heard myself saying, 'Don't worry, Mr P. *I* know the patter!' He spun round and looked at me as though I had told him he'd won the pools, 'Do you? – d'you think you could manage it with the block?' he croaked.

'Well – er – I could try!' I said shakily.

Work – with – the – block! What was wrong with Miss Well-fitting-overall sitting on the stool and me demonstrating on *her*?

However, that was *out* because she was required to pass the merchanise over for the shillings – so poor old 'wiggy' and I had to attempt to 'go it' alone. What a double act! Me in my comedy overall outfit and poor 'old wiggy' looking as though he had 'the mange'.

Now, if you're not born beautiful, I am convinced God gives you other assets as compensation. One of the assets he kindly bestowed on me is a photographic memory in conjunction with an ear memory. What I mean is, if I hear something often enough, I can repeat it – well, nearly always – and this was one of the instances when it worked. I had heard his nibs doing the spiel so often the previous day that I really did know it DLP (for the uninitiated – dead letter perfect). In any case – and this was the biggest blessing – I wouldn't need to sit and have my hair waved and have to go home looking like a Fiji Islander!

Great! Poor 'old wiggy' would have to suffer – and

look like a 'mangy Fiji Islander'. I ran through the spiel to assure his nibs I knew it and he was so relieved I was glad I had offered my services.

The doors opened and we were ready for business. I felt a bit nervous, especially as the first two might-be customers who approached the stall knew me.

'He-he-he-heee, Hello, Thora!' one of them said.

Please don't get the idea that the 'He-he-he-heee' bit was because they were laughing at my overall or anything – it wasn't. It's something that many Northern people do when they meet to prefix an opening sentence with 'He-he-he-heee!' such as 'He-he-he-heee, what are you doing here?' or 'He-he-he-heee how are you?' and it's meant as a sound of pleasure when meeting anyone and meant very kindly.

After they greeted me, one of them said, 'Are you working on here?' (meaning the stall).

'Yes,' I replied very timidly.

'Are they any good?' she asked (meaning the curlers). Immediately the business part of me took over. 'Any good? They're marvellous!' I stated – with authority.

Overture and beginners, please! by now the people were in clusters in front of the stall. 'Go on then!' croaked Mr P. 'Raise the curler in your right hand!'

If I hadn't been so nervous, I'd have seen the funny side of that and proclaimed, 'I swear by Almighty God that the evidence I shall give', etc., etc., but I didn't – off I started.

'Good afternoon – now this instrument is known as the Ideal Instantaneous Hairwaver – and with it I guarantee to give you as good a wave in two minutes as any hairdresser will give you all day!'

On the demonstration table in front of me sat old wiggy, daring me to continue.

'All you have to do is take a piece of hair' – this bit was rather difficult because wiggy's mangy tufts were not to be compared with my 'auburn cape of hair' and I had slight difficulty in getting hold of a piece of hair to run my tortoiseshell comb through. However, on I went. (The real patent leather shoes in the window at Tyler's would be *mine*, paid for with my hard-earned money, within a few days!)

We did excellent business and by my third demonstration I felt as though I'd never done anything else in my life but demonstrated haircurlers. Never mind my 'crinoline' overall, I was quite enjoying myself – and so was Mr P. About half an hour before closing time, I started on a demonstration – by now it was somewhat of an achievement to find a piece of hair on Wiggy's head that wasn't waved! I got to the bit of spiel where I had to say, 'We are offering you not *one* waver – not *two* wavers – but *three* in the small pink box for – 1/-! Now, who will be first? We have only – '

I *was* going to say 'a limited supply', but before I'd got that bit out, a very quiet but familiar voice said, '*I* will.'

It was my mother! I handed her the little pink box and she gave me her shilling – we looked straight into each other's eyes and I suddenly saw two little tears begin to spill out of hers.

'Thank you, Madam,' I said (nearly crying myself), and then continued passing the little pink boxes over for more shillings as fast as I could, *because*, just behind my mother's black and gold lace toque I had seen a bowler hat. I had seen the expression on the *face* under the bowler as well! Only one man could look at anyone as that man was looking at me – my dad!

Bloody 'ell! Caught in the act!

As the customers moved away, I kind of frantically combed Wiggy's waves. When the stall was deserted, I heard the 'voice that breathed o'er Eden' say very firmly – but quietly – 'Come *here*.'

'Yes, Dad,' I replied like a bullet from a gun and came round to the front of the stall and stood in front of him.

I've already explained that one of the wonderful things about my parents was that they would never let you down or show you up in front of a third party and my dad didn't fail me in this instance. As I stood in front of him, I could see he was furious. Nevertheless, without raising his voice, he looked me straight in the face and said, 'And what, in the name of *hell*, do you think *you* are doing?'

My mother (the peacemaker) was wiping her nose with a lace edged handkerchief as she said placatingly, 'Yes – well, Jim – don't carry on. We can talk when we get home!'

Being a mother myself, I honestly think the sight of the white, starched crinoline overall had upset her – to her I looked pathetic, not comic.

'Never mind about when we get *home*,' said James Henry, emphatically, 'I want to know what she's doing *here*! Who's employing you?' he darted the last bit at me.

'Er – Mr P. – but I only did it so that I could buy those patent leather shoes in Tyler's and he is paying me fifteen shillings and the shoes are only fourteen and elevenpence and he's ever so nice and he's lost his voice so I did the patter and he never asked me to, I offered, would you like to meet him but don't be mad at him, Dad, *please*!'

'Yes, I would *very much like to meet him*,' my Dad said, punctuating each word as though he was playing 'Hamlet'.

By now my mother had fully realized why I had taken on the job – the shoes! As she gave me her handkerchief to wipe my eyes and nose she looked at me so understandingly and lovingly. I introduced my parents to his nibs and after the usual salutations, my dad said, full of authority, 'I suppose you realize how young this child is?'

Mr P. said he did, and that it was remarkable how I had deputized for him, and that he would have been unable to open the stall without me – and so on and so on.

He was most flattering (as he scooped up the shillings and deposited them in his overall pocket). On the other hand, I could see he was well aware that in speaking to my Dad, he was *not* dealing with a 'gormless Northerner' *and*, give the man his due, *he* didn't know my parents were unaware I was working for him.

I know he looked most relieved when my father announced, 'Well – she took on the job and she must fulfil her obligations.'

I took my crinoline off and put on my coat and panama hat.

'Good night, Mr P. – see you tomorrow,' I said – very quietly.

'Good night, Thora, and thank you – thank you very

much, dear! Good night, Mr and Mrs Hird,' croaked Mr P.

We were all rather quiet as we walked home. My father hung his coat and bowler hat up on one of the hooks in the passage and then came into the living-room.

Nobody spoke.

My mother went into the back kitchen to prepare some supper. My Dad took the fireguard from round the fire, which had been left banked up with slack (fine coal). I got the table-cloth out of the table drawer and spread it on the table.

Still nobody spoke.

As my dad inserted the poker underneath the well packed fire and wiggled it about, there was the lovely little explosion of flames that was usually the result of this. There was another explosion as well when my dad spoke – 'I wouldn't *mind*!' he said, 'I wouldn't *mind* – but – BLOODY – HAIRCURLERS! And on a *stall* at the Trades Exhibition! *You* standing there – what the *hell* are people going to *think*? That your mother and I couldn't *wait* to send you out to *work*?' With each word in italics he jabbed the poker into the coal of the fire and beat it into life. The poor slack suffered.

'I'm sorry, Dad,' I said. 'But I'd seen those shoes in Tyler's and . . .'

'You could have *had* the damned shoes – have you *ever* been *denied anything*?' (jab – jab).

'No, Dad,' I replied – the flood gates were beginning to open by now, 'and I only did it because, well, I thought – I –' (Pause.)

'Have you no pride?' he expostulated.

By now, the cups and saucers and plates were rattling in the back kitchen much more than was necessary and it was obvious that my mother was killing time until my dad had had his say.

'Well, I'm sorry, Dad, but I thought if – ' I was crying now, and that brought my mother out of the back kitchen.

'Now, Jim,' she said gently, 'she's said she's sorry – let's have our supper.'

You know – when I got a bit older, I was able to understand my dad so very well – and *appreciate* him, and I wish that during this little cantata I had had sufficient sense to realize that he wasn't cross with me really – he was *hurt* – his pride had been hurt because I hadn't told them about the job. And yet, I know he was really *proud* of me for doing what I had done!

As we ate our supper, Nev arrived home from the scouts or somewhere, and as he was always good for a laugh, things returned to normal.

When it was time for bed, I kissed my mother 'Good night and God Bless' and then went up to my dad who was sitting in his chair by the fire, smoking a 'Gold Flake' cigarette.

'Good night and God Bless, Dad,' I said, as I bent down to kiss him.

Now, I must explain something. When James Henry felt emotional he always showed it because his nostrils dilated. It was his way of suppressing tears, strange as this may seem. I saw it happen hundreds of times. Well, as I kissed him, he looked at me, and I saw his nostrils dilating.

'Good night, love,' he said, and then looked straight

into my face and added quietly, 'Bloody haircurlers!'

The following morning there was a knock on our front door. My dad was just going on the pier to work, so he answered the door on his way out.

A well-dressed man was standing there and after the usual 'Good mornings' had been exchanged, he asked father whether this was where the young lady who demonstrated hairwavers at the Trades Exhibition lived.

'It is!' my father replied.

'Oh good!' exclaimed the well-dressed man. 'I have a Hairwaver stall on the Fairground here and I've a job for her after the Exhibition closes, if she's interested, and if she's at liberty.'

My father informed him politely that I wasn't either interested or at liberty, but thanked him for his enquiry. The well-dressed man voiced disappointment, raised his pale grey homburg and departed.

With a cheery, 'I'm off, see you later!' my dad went to work.

At dinnertime my dad was sitting in his chair scrutinizing a copy of *The World's Fair*.

'Ye Gods!' he burst forth, 'listen to this!'

My mother and I obediently stopped what we were doing and heard him read out the following advert. 'Don't miss this fantastic offer! Metal Instantaneous Haircurlers with tube and clip, one shilling and two pence a gross! With trade name stamped on tube, two shillings a gross! Order now and avoid disappointment!'

Crumbs! And I had been informing the trusting public that, as a 'special concession', we were offering not *one* curler, not *two* curlers but *three*, in the small pink box for one shilling!

'Well,' announced James Henry, 'as you are so good at the demonstrating lark, I've a good mind to send for some. We could run our own stall on the Fairground – 'Hird's Instantaneous Hairwavers!'

He looked up at the two women in his life, to discover us standing there almost as if we had been petrified!

'Well? What do you say?' he smirked. My mother came out of the trance first.

'What do I say?' she asked as she put the cruet down in the middle of the dining table. 'I'll tell you what I say!' She moved towards the back kitchen door then did a beautifully timed stage turn and executing a perfect imitation of my dad, she said, 'Bloody Haircurlers!'

I completed my assignment for Mr P. – and collected my fifteen shillings.

The 'real' patent leather shoes were greatly admired at both Sunday School and Chapel and I faithfully rubbed the toes with Vaseline and stuffed them with newspaper after I had taken them off. The shoes were 14s 11d – so I had a penny left out of my 15s wages. I gave this to my mother.

After she died we found it in her jewel box, carefully wrapped up in tissue paper along with Neville's rather yellow halfcrown.

I would like you to know that for many years Mr P. requested my services 'for demonstration purposes' when he had a stall at the Trades Exhibition. Faithfully he would call at 6, Cheapside, but I was never 'at liberty'.

I would also like you to know that when my father informed the 'well-dressed enquirer' I was not 'at liberty' he was telling the truth, because that very tea time he said to me, 'How would you like to work in the office on the pier, this season?'

I was delighted and said, 'Oh, thanks Dad – my night school shorthand and typing will come in useful and you'll be able to see *how well* I'm doing!'

He looked at me with a twinkle in his eyes and said, 'Never mind about my seeing how well you're doing – I'll be able to see *what* you're doing!'

21

Oh my Papa – to me he was so wonderful!!

Hecky plonk! Have you ever worked for your dad? I'm only joking when I say that – it was great really. I used to report for duty at nine o'clock each morning and finished at five o'clock.

I remember one morning my mother asked me to go for some bread before I went to work. When I arrived at Gibson's in Euston Road, it was to be told 'It won't be a minute, Thora – we're just taking another batch out!' Oh, the aroma of hot bread, isn't it marvellous?

I waited about five minutes and then looking at my watch (*THE* watch, I told you about!) I thought, 'I hope it won't be long or else I'll be late for work!'

Being late for work, or late for anything, as far as James Henry was concerned, was the unforgivable sin! I must say, I never knew my dad to be late for anything. Mind you, I admired him for it and it was wonderful training for us. He used to say that if you were late, let us for argument's sake, say, one minute – that you were as many minutes late as the number of people you had kept waiting. Hence, once when I was a minute late for rehearsal when he was directing the Morecambe Warblers Amateur Operatic and Dramatic Society, he admonished me in front of everybody and informed me that as there were sixty-three people at rehearsal, I was sixty-three minutes late! Red of face and very ashamed I apologized to the whole cast. I was never late again I'll tell you that!

It's a good job I had that training really because I'm married to a man as bad – or good – as my dad! If Scottie and I are going on a journey by train, he has the car hire at the front door so early that by the time we arrive at the station we could comfortably catch the train prior to the one we've gone for! Forgive me for telling you that I am never late for rehearsals, anyone I have worked with will substantiate that. Good old Dad, good old Scottie! My working life runs very smoothly.

Anyway, I've been standing in Gibson's Confectioners waiting for the bread a long time, haven't I? Sorry! As I came out of the shop it was two minutes to nine – oh, crumbs! get your running pumps on, Thor! I ran home, flung the hot bread on the table, kissed my mother ta-ta and flew up Cheapside like a scalded cat! As I approached the promenade the clock tower came into view, its hands were pointing to nine and twelve and gave the appearance of a policeman stopping the traffic, they looked as though they were saying, 'STOP! It's no use you running like that, you should be there now!' and to prove it as I crossed the road on to the promenade the clock boldly struck NINE! Oh I sprinted – thank the Lord, I used to sprint for the school – along the prom, past the Children's Corner and up the slanting forebay of the pier, through the big wrought iron gates at the entrance of the pier, which old Artie Gott had opened – and with a breathless

'Morning, Mr Gott' I whizzed past him up the pier. I was a bit at the panting stage as I flew into Dad's office. Putting my handbag in my desk drawer with one hand, I whipped the cover off the typewriter with my other hand and sat down. I was about to say 'Sorry I'm late, Dad' but I didn't get the chance.

'You're late!' he informed me as though I didn't know.

'Well, I'm sorry, Dad – only a few minutes though, and I had to wait for the bread!'

He wasn't cross or anything, don't misunderstand me, he was what you might call, FIRM!

'Bread!' he said, 'And what's the bread got to do with it – you work HERE and you are late!'

'Well,' I said, 'my mother asked me to go for the bread and it wasn't out of the oven and I had to –' he looked at his watch on his wrist as he interrupted my weak explanation, I'd put the 'My mother asked me' line in, not to put the blame on her, but to add the homely touch. I mean, I was speaking of the woman he loved! I needn't have bothered because it didn't work.

'It's now six minutes past nine and you're supposed to be here at nine o'clock remember – so don't be late again please!' With that he walked out of the office. When my coffee arrived for elevenses I noted that instead of the usual two finger biscuits on the little plate, there was a chocolate eclair! The waitress from the café put the tray on my desk, pointed to the eclair and said with a grin, 'That's from your dad!'

As that particular season on the pier drew to a close, I experienced the same feeling that I do now when a show is near its end. I was sorry it was over. However much I try to console myself with the fact that I have done a job of work to the best of my ability, I am unable to stop myself thinking for an odd moment, 'Oh heck, that's in the past now and won't ever happen again!' It's stupid I know, but nevertheless it's part of the way I am made so there it is. Although I knew I could go back to the Pier Office the following season, I was sad the present one was finishing.

One afternoon whilst I was at work on the pier, there was a knock on the door of number six Cheapside and upon answering it my mother was confronted by a gentleman who had a Drapers and Milliners Shop in Euston Road, which ran parallel with Cheapside. He didn't waste words but came straight to the point. He did the flattery routine by telling my mother he thought I was a very smart and alert young lady and he and his wife would like me to work for them as a shop assistant. And that was how, when I finished on the pier, I went into the General Drapery Business.

22

The EPNS wedding

My parents' Silver Wedding was approaching and Nev and I were in a bit of a quandary as to what to present them with, as a mark of esteem and love from their devoted son and daughter.

We were in an even bigger quandary as to what we were going to use for money!

I was commissioned to 'have a look round the shops for something nice'. Now the 'looking round' bit was easy – and the 'something nice' bit was easier still – it was the looking round for something nice *that we could afford* that was tricky.

Needless to say, the first shop window I planted myself in front of was James Hargreaves, Jeweller. True enough – once again in the window – there was something I thought beautiful (not as beautiful as the watch I was wearing at that very moment and *had* worn every moment since I acquired it!) but what I saw was beautifully suitable for our 'mark of esteem', at least so I thought, and after all Nev hadn't mentioned any article specifically.

It was an oak salad bowl resting on a base of oak, bound round the rim with silver. (It was EPNS really, but I thought it was silver!) The servers were in EPNS with oak handles – like skipping rope handles – *and* – and this was what appealed to me – there was a small EPNS shield on the front of it, absolutely begging to be engraved on.

As I stood there, the old imagination set to work once again and in my mind's eye I read 'To Mum and Dad on the occasion of their Silver Wedding – love from Thora and Neville!' Oh, I could see it! Not only could I see the engraving on the shield, I could see the whole works, salad bowl, servers and engraved shield, on top of our piano! Oh yes – that was the very gift, no doubt about it!

So once again I dashed into Jim Hargreaves' shop and, as always, he was understanding and helpful.

'How much is that oak and silver salad bowl in the window, Mr Hargreaves, please?'

He smiled as he replied, 'Just a minute, Thora, I'll get it out of the window and see!'

As he unlatched the glass door at the back of the window and then moved two or three articles to reach the salad bowl, I was thinking, suppose someone else buys it – I'll never see another one just like that, with a shield on.

He brought it to the counter and turning it upside down perused the price on the little ticket that was stuck on the base. I held my breath!

'Thirty-seven and sixpence!' he said, adding, 'it's very nicely made, isn't it?' I agreed it was.

'There is quite a nice white porcelain bowl inside it, you see, for the salad!'

Cripes! white bowl inside it as well, to protect the real oak!

As I have told you before, we knew Mr Hargreaves, he was 'our' jeweller, so I was able to ask him if he would kindly 'put it on one side'. I told him what Nev and I wanted it for and he agreed that it would be a very nice and suitable gift for Mam and Dad.

So far, so good – we'd decided on the gift. All we had to do now was to get thirty-seven and sixpence. Nev and I had an extraordinary general meeting and decided that as we had some war saving Certificates the ideal thing would be to draw out one each and make the rest up out of our bits of odd cash.

This sounds easy enough, but the saving certificate books were in my dad's drawer and it was an understood thing in our house that Nev and I never – I reiterate, *never* – opened my mother's or father's drawers unless, of course, we were told to. Come to think of it, by the time Nev and I reached our teens, we always regarded the cupboards or chest of drawers in each other's rooms as private.

So how the heck were we going to get hold of the books of certificates? We tried all the obvious approaches, such as, 'Shall I get you a clean handkerchief, Dad?' or 'Can I get your tie for you, Dad' all to no avail until one day, by the grace of God, Dad said to me, 'Nip upstairs and get me my cuff links will you please, love?'

Quick as a flash, Nev said, 'I'll go, Dad!'

I'll admit it took him a bit longer than it should have. In fact, Dad called out, 'Can't you find them, Neville? They're in the leather stud box in the corner of the drawer!'

When Nev replied, 'I've got them Dad!' I was very relieved, I knew what else he'd got as well.

We went to the post office, but of course we couldn't get the money straight away. After signing an application for repayment each, we were informed that a warrant would arrive at our home address and if we took *that* one to the post office, we would get the cash. Crumbs! that meant that the OHMS envelope would arrive in the post at 6, Cheapside!

I wish you could have seen the scurrying, willing and obliging Thor and Nev who, so thoughtfully, each morning when the postman knocked, sprang up from the breakfast table with a cry of, 'I'll get it!' We managed it, I'm happy to say, and in the lunch hour we collected the cash – one pound each! Good egg! We could afford to have it engraved – and buy a nice card as well!

As Nev went off, I shot along to 'our' jewellers and informed Mr Hargreaves about the engraving. I also paid for the salad bowl even though he suggested I should settle up for the lot when the engraving was complete. No fear, I thought, let's get rid of the two pound notes!

So with the halfcrown change in my purse, and the salad bowl paid for I left the shop in a gay and light-hearted mood. I was anticipating the look of wonderment, pleasure, surprise and incredulity on my parents' faces, when the day arrived for us to present them with the oak and 'silver' salad bowl and servers, complete with engraved shield.

My mother finished the ironing that evening and duly put the handkerchiefs on a dinner plate to air on the ledge over the fireplace. Later, when she felt the 'noserags' were aired enough for use, she put them in separate piles and requested me to, 'Take those up and put them in our respective drawers, will you, love, please?'

God bless her for saying that! I nipped upstairs. Nev was in his room and, opening his bedroom door, I hissed, 'Pst! pst! the books, the books!' holding my hand out for same.

As I put Dad's hankies in his drawer, I replaced the saving certificate books under the rubber band that held the remaining ones. It was with love and devotion that I placed the handkerchiefs in the corner of the drawer – well, that's what I thought it was – but it was really with *relief*!

I can laugh at it all now, although, come to think of it, 'old habits die hard' and I still say to Scottie, my husband, 'May I go into your drawer for the nail clippers?' to which he never fails to reply, 'Of course, you don't have to ask!'

The great day arrived. The gift was on the breakfast table, the expressions of wonderment, delight and incredulity were all as anticipated, with the addition of one we had *not* anticipated – as my mother wiped her eyes she enquired, 'Wherever did you get the money for that?'

And believe it or not – we told them!

23

The end of the world

When you were young and the weather was 'thundery' and the sky took on a dark-grey kind of pewter colour appearance, did you ever say to your schoolfriends, 'Oooo, it's the end of the world!' Did you? We did!

And did you get an excitement of sorts when some spooky-minded friend said, 'Oooo-er, all the ghosts will come out of their graves!' We did! Which all goes to prove, and with pride I announce, that I was as daft as any other youngster! And I'm very happy to admit it!

But it wasn't thunder or ghosts or anything ethereal that was responsible for 'the end of the world' in my young life. It was something much more material. My 'End of the World' was brought about by two Bradford businessmen, who owned the Central Pier!

I've related how the Pavilion Theatre had been miraculously changed into the Pavilion Ballroom, and how this prosperous end product was due to the brains, inventiveness and never-ending work of my father. Right! You know all that, so 'new readers start here!' I have no intention of sounding bitter about the following or about the person my father 'tutored' as far as pier management was concerned – because that same person was always very kind to Nev and me, and indeed, he admired my father greatly – so please don't misunderstand or get the idea I am running him down. I'm not! And it really wasn't his fault that he knew nothing about running a pier, until my father patiently and unselfishly taught him. He would admit all that himself! He's dead now, so God Rest Him – it was with sincere respect I went to his funeral.

Things were running very smoothly at the Central Pier. The ballroom was a big success, the bars were always full, the 'spondoolicks' was rolling in and everything in the garden was lovely! It was at this prosperous period that the two Bradford businessmen, dreaming of even greater wealth – and having picked my dad's brain – offered him 'half his wage' if he wished to stay on as assistant to his protege!

My father informed the two Bradford businessmen where they could insert the two small domes of 'The Northern Taj Mahal!' One each!

'Oh, what a lovely smell! what are you baking – gingerbread?' I asked my mother, as I took my coat off. She was in the kitchen and, as she didn't reply, I thought she hadn't heard me.

'*Is* it Gingerbread?' I enquired as I went into the kitchen – and then I saw the expression on her face. There were little tears in the corners of her eyes and she looked so sad that within a second my arms were round her and I was appealing, 'What is it, Mam, what's the matter?' She was rolling a piece of pastry out to cover the top of an apple pie during the above conversation – and why is it, that when a person is upset but continues with the job they are doing, they always look more pathetic than if they just give way and burst into tears? Have you ever noticed that?

As she covered the prepared apples in the dish with the piece of pastry she said, 'Your dad has told the two Mr So-and-So's where to stick the two small domes off the Pavilion – and he's finished on the pier!'

My dad finished on the pier! Impossible! He couldn't be! He *was* the pier! *We* were all *part* of the pier! It had been such a big part of our lives! Hell! It *was* our lives! Nev and I knew every plank of the pier deck, every flagpole and flag, every automatic machine, flower tub, kiosk, bar and deckchair!

And what about the Pavilion? We knew and loved every dressing room, staircase, the ballroom floor and everything? What about the fountain my dad had thought out? What about the six nude women who held the boxes up? They were practically relatives!

My dad finishing on the pier? It was the end of the world – *that's all*! *The End*! (I was always a bit dramatic y'know!) How about dancing in the open air and the dozens of pals I took on there – for nothing? How about Nev on the Lime Perch, and the Spot Dances in which, if the music stopped and the Lime was on you, and you had a current copy of *Answers* in your hand, you could win a canteen of cutlery or a clock? And how about my private Ladies' Toilet with the marble wash basins and the lovely little mirror that informed you 'Mene Towels' were 'for Ladies'? Oh God – it was – *yes it was* – the end of the world!

Have you noticed the selfish touch in all I have just written? My first thoughts were about things Nev and I would have to forego. On the other hand, and I speak in defence of Nev and I, we did love every inch of the Central Pier, it had watched us grow from little children into fairly responsible teenagers, my father had willingly given it fourteen years of his life and knowledge; he had been a slave to the pier, each morning from eight thirty until eleven or twelve o'clock at night. Even in the winter he went back at night to see that everything was safe.

He'd walk round the entire pier and buildings to see that nobody had carelessly dropped a cigarette, he would check and light the warning beacon at the very end of the pier, which involved climbing up on to the high diving platform once used by Madame Rosa Vere. On nights when there was a gale my mother had suffered agony until he returned home safely. And now, suddenly, he was finishing on the pier! What I hadn't realized at the time was that by telling the Bradford businessmen where to put the domes, my father had effectively put himself out of work!

When I grew older I often thought about all I have just told you. I would think of how conscientiously my father had worked, the honest way he always put his job first, and how there was nothing he didn't do. No, I take that back. My Dad just missed doing one thing. He should have told those men from Bradford where to stick the large dome as well!

24

Not guilty, yer honour

Dad had left the pier and I was about to start working in a draper's shop . . . it was a debatable point which was the bigger tragedy. I shall call the shop Glumdell's, that wasn't its name but it will suffice.

The shop structure comprised two large bay-type windows and the floor of the recessed entrance was of coloured quarry tiles in a pattern. The narrow double doors had the usual big brass latch. Upon entering the shop, the counter was on the left and facing it was the millinery department with a large mirror on the wall, surrounded by hat stands, the type that are wall fixtures and welcome a hat popped on them. There were large, deep millinery drawers from where the mirror finished to the floor. Through an archway was the back shop, three walls of which were lined with shelves and packed with boxes of goods. The right-hand wall boxes were huge things covered in dark green American cloth. They pulled out by a big brass handle. There were thirty-four of these handles. I know because I cleaned them each morning.

On the morning I arrived at Glumdell's to take up my duties, the very first thing that impressed me – or *de*pressed should I say, was where we hung our outdoor coats. It was in the passage of the house that was attached to the shop, and ran behind and above the premises. One side of the passage housed a long oak stock cupboard and we hung our coats on pegs on the opposite wall. Everything was spotless, and I mean spotless, but it was the 'smell' that upset me and I couldn't think what it was. I soon found out, the big oak stock cupboard was full of Fustian trousers – all sizes! Phew!

My first duties were explained to me. I had to go into the back yard and get the mop bucket and mop, which they kept in the outside 'loo', bring it in and fill it with hot water and disinfectant then proceed to mop the shop floor, starting at the back of the shop and working my way out backwards through the shop door so that I would mop the entrance to the shop as a final gesture.

It was then explained to me that I must wring out the long mop tightly and wipe the woodwork under the windows 'where the dogs had been!' Right, next item, empty the bucket and don't forget to rinse it out with clean water before returning it to the outside 'loo'. My next artistic task was to clean, with metal polish, the brass latch and letter box on the shop door 'and be careful not to get any metal polish on the paintwork.' Then I had to clean and polish the resident brass yard measure that was secured to the back of the counter. My 'big finish' was cleaning and polishing the thirty-four brass handles on the big boxes at the back of the shop, 'and be careful with these, if you get polish on the boxes it won't come off!'

Behind the counter were the usual shelves filled with cardboard boxes, but in the centre at the same height as the counter was a little display of various haberdashery goods.

Ruling supreme over everything else was a display of steel hatpins; they were stuck in half of an unbustable ball, which had been cut in two and the flat piece used as the base which supported the half dome that was pierced by the hatpins. But these were no ordinary hatpins. Even *then*, when *I* was fifteen and a half, they were period pieces. Mind you, they were lovely, each was about eight inches long and the heads on them were magnificent. Massive, but magnificent.

I can remember the head of one was about the size of half-a-crown (of course, even a halfcrown is a period piece now, isn't it?) with a pastoral scene on it, another one had a cameo head on it, and so on. I'll bet any television wardrobe department would give the earth for them now.

I was told to put a piece of paper on the counter top and emery paper the hatpins! 'Because they soon go rusty being steel, and we don't want that, do we?' I will admit I didn't mind. I thought they were being preserved because they were antique. Not on your nelly! I had to clean them in case anybody came for a hatpin!

Now who in the name of goodness would want an eight-inch-long hatpin, in steel, when everyone was wearing toques? Never mind, I emery-papered them each morning, gradually wearing the steel away. By the time I left Glumdell's the steel pins were so thin I was afraid they would break. Nobody had ever purchased one.

You'll notice I said, 'by the time I left Glumdell's?'

Well that isn't quite correct. I was *sacked* from Glumdell's – for *stealing*! Put on a record of 'Hearts and Flowers' and I'll tell you what happened.

On a Saturday night it was Glumdell's who 'shut Euston Road up!' We were always, without fail, the last shop to close; we would be mopping out the entrance and wiping down where the dogs had lifted their legs long after every other shop had closed and their assistants had gone home. It was a very prosperous business, but, even so, during the last hour we were open on a Saturday very few customers came in.

I had been working there just over a year, so was about to take some 'Iron Tonic' in preparation for my second Christmas at Glumdell's. We really did work like mad preparing for Christmas. There were only two assistants and 'himself'. 'Madam's' contribution was to come and stand under the archway, her hawk eye watching that we never stopped, and saying, 'How do you do,' to the customers.

One job I was not mad about was making balls of cotton wool, about the size of sago, and sticking them on the Millinery mirror with spit to form the words, 'A Merry Christmas to all our Customers!'

The Benefit Boot shop was opposite Glumdell's on the other side of Euston Road, and I had seen a very pretty pair of red bedroom slippers right in the middle of their window – four and elevenpence halfpenny they were. I wanted to give them to my mother as a Christmas gift, so about a week before Christmas I asked the Manageress to keep them for me.

Our uniform at Glumdell's was a navy blue serge dress, which reached nearly below our calves; it was embarrassing really, because the short skirt was in fashion then, and although we requested to have the length shortened 'Madam' wouldn't hear of it. What, she asked, would it look like if you had to go up the steps to get a box from the top shelf! I'll tell you what it would have looked like – the black hole of Calcutta, that's what, because we wore black knickers and stockings!

Over the long serge dress, to preserve it, we wore a black sateen 'pinarette', yes, that's what they were called. It was an apron with a bib top. There were two pockets in the pinarette that were neither use nor ornament because they were so shallow. It was because they were so shallow I was sacked for stealing! Let me explain.

We were very busy on Christmas Eve and I hadn't collected the red bedroom slippers. I'd been over during my teatime but the shoe shop was packed, so I thought I'd pop across later. I did, and paid for my mother's present with two halfcrowns, which I had brought to work out of my savings. The halfpenny change I put in the shallow pocket of my pinarette.

As I came back through Glumdell's shop door I saw we were busy, so I rushed and put the slippers with my outdoor coat in the smelly passage. I didn't waste time by taking my purse out of my coat pocket and transferring the halfpenny from my pocket to the purse, but went straight back behind the counter to serve. About half an hour later I was serving a customer and, as she had bought rather a lot of goods, I needed a large sheet of brown wrapping paper. This was something else that embarrassed me; we always used large sheets of brown paper that goods had been wrapped in when they came from the warehouse; they were always creased and crumpled, so we were never able to make a tidy parcel. I always thought it was a cock-eyed way of doing things. Bending down to get a piece of crumpled brown paper from under the counter where it was kept, I heard something drop out of my pinarette pocket and roll into the back shop, I realized it was my halfpenny change from the five shillings I'd paid for the slippers, so I didn't bother to go and find it immediately because I was serving. I could find it later.

The slippers were a big success and my mother was delighted and, of course, I was delighted that she was delighted. The loving incident I will now relate happened on about the seventh of January on a Saturday morning. We were into a new year and as per usual I was going into the back yard 'loo' for the mop bucket and long 'mop' I was on my way back into the shop when 'Madam' halted me.

I must admit, she terrified me – honestly. I was frightened to death of her, so you'll appreciate that when she ordered, 'Just a minute!' I nearly dropped the ruddy bucket! She then proceeded to say that a customer in the shop had noticed 'some money' fall out of my pocket on Christmas Eve when I was bending down to get some brown paper, and had thought it was strange that an assistant should have loose cash in her pocket and so on and so on and so on.

As I looked at her, I *knew* no customer had ever said anything of the sort. I could tell by her face, don't ask me how, but I could.

In retrospect, I know that as she said what she did, I

changed as a person or perhaps it would be more correct to say that it was a changing point in my life.

Suddenly, I was no longer frightened of her. I stood there clutching the handle of the long mop, I could have cried, but I wasn't going to – *how dare she*? She was as good as accusing me of being a thief! *Me*! I'd never taken anything that wasn't mine in my life and I'd never wanted to – and I never would! Clutching the mop handle until my hand hurt, I said, 'Are you calling me a thief?'

It was her reply that *did* it, she said, 'Well, *I'm* not but it's very funny that this – er – customer should remark that some money fell out of your –' she got no further, because I heard somebody say – and it must have been *me* because there was only me there, 'You bloody bad old bitch!' I thought she was going to faint! I thought I was going to as well, when I realized it was me who had sworn at someone for the first time in the sixteen years I had lived up to then! Need I say that, as I was given my meagre wage packet that night, I was also given my notice! I was out of pocket as well – because I never found my halfpenny!

You are bound to wonder why one of my parents didn't go to Glumdell's and knock Madam's teeth in! Well I'll tell you why.

When I went home for my dinner on the day of the accusation I hadn't got my coat off before my mother enquired, 'What's the matter?' I unashamedly admit I burst out crying. 'Oh, love,' my mother murmured as she embraced me, 'whatever's happened, what is it?' In the comforting safety of my mother's arms, I told her. I think it was a 'changing point' in her life as well because she immediately seemed to become a *tigress* protecting her young.

'*She said what?*' she demanded. 'Right, you sit down and have your dinner. I'm going round there *NOW*! How *dare* she, the old faggot! Accusing one of *MY* children –'

All this was being said as she unhooked her coat off the peg on the partition. It was at this juncture I started to plead, 'No, don't go round, Mother, please, I'd rather you didn't, it will only cause more trouble and . . .!'

James Henry came through the front door, before I'd finished. You can imagine the following five minutes of our lives, can't you? He was furious! My mother was told she could take her coat off because *he* was going to see Mr and Mrs Glumdell! By God! They would be sorry they had accused me of the lowest crime on earth when *he* had finished with them, by God they would. His children had been brought up to know the difference between right and wrong, we were a family that was well respected in the town and to dare accuse his daughter . . . on and on he went, I was crying and pleading, 'Don't go, Dad, it will make it worse for me, *please, please* don't go!'

Well, he didn't go, not because he didn't want to, but because I was so upset at the thought of him doing so. I assured them both that I was no longer afraid of Madam, so things would be different. Even so, he only refrained from the attack on the understanding that when I had dutifully finished my work that evening I would give in my notice. I have already told you – I didn't get the chance – *they* presented *me* with it!

I started to work my fortnight's notice without any

embarrassment, I was a changed young lady, albeit I worked harder than ever, if that was possible. Jobs that were automatically done each day I did with gusto, adding many other little jobs to them.

It would be untrue to say there wasn't an atmosphere because there was, but the fact that I never stopped doing *something* did leave a bit of egg on their faces.

Actually, 'himself' was sorry I was leaving and told me as much as I helped him to dress the window. As we artistically arranged 'Ladies' combinations, with bust inserts' he told me, 'It's nothing to do with me, you know.' 'I know,' I said, using an inflection that left him in no doubt I knew he was frightened of her as well! Poor, henpecked old soul!

On the Tuesday, which was only the second day of my 'atmosphere fortnight', he enquired, 'What do you think you will do?' He asked this rather sadly, really, and I felt a bit sorry for him.

'Do? Mr Glumdell,' I exclaimed, 'I shall find another job, of course!'

He looked at me, then looked at the floor as he said, 'That won't be too easy – without a reference!'

25

'Change please'

'*Wanted,* young lady cashier for the Queen's Square Branch of the Lancaster and District Co-operative Society Limited – *must be eighteen*. Apply in own handwriting to the secretary, etc. etc.'

The above advertisement appeared in the *Morecambe Visitor* on the Wednesday after I had received my notice at Glumdell's. I applied immediately.

On the Friday morning I received a letter asking me to be at the Co-op offices in Lancaster at 7.30 that evening. I was there. So were another million hopefuls! The big room was full of long tables and the applicants were instructed to sit down. It was then explained to us what we were to do. In front of each person were papers and pens, and piles of 'gum sheets'.

For anyone not familiar with the system that was used at certain Co-op Societies, I will explain. A 'gum sheet' was a long narrow piece of paper about three inches wide and about eight to ten inches long, gummed on one side. After each purchase made, the member was given a narrow slip of paper, called a check, stating the amount they have spent, the shillings amount being written in words and the pence amount in figures. These amount slips were stuck on the gummed sheet and, when full, the member took it to one of the Co-op shops or offices, where it was added up and the full total written on an orange-coloured slip and stuck on the top of a new clean gum sheet, and off you went again, sticking your checks on. In my Co-op days, at the end of each quarter, your gum sheet was taken to the office and you received two shillings in the pound dividend on all you had spent, and sometimes a twopenny bonus as well!

On the night I am telling you about, the pile of 'gum sheets' in front of each applicant had to be added up and summarized on a sheet of ruled paper which was provided. All I can add to that is – there seemed a lot of 'gum sheets'!

At the 'off' we all started, heads down and pens at the ready – it was just like a school examination. All was silence with the exception of the scratching of pens on paper and the near silent murmurings of lips as the adding up took place.

I was enjoying myself; I wasn't bad at arithmetic and here was the opportunity to use a little of my book-keeping and accounts knowledge I had acquired at night school. Oh, yes, the thin red line!

Eventually the sound of chairs being pushed back could be heard as first one and then another future Chancellor of the Exchequer took their papers up to the little gentleman who was presiding behind a desk at the far end of the room. I was to discover he was the Lancaster and District Co-op Secretary.

Everybody present finished before I did. It wasn't because most of the amounts to be added up were written in words, although that can be quite difficult until you get used to it. It was because I was so anxious to make the end product neat and businesslike. I might still have been sitting there, if a quick glance at the old-fashioned clock on the wall hadn't reminded me that the last applicant had left the room twelve minutes previously!

Using a pencil as a ruler I drew a final thin red line under the grand total. I looked at my effort, then added another thin red line under the one I had already done. Yes, that looked better, much more professional! I blotted it carefully and then gathered my papers together and took them as an offering to the gentleman, who was still sitting waiting patiently behind the desk at the end of the room.

'Thank you,' he said as he accepted my papers. 'It took you rather longer than anyone else, didn't it?'

This was not a reprimand, it was just a quiet statement of fact, and even whilst he was saying this his eyes were taking in my efforts.

'This is all extremely neat,' he stated, his eyes leaving the papers and looking up at me.

'Thank you, sir,' was all I said.

He turned to the last page where the final column was penned, and as I saw his eyes start to move down it, I realized he was adding it up – so I added it up as well, to discover that where I had put three farthings in the grand total, it should have been a halfpenny!

Before I could stop to remember 'my place' I had touched his arm and then pointed to the total.

'Oh! excuse me, sir – that should be a halfpenny, not three farthings,' I dared to volunteer. He looked at me so very kindly and said, 'You went up that column of figures very quickly!'

In normal circumstances I might have been tempted to say 'No I didn't, I went *down* it!' but I refrained. He thanked me for attending, said he was sorry it was so late and wished me 'Good night.' *He* was sorry. It was my fault.

I caught a bus in Dalton Square and went back to Morecambe. By the end of the following day I would have worked one week of my notice at Glumdell's. One gone, one to go!

On the following Tuesday a letter arrived asking me to go for an interview on the Wednesday evening, same place, same time, with references. These were acquired by my father from a JP in the town, my Headmistress, the Headmaster at night school and our doctor, who was also a JP. My father was prepared to provide one re my office work on the pier, if necessary.

When I arrived at the Co-op Head Office there was only one other young lady there, so I thought perhaps as we were rather early the rest would arrive later. A Co-op official (they all look alike, don't they?) collected our references and asked us to wait in a small anteroom – we did, for ever it seemed.

There were only the two of us for the final round. My opponent was a very pretty girl and certainly looked more intelligent than I did. She told me she worked in the Borough Treasurer's Office in Lancaster Town Hall (goodbye job, I thought!) – but as she suffered from every kind of travel sickness she wanted to work in Morecambe were she lived.

She was summoned to the inner sanctum first – it was the committee room. I sat there waiting – it didn't half feel lonely! I had put my long hair up into earphones for the occasion, as I thought it would make me look a bit older, remembering the advertisement had stated *must be eighteen*! Eventually my pretty challenger came out of the committee room, and smiling very kindly, she wished me 'Good night and good luck!'

In I went. The scene was a large comfortable room governed by one of the biggest polished mahogany tables I had ever seen – I was later to appear in plenty of rooms like this one when I played Councillor Sarah Danby in *The First Lady* on the telly. About twenty Co-op committee members were sitting round the table – I won't bother to describe them, they all looked alike, and at the far end sat the Secretary of the Lancaster and District Co-operative Society, my former kind inquisitor, with what were obviously my references in front of him. I was asked to sit in a corresponding chair to his – at the opposite end.

After general Good evenings, the Secretary explained exactly what the job entailed, and then out came the first question, 'How old are you, Miss Hird?' Just as quickly as it was asked, I answered, 'Sixteen, sir.' I wish I could describe the intakes of breath, the heads turning to each other, the mumblings of derision! It was reminiscent of a Labour conference! The Secretary kept his eyes on me – that was all he did, it was enough.

'Er – we did state in the advertisement that we required a person of eighteen – it was stated very clearly,' he said. 'I know, sir,' I defended myself, 'but I think I can do the job!' There were a few more mutterings at this point.

'Your references are excellent, but this position

involves handling large amounts of money and you appear rather young – are you working at the moment?' I replied, 'Yes, sir, but I finish on Saturday.' 'Why?' he asked. 'Why are you leaving your present position?' I took a deep breath and then I swallowed – here goes, I thought, don't waste words, Hirdie, you've nothing to be ashamed of.

'I've been sacked, sir!' I heard myself say in a firm voice. Hecky plonk! The mumblings and mutterings all started again and were only silenced by the Secretary tapping on the table with his pencil. All went quiet, he looked down at my little pile of references, cleared his throat and informed me, 'There doesn't appear to be a reference here from your present employer – why is that? What are you being sacked for?'

By now, the 'might is right' chorus were looking at me with steely eyes, and a couple of them were looking at their watches with some impatience. I suppose they had every right to feel I was keeping them out of the 'Cross Keyes' but wasn't their slogan 'Equality for all?' All right, I'd tell them why I was being sacked. They had every right to know.

Looking at the full table as though it was a full house in a theatre I said, 'For stealing, sir.'

You could have heard a pin drop! God 'strewth! Some of them nearly slithered under the table!

'I . . . er – I think you had better explain,' said the Secretary after he'd regained his composure – and I did – and I told them the whole story, every detail. As a matter of fact, if it hadn't been so serious, I could have almost felt I was telling a bedtime story to a lot of little children, so attentively did they listen – but it *was* serious, and I *knew* it was, so after strenuously defending my honour I finished off by saying, 'So you see, gentlemen, I have nothing to be ashamed of – *I* know the money that fell out of my pocket was my own.'

At this point you could have heard another pin drop! – and then – 'Thank you, Miss Hird,' this came from the Secretary, quite quietly really. I was politely dismissed and thanked for coming along. With an equally polite, 'Good night, and thank you,' I left the room.

I cannot remember the journey home on the bus, but there must have been one.

As I hung my coat up on the varnished partition in our living-room, my mother asked me, 'How did you get on!' She was preparing a cup of cocoa for me.

'I don't know,' I replied as I pushed a dislodged hairpin back in place, 'I told them why I had got the sack – that seemed to shake them a bit, but I did tell them everything!'

'That's a good girl,' my mother said proudly as she poured the hot milk into my cocoa mug.

It wasn't until I was in bed, that I suddenly realized I hadn't told them everything, I hadn't told them that I had called Madam Glumdell a bloody bad old bitch! Which was probably the *real* reason why I had got the sack!

On the Saturday morning, my last day at Glumdell's, a letter arrived at 6, Cheapside, requesting me to report for work at the Lancaster and District Co-operative Society's Queen's Square Branch, for duty, at eight thirty on the following Monday morning! I'd got the job as cashier!

As I unhooked my coat from the rail in the Fustian-smelling passage, Madam stood like a wardress in the shop. I buttoned up my coat as I proceeded to walk out of the shop for the last time. I opened the door with the big brass latch I had cleaned so often as she called after me, 'I can't see you getting another job in a hurry, we are not giving you a reference, you know, so don't bother to come back and ask for one!'

I turned and looked at her, and with all honesty I said quietly, 'No, Mrs Glumdell, I won't do either – good night!'

The door of Glumdell's closed behind me for the last time.

In my fan mail on 9 October 1970, was a charming letter from an equally charming lady, I should think. She added a postscript which read, 'I believe that when you were in your teens, you worked in my aunt's draper's shop in Euston Road, Morecambe. I gather you were the only one she couldn't boss! Hearty congratulations!'

Thank you, dear lady, but you have been misinformed. Your aunt *did* boss me, which I suppose she had a right to do, as she was the boss. But she also awakened in me the knowledge that I had a life ahead of me that would probably hold many undeserved accusations and rebuffs, in fact, she really assisted me to grow up! At least I'm grateful to her for that!

26

'Fierce flames are raging'

(Il Trovatore)

I stood on Morecambe Promenade on 31 July 1933, as the Central Pier Pavilion burnt down, watching a very happy slice of my life go up in flames.

As the small dome on the left-hand side pathetically crumbled like a deflated paper bag, the little balcony in front of it collapsed in sympathy and disappeared.

'That's our mustard and cress balcony,' I thought.

The gallant centre dome stood proud and magnificent, trying to defy the flames as they curled round its base, but the orange and red arms of fire reached greedily upwards and embraced it in a cruel bright red cloak. The big dome was soon entirely ablaze and as the massive flames reached to the sky it looked as though it was frantically trying to cling or clutch on to something – or perhaps it was raising its arms to the audience on its final curtain.

With a heartbroken wail of agony, it collapsed, and took the small dome on the right with it for company. The balcony where we'd kept the doves went, too.

A tumult of memories rushed through my mind as I stood there amongst dozens of people, but alone, 'Programmes, threepence each – perfumed with Amo-Del!' 'Two more jellies, please!'

'Oh no, this is not I!' sang Miss June, in her navy blue costume and panama hat!

'Sorry I'm late, Dad, but my mother asked me to go for the bread!'

Regardless of my thoughts, the fire didn't stop to think, it was greedily eating into the Pavilion and unashamedly belching black smoke. The place where Devilshoof had carried me over the scenery rocks was devoured quicker than it takes to record.

I ached with sadness as I wondered how much longer my Vestal Virgins could hold the boxes up! Of course, they had never held up the boxes really, had they? I can remember thinking – I'll bet they are valiantly trying to hold them up now! But the inferno was too much for them and the part of the Pavilion they had graced so well, crashed as I thought of them lovingly.

Within a few minutes the entire structure was a mass of flames.

The papers reported that it was Morecambe's biggest fire to date! How like the Central Pier! Nothing but the best! 'Everyone on stage for the finale, please!'

The northern Taj Mahal in true Indian fashion had held its last rites on a burning funeral pyre.

It was there. It was there no longer. All in ninety minutes!

As I sadly walked away, I was thinking of my dad. He was in Lancaster that day so was spared the devastating sight I had just witnessed, I was grateful for that.

I knew the question I would ask him, 'D'you think some silly devil carelessly dropped a fag end, Dad? If you'd been there you'd have found it, wouldn't you?'

I ambled along the promenade, dejectedly pushing against the wind, thinking, 'The domes have gone – it's no use my dad telling anyone where they can stick 'em any more!'

I looked at the raging sea, it pounded deafeningly against the sea wall, madly furious at the disaster it had witnessed during the past two hours. As it thundered its way up the ramparts it suddenly pulled back savagely, leaving its white spume running down the walls like giant tears. I held on to the promenade railings and looked at it. Dark grey, almost black. It was already wearing mourning for the late lamented Central Pier Pavilion!

27

The drummer boy

When the Winter Gardens, Morecambe, was taken over from the Broadhead Circuit in 1933 by a group of wealthy northern businessmen, it was given a face lift, an uplift and every other lift you can think of. The old place was really transformed.

Credit where it is due, it had been looking like a poor relative, which is always a sad thing to write about, especially when one can remember the glittering years of variety and dancing there. However, unlimited money was spent, splendid ideas used and the result was worth all the praise showered upon it. It was back in its place as a first-class variety theatre and ballroom.

The new orchestra, under the leadership of Cecil Hodgkinson, was installed in the band pit and it was to become so popular that the Theatre would be full at seven o'clock, just to enjoy the music prior to the curtain going up at seven-thirty. I was invited to the exciting opening night. It really was a wonderful evening, the entire place had been redecorated, the seats renewed, everything gilt had been regilded and there was a wonderful atmosphere of opulence.

If I tell you that I didn't really notice the drummer in the orchestra, that would be a big fat lie. I did. But it wouldn't be a big fat lie to say that although I noticed him I didn't suddenly think, 'Ah, there is my fate!' It was quite a few months before I thought, 'I *think* that's my fate!' by which time, you will have gathered, we were 'going out' together.

Anyway, I won't recall in detail the three years we saw each other every day but I will tell you that after three years we became engaged and I was taken to Forfar in Scotland to meet his father. (It's usually the other way round, isn't it? Only as Scottie had had his supper at our house for three years one might say he already knew my father and mother. And they knew and loved him as I did.)

If ever Scottie had a rival it was his father, 'The Chief', because from looking at his dear face for the first time, that night long ago, on Forfar station, my love for him increased daily, as his did for me, until he died. See what I mean about being born lucky? A wonderful set of parents of my own and a loving father-in-law as well. (Scottie's mother had died when he was seven.) When he came to live with us, by popular demand, I could do no wrong and he always stuck up for me. This was counterbalanced, however, by my mother, in whose eyes my husband could do no wrong and she always stuck up for Scottie. A wonderfully balanced arrangement, you must admit.

There was something else that was very lucky for us about my parents and Scottie's dad . . . they all got on extremely well because they had so very much in common.

By this time I had begun to work in the theatre, and Scottie and I used to have a favourite stroll after our respective curtains had come down. If his Winter Gardens show was down earlier than mine at the Royalty, he would collect me at the Theatre. If my show was down earlier than his I would wait at my mother's and he would collect me from there . . . all very convenient.

We agreed that this little stroll was a good way to clear the theatre air out of our lungs – but who am I kidding? We were young people in love, and, quite honestly, didn't give a damn about clearing our lungs!

Our walk or stroll was only about half a mile, if that, and ended on a little hill known as Woodhill. I suppose there had been a wood there at one time and that is why it was so called. I had known it since I was a little girl and used to picnic there, with my lemonade bottle full of milk, and my brown bread and banana sandwiches, but I could never remember it as anything but a sort of meadow on a hillside. A meadow that smelt of fresh grass and clover. As I grew older I discovered that the full moon shone on it, too! Smashing!

Most of the surrounding area around had been built up, and part of Hodgson's Meadow, another of my picnicking spots when I was little, was by now a road of spick-and-span new semi-detached houses.

Perhaps it was the moon – or perhaps we'd cleared our lungs of theatre air – perhaps it was because Scottie was in digs, but whatever it was, he once again got on to the 'marriage chat'.

How do I explain that although I knew he was the one destined to be 'the one that *didn't* get away!' I was not mad keen on getting married too soon. I had a wonderful family life at home into which Scottie was welcomed and I loved him dearly, so I said, 'I'll marry you if you'll have a little house built for us, on this hill!'

I suppose it was about two months later that, as we arrived at Woodshill one night, I saw that the foundations of a house had been dug! In the middle of the well of earth and clay there was a small piece of wood stuck up, and nailed across it horizontally was a smaller piece of wood bearing the word, 'Sold'. The 'S' was the wrong way round, which made it look a bit sad, but it fitted with my mood as I said to Scottie, 'Aw, what a shame! There you are you see, someone has beaten us to it!'

My man is very undemonstrative really, but on this occasion he put his arm round my shoulder and said, 'Did you ever think you would *have* to get married?'

'No I didn't!' I shot back, 'and what a thing to say!'

'Well,' he laughed, 'you'll have to marry me now, because this is *our* house!'

I flung both my arms around him! Within three minutes I knew what sort of curtains we would have and which tree, in the non-existent garden, we would sit under!

An obliging cow had 'dropped its card' in the foundations. Muck for luck, I thought, and it was!!

We called the house, 'Prompt Corner' (but of course) and it cost the amazing sum of four hundred and ninety-five pounds!

Scottie and I returned from our honeymoon on a train from Forfar that arrived in Morecambe around lunch time. As the station was midway between my parents' house and our own brand new little house, you may wonder why we made for 6, Cheapside, first. Well, that's easy to explain. I wanted to see my parents and tell them all about our honeymoon (well, not *all* about it – but at least about the lovely scenery!). And also, as it was lunch time, I was anticipating a 'free nosh!'

I shall never forget the aroma of roast lamb, mint sauce, and new potatoes rolled in butter, that wafted up our nostrils as we opened the front door.

After loving hugs all round, my mother informed us that they had already eaten. 'We had lamb chops,' she said, 'and I would have prepared some extra if I'd known you were going to call here on your way from the station, but there are plenty of new potatoes left and some mint sauce. So why don't you nip round to the butchers and get a couple of lamb chops? You can grill them here and we can hear the rest of your news while you eat them!'

Quite simple and straightforward, really, only she didn't know that the newlyweds had but three shillings and eight-pence between them! Which had to last until the Friday. (And it was only Monday!) Never mind, I bought two lovely thick chops for *tenpence* (doesn't *that* sound like a bit of ancient history!), reducing the housekeeping cash to two shillings and tenpence!

There was apple pie and custard on the table so after we had eaten the two succulent chops I said to Scottie, 'Apple pie and custard, love?' as I cut him a generous wedge. As I was about to put his plate in front of him my mother said, 'It's threepence a portion!' I nearly dropped the plate on his lap but then started to laugh as I said in a very assured way, 'Yes, I'm sure it is! 'But it *is*!' protested my mother with a very straight face. In fact, she was so serious that I asked, 'You're kidding, aren't you, you don't really mean that you're charging us for it?'

'Yes. Two portions will be sixpence!' she assured me.

I gave her sixpence, and didn't enjoy my three-pennyworth at all. My own, dear, generous mother, who gave everything, charging *me*, her own flesh and blood, her own loving daughter, blasted threepence a portion for blasted apple pie and custard! Ah well, you live and learn, I thought.

As we walked to our new house, poor Scottie had to suffer my martyr-like moanings, such as, 'I'd never have believed it!' 'My *own* mother charging us for a sweet!' etc., etc. However, I can honestly say that as we entered our newly-painted front door for the first time as Mr and Mrs James Scott, I was so happy that I wasn't bothering about anything . . . not even how I was going to manage until Friday on two shillings and four-pence housekeeping money!

Scottie returned to work at the Winter Gardens that same evening and as I wasn't playing in the rep. company that week, I met him after his work. We called at 6, Cheapside, to say 'Goodnight' as we were on our way home.

In the centre of the dining table were two large plate pies, a savoury one and an apple one. My mother started to wrap them in greaseproof paper and burst out laughing as she did so. I pretended I didn't see the joke, but as it was hard to keep a straight face because my mother's infectious laugh had started Scottie laughing as well.

'It was worth it to see your face at lunch time,' my mother explained.

'Well, there was no need to charge me!' I retorted.

'Oh yes there was, you're a married woman now and you'll have to learn to make your money spin out . . . if you want anything badly enough and can't afford it, you'll just have to wait until you've saved up for it!'

How right she was, and how often Scottie and I have saved for some special item, enjoying the anticipation of buying it as much as the actual purchasing!

We unwrapped the pies when we arrived home, to discover that the apple pie had a centre decoration. Nestling there, as though it had laughed itself into my mother's fabulous pastry, was my sixpence!

28

The pioneers

It was a great moment when we discovered that 'The two James's' (my dad and Scottie's dad were both called James) had both at one time been managers for Pooles. Not Vernon's Pools or Littlewoods' Pools but the original Charles Poole, the pioneer of the Panorama, Cyclorama and Mirrorama, which were the forerunners of the film industry.

A Panorama, to describe it as per dictionary, is a continuous revolving landscape, circular or semicircular view, inside of a cylindrical surface painted with scenery.

To describe it as per Thora, a Panorama was two massive rollers like tall pillars and the scenic canvas was wound from one to the other by means of a big handle. (By the way, I know I'm not twenty-one any more but neither am I old enough to have seen one of these wonderful contraptions in action. All my knowledge of same was gleaned from my father.) When the aforementioned progressed even further it was called a Cyclorama. The next step was the Mirrorama and by the time it reached this stage it was really something! Scenes were projected from a magic lantern on to the revolving canvas. There would be moving clouds going one way, while cut out figures, carriages and horses, fixed to a gauze, would be moving the other way. 'The Siege of Mafeking' was produced quite realistically by adding gun noises, flashes, and a background of smoke. A gentleman would stand at the side of this living miracle and describe to the open-mouthed audience what each scene depicted, pointing out various interesting details with a billiard cue.

There is no doubt at all that this was the forerunner of the modern motion picture industry, and our parents were in at the conceiving, just as they had both operated Lumiere cinematograph machines at the dawn of the twentieth century. How interesting they were to listen to and how patient when we would ask them to describe some intricate detail more fully.

James Henry even appeared in a film in those early days. The part he played demanded that he should ride up into the clouds on a bicycle! This effect was achieved by laying a sky-and-cloud painted backcloth on the ground and riding across it normally. Clever stuff eh? and the beginnings of trick photography and stunt men all rolled into one!

When I first started in films, I was greatly befriended by Thorold Dickinson and his wife Joanna. It would require a separate book to record their many kindnesses to me.

One night when I was dining at their house, we were discussing the early days of filming and I told them about the two JAMESES and their involvement with the 'industry'. Thorold was so interested, that he asked my father to write about his experiences during those pioneer days, which he (Thorold) eventually incorporated into an article in a film magazine.

I have already told you that my father moved along in the entertainment business from artist to manager. Parallel with that, Scottie's dad moved on to the musical side and was to become Musical Director at various theatres. He also taught the cello, which he played very well himself.

So there you are. Scottie's dad played the cello and my dad played the banjo. A great pity they didn't meet years earlier. What a double act they'd have made! 'The two Jimmys'. From Schubert to Jazz: open for offers for summer season or Royal Albert Hall Concerts!

29

'Morecambe's Royalty'

Although my father had left the Royalty Theatre so many years before, it continued to be quite a part of our lives. I was in my teens when I made my debut into 'rep.' at the Royalty, it was during the time I was a cashier at the Co-op. What happened was, the repertory company was presenting a play that required a larger cast of artists than they had in the resident company and they asked me 'would I oblige?' I did. It was the thin end of the wedge. Eventually, as I've mentioned, I appeared in rep. there. At first the parts I played were always very small (come to think of it, the parts I played were *always* very small, but we won't go into that), so, consequently, I was off stage more than I was on, but even that had its advantages because by the time I had joined the rep. the dressing rooms were under the stage, my childhood hunting ground, so whilst all the artists with the big parts (pardon the expression) were acting their socks off, I would wander around my old haunts happily reminiscing! You are well aware by now that the stage door to the Royalty was in Cheapside, so what better door to venture through when I went into rep? A stage door in 'our street'. Of course I had been through that door hundreds of times before but never as a wage earner.

My first part in rep. was in *Yellow Sands* by Eden Philpots. I played one of the twins. As one twin says most of the words and the other is only an echo, the Morecambe Repertory Company weren't risking their reputation when they cast me as the echo! It was great fun really, because the other twin (poor soul) had to study all her lines but all I had to do was wait until she had said them and then echo the last two words – e.g. if she said, 'Happy birthday, cousin Jennifer', all I had to say was, '. . . cousin Jennifer!' If she forgot to speak, I was laughing bags because I couldn't echo nothing! It was money for old rope really. Come to think of it, a bit of old rope is about all I could have bought out of my wages. One pound a week I got. On my first pay day I celebrated by treating myself to a bottle of L'Onglex nail varnish . . . it was sixpence.

I could easily fill a book about my experiences in rep. but I'm not going to. All I will say is that they were great days and nights and hundreds of funny things happened to me. I shall have to refer to my rep. days during one or two of the little stories I want to tell you, so that will suffice.

It's extraordinary how one looks forward to, anticipates and talks about, one's first wedding anniversary, perhaps a little more than, let's say, one's third, eighth, or fourteenth. Most wives will agree with me, I think, that a couple of weeks prior to the first anniversary one is inclined to say in a rather offhand way or manner, 'Just imagine, in *two weeks* we will have been married for a *whole year*!' or 'It doesn't seem *nearly a year* since we were married, does it?' or 'Who'd have thought . . . it's our wedding anniversary in *two weeks* . . . hasn't the time flown?' The husband usually agrees with all the aforesaid remarks because it is the safest and easiest thing to do. He's also very grateful that the little woman has reminded him! In plenty of time!!

There's another thing about the first wedding anniversary, too. The bride of last year is rather inclined to look at the clock (which was a wedding present), sigh nostalgically and breathe, 'A year ago today, at this very minute, I was putting my wedding dress on and being zipped up the back!' or 'I shall *never* forget, I laddered my new nylons as I pulled them on (titter-titter), I thought I should never be at the church on time!' Little did she know that within a few hours the brand new bridegroom would throw his 'L' plates away and with fumbling fingers would be frenziedly and legally laddering 'em again!

Any road up – that's enough of that sort of talk – as my mother would have said!

About a couple of days before our first wedding anniversary, Scottie said to me, after I had brought the subject up, accidentally on purpose, about a dozen times, 'Good God, is it *really* a year?' It struck me at the time, that he used exactly the same expression he would have used had he said, 'Good God . . . is it *only* a year?' But we'll pass over that!

There's an expression, common to the north, 'We haven't much money but we do see life!' Well, that applied to us!

On the day prior to the anniversary, Scottie asked me, 'Would you like a mink coat or a diamond solitaire ring?' I add quickly, there was a twinkle in his eyes as he said it! I replied that I had so many mink coats and diamond rings that it would be ridiculous to buy me any more!

Then we both burst out laughing. You see, this was the wonderful period when everything we wanted had to be saved up for. We hadn't a bank account but we weren't in debt either . . . except for the house, and we religiously put the thirteen shillings and eight pence halfpenny rent away each week so that it was there to pay the mortgage on the specified date. I had a series of empty cigarette tins in the top drawer of the desk, each one labelled neatly and clearly. I can remember those tins like old friends. The fags they had contained were called 'Ashton' and they were thirty for a shilling. I've still got one of the tins amongst my 'treasures'. The great advantage about them was, the lids were half red and half white, divided obliquely, and, if one so desired, one could print the description of the contents on the white half instead of going to the trouble of making labels of stamp edging. The tin I still cherish has 'Papers' printed on it, but that doesn't mean it contained toffee papers, the Aspen papers, curl papers or cigarette papers – oh no, it meant that it was the receptacle for the weekly money for the newspapers. The money was put into the tin each Friday when we were paid our respective wages, so that it was *there*, waiting to pay the newsagent.

Another tin displayed the word 'Windows'. I used to put fourpence a week in that tin, because Edward Fern, the window cleaner, used to do our windows, front and back, inside and outside, every fortnight, and he charged eight pence! (*Eight pence*! I haven't as many windows in our present house and it costs two pounds and the bloke only does the windows outside! There's another thing, apart from the price, where our present bloke can't compete with Edward Fern – Edward was an artist at his job who always 'got in the corners!').

'Clothes', 'Insurances', 'Garden' (that was for seeds, etc.), 'Rates', everything was covered by my 'tin system'. But my favourite tin was the 'Weekend in the Lakes' tin. It meant, of course, the Lake District, and every time Scottie did a broadcast with the orchestra, and there were many, the money was put in that particular tin. You'll notice, if you please, I had put 'Weekend' in singular, so that we wouldn't be disappointed if we only managed to go once!

'Weekend in the Lakes' sounds as though we were going to take our shoes and socks off and 'paddle or stand in the middle of Lake Windermere for the weekend. Doesn't it?

Right! Now where the 'ell was I? Oh, I know, Scottie had just asked me whether I wanted a mink coat or a diamond solitaire ring for my first wedding anniversary present and I had replied in a rather facetious manner that I had too many minks and diamonds!! Well, after we had stopped laughing, and I think there had been a bit of a kiss and a cuddle, I asked him, 'Would you like – and you have a choice – a navy blue Hillman Minx with a gilt "S" on the door, or a three and elevenpenny ha'penny evening shirt from Greenwood's in Euston Road?' He thought for a minute, then (melodramatically acting out his indecisions) finally said he would prefer the shirt because he needed a new one to wear in the orchestra.

On the great day itself, I presented him with the shirt, carefully gift wrapped in a piece of fancy paper. I'd also bought a most beautiful card for three pence . . . honestly . . . *THREE PENCE*! He in turn presented me with some flowers and a card, which I've still got (the card I mean, not the flowers).

During lunch, he remarked that he wished I would tell him if there was some little thing that I would like that he could give me because he didn't feel the flowers were enough. 'Right!' I said, 'there *is* a little thing that I would like that you could give me!' 'Good!' he said. 'What is it?' 'A baby,' I answered, as I chewed on a chip. 'And I want us to make it tonight!'

The doctor called me into the surgery. I knew her well and I knew her dad before her. Her dad had known me very well too, he'd brought me into the world, and you can't know anyone better or more intimately than that!

'Now then, Thora, what's wrong?' she asked, lighting a State Express 333 and offering me one.

'Nothing,' I replied, 'I'm just in an interesting condition, that's all!' She bounded up from the desk, said how happy she was for Scottie and me and my mother and father, and then instructed me, 'Get on there!' 'There' was that dark green, leatherette covered couch thing. She turned away from me to put her cigarette out in an ashtray on her desk and whilst her back was still to me she asked, 'How far?' 'Three days,' I replied confidently.

'Three da . . . ! Get off there and pull your skirt down. *Three days*! Come back and see me in a couple of months.' 'All right,' I said, ' . . . but I'll bet you one hundred State Express 333 . . . that I am!'

'Right!' she said, 'and I'll bet you . . . one hundred . . . Players it is you smoke isn't it? . . . that you're not!'

I got my hundred Players and *we* got a wonderful baby girl. Doctor Jo delivered both. 'It was,' as I said to her, 'it was daft of you to take the bet on – you see I know Scottie better than you do and when that lad makes up his mind to do a job – he does it properly!'

On our seventh wedding anniversary I gave Scottie a navy blue Hillman Minx with a tiny gold 'S' on the door. A lot more working water had to flow under the bridge before I got my mink coat, and when I *did*, for my twenty-fifth wedding anniversary, I lent it to someone before I ever wore it myself.

When the curtain rose on the biggest drama of our lifetime, the war, Scottie joined the RAF and for the first time since our marriage we were parted. I had the comfort of our ten-month-old daughter, but, like most people I wanted to 'do my bit' in some way.

I went to the Clarendon Hotel, which was the RAF Headquarters and Billeting Office and offered my services to help win the war. I became a civilian clerk. You will obviously assume that it meant my finishing in the repertory company. Not at all. The parts I played were so small, it was arranged that I could rehearse in my lunch hour!! I worked things out to the second; I would leave the office at 12.30 – rush across the road to the bus stop in time to catch the 12.32 from the Battery, which was further back along the promenade. It was only a short journey to Euston Road Central and I'd be on the Royalty stage at 12.42! Not bad, eh? On arrival at the theatre, the rest of the company, very accommodatingly rehearsed the bits that concerned me, and Bob's your Uncle!

As my parents still lived next door to the theatre at 6, Cheapside, I was always sure of a bit of 'nosh', free, gratis, and for nothing (although I always offered my meagre share out of the rations I got on my own and the baby's ration books, they were never accepted – that's parents all over, isn't it?). It also meant I could see our baby daughter who was contentedly being loved and cared for by her doting grandparents during my working hours. If my role in the play involved more than two entrances my mother kindly provided me with sandwiches wrapped up in greaseproof paper, which I would eat when I got back to the office. The sandwiches I mean, not the greaseproof paper.

30

'Ring down the curtain – I can't sing tonight'

The old Victorian Music Hall song with the above title is inclined to get a laugh in 1975 and remarks such as 'The show must go on' and songs such as 'There's no business like show business', 'Laugh Clown Laugh', 'Close the Shutters, Willie's dead', 'Smile though your heart is breaking' are a bit mushy and I've laughed and made jokes about 'em as often as anybody else.

All the same there *are* occasions when it would be both comforting and convenient if one 'hadn't to go on' – the stage I mean – but one does 'go on' because – excuse the expression – 'The show *must* go on!' I recall, very vividly, the day my mother died. I was in rep. and, would you believe it, on my first entrance in the play we were doing I was attired in black for a funeral, and my opening line was, 'If we're going to mourn the departed, we must do it completely!' Nobody could or did love their mother more than I loved mine and the fact that I played that night will be understood by all my fellow workers. I wasn't playing 'a big important part' – it was very rarely that the repertory company cast me in such a part – but you see, there are no 'understudies' in rep., and in any case my dad, Mr Professional, said 'Go on, love, go to work, your mother would have wanted you to!' So I did. The strange thing was that, as I walked on to the stage and said the line, I said it without any additional emotion; in other words, I said it as I had rehearsed it, it was the *rest* of that wonderful band of players who could hardly speak. When the final curtain was down, I went to my dressing room, excuse the *my* dressing room bit, I *shared* a dressing room – and my dad was sitting there. 'Hello, Dad! What are you doing here, love?' I asked ever so brightly. 'I don't know,' he answered. 'Well, just let me clean off and we'll go into the Rat Pit and have a drink,' I replied.

'The Rat Pit' was the pit bar at the Royalty Theatre, and the artists had access to it from under the stage. It was aptly named, we had to pass the gentlemen's urinal to get to it and believe you me the effluvium was enough to make anyone join the 'Blue Rubber Band' or 'The Band of Hope' and cry off drink forever! But we didn't notice 'the perfumed passage' much that night.

As we walked home (I had insisted that James Henry stayed on for a while with us because my mother had died in our house, 'Prompt Corner') a lump of pain, like a brick, formed under my ribs. I suppose the same thing has happened to lots of people reading this. In my case it *stayed* there for five whole weeks until one day, after carefully saving my meat coupons for weeks (because this story happened in 1942), so that I could give Scottie a mixed grill for his lunch when he arrived home on leave from the RAF, I gazed at the little kidney, the weary sausage and minute piece of steak and the bit of shrivelled bacon, that were all huddled together on the plate as though they were ashamed of their size, and I can remember thinking, 'Oh, he *will* enjoy this!' As I grabbed hold of the plate, my anticipation of Scottie's joy was so great that I forgot to use a towel or an oven glove and as the red hot plate burned my fingers I dropped the blasted offering – it fell upside down on a piece of coconut matting! The brick under my ribs started to dissolve and I cried for two hours!

My darling Scottie sat at the dining-room table in his RAF uniform, picking coconut matting hairs out of the mutilated sacrifice, faithfully eating the 'surprise' I had cooked for him and saying, 'Don't cry, love, it's lovely – *really*!' He knew, of course, I was crying because I'd lost my mother five weeks before!

I am never likely to forget the week we played *As You Are*. I was cast in the character of the mother-in-law, Emma Pearson. She was a woman of sixty, so after I had made myself up, complete with paste nose, I nipped out of the back door of the Theatre, ran the ten yards to our back yard door, and into the house. There, confronting my mother, I appealed anxiously, 'How do I look? I've not overdone it, have I?' She assured me I had done very well, as she smoothed a rather harsh line of greasepaint, which I had applied to give the effect of wrinkles, with her little finger. You see, that was just one of the lucky and wonderful assets I was blessed with; I mean, how many actresses have the advantage of nipping out of their dressing rooms and within a count of twenty are able to be in their own living-room asking their very experienced and professional mother, 'How do I look? I've not overdone it, have I?'

When the curtain was about to rise, the buzz was going round the company, 'George Formby's in front!' and quite a bit of excitement prevailed, because he was a big name. The leading man said to me, 'I'll bet he's in a box,' and I said, 'I'll bet he hasn't paid!' (I said this with a laugh and not with disrespect, I assure you!)

After the show, the manager of the Threatre brought Mr and Mrs Formby down under the stage because they had asked to meet me. I was just taking my paste nose off when I was informed that they wished to speak to me, so with my paste nose pointing towards my left ear I was introduced.

I won't bother to tell you what they said about my performance but I will tell you that I heard him saying he was going to make a film of *As You Are* and that he would like me to repeat the part I was playing on the stage in it. He then said he would arrange for me to go to Ealing Film Studios for a film test.

I was dumbstruck but I managed to thank them both very much. I stood there like someone in a trance.

I was still standing there with my paste nose pointing towards my left ear after they had gone, when it really dawned on me what George Formby had said. I didn't know whether to laugh or cry. Instead I gave a great sigh, and as I did so my head went back and my eyes looked up. I was standing underneath 'the grave drop'. '*I* know *you*, don't I?' the grave drop seemed to say in our Nev's voice of years ago.

Then I *did* cry!

Opportunity knocked on the Monday and on the Friday night while I was removing my makeup after the show, there was a knock on my dressing-room door. I called out. 'Come in!' but nobody did, so, grease towel in hand and face covered in cold cream, I opened the door.

I'm not one for flattering, but the gentleman standing at the door really *was* well dressed and very smart, added to which, he was very handsome as well. I didn't know who he was so I just smiled through the cold cream, whereupon he enquired, 'Miss Hird?' 'Yes,' I answered.

He gave me his card. I'm short-sighted anyway, but it doesn't help much when one's eyelashes are sticking together with cold cream. Anyway, I managed to read 'Gordon Hamilton-Gaye, Casting Director, Ealing Film Studios.' The casting director! And me covered in cold cream! Sod it! Then I suddenly thought, as I'd never kidded myself I was in the front row when good looks were being given out, perhaps the cold cream was covering a multitude of sins!

As Morecambe is a seaside resort, my first thought was that he was on holiday, so, like an idiot, I asked him, 'Are you here on holiday?' 'No,' he replied, smiling, 'I travelled up from London especially to see you!' 'Just to see me?' I stammered. 'Yes, just to see you!' My mouth was open a bit, I was nervous, I was dithering, I was embarrassed because of my greasy face and I was young, so perhaps it is understandable and forgivable that I just looked at him and gasped, 'But the fare is three pounds seven and nine!' Hey, d'you know, I couldn't imagine anyone going to that expense to see me! He didn't half laugh. I wonder whether he would have laughed had he paid the fare from London today!

If things go on as they are doing, it's going to cost three pounds seven and nine to travel from Marble Arch to Oxford Circus by tube.

'Is there somewhere we could go to chat for a few minutes?' he asked. As I was sharing a dressing room I replied 'Yes – er – well – er – where would you like?' (What a daft thing to say.) 'Well,' he said, and this was the moment when I knew I had a friend for life, 'What about the prop room?'

Sitting amongst the props, he voiced his own love of prop rooms, having been connected with the live theatre before he was in the film business and as I sat and listened to him, I wiped the remaining cream off my face.

I looked around the room, a room that I knew so well, a room that had given so much pleasure and was now witnessing the germ of something that could end in a lot more pleasure. I'm not going to excuse myself for feeling like I did. I felt I wanted to say, 'What shall we play at being now, Nev? Film stars?'

Years later, when I was the subject of *This Is Your Life*, Gordon Hamilton-Gaye was one of the mystery guests. When I heard that voice off-stage say, 'But the fare is three pounds seven and nine,' I didn't need to guess, I *knew* who it was!

31

As Dick Whittington said, 'Ten miles to London? Come on, Puss!!'

So, hey up Metropolis, here I come! Now just hold on a minute whilst I describe the ensemble I was wearing. The main bit was, of course, the suit, it was from the 'Fifty Shilling Tailors', it was navy blue with a white pin stripe, my blouse was made of white pure silk, I wore white gloves, black patent leather court shoes and my hat was in navy felt and rather large. Nothing about that outfit to cause alarm or make you laugh, is there? Not yet, but read on please.

My Auntie Molly and Auntie Martha (who weren't relatives in any way, only their back yard door backed on to our back yard door), were dear, kind neighbours and I loved them both very much, hence the title of Auntie. God bless 'em!

They had each of them just acquired a black, silver pointed fox fur and with their usual generosity they insisted that I should wear *both* furs for my debut into the moving picture business!

My mother said, certainly not, it was most kind of them both but they had saved up for the furs and supposing anything happened to them, she would never forgive herself.

Both furlenders said I must wear them. My mother

said I mustn't. The furlenders said they would like me to wear them and it was nothing to do with my mother. My mother said she *wouldn't* like me to wear them and it would have plenty to do with her if I lost them. I just stood and listened. At the end of the final round, the referee's decision was a draw. All the aforesaid argument had been in the most friendly way.

Both fox furs had a snap-clip mouth so one mouth could clip to the other, rather as though they were eating each other, and the two bodies and brushes could hang down my back, nothing about *that* to make you laugh either if I happened to be tall and willowy, but I am only five feet and one inch tall and the brushes of the luxurious furs were hanging well below my bottom, so the effect was er . . . well er . . . rather top heavy and grotesque.

The gates of Ealing Studios opened to welcome me (well, that's not quite correct, the *small* gate at the side of the big gates was pushed open by me) . . . the air raid warning sounded as I did so, everybody started running so I did as well, I had no idea where we were all running to but I guessed it was a shelter. It was and we sat there for over an hour. A woman sat next to me shelling peas for the restaurant as though she always went there to shell peas!! There was a lot of joking and rude remarks passed about what should happen to rotten old Adolf!

A film test is not like a driving test, a breath test, or an eye test, it's like er, well, er, a film test, and I am here to tell you that 'not nobody nowhere' knew less about a film test than I did! Which I will prove!

After being made up and costume I was taken on to

the set, where I was looked at, talked about and photographed and then tested as the sixty-year-old mother I had played in the play. After all that it was decided to send me back to make-up where I was to be given 'the glamorous treatment' – it seemed to take hours (which is not surprising, with my face!), false lashes, hair styled, all little bits of curls over my forehead and the prettiest of 'juvenile lead' dresses.

When I returned to the set I was informed that I was to be tested as Lynda (who was the female lead in the play and daughter-in-law of the part I had played). They had employed a young actor to play, for the test, the part that George Formby would play in the film.

He was standing in the middle of the little set they had built, looking distressed. I had to walk on, looking equally distressed, whereupon he asked, 'Where will you go, Lynda?' and I had to reply, 'I shall go to London!', and then exit. Not much, you will admit, to give 'em an idea of whether you can act or not. We did the scene about ten times, so I'm sure you'll understand when I say that I thought we kept on doing it because I was doing it wrongly. I'd no idea that they were shooting close-ups, medium close-ups and long shots. The young director of the test was very kind and helpful and after the tenth attempt came up to me and said, 'Splendid, now in this next take, I want you to say the line with more anger, sort of, "I shall go to London and bugger you!" Get it?' I said I would try.

By now, I was convinced that they were just being kind and patient. On I went for the eleventh time, my young leading man asked me, 'Where will you go, Lynda?' and I replied, 'I shall go to London, and bugger you and bugger everything because I don't think I'm any good at this . . . if I haven't done it right after ten attempts I never will, after all I was *asked* to come down here, *I* never asked if I could, I was quite happy in rep, I mean, I'm sorry but *you* did ask *me*!' At that moment the director said, 'Cut!' As I didn't know what that meant, I just stood there with egg on my cupid-bowed lips, false eyelashes, and curls-over-my-forehead face!

I was requested to go and change into my own clothes, and I was glad to escape for a breather after my pathetic outburst. I was then tested as a secretary.

After all that, I was thanked most profusely and everyone treated me very kindly.

I was staying the night at 'Kenmare Cottage', which was only yards from the studios. It was a wonderful old place, all authentic old oak beams and ingle-nooks. Great food. But great or not, that night I fell asleep at the table during the soup.

The following morning I had to go to the studios to see the result of the test. I arrived and was directed to the Rushes Theatre. Quite honestly I didn't know what rushes meant and wondered whether I should have to rush into the theatre and rush out again. The place seemed full of people, mostly men, but as soon as I spotted Gordon Hamilton-Gaye I felt a bit more at ease. I was introduced to Mr Shandos Balcon and sat on his left.

Then it all started. The screen flickered and the first person I saw on it was the clapper boy, holding the clapper board and saying, or announcing would be a better word, 'Screentest-thorahirdtakeeleven!!' Then he clapped the board.

I can't really describe the next bit adequately, because I had gone sort of numb all over as I saw and *heard* myself on the silver screen.

The curls on my forehead were bobbing up and down, my false eyelashes were being blinked at the rate of knots and my cupid-bow mouth was saying, 'I shall go to London and bugger you and bugger everything because I don't think I'm any good at this, if I haven't done it right after ten attempts I never will, after all I was *asked* to come down here, *I* never asked if I could, I was quite happy in rep., I mean, I'm sorry, but *you* did ask *me* – A quiet voice interrupted me with the word, 'Cut!' and the screen went blank. The lights went on. I was sitting there petrified, clutching Mr Shandos Balcon as though we were in the back row of the cinema! There was quite a bit of mumbling and subdued laughing. I felt *awful*!

Hamilton-Gaye came up to me, encouraging as always. He looked at me, rather seriously I thought, and said that Mr Michael and Mr Shan would like to see me in their office. I went, feeling just like one felt at school when the Headmistress requested, 'Stay behind after school please, I want a word with you!'

I knocked on the door of the office of Messrs Michael and Shandos Balcon feeling as though they might tell me to write, 'My name is Thora Hird and I must not be rude' five hundred times. A quick and very businesslike 'Come in!' changed my thoughts completely to, 'Thank God I have my return ticket home!'

The Brothers Balcon were marvellous, businesslike but marvellous! Before I had a chance to apologize, Mr

Shandos explained why I would not be playing George Formby's mother and how one can get away with so much more, make-up wise, on the stage than on the screen. *I was too young!* (What a wonderful thing for an actress to be told, I can't recall anyone saying it to me recently!!!)

I swallowed hard hoping that he wouldn't notice, and by now I was *more* than grateful that I had my return ticket home. Giving me no time to feel sorry for myself, he continued in the same businesslike way to tell me that, all the same, *they were putting me under contract*! – *Under Contract*!!!

He explained they would pay me ten pounds a week whether I worked or not, plus ten pounds a day when I worked on a film. I thanked him very much but added that I didn't think it fair to them if they paid me when I didn't work and that I would return to the repertory company in Morecambe until they needed me. I also added that as the repertory company only paid me one pound for a week's work why should he and his brother pay me for doing nothing?

His face was a picture! He looked straight at me as if I were a specimen of rare imbecile he had never seen before. Then he turned and looked at his brother Michael as though he wanted confirmation that he had heard me correctly. Putting his hands on my shoulders he gently steered me into a very large and beautifully carved chair. 'Thora Hird,' he said, quietly but firmly, 'don't ever let me hear you saying a thing like that again. You are going to go a long way in this business and I have not the slightest doubt that some day in the future you will be in this office, *not* to tell us we are paying you too much . . . but to argue that we are paying you too little!'

Years after that day I *was* sitting in the same office. Our daughter, Janette, was ten years old and under contract to Associated British Picture Corporation. Ealing Studios were interested in her for a film. I reminded Michael Balcon of the day I had told Mr Shandos I thought they were paying me too much! He remembered, and jokingly informed me that he didn't particularly notice me arguing that Jan's fee was too high! I was sitting in exactly the same chair that Mr Shandos had steered me into many years before.

Mr Shandos is dead now, God rest him, and Mr Michael is SIR Michael, and deserves to be.

Thank you Brothers Balcon, you obviously agreed with something my Dad had told me years before: 'If you work for nowt you're worth nowt!'

32

Many happy returns

Right then – after my three day stay at Kenmare Cottage next to Ealing Studios, a film test, the offer of a contract and fifteen air-raid warnings, I made my way to Euston and caught a train back to Morecambe. I was weighed down with good news and Auntie Mollie's and Auntie Martha's silver pointed fox furs.

I sat in a window seat of a third-class carriage, thinking. I tried to put my head back but the large brim on my hat prevented this, so I sat up straight. Had I been in the carriage alone, I would have taken my hat off and put it on the luggage rack, but the carriage as well as the luggage rack was full and I hadn't the nerve to take my seven and elevenpenny model off because I was afraid my hair might look untidy. Earphones and figure eight coils were all right without a hat, but a hat always mussed them up!

Aye dear, what a chump I was, wasn't I? I mean, what the 'ell did it matter how my hair looked? I didn't know any of the passengers, and they didn't know me, I doubt if any of 'em had given me a second glance, so who would have cared? *I* would – that's who.

Of course – er – and pardon my mentioning this – they were totally unaware that, sitting in that third-class window seat was a woman of wealth, a plutocrat, an actress with a promised film contract, two borrowed silver pointed foxes and a pair of patent leather court shoes that were crippling her! But that, of course, was their loss.

As we pulled into Crewe station, I asserted myself and with all the assurance of a 'Ten pounds a week if I didn't work and ten pounds a day if I did,' I stood up and pulled the carriage window down and hailed the tea trolley attendant. Putting my 'lace curtain voice' on, I ordered a cup of tea (twopence) and a pork pie (threepence). I took a red ten shilling note out of my purse and offered it in a nonchalant manner, and as I did so the two foxes slowly slithered off my shoulders as though they were doing a high dive, and ended up on the platform in a heap one on top of the other, as though they were copulating.

I returned to Morecambe, I returned the silver pointed foxes and I returned to the rep. company. According to everybody I met, I was now a film star. The repertory company put up my wages by five shillings but although my wages increased the size of the parts I played didn't.

Before long I was requested to return to Ealing Studios to 'appear', which is about all I did, in a film. It was known in casting jargon as a 'two-day part' and I would never have got it had it not been for the persistence and perseverance of Gordon Hamilton-Gaye. (I shall refer to him from now on as Gordon H.G. I mean I *can't* keep writing Gordon Hamilton-Gaye, it sounds too bombastic for such a lovely person – God rest him.) The film was called *The Black Sheep of Whitehall* and starred Will Hay.

Over a dozen young, well-known character actresses had been tested, but apparently, though capable, they weren't exactly what Will Hay had in mind for the part of 'Joyce', his secretary in the film. After each unsuccessful test, Gordon H.G. would dart in with the request, 'Will you see the test of this girl from the North, Will?' Each time he got the same reply, 'No Gordon – because I want an established actress in the part!' Any road up, after more tests, of established artistes, Gordon H.G. said, 'Just see her test, I'm not asking you to give her the part.' So, Will Hay saw the test. According to what I was told, it had only run about half a second when he turned to Gordon and said, 'What a face – who is she? Send her a telegram!'

I think I should point out that the test he saw was where I'd been 'glamoured up', and it's best not to dwell on what he might have said had he seen me in my natural beauty!

So, thanks to Hay and Gay, I played in my first moving picture. My pattern of living after that was to return to my home in Morecambe and appear in rep. between film 'engagements' until I was recalled to the studios. The second film I appeared in was with Frank Cellier and Michael Redgrave in *The Big Blockade*. I was a barmaid at a German railway station buffet. I had about eight words to say. My own hair being a good length, the hairdresser plaited it and wound it round my bonce to help me look like a Frau.

My contribution to the film took only one day to complete. So however you add up, my first film role was two days' work, and my second, one day's work. Was I slipping? Watch it, Thor! Happily, my third film role was a good 'un. It was a film made by the Studios about security on the 'Careless-talk-costs-lives' theme, and it was directed by Thorold Dickinson who was a joy to work with.

However, back to the film. We all worked for half pay, and the studios contributed handsomely, as part of the war effort. I knew the finished film was to be shown to the forces as well as to the public, and I thought to myself, 'Oh good, Scottie might see this!' He did. Seven times, because the forces were *forced* to see it!

The above makes it sound as though it was a rotten film. Well it wasn't. It was a good film. What I mean is, although he was pleased to see the celluloid me once or even twice, seven times *is* a bit much, isn't it?

Once when we were visiting our daughter in Beverly Hills, she and I watched a late, late film – *The Big Blockade*. How we fell about at my plaits and my 'Frau' accent!

33

Way out West

My first appearance in the West End was in *No Medals* at the Vaudeville Theatre. The stars were Fay Compton and Frederick Leicester, and the play ran for nearly two years. This all started in 1944/45. I played Mrs Gaye, the comedy charlady, a cockney woman of about sixty, so it gave me a chance to apply the 'slap' (make-up) to the best of my ability.

I enjoyed playing the part and equally enjoyed playing it in the film version, which was called *The Weaker Sex*.

Looking back, I cannot honestly say they were two of the happiest years of my life. How could anyone be perfectly happy when one's husband was in the Air Force, one's four-year-old daughter in Lancashire (albeit she was being expertly and lovingly cared for by our nanny Vera). Thank you, Ve, I shall never forget the care you took of our little girl and neither will she. You really were the best Nanny in the world, whilst you yourself, personally, were living alone for the first time. 'Alone in London.' Hecky plonk! That sounds like a chapter heading in a Dickensian serial! Well it does, doesn't it? Apart from which, I don't like my own company and I'm not the sort of person who will go to a lot of trouble over meals if I'm only cooking for myself. But of course that never came into the routine of things during the war, being rationed to one ration book.

What I mean is, well take a 'ferinstance', on the rare occasions that Scottie is in America and I am here in England, although I will grill myself a steak or poach myself an egg or something like that, I will prepare a salad rather than bother cooking vegetables, whereas Scottie, if he is alone will grill himself a pork chop, automatically make stuffing and apple sauce, cook two veg and spuds, follow with a sweet or cheese and find it no trouble at all. Mind you, he's a smashing cook and the lad does enjoy a spot of good food. No, it's not that I'm lazy, God forbid, I'll take time and care to set myself a table plate or a tray nicely, whereas Scottie will probably eat in the kitchen off the top of the fridge, even so, if marks were being awarded for self preservation he would deserve the most!

Oh dear, I went off the subject again, didn't I? Sorry! Now where was I? Oh, I know, 'Alone in London!'

Anyway, there's one thing I will say, and that is, although it wasn't the happiest time of my life, I made a lot of very good friends and I've still got 'em!

I have no intention of making this book one of those 'when I was appearing at such and such a Theatre'. Let me just tell you some of the amusing anecdotes that come to mind.

One night when I was going into the Vaudeville Theatre stage door (I was appearing in the play *No Medals* at the time) a rather large dog paused and appeared to read the billboard. Then it lifted its leg, and wee-weed all over my name, which was in very small print at the bottom of the bill. There were a few other names as well but it appeared that my name was the bull's eye, because that's where most of the wee-wee had hit before running down. Laughingly I said to one of my fellow artistes as we entered the theatre, 'I don't think that was meant to be taken personally, do you?' That night as I made my way to Trafalgar Square tube station through blackened Maiden Lane and the Strand, I thought about the dog christening me, and I started to laugh. I was on my own remember, but it's something I am very guilty of, having a bit of a laugh to myself. By the time I arrived on the platform for the tube, I had forgiven the dog and excused it by telling myself that it wasn't its fault that my name happened to be in 'the wines and spirits' at the bottom of the bill.

Please believe this next bit. As I stood there with my gas mask jauntily slung over my shoulder, I looked round and there was a day bill advertising *No Medals*. I found myself hypnotized as I watched the smallest Yorkshire terrier I have ever seen pull on the lead its mistress held and go up to the bill and have a sniff. It started the sniffing routine at the left hand lower part of the bill, moved with a sniffing motion to the right, found my name, read it, lifted its little three-inch hairy leg, and, direct hit, it wee-weed all over it. I couldn't believe it! Twice nightly! I started to laugh, and I laughed so much that the owner of the dog moved away pulling her dog with her. I think she thought I was drunk or had air-raid shock.

34

Lease and Lend

I have been taken for a mug many times. I have been taken for a ride, as far as lending money is concerned, many times. I have been taken advantage of (in the nicest possible way) many times . . . but I have only been taken for a prostitute once.

It happened on a particular night, when, as part of the war effort I had been to the Nuffield Centre to do a show for the Service lads after our show *No Medals* at the Vaudeville finished. I was living in Ealing at the time, and as I arrived on the platform of the underground station to get my tube home, I saw the usual camp of citizens: some in bunks, some bedded down on the platform itself, old people and tiny babies sleeping, middle-aged people trying to sleep, and young mothers keeping vigil and not bothering to sleep at all. The brave undefeatable people of London, who are so capable of setting an example to any other country in the world, had taken food, thermos flasks of tea and coffee, and bedding along with their wonderful sense of humour and were calmly defying Hitler to drop anything that night! At the end of the platform, where I went to stand and wait for the train, there was only me and a weighing machine. I was wearing a bright red coat, my hair was nearly the same colour, and I wore it in the fashionable Veronica Lake style which was, as people my age will remember, a side parting with a slight wave covering one eye! It was a silly style, really, but one might as well be dead as out of fashion, as the saying goes, and anyway, come to think of it, the present fashion for hair is like curtains that cover both eyes!

Anyhow, there I was, complete with gas mask in case slung over my shoulder, ready to defy Hitler, Goering or anyone else. Well – so I thought.

Down the flight of steps at the right hand end of the platform weaved a GI, rather 'under the influence' – if you follow me! He was smoking a huge cigar.

Let's be fair, it would have been impossible for him *not* to have seen me with my bright red coat and matching hair. On the other hand, and with the greatest respect for our lease lend friends, he couldn't in any event have been called shy or retiring. With a slight roll to starboard, he came up to me, took the cigar out of his mouth with stiff fingers, and enquired, 'Hiya, Red?'

Let me record here and now, I have always been afraid of drunks. Nervously, I moved from one side of the weighing machine to the other. (What the 'ell protection I thought *that* would be I don't know!) Not in the least put off, he followed me and, sticking the cigar back in his mouth, he once again enquired, 'Hiya, Red?'

With British politeness I requested, 'Will you go away please!' (Honestly, can you imagine a more barmy request to an inebriated GI?) But, he had no intention of going anywhere, except with me. 'Hey,

Red!' he repeated, 'I'm *talking* to you!'

'Well, *I'm* not talking to *you* and I don't *want* to talk to you,' I informed him – which was a stupid remark because I *was* talking to him – I mean, I was *compelled* to talk to him to tell him I didn't *want* to talk! I then heard the distant rumble of the train and immediately assumed a courageous façade! As the train pulled into the station he said, 'Waal, don't talk – jus' tell me, wadda yew charge?'

The tube train doors slid open, and as I stepped into the comforting safety of a full compartment I turned and replied, 'I haven't the faintest idea – what do your mother and sister charge?'

'Lady!' he answered, 'my mom is the greatest!'

The doors hissed to – shutting him out and leaving him protesting on the platform, cigar in hand – nearly in tears at my mention of 'the old Rocking Chair'.

As the train rumbled on I began to feel a bit sorry for him – he was a long way from Tobacco Road or wherever it was he came from. But so was my husband who was in Belgium with the RAF.

I suddenly sat up very straight as I wondered what *he* was doing at that moment!

In 1948 a play called *Flowers for the Living* by Toni Block was to be put on at the New Lindsey Theatre, Notting Hill Gate, and I was asked to go along there to see Frederick Piffard who was presenting it and John Oxford who was directing it.

Now there used to be a very good shoe mending shop at Notting Hill, so, as I'd been 'resting' for quite a few weeks, I thought I'd take the shoe mending (a pair of Jan's and a pair of mine) along with me, therefore using the same three halfpenny bus fare to cover both jobs!

The foyer of the New Lindsey Theatre was very small and looked even smaller because it was packed like sardines with actors and actresses. At this point I had no idea that I had gone for an audition. Suddenly, a dark-haired young fellow came bustling through the doors that led from the auditorium – he saw me and handing me a script he requested that I read pages five and six in act one, page twenty-three in act two and pages fifty something or other in act three. I thanked him very much and opened the script at page five to discover that most of the dialogue on that page was for a character called Shirley. Turning to the front of the script, I read the description of the characters and discovered that Shirley was the fifteen-year-old cockney daughter of Mr and Mrs Holmes. Well, hell, I know that 1948 is twenty-eight years ago, but in all honesty I cannot claim to have been only fifteen even then. So I closed the script, picked up my basket on to my knee and sat waiting patiently to give the script back to the dark-haired young man the next time he burst through the doors, which he did almost immediately.

'Miss Hird please, can you come through?' I could and I did. Sitting in the auditorium were Messrs Piffard and Oxford who greeted me most kindly. I explained that I felt rather long in the tooth to play Shirley, but they hardly let me finish before Freddie Piffard interjected, 'No, no, you're not here to read Shirley, we want you to read Mrs Holmes!'

Now just let me tell you this next bit. I was wearing a

cream tie belt overcoat and my hair was still *à la* Veronica Lake.

The description of Mrs Holmes (which I hadn't read) went something like this: Mrs Holmes is a shabby, hard-worked, middle-aged cockney woman who looks as though she is going through the change, etc., etc.

Well, I might not have been fifteen but I wasn't that old either! However, back to the New Lindsey auditorium and Messrs Piffard and Oxford.

I approached the stage and stepped up on to it, it was only about a yard off the floor. I faced out front and I started to read the part of Mrs Holmes. Not having seen it until that moment, I wasn't prepared for the sadness of this poor woman. As I read, I cried. (I'm a real silly maggot and easily moved.) I tried to stop crying but I'm afraid by the time I'd finished, my nose was running, my mascara was running and *I* felt like running. There wasn't a sound in the auditorium as I stepped down from the stage and walked up to Messrs Piffard and Oxford, handed 'em the script which they took, and said, 'Sorry about that. May I suggest that you tell whoever you give the part to not to bother to act it – just feel it!'

'That's why we are giving it to you,' they replied as they handed back the script to me.

'How did you get on?' asked Scottie as I walked in home. 'Hey – I've got it!' I replied, my face covered with a grin as I put my basket down. 'Er – what about the shoe mending?' he enquired. Oh cripes! I'd forgotten to call at the cobblers. Never mind, I could afford another one and a half penny bus fare now I was in work.

I've called the cobblers' shop 'the shoe menders'. I suppose some people call it the shoe repairers, but it doesn't matter does it, whichever it is – it's all a lot of cobblers.

Flowers for the Living was really my Cinderella story, and I shall always be grateful to Frederick Piffard for risking me in the part of Mrs Holmes. Everything seemed to stem from that. My contract with J. Arthur Rank, the many plays and film parts I was offered. My dad came to London to see the play and I particularly asked him not to come to the opening night because although he had taught me everything I knew about the business up to that point, I felt I wanted him to see me give a performance worthy of his care and patience, and I knew that wouldn't be on the first night.

After he had seen the first night notices, though The New Lindsey was only a little theatre it was one of the best shop windows for a play possible and all the London critics were there, my dad asked, 'Do you think I can come and see you tonight?' 'I'll tell you what,' I replied, 'come tomorrow night, Dad, and I'll try and be ready for you!' That was agreed upon.

After the show the following night we went into the bar. Everybody was being very kind about my performance and I watched James Henry trying not to look too proud.

When we got back to our little mews house, Dad was full of praise for the performances of the rest of the cast. I can remember thinking 'It's any minute now, he'll say I was all right.' There was no feeling of conceit about this, it was merely that I valued his opinion more than anyone else's, because my dad had never ever said to me, 'Oh, you are good!' or, 'You were the best.' He had always given me constructive criticism and had always told me I could do better. When no word of praise was forthcoming I began to wonder if everyone else, critics included, had been wrong.

He got up from the chair, saying he was going to bed. As he went through the lounge doorway he half closed the door and then pushed it open again. Looking straight at me with those smashing blue eyes of his he said, 'You're a wonderful artist. I've lived to see you perform like you did tonight. Good night and God bless, love!' And he closed the door gently.

I was so happy to know he was pleased with me that I laughingly called after him, 'Hey – can I have that in writing?'

He died early the next morning.

During our final week at the New Lindsey, I was requested, 'Don't bother to clean off – Mr Sydney Box is coming to see the show tonight and can only stay for a few minutes afterwards to have a little chat with you in the bar!'

I did clean off – Mr Box stayed three quarters of an hour – and he was the instigator, the thin end of the wedge, or whatever you like to call it, of my being put under contract to J. Arthur Rank! *Flowers for the Living*, eh? I just wished my dad could have been there.

R. F. Delderfield had written a play about life in a general draper's in 1887, Queen Victoria's Jubilee Year, and the play was called *The Queen Came By*. You know, I've been very lucky really, I keep telling you this, don't

I? But I have. The part of Emmie Slee is an actress's joy – I played it at the Embassy Theatre in Swiss Cottage prior to us moving into the Duke of York's in the West End, and I have played Emmie on the two occasions the play has been on television.

During our run at the Duke of York's, our very small daughter Janette was allowed to watch the play one matinee. I can see her now as she came to my dressing room to have tea. She was wearing a kilt of my husband's family tartan and a little tailored tweed jacket with elkhorn buttons, her long plaits sporting tartan ribbons. The play had upset her because she didn't like me being ill at the end.

There is a loving little girl in the play called Kitty Tape. I say little girl, actually she's about sixteen or seventeen. The feeling between her and Emmie is such that when you come out of the theatre you may think that Emmie may or may not be her mother and either would seem acceptable. That all sounds a bit Irish, but you know what I mean, don't you? Well, Jan just loved the character of Kitty and told me over her sandwich in my dressing room that when she grew up she was going to play Kitty Tape. I explained to her that by the time she was old enough to play Kitty, sadly, the play might have been forgotten.

Years later, in 1955, I played Emmie when *The Queen Came By* was done on BBC television. Happily it was successful. They invited me to play in it again the following year, but I graciously refused because I thought it was too short a time since we had done it previously. It was postponed and the following year I was again asked to play Emmie. This time I accepted.

About a week before rehearsals commenced, Jan rang me up and in conversation said, 'You're doing *The Queen Came By* again on telly, aren't you, Mummy?' I said I was. 'Who's having first billing?' she asked, laughing. 'Who's what? Well, *me* I should think, why?' There was a real burst of laughter and then she said, 'Why? Because I'm playing Kitty Tape, that's *why*!'

My breath went. I was *delighted*. Then it dawned on me that it was Janette Scott – *film star* who would be appearing, by kind permission of Associated British, as well as it being my own daughter who had, as a little girl, informed me that she would play Kitty Tape when she grew up. I really was overjoyed. 'Mummy – are you still there? I was only joking about the billing, darling, I mean, nobody could ever star over you in that play!' That was daughter talk, but I got first billing anyway at least, we shared, we both starred. It was the only play we ever did together and it was probably as good a bit of work as either of us has ever done.

35

'Upstairs – Downstairs'

(With apologies to that splendid series)

So, once again, as one door closed, another one opened, and as *The Queen Came By* passed by, I went back to the land of the silver screen. *Fools Rush In, Boys in Brown, The Conspirators* and *Cure for Love.*

I've just remembered something about one film I was in, I won't bother to tell you which film it was because that's neither here nor there and I don't suppose the director of that unfortunate epic is ever likely to read *this,* but if he does – he'll know the name of the film all right.

We had two American stars in the picture and the poor director had no skin left on his hands through stroking them (the stars I mean). It was pathetic to watch him, honestly, but you see, those sort of situations start me off tittering and I used to enjoy the performance he gave. He also sported an American accent! *An American accent*! He was an East-end cockney! I could understand him wearing a trilby on the back of his head, *à la* Bogart, because he was bald. I could understand his chewing gum and the 'Yeah! sure – okay, baby – roll 'em!' But what I couldn't understand was the way he treated the small-part artists.

On the first day of the film we were all assembled to

start on yet another happy adventure. I was in the very first shot. I had to walk down a beautiful staircase, supposedly in the hall of a house in Belgravia, and answer the doorbell. By the way, I was playing the housekeeper-cum-everything. I've forgotten the script, but whatever it was it had to be spoken as I descended the staircase. 'Shall I start to speak as soon as I'm in shot?' I enquired, most politely I thought. 'Oh, just say the speech as you come down the stairs,' he threw away. So that's what I did. I said the speech as I came down the stairs! 'Stop! Not like *that*!' I heard him bawl, 'Oh God – don't – start – to – speak – until – you – are – halfway – down – the – stairs – now go back and start again!' These dictated to me as though I was a stone deaf idiot!

Now bear in mind, I was only about four stairs down when he stopped me with his bawling, so after his dramatic performance, I continued walking down the staircase (rather majestically I thought), all five feet and one inch of me, and kept on walking until I was standing in front of his nibs who was sitting in a chair with his name on.

'Don't speak to me like that, please, and don't shout at me either, I'm not deaf!' I said quietly. 'If you will kindly direct me as to how you wish the scene to be played, I will try and do it to the best of my ability. Just because I have a Lancashire accent doesn't mean I'm a fortune teller with a tent on the sandhills at Blackpool, y'know. I can't foresee what you want!' And with that I went and sat in the chair with my name on. The unit applauded! They'd worked with him before. The director and the small-part player got on like a house on fire for the rest of the 'twelve days over seven weeks!'

That was the only occasion I ever 'had a few words' that I wasn't paid for in any film studio. And considering I chalked up my hundredth film a couple of years back, that's not bad going is it?

I don't know how familiar any of you are with the play *Tobacco Road*. Come to think of it, I don't know how familiar any of you are, period. But just in case you don't know anything about it at all, please allow me to 'fill you in'.

Tobacco Road is situated in Georgia in the 'Deep South' – yes sur! To depict this, the stage of the Playhouse Theatre was covered with fine sand about eight inches in depth. The Lester Family lived *in* a broken down old shack and *on* turnips. Jeeter Lester was played by Mervyn Johns and Ada Lester his pellagra-ridden wife with the twisted crippled foot (due to pellagra) by yours truly. Ada Lester had seventeen children, if you read up any Tobacco Road history you'll find that there's not much to do during the winter months!

Now I am not going to decry the play – like almost everything else I do – I enjoyed being in it, but I must hurry and get to the bit I want to tell you about. You couldn't, in all honesty, have called any of the poor pellagra-suffering Lesters, *bright*. In fact, they were all a bit dim, due to the continual diet of turnips (because pellagra is a deficiency disease which is probably the reason their brains were a bit deficient as well). So it came as a shock to nobody when one of the sons, Dude (whose sexual desire had been unleashed by Sister Bessie the preacher), having acquired an old motor car, backed it into poor old Mum, knocking her flat, then continued backing over her stomach until she *is* flat. (All good stuff.)

At this point I must make a little admission. If I have to scream in a play I always ask my understudy to do it for me. I just cannot scream without my voice going after I have done so, honestly!

Right, so back to flat Ada Lester having been run over by her sex-ridden son 'Dude'. All that motor car business was done off stage and my understudy used to let out a piercing scream as she held out a saucer on which lay about an inch and a half of Gordon Moore's red toothpaste. You've probably used it at some time or other to make your gums nice and pink. It's very good. However, it's also very good to give the effect of 'spitting blood' and after I had scooped it off the saucer with my little finger and put it in my mouth, I had to sort of crawl on to the stage on my flat stomach, clawing at the sand (you're getting the picture, aren't you?), and that is one of the reasons we had seven or eight inches of sand so that one could claw at it or walk on it and not reveal the wooden stage underneath.

So, having crawled along into my final position which was almost centre stage, I would try to look up at Jeeter (brave little woman) and at the same time release the red toothpaste which would very obligingly spurt out and then dribble down the side of my mouth. When I felt the audience had seen it, I dropped my head on one side in the sand and expired.

Jeeter had a speech that seemed to last for ever after

I'd 'popped off', but it was easy enough for me to lie there until the final curtain. Well, as a rule it was.

I forget how many cats they had at the Playhouse and it really doesn't matter because, let's face it, it only needs one cat to use the sand to cover up its 'buried treasure'. Phew, mate! D'you know, it became a nightly challenge for me to expire, and if, as my head dropped on the sand, I realized my nose was within an inch of one of the theatre cats' deposit accounts, I would add a death twitch which would move me slightly away.

By the time the play was ready to fold, and because the sand of *Tobacco Road* was the same sand we had opened with, my death twitches were becoming increasingly numerous, because it was difficult to find an unpolluted spot.

Oo, I love being an actress, it's all so *glamorous*.

36

What'll you have?

During the Festival of Britain year, 1951, Jack Hylton presented the play *The Happy Family* at the Duchess Theatre. Henry Kendall and I starred in it and one day, during the rehearsal period, we were lunching in Rules Restaurant in Maiden Lane, when Henry happened to bring up the subject of birthdays, and, would you believe it, we discovered we shared the same birthday, 28th May. We opened at the Duchess on 14th May, so the play would have been in production fourteen days when our birthdays came around.

I shall never forget Henry coming to my dressing room and saying, 'Well, I suppose we shall have to give the company a drink.' Now don't get the idea that he said this in a mean way, Henry Kendall was a generous man and a very clever man and I liked him and respected him a lot. But he did have the ability to make me laugh even when he was being serious, which explains why every time I think of the following story, I burst out laughing.

It was decided upon that we would invite the company into the Stalls Bar after the show the coming Saturday night for a glass of 'Champers'. 'We're not having any cards printed or invitations or anything,' announced Henry. 'Well there's no need,' I replied. 'We'll get the young ASM (assistant stage manager) to invite the company through the tannoy (public address system) at the side of the stage.' Agreeing with all this, Henry left it to me to see the ASM which I promised to do when I went down to open the next act. This all happened on Tuesday night, 24th May. On Wednesday night we were in our dressing rooms during the interval when we heard the tannoy click and then the ASM announce, 'May I have your attention, Ladies and Gentlemen, please. Miss Thora Hird and Mr Henry Kendall invite you to a glass of Champagne in the stalls bar, after the show on Saturday night next. Please come and join them in celebrating their joint birthdays – thank you!' Click. Henry and I agreed that the announcement was most satisfactory.

Most satisfactory? Hold on a minute whilst I tell you what happened.

After the show on the Saturday night, I changed quickly and cleaned most of my stage make-up off, leaving only sufficient on as a base which I powdered. Adding a touch of fresh lipstick, I was ready for the fray. Jack Hylton had given us a large, square, iced cake – in fact, he had rung me up that very morning and *enquired* how many candles were required. He was a Lancastrian as I am and I think I understood him very well. I told him one hundred. His words were, 'Why's that then?' and I informed him that Henry was eighty-five and I was fifteen!

On the Saturday night, Scottie came along to my dressing room after the show with a friend of ours called Kay. As we left my dressing room we were joined by Henry and, getting into the lift, we descended to auditorium level. The happy little birthday boy and girl!!

Of course we ought to have known that something was amiss when we had difficulty in opening the doors of the Stalls Bar. But we didn't think. The bar was packed! Champagne corks were popping at the rate of knots, and gay, abandoned laughter greeted us from the happy throng. Henry's face was a picture. Grabbing me by the arm he tried to pull me to one side but there wasn't an inch of spare room anywhere so he hissed into my ear, 'Good God, how many guests have you invited!' 'Only Kay and Scottie,' I shouted back. The noise and gaiety was your full Victorian naughty house. POP! Every time, a cork popped Henry flinched.

At that moment a couple of ladies pushed their way through the masses to thank me most sincerely for inviting them. They had come from Southall because they had never been to a party like this before. They kindly pointed out a batch of people who had travelled all the way from Beckenham, specially. One of the ladies added that she thought she and her friend and neighbour were very lucky to have been in the Theatre on Wednesday, the night that the invitation was announced, and had the announcement been made every night this week? Oh, cripes, it dawned on me what had happened. However, to make sure, I bawled out at her, 'What invitation?' To which she replied, equally loudly, 'The invitation in the interval on Wednesday night, we were in the stalls.'

Well – let's be fair – they had been invited! 'May I

have your attention Ladies and Gentlemen please – Miss Thora Hird and Mr Henry Kendall invite you to a glass of champagne in the Stalls bar, after the show on Saturday night next, please come and join them in celebrating their joint birthdays – thank you.' The tannoy had been plugged through to a theatre full of people as well as the dressing rooms!! I mean, you couldn't blame the uninvited guests for thinking they were invited could you? 'Cos they had been.

Although I saw the funny side of it all, Henry didn't. He pushed his way out of the bar through the doors that led into the empty auditorium and sat on the front row of the stalls looking at the curtain, which was down. I joined him, trying my best not to laugh. 'Well I'm not paying for this lot!' he exploded. 'It's that stupid bloody ASM's fault,' he said. 'Fancy having the thing plugged through to the auditorium!' 'Never mind, love,' I comforted, 'it is our birthday!' And then I started to laugh and couldn't stop.

He didn't laugh, he didn't want to laugh, he tried not to laugh but then he *did* laugh. So we returned to the bar and to the popping of corks and to the host of people we didn't know but who felt they knew us, and we cut the cake!

Everybody raised their glasses and shouted 'Happy Birthday!'

It cost us – oh mate, it cost us! But you can't help laughing can you?

After *The Happy Family* I played in *This Same Sky* (by that clever actress Yvonne Mitchell) I certainly enjoyed playing Momma Brodsky to Frederick Valk's Poppa

Brodsky and it was this play that took me to the Duke of York's Theatre for the second time. The only difference was that number one dressing room had acquired its own 'convenience' which was you'll agree, very convenient! Then I played in *The Troublemakers* by the American author George Bellak, who also directed it. During this time I 'partook' in numerous films – well, it's true, you name 'em, I was in 'em! Of course, many of the parts were just a cough and a spit, and frequently the same sort of coughing and spitting. The wardrobe departments at various studios took to calling me prior to my going to the Studios to say, 'Same sort of thing as usual, Thora, wrapover apron, head scarf and curl pins?'

Then, in February 1954 something happened that I shall never forget. I met Charlie Chaplin! Magic! There's no other word to describe it. He is now Sir Charles Chaplin, which I think he should have been years ago, but that's beside the point. I was in America during the period they gave him an Oscar and as I watched the ceremony on television, I could have wept, well I *did* weep and I'm not ashamed to admit it. I remember sitting there thinking, 'What took them so long?'

How did *I* meet him? Well I'll tell you. Our daughter, Janette, was an important asset of Associated British Film Corporation and Mr Chaplin had a script he wanted to make into a film in England. After the initial chats with ABPC, his secretary rang us from Switzerland to say that Mr Chaplin was coming over and would be staying at the Savoy and that he would like to meet Janette. Scottie had looked after Jan's business matters since she was nine years old, which was really splendid because it meant she had had affection, she was obedient (good old Dad), and she also had a good education.

When the appointment was being finalized, the secretary said that Mr Chaplin would like both Jan's parents to go along and have tea with him and Mrs Chaplin. So the three of us went.

It really was a fantastic afternoon. He was very anxious for Jan to play the part in the film of the fifteen-year-old Irish girl who eventually became a saint. We all sat like children at bedtime whilst he told us the story and as he read every character in the film for us, he literally turned into that character before our very eyes. He even played the part of the young girl, it was almost unbelievable. During tea, we talked about his early days in England and we listened enthralled, practically ignoring the paste sandwiches and the scrumptious cream cakes.

He told us how he came to write the music of 'I'll Be Loving You Eternally' (I think the title is 'Eternally', isn't it?). How he had thought of the notes of 'Won't you buy my English Lavender?' which are very similar to the opening bars of 'Eternally'. But it was something else that was unforgettable. While he was singing the notes he was using his fingers as the legs of a ballerina and those magic fingers were dancing along the tea tray. Each time I see his film *The Gold Rush*, and I do so whenever possible, I am reminded of that afternoon. Most of you will have seen it at some time or other, and you will remember the scene where Chaplin sticks a couple of bread rolls on two forks and manipulates them so that they do a tricky little dance ending in the splits! Well, as I watched those magic fingers I thought, 'Hecky plonk! I'm actually watching this genius at work!'

It really was a smashing afternoon and as we rose to leave he took Jan's face in his hands and said, 'If I can't get you for this part I won't make the film.' Unfortunately there was some kind of unpleasantness and trouble at the studios (not ABPC studios; the studios where Chaplin wanted to make his film). So, of course, it never got off the floor. To be more correct, it never even got *on* the floor!

Never mind, we did have those few illuminating hours for which we thank you very much, Sir Charles and Lady Chaplin!

37

'World premiere'

When Walter Greenwood died at the end of 1974 the world lost an extremely clever author and playwright and I lost an extremely intelligent and humorous friend. Walter could make me laugh and equally make me cross; and though we could and would argue like mad about a line in any of the plays he wrote for me, we never fell out, and there never was a time when we weren't speaking. His knowledge of English history was fabulous, and there was nothing I enjoyed more than listening to him when he was on the right side of a couple of 'whiskey all-ins!' He talked of our historic island in the same truthful and colourful way he wrote about Lancashire, mingling sadness with humour. I was in America when he died, and I learned of his death through an obituary in *The Times*. I shall miss you, Walter – our loss is the other side's gain, and I'll bet you have already told whoever is on the other side that *Love on the Dole* was returned to you thirty-nine times before it was published and that you didn't become the proud owner of an overcoat until you were nineteen. Oh, and another thing, you will have found out whether Richard III did or did not send those little Princes to the Tower. You always swore blind he didn't!

(I always felt that was on account of your Lancashire softness coming out, y'know, because he was a hunchback.)

Saturday Night at the Crown, surely one of his funniest plays, seemed to punctuate my life for many years. The first time we presented it was at Oldham Rep. I went up there to rehearse with the resident company and stayed at The Grapes. The people who ran the place were wonderful to me, informing me that, 'You've got the bedroom and sitting-room Nellie Wallace had, you know!' (And I can't blame Nellie for staying there; she was no fool, every Lancashire comfort including fantastic grub and a big coal fire in my sitting-room!)

When I saw the billing in front of the Theatre, I nearly collapsed laughing, there in large letters it said: WORLD PREMIERE OF WALTER GREENWOOD'S *SATURDAY NIGHT AT THE CROWN* STARRING THORA HIRD.

World Premiere! In Oldham!! Now don't think for one minute I am running down Oldham, I'm not, I love Oldham, but the World Premiere bit struck me as a bit ambitious. However, walk tall, as they say.

Mrs Kathleen Williams, who did all the bookings for the Blackpool Tower Company came to see the show on the Saturday night (the world premiere was only there for a week), with George and Alfred Black, the impresarios. In the first interval Kathleen came into my dressing room and said, 'Oh, we're having this for Blackpool!' At the end of the show George and Alfred confirmed it. All in happy mood we went over to The Grapes.

In the second act of *The Crown* (I shall refer to it in

that manner from now on because it's such a long title to write and I shall have to keep mentioning it because so many funny things happened to me during my life as Ada Thorpe). Well, as I said, in the second act of *The Crown* we talk for the entire act about Annie Cross and Fanny Butler, who never appear in the play but are certainly a big part of it. They are ensconsed up in the 'Singing Room', which, as we all know, is the room in the pub where the small stage is, for the 'turns' who appear to entertain the customers whilst they 'sit and sup'.

Now The Grapes had a smashing singing room – and at this point allow me to mention that in 1955 not every pub boasted one; but The Grapes did and the singing room was in full blast as Kathleen, The Blacks, Walter and I entered the pub itself for a celebration snifter. Kathleen was very keen to see it – the singing room, I mean – because of the singing room in the play, so we took our drinks and just stood in the doorway.

A man on the stage was belting: 'Hone-lee a rose, hi give yew' from *The Vagabond King*, and as he burst into the second line of the song 'Hone-lee a flow-wer . . .' the master of ceremonies put his hand on the singer's arm and stopped his vocal efforts.

Pushing the singer gently to one side, the MC spoke into the mike as follows, 'Ladies and Gentlemen, excuse me for that [meaning stopping Caruso in the middle of his aria], but there is somebody wot has just come in this room who, and I think I speak on behalf of us all, we love very much [cough]. She has been in Oldham for the past two weeks entertaining us in a play at the Coliseum, so I'm going to ask her to come up on here [the stage], which I'm sure she will, and say hello and goodbye to you all, because she is going home tomorrow, ladies and gentlemen [at this point his hand and arm were sort of beckoning me on to the platform]. It gives me great pleasure to present – Janette Scott's Mother!'

Do you wonder I have never had any conceit?

P.S. One morning recently I was listening on the radio to Pete Murray's *Open House*. He played one of Mel Tormé's records and announced afterwards, 'And that was the velvet voice of Thora Hird's son-in-law – Mel Tormé!'

See? Everything evens out if you wait long enough!

The Love Match was written by Glen Melvyn, a clever writer, a wonderful comedian and a helluva nice fellow. It seemed like fate that eventually I would have to be part of *The Love Match*. Glen asked me to be in it so many times, but each time I was busy. However, the moment arrived when I was able to accept his offer. First of all we did a week at Wimbledon. It was a treat! We then did a short tour. Jack Hylton saw us play in Brighton, and presented us the following year at the Grand Theatre, Blackpool, for the season, my introduction to that lovely theatre.

After a very successful season in Blackpool, Jack Hylton decided to bring *The Love Match* into the West End. We opened at the Palace Theatre, Cambridge Circus, playing twice nightly. I travelled to Manchester every Sunday morning for six weeks to be part of a radio show with Ken Platt and Billie Whitelaw, appeared in a film called *Tiger by the Tail* then started on the Norman Wisdom film, *One Good Turn*.

John Paddy Carstairs directed the Wisdom film, and anybody who ever worked with John Paddy will tell you what a love he was, never lost his temper and could get the best out of anyone. Little did I know then that when Freddie Frinton and I started the television series *Meet the Wife* he would direct the first batch. Come to think of it, little did I know then that I would ever be asked to do a television series.

I enjoyed making *One Good Turn* very much indeed . . . never a dull moment, by the time it was finished we were ready to start the film of *The Love Match*.

We had transferred from the Palace, Cambridge Circus, to the Victoria Palace by the time we started to film the play.

When at the end of August, we finished the film I was free to do one of my candid cameos in the film *For Better or Worse*. In my spare moments I used to nip to a recording studio to do my 'voice over' for 'Mother's Pride' bread, which was a job I had for many years. I've been known to catch a London train from Blackpool or Bournemouth on a Sunday, when I was playing a season, record, 'I'm the Mother in Mother's Pride, y'know!' on a Monday morning, and catch a train back to wherever I'd come from in time to play the first house at six-fifteen. I was never bored – I had not time to be.

Doing 'bits of parts' in films has always been fun – I don't mean 'bits of parts', 'parts that were bits' would be more descriptive. I loved 'em because when one did as many as I did, it was always a challenge to try and alter the way I played a charwoman or a daily or a landlady, and I must confess, I was always treated well and with quite an amount of affection at the various studios.

I hesitate to say 'Of course things were better in those days.' I mean, who knows if they were? I'm quite sure there are thousands of people today who enjoy their work as much as I do and are treated just as well as I was and am. I'm not referring to the folks who think the world owes 'em a living. Life's too short to waste time writing about them.

All right then, I'm still treated well and kindly in the television studios, in the theatre and in the film studios. Oh, and I nearly forgot, sound radio. Well, I think I am anyway. Perhaps it's because I am very old fashioned and believe in giving a fair day's work for a fair day's pay. Hey, I sound like a union leader don't I? Well I'm not. I'm not rich enough for a start, and I only own one house, I've no telephone in my car and it took me a much longer time than it did them to get on to the telly!

38

'SNATC'

Saturday Night at the Crown. In the spring following the 'World Premiere at Oldham', G.B. and A.B. (everyone who knew or worked for the Blacks lovingly referred to them in that way while they in turn called me 'Thorird', because they said that was the way Northerners always referred to me) took the play out on tour. This enabled us to tighten it up a bit, and it also enabled a lot of comic bits to be added. In the last act of the play Ada, the character I played, is definitely the worse for wear, having consumed quite a few glasses of stout. I had to eat a pork pie, and during the week we played the Alhambra, Bradford, a little incident happened. I would break the pie in half very carefully so that the half I gave to Herbert, my husband in the play, was only an empty crust. You ought to try that sometime, it really is possible, with care, to leave all the meat in the half you keep for yourself! Well, one evening, a little piece of my meat fell on to the stage. I bent over and picked it up, wiped it on my coat, took the piece of empty crust off Herbert, stuck the bit of meat inside and gave it back to him! It stopped the show. So of course I dropped a bit of meat every performance and it always had the same effect. I am unable to write about the added business in a way that is convincing enough to prove to the reader how very funny some little things that happen by accident can be. All I can say is, that by the time I played Ada Thorpe for the thousandth time, and that happened to be in Australia, most of the big 'business' laughs had 'gone in' after we originally opened with the World Premiere in Oldham. Most actors and actresses will agree, I think, that the perfecting process of a character in a play is really quite exciting. Well, *I* think it is, for the simple reason that however often you play a part you are always striving to make it just that one toot better.

So, we prepared for the tour. Let's be honest, apart from the tightening up effort we all hoped to make a bob or two. Fond though I was of G. and A. Black, I knew they hadn't got where they were through putting shows on just to tighten 'em up a bit!

Mr Harold Boyes was their business manager, he was one of the keenest and shrewdest business men I have ever met, I admired him tremendously and we were and are very good friends. Now we had no reason to think we would play Blackpool that season, because a show was already booked there for that year. However, unfortunately for the show that opened it didn't do the expected business and folded after five weeks, so our tour was cut short and we took over. No artist really likes doing that, y'know – I think most of my fellow rogues and vagabonds feel a twinge of sorrow when their 'in' means someone else's 'out'!

So, Blackpool here we come! Wotta season. The part of Ada Thorpe, which I played, is as long as Hamlet. I was drinking ten glasses of Dandelion and Burdock (five each show we played twice nightly) until we got the prop glasses, which of course look full but aren't. As I wished the company good luck on our first night in Blackpool, I finished up with the request, 'If you love me will you please, when the curtain drops for the interval, wait to go to the toilet until I've been. Thank you!'

Incidentally, Dandelion and Burdock pours out looking like stout, but it's non-alcoholic and I think if you are drinking ten glasses a night you should go easy on the Beechams and Senna Pods. I'm not certain of this, I'm just speaking personally.

Blackpool is only thirty miles from Morecambe, my home town, so can you wonder that I enjoyed playing a season at The Grand Theatre so much? It's a lovely theatre, designed by Frank Matcham who designed the Royalty Theatre, Morecambe, which is now a memory. The clever Mr Matcham must have known what he was doing acoustically, because I have worked in three theatres he designed, The Royalty, Morecambe, The Grand, Blackpool and The Kings, Hammersmith, and in any of those theatres you could literally whisper on the stage and be heard quite clearly at the back of the gods!

On Sunday a few of us had gone over to Morecambe to see various friends, and Walter Greenwood and I decided to have a long walk! We started out at the Golf Club at *Bare*, walked the length of the promenade past the Battery Hotel onto Sandilands promenade and finished up in lovely Heysham Village. We refreshed ourselves with a glass of nettle drink – it used to be called nettle beer when I was a kid, but somebody put the kibosh on that. 'Right!' I said, 'shall we get a bus back?' 'A bus!' exploded Walter. 'What's up with walking!' We walked, and I'm glad we did because if we hadn't, I wouldn't be able to tell you this typical 'Greenwoodism'.

As we strode out along Sandilands Esplanade, the picture of the bay was really wonderful. You don't have to be born in Morecambe to appreciate the breathtaking views across the bay, the sunsets, and the shrimps. The afternoon was closing in, the tide was out and the ripples of sand were broken up by small pools which reflected the dying sunlight. A few birds hopped about amongst the screeching seagulls. We stood by the esplanade railings and looked at the purple and gun-metal hills across the bay backed by the soft pink and orange of the sinking sun's rays. 'I'll bet you don't know what *that* bird is!' stated Walter, pointing to a little thin-legged creature that was stamping its little clawed feet up and down on the wet rippled sand as though it were doing a Spanish dance.

'Well, as a matter of fact, I do!' I replied. 'Remember I was *born* here, I'm a sand grown'un y'know, it's a sand piper!' 'Yes – well – just watch it a minute!' he ordered, 'You'll learn a lesson well worth remembering.' This was typical Walter Greenwood talk and I always enjoyed it.

'What have I to watch?' I asked. 'There . . .' jumped in Walter, 'you see it hammering on the sand with its beak?' I said I did. 'Well now, watch.' At that moment the sand piper was standing like a statue staring at where it had been hammering, then, with a swift downward movement of its head, it collared a worm and stood dead still again, only this time with the wriggling worm in its beak. It was standing there posing as though it was trying to say, 'How about that then, look what I've found!' 'So what's the lesson – God helps those who help themselves?' I asked. 'No – it's not,' replied Walter, quietly but definitely. 'The lesson *is*,' he continued, 'when the sand piper hammered on the sand with its feet (as soon as he said "feet" I started laughing), the nosy worm underneath thought, "Hello, what's going on there, what's that knocking?" and it poked its head up through the sand to have a look, didn't it?'

'Yes!' I agreed, '. . . but –'

'Well, there's the lesson to remember,' he said. 'What?' I asked. 'If that worm hadn't been so bloody nosy it would still be alive!'

However you look at it, he was right!

39

'The Crown'

There were so many small anecdotes about *The Crown* and I really would like to write about them all but that's not possible – because if I do this book will never come to an end! – so I'll just slip in the one about the night a woman in the upper circle at The Grand, Blackpool, laughed so much her false teeth fell out and hit a bald-headed man in the pit! It's *true*!

At the end of a wonderful season G.B. and A.B. asked me would I play Sunderland (Oh Gawd!) and Manchester Palace. I was very tired but the word Manchester revived me! I had never played Sunderland so I thought, 'Well, I'll have a go – it will be an experience!' It was.

Bernard Fox, who is now very happily married and very successful in America, and lives about half an hour from our daughter in Beverly Hills, was playing Harry Boothroyd in *The Crown* and playing it very well may I add. He had a Mercedes car that I reckon was an antique *then*, but that's beside the point, he offered to run me to Sunderland and believe you me it can be a really beautiful drive. We arrived at the theatre and entered the stage door just as the stage door keeper was filling his kettle. He ignored us until it was full and on the gas ring and he'd found the matches, struck one, lit the gas, blown the match out and chucked it on the floor. Then he turned and looked at us. It was a look of pity.

I noticed that his pullover had about three four inch wide 'ladders' in it as he said, 'What number?' (meaning what number dressing room key did I want). 'Oh good morning!' I replied. 'Er – number one I should think, at a guess!' I was being far too bright and it was getting me nowhere. 'Two as well please whilst you're there,' requested Bernard as his nibs went to the key rack. He passed us the keys, looked us up and down as though we were hobos, shook his head slowly from side to side, did a couple of 'Tut-tuts' and said, 'Oooo, you'll do nothing here!' He was right! We didn't. But we made up for it the following week in good old Manchester.

After Manchester we put *The Crown* to bed, but it rolled over and woke up again in 1957 and we went into the Garrick Theatre in the West End where we played twice nightly happily and successfully.

I had a line in the show referring to the Halle Orchestra, which was written as follows: 'Herbert doesn't care for that kind of music,' which I altered to, 'Herbert doesn't care for that kind of music, that Sergeant Malcolm and his band!' Well, one night Sir Malcolm Sargent was in front. I didn't know he was, but he thought I did, because after the show he dashed round to my dressing room, delighted that I had mentioned him. Before I had a chance to inform him that the Sergeant Malcolm line was in every performance, he requested that I put the line in the following

Friday, second house, as he was bringing the Prince and Princess of Denmark and a couple of members of the Bowes-Lyon family to see the show.

Well, of course, the line tickled them pink, they all came round after the show and had a drink in my room. I'm glad he thought I had put the line in specially for him the first time he saw the show and I'm glad I didn't tell him I hadn't, because if ever there was a gentleman, 'Flash Harry' was he.

After *The Crown* closed its doors at the Garrick we thought we were about ready to shout 'Time Gentlemen Please!', but in 1960 we took the play to Scarborough for the season where one little incident occurred that I'd like to tell you about.

Two theatres stand next to each other on the promenade: The Arcadia, where we played, and The Futurist, where The Black and White Minstrels were appearing. The same stage door is used for both theatres and the parting of the ways is just inside the stage door – a case of our company going to the left, and the other to the right.

The minstrels were a great band of people and our small company got to know them very well. Their season ended a week before ours, and on their final Saturday night, I was sitting on our stage during Act III getting on with my drunk scene, when the door was flung open to admit the Black and White Minstrels in their entirety, singing, 'Thora, how we adore her' to the tune of 'Ida, Sweet as Apple Cider'. It really was an unforgettable moment. When all that lovely lot in white tail suits and white tall hats made their entrance on one side of the stage, the applause started and went

Me (*notice the low waistline*), my cousin Glad (*who wasn't my cousin, really*) and Neville (*the Admiral*).

Happy, happy wedding day. Notice my clutching fingers holding his arm so he couldn't get away…the lilies seem to be wilting a bit!

This was the first film my daughter Janette and I appeared in together (*They Came in Khaki*). She was four, but I was a bit older.

As Mrs Holmes in *Flowers for the Living*, the play that did everything for me.

This is him! That fella! My husband Scottie. He's just been cueing me with my words. It looks as though I know them. (Keystone Press Agency)

Top left As Salvation Army Captain Emily Ridley in *Hallelujah!* I quite fancied myself in that bonnet! (Yorkshire Television)

Bottom left Kathy Staff, Jane Freeman and I in *Last of the Summer Wine*. What fun we had doing the series over the years! (BBC)

Above That wonderful role in *Cream Cracker Under the Settee* which did so much for me. I'll always remember how surprised I was at receiving the BAFTA for that – at my time in life! (BBC)

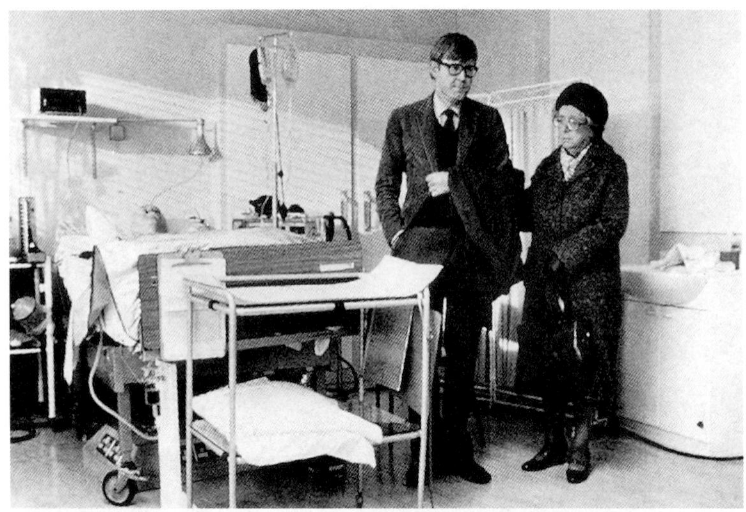

Top Here I am with Alan Bennett, playing his mother in another one of his plays, *Intensive Care*. (BBC)

Bottom 'Dame Thora gets her Dameship'...and what a wonderful time we had at Buckingham Palace. James and Daisy flew over specially and darling Scottie gave up his seat so that both grandchildren could be there. (Press Association) on and on while they crossed in front of the audience and made an exit on the opposite side – I wouldn't know exactly how long it all took but what a compliment they paid me!

Talk about 'Follow that!' When the ovation died down, we'd nearly forgotten where we'd got to in the play before they came on. The actor playing Harry, the landlord, looked at me and said, 'What about that then, Ada?' to which I replied, 'Lovely, Harry, most touching – and I have no colour prejudice!' Which got another round of applause. Oh! Happy Days!

And that was the title of the next play Walter wrote for me: *Happy Days*. We'd had quite a few meetings about the title and suddenly Walter said, 'You always put "happy days" before your name when you give an autograph. Let's call it that!' So we did.

Coliseum, Oldham, here we come with another World Premiere! George and Alfred Black again made a pilgrimage up north, saw it, liked it, bought it, and by arrangement with the Blackpool Tower Company, presented it the following season at The Grand, Blackpool. Great, twenty-two weeks, twice nightly and never an empty seat.

It was during that particular season that our daughter got married, and one day G.B. and A.B. and I were going into the Opera House Restaurant for lunch when I said, 'Er – there's something I want to ask you. Do you think I could. . . .' They didn't let me finish. I can't remember whether it was A.B. or G.B. who said, 'No, sorry Thorird!' I informed them that they hadn't the slightest idea what I was going to ask for, but they informed me they had because they read the newspapers as well. I wish I was clever enough to capture with a pen the humour of these two gentlemen, you see, they laughed through all that last bit of print you have just read. They *knew* I was going to ask if I could possibly have a certain Saturday off to go to my daughter's wedding, just as they *knew* they couldn't give it to me. I was starring alone, and it *was* a Saturday in Blackpool. And here is the strange thing, I *knew* they were right.

All right then, on the wedding morning I felt like any other loving Mother feels on the day her child (an only child in this case) is getting married, but I must say our daughter made me feel I was in London because from seven thirty in the morning she rang me about every ten minutes until nine o'clock. Lovely bits of chat like 'I'm just putting my dress on, Daddy says it looks lovely!' and 'I wish you could be here, Mummy!'

Now I must explain that in the play *Happy Days*, my husband, Peter Sinclair, who played Andy Mactagget, and I, who played Maggie Mactagget, celebrate our silver wedding. I think he's forgotten it, and when a telegram arrives from our son, Malcolm, I burst into comedy tears whilst I am reading it and rush off the stage. Right, are you with me so far? Well, while I'm off stage (drying my eyes), I discover a fur coat and twenty-five red roses (in cellophane, so that they would last for the entire run of the show!), and I burst back on to the stage wearing the coat and hugging the roses. On the particular night we are talking about, my husband had been to the wedding in London, and managed to get back to Blackpool for the end of the second house and was literally standing in the wings as I ran off crying. I had two dressers because my quick changes during the show were just that, *quick*! As one dresser passed me some tissues to blow my nose and wipe my eyes, the other dresser put my free arm in the fur coat sleeve and as I threw the tissues down and put my other arm in the other sleeve, the first dresser passed me the roses. Phew! I don't know about you but I'm tired out just thinking about it!

Well, as I said, Scottie was standing there as I made my exit crying. He was holding Jan's wedding posy of tiny little rosebuds, lily of the valley and forget-me-nots. As Florrie, the dresser, handed me the twenty-five extremely life-like red roses, Scottie said, 'Take this on, Jan sent it for you!' And he handed me the posy, which of course I took on.

The audiences in Blackpool are a joy – that isn't only *my* opinion, but the opinion of very many artists who have played to them – on that particular occasion, however, they surpassed themselves. As I started my curtain speech, I held the posy and when I told them, 'We have had a wedding in our family today' – the roof went off. I'll never know whether the applause was because they loved Jan or because they knew I hadn't been able to be at the wedding or whether it was because they just felt like it – or what. I went on to tell them that I usually brought red roses on for the final scene, but that my husband had rushed back in time to give me the posy from Jan. Handkerchiefs were being flicked out of breast pockets, women were opening their handbags to root for a tissue, noses were being blown. If ever I felt the understanding of an audience, it was that night. The curtain came down, went up, came down and went up to tumultuous applause and whistles. On the final curtain the stage director, Chris May, dashed on stage and threw his arms round me, the company were just as loving and it dawned on me as the audience trooped out of the theatre to the recorded music of Syd Phillips' *Happy Days!* that there are a lot of kind people in the world. I can't finish this chapter without telling you that every member of the company bought me a small gift that day – it was as though *I* was getting married. The young ASM came to my dressing room with her present – a small punnet of strawberries and a carton of cream. And I still have three very pretty little white china angels that three of the girls in the company bought for me on that day. I wonder if Pat Phoenix remembers she was one of the donors? I remember!

Each time 'the end of a season' in Blackpool approached, I always had a little heartache, whether it was because I was leaving my lovable Lancashire, whether it was because whenever I finish a job, I feel it's a part of my life I can't enjoy again, or whether it was because I always used to wonder when I left the theatre whether I'd ever play there again.

We only played once nightly during the final week, which was a piece of cake, and, as it was usually October by then, the shops were displaying Christmas goods – so you could buy your Christmas crackers if you felt inclined to do so.

We didn't ever buy crackers, but we always arrived back in London with a great hunk of Lancashire extra-strong farmhouse crumbly cheese. (Did you notice that? 'Cheese and crackers' in one sentence.) Oh mate, that cheese! And I can't get it anywhere in London. If you really want a feast for the gods, try some of the aforementioned cheese on an oven-warm barmcake that has been liberally spread with farm butter!

Excuse me, whilst I go and make myself something tasty to eat – the thought of all that has set me off!

40

'Emergency ward – Sfax!'

I often wonder if it was the piano copy of 'In a Persian Market' by Albert Ketelby that did it – or, of course, it could have been Rudolph Valentino in *The Sheik*, or the bit in the overture of *Samson and Delilah*. Any road up, whichever it was, from quite a tender age I have been hooked on souks. And it makes a happy state of things that Scottie is also hooked on souks, otherwise perhaps I should never have been able to visit so many.

'Souk', described in the dictionary as 'an Arab market place'. I love a souk. Well, perhaps *love* is the wrong word, so I'll say I enjoy a souk tremendously. We really have visited very many and always found our trips most interesting and entertaining – with one exception. It happened like this. We'd been 'souk sight-seeing' in Tunis and travelled on to Djerba, that little fly speck of an island off the northern coast of Africa in the Mediterranean. One afternoon after sunbathing we entered our room for a siesta. Scottie flopped on to the bed and I went to have a quick shower. It was as I stood under that welcome cool spray, soaping my birthday suit, that I thought to myself, 'Aye, Thor, your stomach is sticking out a bit!' In fact I was so convinced that it was sticking out more than it should, that I turned the shower off, wrapped my protruding abdomen in a bath towel, went into the bedroom, exposed myself and enquired of Scottie, 'Should my stomach look like this?' I must quickly explain that after thirty-eight years of being married to me, that sort of question doesn't surprise Scottie – and although we hadn't been married more than about twenty-four years the afternoon I made the stomach enquiry, it didn't surprise him. But my domelike abdomen did.

'Have you got any pain?' he asked, quickly sitting up in bed.

'No – well – er – I don't think I have,' I answered. 'You're not constipated are you?' he enquired. 'Quite the opposite after all that couscous,' I said. 'Well, I don't know what to think,' he sort of muttered, gazing at my navel as though he'd never seen one before. 'There's one thing for sure, you're not pregnant! Ha! Ha! I mean you're *not* – are you?'

I assured him that there was no chance of the patter of little feet.

We sat outside and had a cup of tea (Pardon the expression! Tea! made with one teabag and warm water) and I began to feel 'not so well'. By six o'clock I felt 'not so well at all,' and enquired if the hotel had such a thing as a hot-water bottle. All right, I know it's like asking for a refrigerator in an igloo but believe it or not within thirty minutes there was a knock at the door and there stood the hotel porter, grinning all over his happy face and looking like an adver for toothpaste. He was holding his right arm and hand up high displaying a little pale blue rubber Teddy Bear which also acted as a child's hot-water bottle, obviously left behind by some previous guests. 'Yes please?' he smilingly enquired . . . 'Yes thank you,' I gratefully agreed and, took the bottle from him. It was filled with cold water which had probably been in the little blue Teddy Bear since the previous patrons absent-mindedly left it behind. Poor old Teddy, all that cold water in his tummy – and poor old Thor – all that rotten pain in *her* tummy.

We left Djerba the following morning at seven o'clock. As usual, I was looking madly attractive and sexy, I was wearing a white tailored coat from Simpson's, Piccadilly, and clutching a bottle of Vichy Water in my right hand. My coiffure was – well how can I describe it? Rather as though I had been pulled through a hedge backwards. The reason for this unusual style being, I'd been so ill the previous evening I hadn't bothered to 'put my curlers in!' We arrived in Sfax at four o'clock in the afternoon.

Scottie settled me into bed in our hotel and then set about getting a doctor. The heat was suffocating. My pains were spifflicating! Was I glad when the bedroom door opened to admit Scottie and the Sheik of Araby. Well, of course, it wasn't the Sheik of anywhere but he was an Arab doctor who only spoke a bit of French (thank God for Scottie in that case). Why, oh why, did I always play noughts and crosses during the French class at night school? Though I had passed my French exam, because I was able to mime, '*Voici le tableau. Le tableau represente le grand-père, la grandmère, le père, la mère, le fils, la fille et le bébé.*'

He, the Sheik, was wearing a white overall buttoned at the side of the neck and, ill as I was, I remembered that the first overall like that I had ever seen was worn by Mr P. on the 'Instantaneous Hairwaver stall' at the Trades Exhibition at Morecambe. All in my past! Oh dear, the pains, was I to see a future? The Sheik wore what I believe are described as butterfly-wing lensed tinted glasses.

After prodding at my tummy he turned to Scottie and said, 'Apen-dee-cite kron-eek!' and went on to tell Scottie to go out and buy an ice bag. *An ice bag in Sfax*!! He added that if I was no better after the application of the ice bag on my tum, we'd better get in touch with him again. Scottie argued that something ought to be done at once, but to no avail. The Sheik rode off into the desert night eating his piece of Turkish delight.

Will you believe it that Scottie was able to purchase an ice bag in Sfax? Well you'd better, because he did, but even that didn't help much and Rudolph Valentino had to be recalled. He gave us the choice of the native hospital (straw palliasses on the floor) or his own private clinic. Need I tell you where we went?

I was taken into a twin-bedded room. As I was already in my nightdress, all the nurses had to do at that point was remove my coat and sandals. The next bit was off-putting. They produced from nowhere a rather rusty old safety razor. One nurse shot my nightdress round my waist, whilst the other one started to give a 'short back and sides' on my most intimate possession! Right, we all know those things happen prior to an operation but dear God, when she started blowing the cut curls away in the same manner one blows used india rubber away after erasing something, I thought, 'What would the London Clinic say!' By now

I was 'very poorly', but on her last 'blow' I looked at her lovely black face and winked and managed to say 'Hi Jean!' (hygiene). She didn't see the joke.

They got me off the bed and in my bare feet walked me down a long passage. I can vividly remember the biscuit-coloured, brown-patterned tiled floor. At the end of the passage we entered a room which I thought was a laundry because there was an ironing board standing in the middle of it. With Arabic sounds they guided me to the ironing board which had three little white steps at the side of it, and holding my elbows they gently guided me up the steps and laid me on the board. Between throwing up and wondering where the hell I was, it suddenly dawned on me that I was lying on an operating table!

On my right (in the blue corner), was an Arab doctor all of six feet four inches tall, and on my left (in the red corner) was a shorter Arab doctor who had a very kind face and looked to me just like Robert Lennard, Casting Director for Associated British Pictures. I'm not suggesting that Robert Lennard looks like an arab, but Bob has a kind face! The tall one fastened my right ankle to the board with a leather strap and buckle, and one of the nurses fastened my left ankle likewise. Honest! Meanwhile Robert Lennard appeared to be sticking something in my arm but I didn't mind because he was smiling at me with his kind brown eyes, but I *did* mind the ankle strapping lark because it reminded me of the silent film days when Pearl White was left strapped to the railway lines until the following week's episode.

Robert Lennard and the six-foot-four gent must have

only been 'small part artistes', because there was no sign of the Sheik of Araby. I suppose once I was strapped to the ironing board he would make a big entrance! Chord on, please – ta-rah!

At this point I lost interest. In other words, I don't remember anything more until I came round in one of the twin beds about 3.30 in the morning. Scottie was in the other bed; he had never returned to the hotel. As a matter of fact he only went back to the hotel once and that was the following day, to collect our luggage which he brought to the clinic, where he stayed with me until I was fit to travel back to the old country.

On the night I was admitted, the Sheik of Araby had taken Scottie out on to the balcony of the clinic and informed him that I had peritonitis and a gangrenous appendix and he would operate on me for two hundred and fifty British pounds – he was very curious to learn if Scottie *had* that amount of money on his person, which between you and me, dear reader, Scottie had *not*. However, having married me for better or worse and having promised in the Wesleyan Chapel to endow me with all his worldly goods, Scottie implored, nay, ordered, the Sheik to operate at once, thinking that the following day he would find a bank and get some spondoolicks. Little did that Scottish lad realize that Ramadan had started that very evening and that he had no chance of a bank being open for the next few days. So what did our brave lad do? By various means he discovered where the British Vice Consul could be found – and he found him – in a little shack full of tins of dried milk on the side of a harbour – and he was a Maltese. Rule Britannia! Any road up, the

Vice Consul was able to send a frenzied cable to our National Provincial Bank manager, who came out of his wardrobe and acted immediately so that the money arrived just in time to stop the Sheik of Araby pushing my appendix back in and stitching me up!

I will say this – and I mean every word of it – I shall always be grateful to the Sheik because he obviously saved my life, and to prove it he carved his name in Arabic as an operation cut! As God's above that's the truth and any London doctor who has had to examine me will tell you that after the 'shock' of seeing my operation scar, and the remark 'Wot the 'ell's that?' I have explained fully.

When I was in Perth, Western Australia at the Theatre Festival, I did a television quiz show called *What's my Secret*, and my secret was that I had 'The Sheik of Araby' cut on my stomach. Of course, as I've already said, he *did* save my life so I'll keep him anonymous. When I tell you that his first name was Mohammed you'll appreciate that I carry a longish scar, kid!

Isn't it amazing what the human body can stand? Six weeks after the little drama I have just related, I was to open in Blackpool for a season, and here we were next to a Mosque hearing them call to Allah and wondering what we were going to do. A cable arrived from A.B. and G.B. which read: 'Hey Thorird what are you doing out there – hurry up and get well and come home – Fond love A.B. and G.B.' I wept.

Scottie arranged for a taxi to drive us to Tunis Airport where an invalid's chair would be at the ready. What he hadn't arranged was how I was going to get out of bed to make the four-hour journey on shell pot roads. You see I had all these drainage tubes hanging out of my stomach! He awakened me at 5.30, well that's not quite true – at five thirty we were both awake because of the wailing of a man whose wife had given birth to twin *daughters* – daughters! not even one son!

I had only been out of bed once, for five minutes, and although I was not really fit to travel, the Sheik was quite anxious that I should get to London because his admiration of English doctors and hospitals was really sincere.

No way can I describe the next few hours – Scottie trying to dress me, getting me to the taxi, where I was in such pain I couldn't move a muscle, and couldn't bear to be touched. Arriving at Tunis Airport, they wheeled *me* to the Caravelle first and made Scottie wait until the healthy passengers boarded.

The pilot radioed Orly Airport to have an invalid chair standing by. And they had. They were marvellous. The next pilot radioed London Airport with the same request, but unfortunately when we touched down at Heathrow Airport we had to sit in the plane for twenty-five minutes after everyone had disembarked – and wait.

Eventually a little green van came scuttering across the tarmac and pulled up at the bottom of the staircase leading up to our aircraft. By this time it was almost eleven o'clock at night and I would have been quite content to sit in that plane for the rest of my days, because by that time I was nearly beyond caring about anything.

After carrying me down the stairs, or steps or ladder

or whatever it's called, they put me in the invalid chair and pushed me up a ramp into the van. I can only make a rough guess that the feller who had been told to get the chair and the van and bring it to the aircraft was *not* a fan of mine! As he pushed me up the ramp, he pushed me and the chair into the side of the van – bang! No apology – Scottie was furious and by now was looking almost as ill as me. But not quite. You see, I had the 'ether scabs' all over the lower part of my face, due to the fact, that, although the Sheik was a clever surgeon, such things as 'pre-op' pills' and all the clever things we use here prior to an operation were not part of their plan of campaign. All they did was bung a schimmel-busch mask over my nose and mouth and pour ether on to it. I'll admit it was in a beautifully shaped glass flask, but that's no help is it? Consequently I was a real old 'scabby chops'.

Where was I? Oh, I know, being banged into the side of the little green van. As we arrived at the buildings about half a minute later, our Christian driver pushed the chair and me out of the back of the van, held his hand out with the palm upwards and announced, 'I don't go no further than this, see, 'cos I ain't allowed.' Scottie had to put hand luggage, his and mine, mackin-toshes and various other objects on the ground to enable him to get a hand free to dip into his trouser pocket for a tip. Ill as I felt I can remember thinking, 'What's he tipping him for? All he's done is almost knock the tubes out of the Sheik's autograph!'

Picking up all the articles he'd put down, Scottie managed somehow to hang everything on himself – he looked like a loaded camel. With a, 'Never mind, love –

we're home now,' the caravan moved off the thousand miles' trek to customs.

I know our customs officers are acknowledged to be the best in the world, but the one who recognized me under the scabs was brilliant – and humorous with it – well, he made *me* laugh when he asked, 'Anything to declare, Miss Hird?'

So there you are – I opened at Blackpool, tubes hanging out of the 'Sheik's autograph' and all! I had two rehearsals only, in the dress circle bar at the Grand Theatre, and played twice nightly for the season. The only thing that was 'cut out' of my part, in the play I mean, was where, during a Curry's Water Scene in the bathroom, I had to sit on the toilet lid and a spout of water lifted me four or five feet into the air. A.B. and G.B. wouldn't let me risk that! I was inclined to agree with 'em!

By the way – and I nearly forgot to tell you this – while I was in the Sheik's Clin-eek, one of the nurses presented me with a very large glass tube. She was sort of pushing it at me and I was pushing it back at her. You see, the contents of the tube looked, well, a bit nasty. Will you believe, the contents were my *gangrenous appendix*!!! The Muslim religion does not believe in one being buried incomplete, and they thought I would want to keep the tube with its enclosed souvenir until such time as . . .

I gave it back – besides, my charm bracelet is full!

41

'The best laid schemes'

You will have gathered by now that I was always a fan of my brother with regard to his humour. All right, perhaps I was a little biased because he was my brother; but it's a fact that anyone who knew him well will verify that he was a real funny devil!

Scottie and I had often remarked that he should write a comedy, not particularly for me; but that he should use his talent in this direction by putting pen to paper. Well he did, and he called it *The Best Laid Schemes*.

When I was preparing for a summer season, the play I was going to embark on was usually decided upon by the November prior to the June I would open in it. The Brothers Black had got hold of a comedy that I won't mention by name because, quite candidly, I thought it was about as funny as a dose of mumps. I was invited to lunch at the Pastoria by Harold Boyes and I knew he was going to hand the play to me.

Neville had finished his play and, honestly, it was very, very funny. And, of course, he knew me so well that all the situations he had written with me in mind I felt capable of handling. I didn't feel, and neither did he nor Scottie, that I could push his play because he was my brother, so we took a bit of my Dad's name, James

Henry, and a variation of my mother's maiden name, which was Mayor, and Neville Hird suddenly became Henry J. Meyer. It looked good and it sounded good.

Mr Boyes had entertained me to a splendid lunch and during coffee he said, 'Oh, take this play with you and read it again will you?', meaning the not very funny play. Nev's play was in an envelope at my side, so handing it to Harold I said, in a very couldn't care less tone, 'Have a look at this one will you, Harold, when you've time, and let me know what you think of it!' He took the envelope, slid the play out, looked at the title and the name of the playwright and said, as only dear Harold could, 'Henry J. Meyer, who's he? Never heard of him!' I agreed, but added, 'No, well, you won't have, it's his first play but *I* think it's very funny. Anyhow, just have a read and tell me what you think, will you?' He said he would – when he had the time.

It was about a quarter past three as I got into a taxi to come home, and as Harold closed the taxi door on me he requested that I read the 'funny as mumps' play again because they all thought it could be hilarious with a few alterations here and there. As the taxi moved off I put my head out of the window and shouted, 'Yes, and you read that one because I think it's very funny *without* any alterations here and there.' And that was that. At six o'clock that same evening Harold rang me, the first words he said were, 'Who is he?' 'Who's who?' I enquired, as if I didn't know, 'The fellow who has written this comedy?' Let me state here and now, there are two things I am NOT: beautiful or a 'stranger to the truth'; so without lying I replied, 'Oh, it's a chap who has known me – well – all my life' to which, to my great relief Harold said, 'Well, never mind who he is, he has written a very funny comedy.'

It was at this period that A.B. and G.B. asked me how I would feel about Freddie Frinton being in the Blackpool show with me, explaining that he had worked for them in variety but would like a 'little go' at the acting lark. I agreed immediately. I'm no fool. Now it had come to pass that in *The Best Laid Schemes* Nev wrote a drunk scene for the husband. Well, who better to cope with that than Freddie? I mean to say, it was a piece of cake for him, and he was a great asset to the show.

And so, my friends, *The Best Laid Schemes* was chosen as the show for the Blackpool Season, 1962. But tarry awhile – at that stage nobody knew that Henry J. Meyer was my brother! What I mean is, nobody except Scottie, Nev's wife, his agent and me!

As the season progressed and, do forgive my saying this, we played to two packed houses every night, whenever A.B. or G.B. nipped into my dressing room for a 'sip', one or the other of them would always remark, 'Hey, Thorird, it's a funny thing that Mr Meyer hasn't been to see the show, isn't it?' and I could always truthfully answer, 'Oh he has! He booked six seats for last Tuesday!' or, 'He booked four seats for last Friday,' which was true, he never had a complimentary seat all the season, and he couldn't have had if he'd wanted to, which he didn't, because there weren't any!

On the very last night of the show, Neville and his wife Lily were in the little sitting-room attached to my dressing room. They had brought large boxes of chocolates and flowers for the company and as I looked at the

'Admiral' sitting there having a mug of beer I thought, 'You clever thing, our Nev. I'll tell 'em tonight who Henry J. Meyer is!' Believe me if I'd rehearsed 'the revelation scene' for a month it couldn't have played better.

I have a habit of always, on the last night of any show I'm in, seeing to it that my dressing room stuff – make-up, covers, etc. – are all packed before the last act. It suits me that after the final curtain there is none of that rather depressing business to do. Right, I changed into my going home clothes, and my dresser took my last act dress, shoes and coat up to wardrobe. So there I was in the empty dressing room as G.B. came through the 'drapes' from my sitting room with a whisky in his hand.

'Well, Thorird,' he said, 'the end of another good 'un eh?' 'Yes – thank you,' I answered. 'You'd have thought Meyer would have come in tonight wouldn't you?' he questioned, with a real twinkle in his eyes.

I was about to spill the beans when he added, 'Of course, he *has* been in hasn't he? I know who wrote it y'know!' I was just going to say 'Do you?' when he continued, '*YOU* did!' 'I didn't, y'know,' I assured him. 'Oh, yes,' he continued, '. . . nobody knows you well enough to write like this for *you* but *yourself*, do they?' And he started laughing. At that very moment Nev walked in to join us and I was able to say, '*He* does. Mr Black meet Henry J. Meyer.'

That lovely George Black, who should have lived for ever, looked at Nev, whom he knew, shook hands with him and said, '*Are* you him, Nev? Well get your pen out and write another!'

It goes without saying that Neville – ahem – sorry – Henry J. Meyer – did just that!

42

'The Bed'

We took *The Best Laid Schemes* to Torquay for the season following Blackpool, and it was there that Ronnie Chesney and Ronald Wolfe came down to see me and Freddie about a television script they had written called *The Bed*. Freddie and I felt that the idea was just up our streets.

It was arranged that we should make *The Bed* more or less as a pilot for a comedy series. For the uninitiated, that means it would be shown in the *Comedy Playhouse* series and then, if the comics were comic enough and if the television company could manage to find a slot for it, we might be given a series. We *might*!

We finished the season at Torquay and came back to discuss rehearsals of *The Bed*. We started to rehearse on Sunday 1st December at Sulgrave Boys' Club where I was to spend a lot of my life in the following years, and we went to BBC Birmingham on 9th December to play it to an audience and 'put it in the can'. I shall never forget that day. Freddie had been rehearsing *The Bed* from 9.30 to 2.30 each day, then driving back to somewhere or other to appear in Pantomime in the evening. Well he was *so* tired he could hardly keep his eyes open, and as most of *The Bed* took place *in* bed, you can imagine the difficulty I had in keeping him awake. Every time we stopped for anything during the recording, Freddie would drop off and I had to keep nudging him with my knee or my foot and whisper, 'Wake up, Fred love!' We laughed very often when we recalled that first recording.

Regardless of all that, the BBC must have been satisfied because the result of *The Bed* was to be the very happy and successful television series, *Meet the Wife*. Of which more later.

43

'This is your life – No it's not – It's his!'

During dinner one evening after we had returned from playing the season at Torquay, Jan enquired, 'Mummy, can you keep the most *secret secret* you've ever heard?' to which I promptly replied that I could. I'll tell why I replied promptly – because I *can* keep a secret! D'you know, when I was a school girl aged ten, a friend of mine who was couple of years older than I, told me a secret and with our little fingers locked I swore I would never utter it to anyone. And I never did – torture wouldn't have dragged it out of me, money or jewels couldn't have bought it, because you see we'd locked our little fingers and sworn an oath! I met this old school friend a couple of years ago, and I was proud to inform her that her 'secret' was still safe with me. She's a good sport and she said, 'D'you know, Thor, I remember us hooking our little fingers but I can't remember what the *secret* was!' I lowered my voice to inform her, 'You had got the *curse* – started on your periods!! Sh!' We exploded with laughing. When we'd contained ourselves, dried our eyes and blown our noses, she informed me that I was freed from our finger-hooking secret as she had just 'gone through the change!'

Sorry – I sort of went off the subject again didn't I?

Right! Jan had asked me whether I could keep a secret. Well, the secret *was* the BBC were about to do a *This is your Life* and the culprit, sorry I mean subject, was David Frost, and I was the chosen body to get him to Shepherd's Bush Theatre by hook or by crook – if I could.

A few nights later we were again having dinner (we don't care, y'know, we often have dinner), and David, who was dining with us, was munching away when I said, 'Hey, David, we were having a discussion at rehearsal today and someone remarked that as we made our living on television, we really ought to visit each programme that plays to an audience and see the various methods of producers, etc. Do you agree?' Before he could get rid of his mouthful of food and answer, I continued, '*I* do – I mean, for a start, *I've* never been to a *This is your Life*, have you?' By now he had cleared his mouth of food and informed me in no uncertain terms that he hadn't and had not the slightest intention of ever doing so! 'Oh, come on,' I wheedled, 'let's go and see one made. I'd love to, honest.' Eventually he agreed.

I excused myself from the table and ran into the lounge to look at the diary. I *knew* which date they wanted him there because I had it marked with a sort of spy-like sign, so I had to use my histrionic ability a bit more. 'I can only go on the so-and-so,' I called out. 'It's the only night I have free when they'll be doing one – is that all right for you?' He took out his pocket diary – scrutinized it and very begrudgingly agreed, that yes, it was all right for him. Tee-hee, I thought, little do you know Frostie, that it's *you* they're doing. So that was that.

When we returned from Torquay I did quite a few little bits – the *Vic Oliver Show* on sound, *Woman's Hour* and so on, and – I'd started to rehearse the play *All Things Bright and Beautiful.* The famous 'David Frost. This is Your Life' day came during the rehearsal period, so I would need to leave rehearsal early on that day.

As we say in the north, 'I took the director on one side' and explained to him that many are called but few are chosen to convey the subject of *This is Your Life* to the appointed execution ground! I did *not*, repeat, *not*, tell him who the subject was. The director, John Moxey, agreed immediately to let me leave early. In fact, he started to direct my means of getting across London to the hairdresser's by suggesting I order a taxi for three o'clock and so on. On the day it all happened beautifully.

Arriving home from the hairdressers, I put two voluminous bath caps over my 'shampoo and set' and had a quick bath. I had the house to myself because Scottie was out at a Masonic Luncheon and Jan was at Pinewood filming *The Beauty Jungle*.

David's mother and father had come from Beccles to spend a few days with him (tee-hee, little did he know *why* they had chosen these few particular days!) and were to come to our house, with David, and collect Jan and me around five-forty. About five-thirty a Rolls-Royce pulled up outside our front door. Jan got out and burst into the house looking (excuse me, as it's me daughter) gorgeous! I was ready. I cannot ever remember up to that point in our lives, Jan *ever* saying to me or Scottie, 'Let's have a drink shall we?' And that's the truth.

But that evening she said, and I shall never forget it, 'Oh Mummy you *do* look nice shall we have a drink?' All in one breath! So we did! David and his parents arrived in another Rolls-Royce, so Jan sent hers away. David had a sherry and his parents orange juice (his Dad was the dearest of Wesleyan Ministers, and God will rest him), after which the caravan prepared to move off.

As we drove along the Bayswater Road and approached Shepherd's Bush from Holland Park, David said, 'Well this is all very nice – I wonder whose life they are doing tonight – some poor soul is, at this moment, totally unaware of what the future holds!' We all laughed – as I, 'cleverhead', nudged Jan on one side of me and Mona, David's mother, on the other! *Some Poor Soul*! Tee-hee, it won't be long now, I thought.

We arrived at the Bush and got out of the car and, as arranged (secretly), we just walked in like anybody else – but we were put on the front row. The moment arrived. Eamonn Andrews appeared, to loud applause, and started on his spiel. He was standing in front of us, more or less. He chatted away and gawd knows there is nobody better than he at this particular kind of thing. David was looking round and whispered to me, 'I can't see anyone behind us who it might be.' Oh dear, I was very near the tittering stage. 'On the front row ladies and gentlemen,' I heard Eamonn say, '. . . . we have the King of Satire, David Frost.' (Loud applause.) 'The Queen of Comedy, Thora Hird.' (Quite loud applause.) 'And Britain's most beautiful film star, Janette Scott.' (Whistles and applause.) He looked at David and said, 'Did she have a lot of trouble getting you here tonight,

David?' indicating me. 'Well, er, yes – quite a bit, really,' replied David. 'Oh well, never mind,' said Eamonn, '. . . the most important thing is that she got you here, because now we are able to say, *This is Your Life*!' And at this point he sort of showed the big red book to David, and then moved it over to me, as he concluded, 'Thora Hird!'

'No, it's not!' I argued. 'It's *his*!'

Talk about he who laughs last, eh? Scottie was *not* at a Masonic luncheon, he was at the studios waiting and *he* knew all about it; John Moxey, who had so willingly let me off rehearsals early, *he* knew. My brother Nev, who was brought down from the north (or up as the case may be), *he* knew; Jan, who was so nervous for me she suggested we had a drink, *she* knew; the Rev and Mrs Frost had been acting their socks off, *they* knew! and – from before the moment Jan had asked me if I could get David there – the King of Satire *knew*!

Do you wonder our country produces the finest spies and the most brilliant actors and actresses? Mind you – we do occasionally produce a real, gormless, egg-headed, dumb cluck – like, for instance, ME!

There was a smashing 'marble hole' under the street lamp opposite 6 Cheapside, Morecambe, Lancs, England, Europe, the World, and when the BBC made me the subject of *This is Your Life*, they and the Morecambe Corporation couldn't give me the marble hole but they did give me the street lamp! Honest!

44

'Meet the husband'

We were still 'laying schemes' to the best of our advantage when we took *The Best Laid Schemes* to Bournemouth in 1964, for by then Freddie and I were making a batch of *Meet the Wife* for television between each summer season we played. In fact, 'Fraid' was doing twice daily pantomime each Christmas as well, and I'd do a television play. There really were so many funny things that happened during *Meet the Wife*. For a start, half the viewing public seemed to think that Freddie and I *really were married* to each other. One Sunday, this was during our season at Bournemouth – Scottie and I had lunch out in a very old country pub that was noted for its food, and we were having a drink in the bar before lunch when it became obvious that five ladies who were sitting round a small table, having a drink, were talking about me. Anybody who appears on telly will tell you that you have to 'behave yourself in public because everybody knows you'. The Manager of the pub told Scottie our table was ready and added in a whisper, 'I know you want a bit of peace, Miss Hird, so I'm not letting on who you are!' We moved off towards the restaurant, which meant passing the five ladies, and one of them grabbed hold of my hand.

'Eee-eee!' she verbally grinned. I grinned back, I mean let's face it the viewers and theatre audiences are our bread and butter, aren't they? I mean that sincerely. 'Eee we were just saying . . .' At this point all five ladies burst out laughing. So I laughed – Scottie had not seen the hand grabbing and was by now standing by our table in the restaurant. 'Eee – we were saying – weren't we?' She turned to her buddies for confirmation. 'Who's *he* then?' and with this she nodded her head directionally towards Scottie. 'Oh,' I said, '. . . that's my husband!' The shrieks of laughter were like an explosion! I tried to move away but unfortunately lady number one still had my hand in the famous 'Indian toe hold'. 'Now come on, darling, we're not going to say nothink to nobody – yer boy friend is it?' enquired lady number two. More uncontrollable shrieks! 'Naughty girl, I'll tell Fred,' added lady number three. 'Oh I do hope you won't!' I implored as I escaped to join Scottie.

We had a good lunch and, as we came out of the restaurant, I didn't need to *see* the five ladies, I could *hear* 'em! A few bottles of Guinness and a few gins had worked wonders. 'Hey, come here a minute, Thora!' one of them bawled as I passed. Not wishing to be rude I enquired, 'What is it?' 'Well,' said one of the five, 'she didn't mean what she said about telling Fred. Don't you worry, Thora, just go and enjoy yourself, he (meaning Scottie) looks smashing – you deserve it, you work hard!' I thanked them very much and went and joined my lawful wedded husband for a dirty weekend.

And it came to pass that Henry J. Meyer did get his pen out and wrote a comedy equally as funny as *The Best Laid Schemes*. The fact that Freddie and I were so happily successful in *Meet the Wife* prompted us to entitle it *My Perfect Husband*. I mean, fair do's. In any case, as soon as we finished in Blackpool we were due to start yet another batch of *Meet the Wife* for telly.

Whilst I was playing that particular season I was asked to read a script of a play for the West End the following year. Felix de Wolfe, my agent, flew up to Blackpool with this particular script and said that I would either 'madly' want to play the leading part or I'd want to be sick! Well, I read it that night, in bed, and let's be candid, I felt a bit sick! However, to cut a long story short, the clever author, and make no mistake he *is* a clever fellow, re-wrote a lot of it for me and the second time I read it, I didn't even feel faint.

Now you must be wondering why I haven't mentioned the title of the play! Well, just hold on while I put you in the picture as regards what happened when we returned to London. As I've said, we ploughed into another happy batch of *Meet the Wife* and whilst we were doing them we were asked if we would like to be in *London Laughs* at the Palladium, opening the following May for thirty-two weeks.

I'll bet you are thinking that I jumped at it – I mean, let's face it, starring in a Palladium show with lovely Harry Secombe, Russ Conway and up and coming Jimmy Tarbuck, and for thirty-two weeks! Any artist who refused that would want his brains washing – eh?

Well, folks – believe it or not, I wanted to do the play. Oh yes, very much I wanted to do the play, but

I couldn't do both. I had to decide.

Have you ever looked at a child when it has been deeply disappointed? Of course you have – well – Freddie Frinton, bless him, looked about six years old when I told him I'd have to choose between the Palladium and the play. We were walking to our respective dressing rooms in red section at the TV Centre, having put yet another *Meet the Wife* in the can, when Freddie said, 'I wish you'd do it, Chuck! (Meaning the Palladium season.) I've never been in the West End.' Incidentally, he always called me Chuck. As he said that I *knew* what my choice must be. We played the Palladium.

There's a wonderful saying my Mother used to use, 'Cast your bread on the waters and it comes back buttered!' Well, that's a fact – no kidding. As I decided to take the Palladium I *knew* how much I wanted to do the play but what I didn't know was how much I was going to enjoy those thirty-two weeks. Bliss!

We would rehearse *Meet the Wife* in the morning from 9.30 to 2.30. Scottie would collect me from rehearsal in the car and we'd come home for lunch and then try and have a walk – otherwise I'd never have had any fresh air. I'd be at the Palladium for 5.30 and we'd play two houses nightly (three on a Saturday, because there was a matinee) and on Sunday we were in the TV studios all day recording the *Meet the Wife* we'd rehearsed all week. The only day we were free of *Meet the Wife* was Monday, and on that day I had a sound show which we did at the BBC studio on Lower Regent Street, and called *One Born Every Minute*. I was rather proud of that title because I thought of it – I thought it fitted the story line because I played a district nurse who delivered quite a few babies during the thirteen weeks it ran.

So there we were, working day and night as you might say, and getting very little of the 'spondoolicks' we'd earned because, to quote my auntie, the tax we paid was 'an imposition'.

Right, so you are wondering why I didn't mention the title of the play I couldn't do because it clashed with the Palladium! Well the reason is, one of our best actresses played the part I'd been offered wonderfully, and I honestly don't know if she knows it was offered to me first. I hope she doesn't because the first night of the play was during our rehearsals for the Palladium show and I was able to go to it. She was great.

Apart from the enjoyment of that season at the Palladium, and I *did* enjoy it, Freddie and I had a lot of laughs privately. We were always having laughs at rehearsals for *Meet the Wife*, but of course that was all helped along by our director, Robin (they don't come any better) Nash. Robin Nash could direct me through the back of my head. It's a fact. I would make a move during rehearsals, let us say, to the gas stove and although I would have my back to Robin I could 'feel' if he wanted me to change the direction and let's say, move to the table. It was incredible. I used to say that he was the youngest Svengali and I was the oldest Trilby in the business. Any artiste will tell you how very important the director you work with is. I mean they can make your work a joy or a misery. Robin Nash understood Freddie and me – he knew our way of working together – he knew our form of timing a comic line or situation – he knew we were disciplined and he knew we were fond of him and respected him. Do you wonder we were such a happy team? Of course we didn't always agree, we would discuss things but we never had a real blazing row and nine times out of ten we finished up laughing. One newspaper man wouldn't believe that we were as happy as we appeared to be and indeed printed that we weren't. I shall never forget, he came to the Palladium to see us in our respective dressing rooms. He saw Freddie first and then came to see me. The series we were making at that moment was our final batch of *Meet the Wife* and – not that any of you readers are interested but I'm going to inform you just the same – the reason I didn't want to do any more was, I wanted us to finish whilst we were still a popular programme, savvy? *Not* because I wanted to leave comedy series for drama series and start *The First Lady*. But this *gentleman* of the press insisted we had had a row and that was the reason we weren't doing any more – he even went so far as to print his story the following Sunday. Freddie and I were at the studios, and someone laughingly brought the paper with the article in it on to the set. D'you know, it really upset Freddie? It didn't upset me – it made me mad as 'ell! But remembering one of the 'twelve bits of advice' my father had given me, which was 'slow time 'em', I did just that.

It would be about four months later that Jan's husband, Mel Tormé, came to star at the Talk of the Town, and prior to opening he gave a cocktail party for the press at the Mayfair Hotel. Scottie and I were invited.

I saw Mr Prevaricator standing with a large gin in his hand and I thought, 'I hope you don't speak to me or I might be rude,' and *then* I thought, 'Hold on, Thor – it's your son-in-law's "do", you are only a guest?' However, a little later, when someone touched me on the shoulder, I turned round and it was 'his nibs'. 'Hello, Thora, how are you?' he asked, grinning with a five-gin flush. 'What do you want to know for?' I enquired very quietly. He ignored that and then said, 'Great isn't he – y'know – Mel?' To which, I replied, still very quietly, 'If I say he *is* you'll say I'm after him; if I say he *isn't* you'll swear I am trying to break his and Jan's marriage up – so just 'op it will you, "Mr Stranger-to-the-Truth?" ' All right, I'll admit it was childish of me, and I'm not proud of what I said, but I really did it for Freddie.

Needless to say he has never written *one* word about me since – true or false – but who cares? I've known a lot of pressmen for a lot of years and they are super. In fact, it has always surprised me that 'his nibs' didn't have his pressman's badge, epaulettes, and buttons stripped off by his fellow writers in the middle of Fleet Street to the roll of the presses!

1966 came to an end and it had been a most interesting and wonderful year. *Call my Bluff, Dixon of Dock Green, The Good Old Days, Jackanory, Late Night Line Up,* a quick visit to France, thirty-two weeks at the Palladium, a meeting with Andrew Osbourne about a drama series, a series on sound, *One Born Every Minute,* my advert for Biotex on telly. We finished at the Palladium on 17 December and on the 22nd Scottie and I flew to Beverly Hills to spend Christmas with Jan and

Mel. Sadly, Jan's first marriage hadn't worked and neither had Mel's . . . happily, they both knew that this one was going to.

They had married in May in Japan whilst all the blossoms were in flower, five days after I had opened at the Palladium – and once more I was unable to be at my daughter's wedding. Hard cheese, Thor! Never mind! I comforted myself with the fact that she hadn't been at mine.

45

'Wherefore art thou – Nursie!'

We returned from America early in the year and I was asked to play the nurse in *Romeo and Juliet*, a Play of the Month, on BBC TV. Any actresses will tell you that there are certain roles they would like to play and that there are certain roles that *other* people would like to see them play. The nurse in *Romeo and Juliet* came under the latter bit. It was amazing the number of times folks had said to me, 'Ooo, I would like to see you play the nurse in *Romeo and Juliet*.' I was flattered, of course, but never did I feel strongly enough about the part even to say to myself, 'Ooo, I *would* like to play the nurse in *Romeo and Juliet*.' Anyway, I was asked to play it. And I most graciously refused.

Stand easy and I'll tell you why. Because I wasn't sure if I would be up to scratch. I mean, just think who had walked away with the part in the past – Dame Edith Evans, Dame Flora Robson, to mention but a couple, and those girls know their Willie Shakespeare backwards, frontwards and sideways. Besides, I had another more important reason for refusing with thanks. Hold on a minute.

Cedric Messina, producer, and Alan Cooke, director, didn't accept my first refusal and a couple of days later asked me again. Upon my second refusal Alan Cooke invited me to lunch. As we took our places at the table in the restaurant, he laughingly said, 'Right – now just tell me the reason why you don't want to play the Nurse!'

'All right,' I said, 'I will – but please don't think I'm not grateful to you and Cedric for thinking of me, it's just that – well – I – er – ' 'What?' he questioned. 'Well, it's just that I can never understand why the nurse is played as an old woman, when she's supposed to have wet nursed Juliet only fourteen years before!' 'And is that the only reason you won't do it?' he asked. 'That and because I feel that I might not be very good,' I stated. He started to laugh.

'If that's your only reason you've lost the argument because we are altering the period slightly and playing the nurse as a woman of fifty!' he retorted, attacking his veal.

'Oh well – I mean – I'm glad you feel as I . . .' I never had a chance to finish. 'Good, so you'll do it then?' He said this without looking up from his plate. There was a short pause.

'I'll tell you what, Alan. At three minutes to ten in the morning I'll ring TV Centre, by the time I'm through to your extension it should be about ten o'clock, so if you could please be near your phone at that time, I will say either, "It's yes, Alan," or "It's no, Alan" – will that be all right?' He agreed.

The following morning I did exactly as I'd said I would do and when I had got through to Alan's extension he picked up the phone and spoke immediately.

'Thora? Well, is it my lucky day?' he asked.

I replied, 'Well, that's a matter of opinion – because I'll do it!' And I did.

Robin Nash asked me to do a comedy sketch with Wilfrid Brambell (Old Steptoe himself). It was about two public lavatory attendants and was called *They Also Serve*. Alan Melville had written it and it was in his programme. The difficulty *was*, it was during the rehearsals for *Rome and Jule* and I didn't want to trouble Alan any more. I felt I'd given him enough trouble before I'd said I'd do the part, never mind giving him any more now I was playing it!

Robin Nash was wonderful, as usual, and even suggested that Wilfrid and I rehearse at my home. I was itching to do the sketch, and I was practically at the scratching stage when Robin told me I needn't go into the studios until four o'clock on camera day. Oh mate, it was too good to miss, so in a diplomatic way and at what I felt was the right moment, I asked Alan would it be possible for me to finish on a certain date around three o'clock?

He was most accommodating. 'Certainly,' he said, 'I shall be doing the sword fighting scenes that afternoon anyway!' I felt, in all fairness I should tell him the reason I wanted off early, so I told him. 'It's just a little sketch I'm doing for Robin Nash,' and left it at that.

You've no idea the fun and pleasure I get out of doing a job like the lavatory attendant sketch. It means I can pop into Wig Creations, have a gab with Mr Brian, explain what I'm doing and then the two of us decide the kind of wig I should have. We have laughed our socks off many a time at some of the comic results. In this case, it was a black wig with a donkey fringe. Let me add quickly that Mr Brian and Wig Creations have been responsible for some very beautiful wigs I've worn as well – for instance the one I wore when I played Mrs Hardcastle in *She Stoops to Conquer*. However, I digress.

When we came towards the end of rehearsals for *Romeo and Juliet*, one day Alan asked me, 'What kind of a sketch did you do for Robin – what were you?'

'A public lavatory attendant,' I replied.

'He just laughed, I don't think he believed me. Then his expression changed to a rather, 'director of *Romeo and Juliet* – Play of the Month' one. 'Not really?' he enquired. 'Yes – really,' I replied, 'and don't look worried Alan,' I added, 'both the Nurse and the woman in the lavatories are *staff* – well aren't they?' He agreed.

I never saw *Rome and Jule* because by the time it was shown I was busy putting a *First Lady* in the can. I enjoyed playing the Nurse and I hope Willie Shakespeare and all the very clever actresses who have played the nurse before I did, will excuse and forgive me for making her 'wetnursable'.

46

'The First Lady

In August 1967 we were ready to start on *The First Lady*. We filmed exterior shots to cover the first four episodes in and around Barnsley in *Yorkshire*. We also used Barnsley Town Hall and Council Chamber. Although I am a Lancastrian right down to my cotton socks, I admit readily that the people of Barnsley and thereabouts were grand and showed me nothing but kindness. Be that as it may, there was nothing in the scripts of *The First Lady*, apart from my accent, to denote that I wear a red rose as opposed to a white one. So after a little chat with Robin Midgley, who was directing numbers one and four, we added six words and they explained everything. It was thus: in the first episode, I got on to the Council and one of the Councillors had to say, 'I don't hold with women on the Council,' and we added a reply from me, which was, 'Especially if they come from Lancashire!' Believe it or not, those six little words gave me a very comfortable feeling!

I really could write a whole book about the sad, funny, serious and dangerous things that happened during the life span of Coun. Sarah Danby. The letters I received were unbelievable – comic, romantic and some rather sad.

One letter requested: 'Please, Mrs Danby, could you have a sewer one hundred and forty feet long laid in our street?'

Another one read: 'I love your clothes, especially the navy blue suit you wore last week, I've got a navy hat and shoes and my daughter gets married in six weeks will you please send me your suit and gloves?'

And: 'When we bought this house the fellow left his pigs in our yard, I've bought his wife a box of chocolates but his pigs are still there, will you tell him to move them Coun. Danby please?'

Also: 'I love your nails and wedding ring, I'm getting married can you tell me where you bought your ring and do you do your own nails?'

And:

'Everybody says I am the image of you.'

'I am always being taken for you in the laundrette.'

'I was asked for my autograph in the grocer's, they thought I was you!'

'I think I look just like you, I think I am as clever as you but my bank account is not as big as yours.'

'I am a bachelor of fifty-eight and would love to take you for a drink in an ordinary pub because I'll bet you've never been in one!' (Author's note: He must be joking!)

'Please, Mrs Danby, *please* try and get us a council house.'

'Where did you get the wallpaper on your lounge wall?'

'Will you seriously consider putting up for our council?'

'Will you please send me a photo with your glasses on, I want to get some!'

And so on and so on. I had literally hundreds of letters from women saying they looked exactly like me or that they had been taken for me or that their husbands said they were the image of me. Eventually, on the back of a fan photograph, which they would always request, I would write: 'Never mind it can't be helped!' or 'Beauty is only skin deep!' or 'Sorry, love – there's nothing I can do about it!'

I shall never forget that one lot of location we did for *The First Lady* was at Castleford Rugby Ground. Storywise, some shots of myself and James Grout (smashing to work with), who played Alderman Kingston in the show, and Henry Knowles (equally smashing), who played my son, were needed, sitting in the crowd watching a match.

We were in the director's room of the club house during the morning, and the president (or whatever it is a rugby club has) and his wife were chatting to us. During the conversation he acquainted me with the fact that I was 'kicking off' the match that afternoon. Laughingly I acquainted him with the fact that I wasn't! 'You *are*!' he argued. 'It's in't programme – in *print*!' It *was*! I'll bet a lot of people in 'our business' will stick up for me when I say I was 'rather annoyed!' I mean, hecky plonk, I don't mind doing anything for anybody, within reason, if I'm told about it beforehand, but the first I knew about the kick off lark was at that moment, when a programme was passed to me. What can't speak can't lie – there it was – as his nibs had said – *in print*!

The match was to be televised in *Grandstand* that afternoon and, as Scottie is an avid viewer, I got to a telephone after lunch and warned him. Please understand that I didn't ring him up so he could *watch* me! Oh, no! I rang him up so that he'd know when he saw me do it there was no need for him to think, 'Wot the 'ell is she doing now!' D'you follow?

Now at this point I must explain about Rose and Lillian. Rose and Lillian must be, nay *are*, two of the finest dressers the business has ever known, added to which they both are blessed with a fantastic sense of humour. Rose can make *me* laugh more than I can make *anyone* laugh – she's cockney, comic, kind and conscientious; Lillian was a dancer in variety and always 'did me a few bars of the Sailor's Hornpipe' to wish me good luck before I did a show. She's softly spoken, affectionate, knows her job and, like Rose, is now retired. It's the BBC TV's loss. I miss 'em at the studios.

On this particular location Rose was dressing me. Paul, the director, wanted me to walk up the grandstand steps and go and sit with Jimmy Grout and Henry Knowles and that was all in that shot. The camera was at the top of the steps in the grandstand, and the idea was to pick me up on film as I ascended the steps with the normal rugby fans as they filed in. Paul wanted to shoot on the crowd arriving and me amongst them. He was then going to pan over as I found my seat and sat down. Piece of cake eh? Well not really. You see all this was a few minutes before I was going to kick off! For the shot I have just explained to you, I was wearing a pencil slim tweed skirt and a sheepskin jacket. No complaints about the jacket – but the skirt – oh mate, it was difficult enough to sit down in it never mind about cock me leg up and kick a ball! Imposs! It was at this point that Rose took over. With my slacks over her arm she informed me that there was no need to worry as she had found four dustbins!

Taking me by the arm she propelled me towards the back of the stand. True enough, near one of the entrances to the stand were four dustbins. She then explained all the details of the operation. 'Now y'see, Miss Hird, you can do the shot with the crowd going up the steps in your skirt and brogues – right? Then nip down here quick, change into your slacks and boots behind these dustbins and then go and kick off – right, gorrit? When you've kicked off, nip back quick round here and I'll be waiting behind these dustbins with your skirt and brogues for the next shot you have to do up in the stand. All right, gel – gorrit?' I assured her I'd gorrit. We did the first shot in the skirt and brogues with the crowd – it had to be a 'one take'.

Rushing back to Rose and the dustbins I took my skirt off and then my brogues – I couldn't put my boots on next because I couldn't get my narrow slacks over 'em – I sat on one of the dustbins until I'd pulled my slacks on sufficiently for my feet to pop through. I was then able to pull my boots on and stand down on the wet ground. I pulled my slacks up over my bottom in a sort of bent double position so as to try and keep out of sight.

It was bitterly cold and wet and I pulled my mink coat on as I ran to join the two teams and the referee under the tunnel thing.

As we marched on to the ground I could hear Eddie

Waring announcing me. It's as well he did because nobody could see me in the middle of those giants! As I took big strides to try and keep up with them my boots sunk into the mud about four inches with each step and as I endeavoured to release each boot a loud squelch accompanied my frenzied effort. I reckon my walk on to that field (sorry, ground) was the funniest walk I've ever done and it hadn't been thought out, it was force-work!

I'd been advised to kick the oval ball rather to the side of it and to give it as hefty a wallop as I could because unless it travelled a certain number of feet or yards (I've forgotten which) the game couldn't or wouldn't start.

Taking off my coat I put it over the ref's arm (to the delight of the crowd). I didn't do it to get a laugh, I did it because it had suddenly dawned on me that as I ran to 'kick off' I might slip. *I* didn't mind slipping in the mud myself, but I didn't fancy my coat covered in what looked like brown chewing gum. I must admit the ref looked very surprised as he stood there with his whistle in his mouth, his eyes wide open and my mink coat over his arm!

The whistle blew – bluddy 'ell– I nearly jumped out of my skin – the captains of each team were crowding me a bit so I linked arms with each of them (it was their turn to be surprised) and the three of us set off at a run and I walloped the ball as far as I could. What a blessing I did hold on to the giants because by the time I had got over the shock of the piercing whistle blowing I realized that I had nearly sunk to Australia. The giants took off with me hanging on to them and literally pulled me out of the ground as they did so, to the accompaniment of an almighty squelch! I had to do the comic knees-up run again. To tell you the honest truth, those mighty men were so strong they nearly frightened me to death. With my boots sticking in the mud, my first thought was we've left my boots, feet and legs behind, they've pulled the top half of me off.

By now the game was 'in play' (did you notice that bit? 'In play?' I rather liked writing that, it sounded as if I know what I'm talking about!) Have you ever felt you weren't wanted? By then, I couldn't have been of less importance. The giants were attacking each other, the ref was running about after them with my mink coat on his arm and I was running about with my knees up trying to pull my squelching boots out of the ground and trying to retrieve my coat from the ref who was doing his best to get rid of it.

Eventually I squelched off like a cat on hot bricks to find Rose and the dustbins.

Faithful Rose – there she was at the side of the ground, tears running down her face she'd laughed so much at my pathetic attempt to kick off and the 'couldn't-be-helped' comic run.

We made our way behind the dustbins, which, let's face it, only came up to our waists, and Rose endeavoured to pull my muddy boots off – because until she had done so we couldn't get my slacks off. Lifting one of the lids off the aforementioned dustbins, we discovered a discarded newspaper which we wrapped round the muddy boots. When we'd got one boot off, we put one brogue on which enabled me to put one foot down on the wet and muddy concrete. It was as I stood in my Marks and Sparks floral elastic knicker roll-ons with one brogued foot up on a dustbin lid whilst I fastened my shoe lace that the belated coach-load of rugby fans passed. 'Good old Thora!' 'I see you've got 'em on.' 'What time is the strip club open?' 'Only a rose I give you!' 'Get 'em off!' etc., etc. I mean, what can you do in a case like that? I know one thing you can't do – you can't win!

47

Tribute to Cheapside

It was August 1970. Scottie and I had returned to the North on business, but we intended to make it a nice long weekend – for my sake. We stayed at our usual hotel in Blackpool. We know 'it' and 'it' knows 'us' and I can ask for toasted *brown* bread, instead of *white* – and I'm not regarded as an eccentric.

It's of no interest to you that my brother Nev's birthday was in August, but it was to me, and of course it does fit in with the bit I wrote about my mother's in April, mine in May, my dad's in June, my sister's in July and my brother's in August! Remember the phenomenon I swanked about at school?

Although we were in Blackpool on the day of Nev's birthday we intended to celebrate the occasion on the following day in Morecambe. Nev and his wife, Lily, picked us up in their car at our hotel, and the four of us set off. We left it entirely to Admiral Hird of the Iron Duke as to where the 'Mystery Tour – back for tea' would take us, but of course I knew the 'big finish' would embrace a view of the Central Pier, the Alhambra, the Royalty Theatre and Cheapside, Morecambe. *En route* I soon discovered that we were driving along country lanes and roads that have now recaptured their former beauty and glory, due to the opening of motorways. These roads and lanes have been quietly pensioned off and are not used now as much as they were. It was all marvellous.

It was a journey of happy memories and exclamations such as, 'Oh, Nev, this is Garstang isn't it?' I remember that little bridge – and us coming here from school to do some folk dancing at a gala – and dancing Helston Ferry all along that road and over the little bridge, accompanied by the local Brass Band playing 'The Floral Dance!'

It didn't seem long before a signpost informed us we were on our way to Wray and Wennington. 'Hey, d'you remember the school nature-study class had a picnic here?' Immediately, my mind flew back to the morning of that picnic. I had implored my mother to pack my picnic lunch in an empty strawberry basket the greengrocer had given me, instead of in a paper bag. And I asked for a little white linen serviette from my mother to cover the food. I was only about eight years old – so I suppose I was pretending to be Red Riding Hood or somebody. I vividly remember I had sixpence to spend and that, after eating the picnic banana sandwiches, the huge wedge of cake and an apple, I had visited the tiny village shop to have a look round and select presents to take back – we always did that. It was easy to decide on my dad's gift – five Woodbines in a little paper packet, *twopence*! My present to my mother was a bit more difficult and a great deal of lip chewing took place before I took the plunge. On the short wooden counter in the village shop, along with the strings of Spanish, sugar mice, kahli suckers and other tempting goodies, was a box of necklaces, made of white celluloid. The chain part of the necklaces was stamped out of celluloid and from it hung a pendant. It was the choice of the pendant I found so difficult as there were quite a few designs with different hand-painted pictures on them. At long last – and I swear no customer buying diamonds in Asprey's or Cartier's chose with greater care – I decided on a small oval pendant that had a little cupid painted on it. The only drawback about the Cupid was that one of its eyebrows was very high up and the other one very low down, giving it a perpetually quizzical look. However, it was the best of the bunch, so I bought it – *threepence*!

I only had a penny left out of my sixpence, so Nev had to be satisfied with a *real slate* pencil, which was a halfpenny, because I rather fancied ten aniseed balls to suck on the way home in the charabanc.

I'm off again about the nice things my mother did. Listen. On the Friday after my gifts had been given and received with great pleasure, my parents were invited out to dinner by some friends, who were called Rawbottom. (It *is* an unfortunate name, isn't it? I spent a lot of time as a child wondering why the very first Rawbottom had been called that – I had my own answer.) When my mother was all dressed and ready to go, she came upstairs to kiss us Good night and God bless. (We had a splendid 'help' at this time and we were never left alone on the rare occasions our parents had an evening out.) When my mother leaned over to kiss me as I lay in bed, something lightly tickled my chin – it was the pendant! She was wearing it! My present! Bought with my threepence! I also remember thinking how *nice* she looked in her lovely brown crêpe-de-chine dress and her tiny pearl earrings.

'Do you think everybody will like it?' I enquired – meaning the chain and pendant. 'Like it? I'm sure everyone will envy me,' she assured me. What a brave woman, a lovely dress and a threepenny pendant! I don't wonder the cupid looked worried!

What I've just told you all went through my mind as we drove through Wray village, August 16, 1970. Isn't it strange? The older one gets, the clearer the memories of childhood seem to become.

After a good few miles of reminiscing we approached Morecambe proper, the feeling I always get on these occasions started at the pit of my stomach – I can't describe it.

'Prepare yourself for a bit of a shock, our kid!' Nev warned me.

'Oh, it's all right!' I said. 'I mean – I know it's not there, is it? I mean, Cheapside, the Royalty, the bottom of Euston Road – it's *all gone*, hasn't it?'

'Yes,' Nev said, looking straight ahead as he drove along. 'It's all gone.'

Quite honestly, we were upon the scene of devastation before I realized it.

'Hey! Just a minute love, go a bit slower please – what was here?' I enquired of Nev. 'Tunstall Street and the bottom right hand side of Euston Road,' Nev informed me. I was ashamed to have to be enlightened. Tunstall Street! In my very early childhood it had been called Back Pedder Street, and the residents of the small cottages had taken umbrage and had it renamed

'Pilling Street'. Apparently, as the years passed by, someone else had got the needle at *that* title, and it was eventually called Tunstall Street, which it remained until the great invasion. When I was cashier at the Co-op, Queen's Square Branch, I used to pass the end of it six times a day: on my way to work in a morning, home to lunch, back from lunch, home to tea, back from tea (when there was always a lovely smell of kippers frying in Tunstall Street) and home again after my day's toil!

And now, it had all disappeared! One side of Tunstall Street backed on to the bottom of Euston Road – and one side of Euston Road backed on to Cheapside – and one side of Cheapside backed on to Sun Street and – what am I bothering to tell you all that for? There was nothing left of any of it!

All I could see was a vast open space. Where was I? On the Sahara? In the desert at Las Vegas? How could I imagine where any individual house or shop had been? It was all a great big nothing! Yes, that's what I was looking at, a great big plateau full of nothingness!

'Pull yourself together, Thora! – don't be sentimental, this is all under the heading of Progress, and you've a bigger shock to endure in about four seconds!'

I got out of Nev's car at the top of Euston Road – they'd left the top half. It was quite blustery, the wind coming from the sea. As I approached the corner of Market Street where Martins Bank, defiantly and proudly, still stands, I started to put my headscarf on – by the time I had tied it under my chin and raised my eyes, I was once again looking at nothing.

Well, not quite *nothing*. I was looking at, first of all,

where Houghton's greengrocery and butcher's shop had once stood. Mind you, to be fair, Houghton's had been replaced long before I left Morecambe, by a smart, modern impersonal Fruit Store, but it wasn't the smart, modern, impersonal Fruit Store that had disappeared in my eyes – oh no, it was Houghton's.

'Please may I have a cut apple for this bucket of peelings, Mr Hadwen?' I wonder which bit of rubble the 'cut apple' bucket used to stand on?

I looked amongst the stones and grey dust and tried to visualize where the entrance to the Royalty Theatre and Opera House started and Houghton's finished. Four more paces and I knew, I just *knew*, I was standing where the entrance to the Royalty had invitingly and proudly stood:

'A compact, comfortable and well appointed place of entertainment, lavishly decorated throughout and one of the most comfortable outside of London, a handsome stone structure, in the classic style. Designed by Frank Matcham. First opened April 4, 1898.'

Finally closed – demolished and erased (when the dust settled) on the morning of Monday, February 23, 1970!

To quote Howard Reynolds, who is so splendid a writer and has a brilliant command of words:

> The bulldozers moved in, their steel jaws aided by hawsers which literally tore the place apart. The event lasted over several days and lunchtime crowds gathered, obviously for many reasons, in a sort of Requiem for a Dead Theatre. The walls came tumbling down, briefly exposing the interior, before

that, too, vanished behind the dust and before the onslaught of men and machines.

I doubt not that several people who were present had hoped one day to see a show which would bring the house down; on this occasion the fulfilment of their hopes must have been somewhat bitter – I only went once – and that was enough. Seeing the inexplicable replaced by the ineffectual is an experience I don't cherish.

Thank you, Mr Reynolds – you clever writer!

Well, Mr Matcham, the theatre you so diligently designed in the classic style disappeared in less time than you sat at your drawing board. Three score years and ten is the expected life span, isn't it? Your theatre – gallant lady that she was – held her head high two years longer than that, Mr Matcham.

Of course, only those who had a sincere affection for her could remember how really magnificent she used to look when she was young. She wore her deep red velvet drapes and gilt ornaments so beautifully – everyone used to pass flattering remarks about her, Mr Matcham; she was, without doubt, the toast of the town! It was heartbreaking to see the state she had fallen into in her later years – of course she had no one to care for her – nobody was interested – d'you understand, Mr Matcham? And although she still flaunted her original style of dress, the red velvet drapes were black with neglect and dirt, her gilt ornaments sadly tarnished. That was the sad part, Mr Matcham, to see her so neglected and uncared for, through no fault of her own, let me add. Our apologies, Mr Matcham.

Please forgive us, Mr Matcham. Progress you know!

I made to move off, but stupid as it sounds, I felt as though the empty site of the Theatre was beseeching me, 'Don't go yet, Thora – stand and look at me for just a bit longer!'

I did so – and then I moved slowly on, past what had been the sweet shop, one window of which had always displayed 'Photographs of the Artistes'.

I had known it before it was a sweet shop. During my school days it had opened as MacGregor's – Herbalist and Drug Store. *Drug Store*! Get that bit – how American. Sure, Baby! I remember I thought it was wonderful. There were always silver and gold pills in glass bottles in one window. I was always asking my mother why I couldn't buy some as sweets and I recall I was always put off with a smart reply of, 'Because you can't – they are not for children!'

Unbelievable isn't it? – in this day and age of 'the pill' and all that! All the same, I got a lot of pleasure from looking at them as they glittered in the window. Thank God I never needed them!

Wait a minute, though – before it was the Drug Store it was Johnson's, High Class Fishmonger and Poulterers. Yes, of course it was. As I stood there I could hear myself, as a child, saying, 'May I have four nice pieces of halibut, Mr Johnson, please – and my mother says will you put in a sprig of parsley, please?'

Before I moved from the spot I was concentrating on what else I used to go into Johnson's for. Oh yes – I remember. 'Fresh garden peas – shelled on the premises.' And what else? (Oh, *do* let me think of something else because it will at least postpone my looking at the wide open space that was Cheapside.) Oh yes – of course – over the sweet shop that used to be MacGregor's Drug Store, that used to be Johnson's Fishmonger and Poulterers – were two floors of rooms that belonged to and were part of the theatre. They were rented out to various business people – Tommy Burton, the Bookie (sorry, Turf Accountant), had his office up there and Withers, the Signwriter, had his workshop up there. His slogan was: 'I made signs before I could talk!'

Oh, and the man who informed me that my mother obviously didn't object to me putting my hands in a bucket of diluted dog shit, he had a room up there as well – up where, Thora? There wasn't anything there any more! There's no point in your looking up there – it's all been knocked into oblivion by a dirty great bull-dozer! By now, Neville had assumed the guise of a guide on a conducted tour: 'And here we have – Cheapside!' he announced. I looked in front of me at another expanse of nothingness. 'Hello, Cheapside that was – and now isn't!' I breathed. But just a minute! I felt it *couldn't* be Cheapside. Cheapside was never a *little* street – was it? I looked carefully – it *can't have been Cheapside*! It all looked so little. If you knock houses down to ground level and clear the rubble away, it should all look so much *bigger*, shouldn't it? – like a room does when the furniture has been moved out whilst you spring clean or decorate? But even the roadway – that has escaped the bulldozer – is *only little*!

No, it can't be the remains of Cheapside – can it? Thora Hird, 6 Cheapside, Morecambe, Lancashire, England, Europe, The World! All gone. No, hold on a minute, be fair – not *all*. Be grateful, they've left the roadway of 'our street', the part where the tram lines used to be – the best repository for horse manure, the part I learned to ride my two and sixpenny Rudge Whitworth bike on (which I painted myself but forgot to sandpaper the already existing chipped enamel of, and consequently after painting over the humps the end product looked rather like a gnarled old tree or someone with varicose veins) – the part I ran across to take the meals to the young mothers that had given birth to brand new babies. They'd left that! – *or it had refused to be moved*!

I wanted to walk down the middle of our street. Wait a minute! what was this? A railing across the top of Cheapside – and worse still, a notice which stated very definitely in red print: NO THROUGH ROAD. Never mind; perhaps one could get in from the far end of what once had been Cheapside – oh no! the notice *there* was even more forbidding: DANGER – PUBLIC ACCESS PROHIBITED. *'Public access prohibited*? No entrance into Cheapside? But everybody used to 'enter' Cheapside, they were either going up Cheapside or going down Cheapside, *to* somewhere or *from* somewhere, or like me and many more they were *living* in Cheapside, having brand new babies in Cheapside, living happy unsophisticated lives in Cheapside – entering and leaving the stage doors of the Royalty in Cheapside! being ill in Cheapside, dying in Cheapside. 'Access Prohibited' to Cheapside because it *wasn't safe*?

Don't be ridiculous! *It was the safest place in the world*! Wasn't our front door open from morning 'til night?

Wasn't I always swanking about Number Six? Weren't all the front steps scrubbed and 'rubbing-stoned' individually and to perfection? Weren't all the grates black-leaded until they shone like diamonds? Hadn't I learned what 'arse' meant in Cheapside? Hadn't I gone to school from 6 Cheapside? Hadn't I been ashamed of the front door key of Number Six and then been more ashamed of myself for being ashamed of it? What about the gold bracelet I won, hadn't that been hidden under my pillow in the front bedroom in Cheapside?

The front bedroom! Hadn't it boasted oil paintings of bullrushes and birds in flight and irises on the panels of the door? And hadn't I come out of the front door of Number Six as a virgin bride to go the Wesleyan Chapel to marry Jimmy Scott? *Access Prohibited – No Through Road*. That's what the 1970 notice on the railings said – KEEP OUT! that's what it implied – KEEP OUT! I stood there, *barred* from my street of happiness and memories. The voice in my mind said, *'Can I come in for a minute, Mrs Hird?'* NO! – NO! – NO: – nobody can come in – keep out! Blink your eyes, Thora – remember you've got your false eyelashes on – push the tears back, love!

'I see the cellar is still there,' comforted Scottie. The cellar – my memories were nudging me again. 'It's your week to bring the coal up, Nev!' 'Have you brushed the cellar steps down, Thora?' 'Let's play in the cellar – you can tie me up with orange box rope and I'll pretend I'm Pearl White in *The Lightning Raiders* and escape – go on, our Nev!'

I could see there was still whitewash on the cellar walls – I wondered how many coats of whitewash had been added to where our last artistic effect adhered.

'Remember our back yard, Thor? Look it's still there!' added Nev.

'Yes, yes, there's our own back yard – no walls left to call over to Mrs Houghton, just the stone base, the part we swilled and then "did" with a yardbrush – they've left that.'

Hey, there's where the 'lav' was! *'Neville, will you fold and cut some newspapers and string them for the lav, please?' 'Did you scrub the seat well with disinfectant, Thora, love?' 'Hey – you needn't sit out there on the lavatory any longer, you can come back in – I've washed up!' 'Neville, come here – have you been smoking in the lavatory? Now look at me – have you? Well, you'd better go and empty some Izal down the pan, before your Dad goes in, because if he smells you've been smoking, he'll go mad!'*

Just the ground left – that's all. Looking like an empty tray, a lonely plateau.

Wait a tick, though – what's that? There! Over there where the orange box full of soil used to stand under the window in the back yard. *That over there!* Growing in our back yard! Can you see what I'm pointing to? Scottie and Nev looked in the direction of where I was pointing.

A bush of weeds had bravely pushed itself through the grey dust and was waving in the breeze – just as though it was beckoning or trying to attract our attention. It couldn't be – surely it couldn't possibly be the *Polygonum Cuspidatum* alias the *Reynoutria Japonica* – defying all adversity? Had it, after years of limited sunshine, burst forth in all its glory in its now wide-open and unlimited space? How marvellous! Long live our back yard! 'Well – 'as my mother would have said, ' – 'it's a nice bit of green and it isn't hurting anybody!' Hurting anybody? It's a crumb of comfort! It's soothing me!

I'm quite sure – or nearly sure – it wasn't our *Polygonum Cuspidatum*. On the other hand, I wasn't near enough to find out, so I'll pretend it *was*. It was on the very spot where our 'nice bit of green' had been. So what matter?

One thing is sure, whichever it was – it will have to go when the new buildings go up. There will be no place for it in the new scheme of things. Mind you, if you *are Polygonum Cuspidatum*, little bush, they'll have a job to get rid of you! When you start to seed in a few weeks' time, I wonder where your seeds will float and eventually come to rest? Please don't float as far as our cottage garden – not even out of affection!

Well, it's no use standing here any longer, just looking and reminiscing.

I wonder what will be built on where Number Six stood? Whatever the end product is, I hope it will contain as much happiness and love as our house did. I hope whoever lives or works on that little area will be as gay and have as big a sense of humour as the Hirds had. Yes, I think *that* will be the best thing I can wish the progress marchers – a sense of humour. They'll probably need it!

'Come on, love,' said Scottie.

'Yes – let's go,' said Nev.

So long, our street. Thank you for everything that stemmed from your having been there, my very happy and colourful childhood, the loving and unforgettable home life that you embraced.

Cheapside! I salute you!

On 28 November 1972, I opened the Arndale Centre, Morecambe. It stood on, what had been, one side of Cheapside (the one step and ordinary flat window side), Sun Street and part of Market St. 'Our side' of Cheapside still remained an undeveloped plateau. The main doors of the shopping centre were graced by two large brass handles. By the time the opening ceremony was completed the same handles had been mounted on to a polished wooden plaque . . . duly inscribed, and presented to me by S. H. Chippendale Esq., of Town and City Properties. You've guessed haven't you? They were the 'solid gold' handles off the mansion doors of one of my childhood fantasies. *The Royalty Theatre dress circle door handles!!*

48

'Round the World in 140 Days'

I'd often thought how nice it would be to be able to go to Australia under the banner of doing a job there. Well, it happened when I was invited to star at the Theatre in Perth, during the Festival. The tempting tit-bit about the invitation *was*, that I was to rehearse three weeks and play four weeks. The reason I mention the tempting tit-bit is that I had previously been invited to work in Australia – on about six occasions – but the periods of work they offered had always been a year or six months and I'd been unable to accept because I never seemed to have that amount of time free – consequently when I was invited to go for a seven week visit, I was delighted.

You are already aware – well I think you are – I'm sure I've written it somewhere in the book, that Scottie and I are both 'travel mad!' So as soon as it was decided that I would accept the Perth Festival job, one could *see* the wheels beginning to turn in Scottie's brain regarding something we had always wanted and intended to do.

'Well,' he began, 'it would seem to me to be a wonderful opportunity to go around the world! Aye? What do you think?' I opened my mouth to answer in the affirmative, but I didn't get the chance. It was one of those odd moments when my quiet Scot's husband was carried away with enthusiasm. 'I mean,' he continued, 'we're half way round the world when we get to Perth, then after you've finished your work there we can fly to Melbourne and then Sydney and then we can fly to Fiji and see the Hacketts, then we can fly to Hawaii and then . . .' 'Hey, hold on,' I interrupted, 'where's Singapore? I've always wanted to stay at the Raffles Hotel.' Scottie kindly told me where Singapore was, and assured me that on our flight out to Perth we could break our journey at Singapore for a couple of days and we could stay at the Raffles Hotel. We did.

Oooo Mate, it's places like the Raffles in Singapore, Reid's Hotel in Madeira and the Fairmont on Nob Hill in San Francisco that convince me I have been here before. Raffles Hotel thrilled me pink! *Full Somerset Maugham period!* I was humming the theme music of the Somerset Maugham television series all the time we were there. For instance, the *hall* of our suite was bigger than most modern hotel rooms and the bathroom was as large as a flat.

And before anyone reading this remarks, 'Ridiculous!' let me add, 'Yes – it is – *these* days – because not many visitors want that kind of place, either the style or the price – but when Raffles was built the life style was very different and believe me or believe me not there's still a great atmosphere of the turn of the century there and I loved it.' Thank God I can still get a lot of pleasure out of what, to some folks, would seem unimportant things. When I looked at the pale grey linen note paper on the beautiful desk in our lounge at Raffles, I saw that under their own crest, which topped the sheet, was Thora Hird printed in gold lettering and on the other side of the desk another batch of note paper bearing the name James Scott. All right, I know we were paying for it – but I was real chuffed and I don't care who knows it.

In the Street of Fame (or shame!) we saw – and I'm not exaggerating, the most beautiful, sequin-gowned, elegantly wigged and made-up women!!! Pardon the expression! The driver of our Trisha, a quaint bicycle with a sidecar for two and a cheerful driver to pedal you around, started to nudge me as he grinned all over his face and nodded his head in the direction of 'the beauties'. He nudged me so much that eventually I had to admit to him that I *knew* they were fellers – mind you, their make-up was smashing and I could have wished for a closer look – and, indeed, nearly got it because one of the 'gorgeous slant-eyed beauties' approached Scottie and was about to offer his/her (delete whichever is not applicable!) wares, when our driver, 'the cycling terror of Singapore', known to his friends as 'the Reg Harris of the Chinese quarter', took off like a catapult. He peddled like mad, laughing his head off, all the way back to the Raffles. I was sorry to say good night to him, his shorts and shirt were spotless, somebody had been using the biological action, he only had the camera right hand side teeth left in his upper set, but this made his grin not only lovable but unforgettable. When Scottie tipped him the 'slice of melon' grin grew even wider and it was a happy man who threw his leg over the Trisha leather driving seat and peddled off – still grinning!

My engagement in Perth was enjoyable for many reasons. The very first morning we walked out of our hotel to go to rehearsal, a lady and gentleman walking along the pavement saw me, and with cries of 'Eee, is it Thora?' approached me with affection. 'Eee-ee-ee, well!' the lady laughed, 'we never thought we'd see you in Australia, did we Dad?' she said, nudging the gentleman with her. Dad agreed, I think he always did! When I remarked that she sounded as though she came from Lancashire, she informed me with glee that a lot of the immigrants in Perth 'were from the north! In fact,' she assured me, 'most of 'em!' And she was right.

Another reason for my happiness in Perth was that I was appearing in Walter Greenwood's *Saturday Night at the Crown*, the play I had appeared in hundreds of times. As a matter of fact, I played the part of Ada Thorpe for the thousandth time on my second night's performance at the theatre in Perth and a huge surprise cake, covered in lit candles, was carried on stage at the final curtain. But wait, I haven't finished about the happiness stakes yet. The director of the Perth Theatre, Edgar Metcalfe (what a clever director, and as nice a person as you would meet on a day's march!), extremely capable and, being an actor, and a good 'un, able to *show* members of the company how he wanted a line delivered. He not only got the best out of me but out of the rest of the cast, too. Steven Porter, who did all my publicity, was fantastic, and as Australian as a kangaroo. I've put that bit in on purpose because Edgar Metcalfe is English with grass roots in Lancashire, and I have no wish to sound biased about Edgar. Bless them for making our visit so very happy.

Another blessing was that my television series *Meet the Wife* and *The First Lady* had both been on the Australian television screens, so people felt they knew me.

One of the many functions we attended was in a sort of Assembly Rooms. Everyone there was British and by the time we arrived, after the show at the theatre, the guests were well into the Saint Bernard's Waltz.

As we approached the room by a long corridor, the MC spotted me – he rushed up to the orchestra waving his arms and silenced the lilting strains with a loud, 'Shut up – she's here!' Everyone stopped dancing as though they were playing 'Statues' or as though it was a spot dance. There were tables and chairs round the sides of the room where refreshments were being fully taken and enjoyed. I was bustled to the mike on the bandstand.

I started to make a very short speech, but there was something wrong with the mike (there so often is). So, using my 'back of the gallery' voice, I said I would go to each table for a chat. This was received with loud cheers. By now everyone was clustered round the bandstand with bits of paper and pens for my autograph. Bless 'em' all, but I've often wondered how many of the bits of paper, fag packets, serviettes and snapshots that folks like me so gratefully sign, are kept! And another thing that always strikes me as strange is, the person who asks for your autograph never wants it for themselves, it's always, 'Will you sign this for my niece', or 'Please – it's for my little grandchild!' or 'If you wouldn't mind, it's for my little boy, he always watches you on the telly!' Well, as I say, bless 'em all, the moment they stop asking us, we'll know we're out of work! As long as anybody is sufficiently interested in me to bother to ask for my autograph, I will be sufficiently interested in them to sign it!

Asking the autograph hunters very politely if they would kindly return to their various tables where I would sign my autograph with pleasure, I then moved away from the mike and made my way to the first table. I asked a lady who was sitting there if she was glad she had emigrated, and she replied, 'Oh yes, Thora love, y'see, we came here with our son and daughter and they have both married Australians and our grandchildren have been born here – so where else would we want to be?' I thought that made sense, all the family and loved ones together. At the next table I asked a lady, 'Are you happy here?' Like a shot from a gun she attacked me verbally. 'I 'ate it!' she exploded, 'I've 'ated every minute I've been here!' 'Oh dear – well never mind,' I said, as gently as I could, 'perhaps you'll be happier when you get used to it – how long have you been here?' She gave me a piercing look as though *I* had persuaded her to emigrate. 'Eighteen years!' she exclaimed. 'And I've 'ated every bloody minute!' I felt it was time I moved on to the next table.

We were shown great kindness in Melbourne and in Sydney, though how the 'ell either place knew I was there I'll never know because after we left Perth I was travelling as Mrs James Scott.

Our next port of call was Fiji.

What can I say about Fiji? Oh, mate! A couple of our dearest friends live in Fiji, Mr and Mrs Jack Hackett. It's a friendship that both Scottie and I treasure. I've known

Jack Hackett and his wife Lena 'forever' as you might say, in fact, it was Lena's bike I used to borrow when we were kids. I'll tell you why. You see, my bike, the halfcrown one, that I had black lacquered without rubbing down with sandpaper first, so that it looked like a jumble of black varicose veins on two wheels – you remember? – I told you about it earlier on in this saga – well, it was not as posh as Lena's – but I scored because I had a tennis racquet and four old tennis balls in a string bag. The bag, rather on the lines of the present-day net jobs that you buy oranges or apples in, *was* for tennis balls.

I would ride around Cheapside, Sun Street, Anderton Street and Moss Lane clutching the tennis racquet and string bag of balls across the handlebars and, in return for the loan of the bike, I'd lend Lena the racquet and the string thing with the tennis balls in for when she rode round. Incidentally, neither of us could or did play tennis – but that never came into it! It was merely that the racquet and balls added a bit of tone. I mean, if it so happened that anyone, seeing either of us riding along with the tennis racquet held with authority across the handlebars and the four tennis balls in their string thing swinging to the rhythm of the peddling, if they wanted to think we were either of us on our way to Wimbledon, that was up to them.

The bit that you might not understand, and come to think of it, neither can I now, so many years after – sometimes I would borrow Lena's nappa gloves that had a bit of beaver or some sort of fur, round the cuffs. Elegance personified eh? Cotton dress, short white socks, racquet and balls on bike – and fur trimmed gloves, on a hot day!! I wonder what a psychiatrist would make of all that. Ambition? Swank? Or being a bit loose in the lid?

Any road, Lena Hackett has remained just as good a friend and just as generous to this day. Jack and his brother, Desmond, used to be in the St Mary's School Concert, and 'our Nev' and I were in Miss Nelson's School Concert. When we were all school children, there was great rivalry in a friendly way, but even so, Jack and Neville became great friends as Lena and I have always been. I suppose 'Hackett' as I call him, is one of the most interesting and intelligent characters I am lucky enough to know. And I'm not saying that because he's an OBE and wears a pair of cuff links given to him by Her Most Gracious Majesty, in recognition of his splendid work. Good old Jack, you're lovely. (If you read this, Lena, so are you!)

Yes, we had an unforgettable time in Suva. One occasion would be impossible to forget. The 'Tabua' Ceremony, it was great! The 'Tabua' Ceremony, at which I was the guest of honour, is really a very moving and important affair and, although I cannot understand why they considered *me* important enough to bestow it on, it *did* happen and it's one of the times in my very happy and wonderful life that I shall be able to tell my grandchildren about without any exaggeration.

When Scottie and I and the Hacketts arrived at the appointed place, which was a thriving Sports Club run by Harry Charman MBE, an Englishman, I was presented with the most beautiful bouquet of small orchids in various colours, by a little Fijian boy. He was extremely handsome and was wearing his best clothes, western style. (I don't mean cowboy clothes, I mean the sort our little English lads wear.) He was also wearing a pair of well-polished leather shoes that should have had laces – but hadn't. He was about eight years old and a real little charmer.

After the usual introductions and photographs the ceremony began. It was all in Fijian but an interpreter, a Fijian headmaster, echoed the words for me in English. I wish I could remember every word that the ceremony embraces, it really was beautiful. They told me that they were not a wealthy race of people but, had they been, they would have given me pearls and precious things. However, they said they wished to bestow on me one of *their* most precious possessions – a Tabua – a whale's tooth.

The man who spoke the ceremonial words had a beautiful, soft voice and I sat there trying my best not to cry. As I looked at these wonderful people who were dressed in native costume – a sort of wraparound, brightly coloured skirt – I thought 'Eee, Thorird, this is all happening to *you* and you used to scrub and yellow stone your mother's front steps!' D'you wonder I felt like weeping?

They then presented me with the whale's tooth, which was hanging on a kind of mayoral chain made of very cleverly interwoven hemp of some kind. It's one of my many treasures and I look at it very often – with affection.

Incidentally, we had to get written permission from the High Commissioner to bring it from the island, or should I say, 'For it to leave the island'. That's how important a whale's tooth is.

Although we still had some travelling to do, I'd like to jump ahead to our return to England where we had to declare 'it' – the tooth – at Heathrow Airport Customs.

'Have you anything to declare?' the customs official enquired.

'Yes,' I answered, '... a whale's tooth!'

He was a very smart and good-looking young man and displayed a smashing set of teeth as he laughingly said, 'Oh, come off it, Thora – you're not on the telly now!'

When the time came for Scottie and me to leave Fiji and the Hacketts, we did so rather reluctantly because we were sorry to leave our good friends. I think as one gets older the 'Heart and Flowers' element creeps in and whether one tries to dispel the thought of, 'I wonder if we shall ever meet again?' or not – you *think* that. Don't you agree? Well, I know *I* do. But there again, I am what is commonly referred to as, 'a soppy 'aporth'.

In the case of the Hacketts, it's daft to think the above because they fly to England to visit their brilliant surgeon son almost as often as I go to Oxford Street. Come to think of it – their journey from Fiji doesn't take much longer than when I go to Oxford Street! And anybody who has waited for an 88 or 12 bus in the Bayswater Road will understand what I mean!

We were bound for Honolulu and we looked like a couple of sticks of liquorice, we were so brown. As the plane took off my excitement eclipsed any heartache, the reason being that our daughter, Jan, and our three-year-old granddaughter, Daisy, were to join us in

Hawaii a couple of days after our arrival.

I think I'm pretty safe in saying it is almost impossible to be bored in Hawaii. Even so, like any mother or grandmother, I was ticking the hours off with loving impatience until their arrival.

Scottie and I arrived at the airport to meet them (much too early – of course). I stood with a couple of heavily perfumed 'leis' hanging from my arm, champing at the bit and ready to fling a lei round their respective necks as I greeted them with the word 'Aloha!' (Oh, Dorothy Lamour has nothing on me, when the mood takes me!) The planes from Los Angeles were touching down like a hail storm, there were so many, and quite honestly it wasn't until a little vehicle, rather like a dodgem car, carrying an airline official, stacks of luggage and our two favourite girls, was under my nose, that I saw it! Even then I'd have missed the joy of the last two yards of their approach if a little voice hadn't called out rather shyly, 'Hi! Ganny! Hi! Popa!'

How in the name of goodness can one write about moments like that? Well I'm not clever enough to do so, and that's for sure. I forgot the leis, even though I had cramp in the arm they were hanging from, I forgot the 'Aloha bit!' (sorry, Miss Lamour) and as I crushed first Jan to me and then Daisy, I crushed the flowers in the leis as well, but I didn't give a damn. We were all together safely and that's what mattered. You can't buy moments such as those, can you? It's a good job really that affection costs nothing. If it did, with inflation as it is at the moment, nobody would be able to afford it! Wouldn't life be awful if we couldn't show a bit of love now and again?

Eventually, after a couple of choruses of 'Goodbye Hawaii', Jan, Daisy, Scottie and I flew off to Los Angeles. Scottie and I of course stayed with Jan and Mel in their Beverly Hills house. Every time we visit them it's lovable and interesting but on this particular visit there was an added enjoyment because we didn't really know how long we were staying. I don't mean we intended staying for ever, I mean we had no idea whether our visit would be two, four, six or eight weeks. Every time Scottie and I opened our mouths to say, 'I think it's time we were thinking of . . .' Jan would throw up her hands and say, 'If you are talking about going back to London, *don't* tell me, I don't want to know until just before you leave for the airport. I can't bear the unhappiness of that "last day you're here bit!" ' It's nice to be loved, isn't it? I mean, it's nice to be loved dearly by your daughter, and it's an added bonus when your son-in-law loves you as well. And it's quadruple green shield stamps when *you* love *them* in the same way.

It was during that particular visit that Scottie and I were taken to the theatre by a couple of very good friends of ours, Bunny and Maurice Charles. It's extraordinary how many friends we have accumulated in Beverly Hills, all of whom willingly go out of their way to give us a good time. Thank heavens most of them visit England, which gives us a chance to reciprocate. On the night I'm talking about, Bunny and Maurice were taking us to see *No, No, Nanette*. We had a splendid dinner before the show, in the theatre restaurant, the food was super, the wines excellent and, add to that, the head waiter was from Preston, Lancashire,

England. 'Nuff said! Well, there's nothing more *to* say, is there?

The production of *Nanette* was very good, and we all enjoyed the show, so you'll gather that by the time we were having coffee and a liqueur in a Mexican coffee house, we were all in a happy mood. And, as my mother would have said, 'We weren't hurting anybody.'

My husband has quite a few traits like my dad and one of 'em *is*, that he has never *ever* said to me with regards to my work, remarks like, 'Oh you *were* good!' or '*You* were the best!' or 'I think you are *marvellous*.' He'll criticize me now and again, and I'll take it because nine times out of ten he's right – the tenth time out of ten, he's wrong, and that's when I argue! However, I have my own way of knowing when he thinks I'm 'not so bad', 'all right', 'competent', or 'a touch of the professional', – he says nowt! I understand him very well.

On the particular evening in Beverly Hills I've just been talking about, as we came out of the theatre Scottie slipped his arm through mine and said, without any emotion, 'If they ever put *No, No, Nanette* on in London, you could eat the part of the maid!' And that was that. I never even answered him.

We eventually arrived back in London after a fantastic holiday. It was only a few months after we returned home that I was asked to play Pauline, the maid, in the London production of *No, No, Nanette* at Drury Lane. Once again, being under the Gemini sign, I had to decide which of two jobs I wanted to do – I couldn't do 'em both – it was a case of telly versus stage. I was inclined a little towards 'the job on the box' but both Felix de Wolfe and Scottie (who, in fairness, I must say, never persuades me against 'my witch's water feeling' – if I feel it strongly enough) advised me to go back into the theatre, especially in the part of Pauline. I did, and I'm happy to say they were right.

There's one little story I'd like to recall. It happened on the last night of the run of *No, No, Nanette.* I was sitting in Annie Roger's dressing room, we'd had a matinee and we always had tea in Annie's room, because we're good friends and enjoy each other's company.

Just before 'the half hour' was called, my dresser came into Annie's room and said there was a lady to see me. I was expecting a lady friend so I set off for my dressing room. *En route* I met Scottie, who was coming to see the last performance, so we both made our way to my dressing room. This little story took place during the SOS ('Save on Something') electricity shortage period, so, of course, I had only left a very small light on in my room.

As Scottie and I entered my dressing room, what we saw in the shadows was a young woman with her arms full of long-stemmed deep red roses and white lilies (I don't mean funeral lilies, I mean the other sort).

I said 'Good evening' to her, and as I did so, she burst out laughing. I knew that laugh. So did Scottie, who at that moment was switching my dressing table lights on. I can remember thinking during the second before the lights came on, 'That sounds just like Jan!' The lights came on – and – it *was* Jan! Honest to God, I've never had such a wonderful surprise in my life – I stood there as though I'd been turned to stone – it sounds silly to say that, but it's true. Jan's voice brought me back to life, she just stood there holding all the lovely flowers and said, ever so quietly, 'Did you think I'd let you fold at the Lane without seeing you?' She'd flown from Beverly Hills, nearly six thousand miles for *one* day just to watch her mum 'having a go!' I reckon her seat for the play was the most expensive ever sold at the Lane, eh? It was a great night for me, I must say – I don't mean *I* was great, I mean the whole evening was great! Where I had to do a little tap dance in the show, the orchestra had prepared a 'farewell surprise' and instead of playing the usual music they broke into 'The Stripper!'

All right then, the London production of *No, No, Nanette* wasn't a roaring success, but *I* enjoyed myself, and as far as (to quote Scottie) 'eating the part of Pauline' went, I perhaps didn't do that – but I spread it on my bread as artistically and professionally as I could!

49

Ours is a nice house . . .

I have a lot of faults. I don't mean evil, wicked, sinful faults, I mean little, everyday, not very clever, 'you'd hardly credit it' faults. I am also incapable of doing a lot of little ordinary jobs that women friends of mine take in their stride.

For instance, I can't mend a fuse, I can't read a road map correctly, I can't drive a car, which is perhaps just as well as I can't read a road map. I have no sense of direction and I am still trying to work out how, when I press a switch, the room fills with light! I should give up trying to work out how, when I lift the telephone receiver with one hand and then put the index finger end of the other hand into a series of little numbered holes which enable me to turn the dial to any number I so desire, in no time at all my daughter's voice in Beverly Hills says, quite clearly, 'Hello, is that you, Mummy?' (I haven't even worked it out how it happens when I ring my next door neighbour!!) As for a gramophone record, radio or television – nuff said!

I was thinking of letting you know that I'm not so bad at pressing flowers, flower arrangement, writing poetry. I'm very good at cleaning of all descriptions, including brass, copper and silver (and I don't leave any deposits of Brasso, or Silvo in the crinkly bits). I'm excellent at washing up, which Scottie says I always make into a production because I always wash behind and round the taps, the top of the cooker, the top of the 'fridge, wipe any splashes off the kitchen cupboards and then wash the washing up bowl and dry it, having poured the soapy water out of the bowl into the sink so that I can wash round the sink with a final flourish! And all that is at each washing up session! Sewing, not bad, not good! Knitting, pathetic! Darning, very good, but nobody does it anymore. I can boast about two things (and don't misunderstand that remark, although I do wear a 38" bra), my handwriting, and my figures – not my own figure, I'm not talking about that, I mean, *fig–ers,* sums and keeping an eye on the building society books!

My husband tells me, and he'd tell you, I am interested in money only to the extent of keeping out of debt. It is due to his enquiring as I go out, 'Have you got some money on you?' that I ever have.

When Scottie is doing jobs such as laying stone paths in the garden at the cottage, a spot of carpentry in our Mews house, or anything of that nature, I am a competent labourer. I know a gimlet from a screwdriver, and a screwdriver from a brace and bit or a bradawl. It is yours truly who holds the bucket of Flash when himself is up the ladder washing anything I can't reach. Oh, and that's something else I'm no good at, going up ladders. Only the other week, I was using the step ladder – I wanted to wash some old fashioned stew jars I have 'on show' on top of a kitchen cupboard. All of a sudden, I cried out, 'Scottie!' He flew into the kitchen and in an alarmed voice enquired, 'What's up?' I replied, '*I* am – and it's making me feel dizzy!' He was most relieved that nothing was really wrong and burst out laughing. 'Dizzy?' he said, 'you can't be, you're only up three treads!'

In other words, though not indispensable, I am quite useful in my simple way and I am always there 'to take it out on' if anything goes wrong, whether it's my fault or not, which does happen occasionally. Every wife must know just what I mean. Credit where it's due – he's the engine driver and I'm the oilrag!

And while we are on the subject of 'things I'm not good at', I'll just tell you a little anecdote which unfortunately was one of those incidents that couldn't be helped. Well, perhaps, it could . . . but let's see what you think.

I'm rather fond of milk-chocolate-covered raisins and I'm more than rather fond of nibbling a few when I'm in bed at night, reading, before I drop off. I don't mean every night, I mean just odd nights. No I *don't* mean 'odd nights', as used in the expression 'What an odd sort of carry on!' I mean, odd, not exactly divisible by two, casual, out of the way, apart!

One day I was in the toffee shop with the intention of purchasing a quarter pound of the little brown beauties, when suddenly I thought, 'Oh, blow the expense, I'll get a pound while I'm here!' (I was in a rather reckless spending mood because I'd received a cheque that morning from the BBC covering a *Meet the Wife* tenth repeat, in some far off Zululand, or some such place. It was for 27p!)

We sleep in a fourposter bed and the head of same is

in front of many rows of bookshelves – are you with me? Well, listen carefully or you won't be. When one is in bed, the most accessible shelf holds a telephone, a radio alarm, the books we are currently reading, a few throat sweets, and some indigestion tablets. It *had* also held, on quite a few occasions a little paper bag with my quarter pound of milk-chocolate-covered raisins in it. Often – as we lay on the love couch, Scottie, my romantic husband, the gay galliard of *my* life, has said to me, 'You're not going to ruckle that paper bag half the night, are you?' or, 'What are you eating?' or, 'Oh, hell, are you going to read and eat chocolate-covered raisins until the early hours?' Now fair do's – he'd every right – because each time I raised my arm and hand over my shoulder to reach the little paper bag, I pulled the bedclothes off Scottie, *nearly* waking him, and the noise of my hand delving into the paper bag *completely* waking him! And he didn't like it . . . Well, he wouldn't – would he?

It was the night of the day I had splashed out on the whole pound of chocolate-covered raisins that a very good idea struck me. This was it. If I put about a dozen milk chocolate raisins in a soft 'rustle-less' face tissue, I could then lay the silent tissue in a small indentation in the duvet and, without a sound, read as well as have my midnight feast! I mean, let's face it, it was the least I could do, as I did not wish to disturb, annoy or hurt my beloved spouse in any way.

Unfortunately, 'the very good idea' did not dawn on me until after I was comfortably and snugly settled in the four poster. To try and see *me* under a large duvet is almost impossible and a sight for sore eyes, because I only use one pillow; so consequently I sort of dissolved into the bed. (Years ago, when we first acquired a duvet, Scottie got into bed one night and as he lay down he nearly jumped out of his skin. *He didn't know I was already in bed until a cold toe touched his calf!*)

Any road, on this 'good idea' night, Scottie was sound asleep so I carefully raised my arm above my head and my hand groped along the shelf for the pound of milk-chocolate-covered raisins. My body remained immobile, like one of the stone effigies you see on top of ancient stone coffins. Only my hand and arm were active, silently slithering along the shelf like a well trained snake. Ah! A finger tip touched the paper bag! Sh! Now all I had to do was to get my hand in the bag, silently, and procure about a dozen tempting morsels. I honestly never intended what happened next but there was nothing I could do to stop it! Like a drip from a tap, two or three milk chocolate raisins dribbled out of the bag – and then – the whole pound cascaded out of the bag like a thundering waterfall – all over Scottie's face! It was like a brown hailstorm! I'm laughing now – come to think of it, I laughed *then* – but Scottie wasn't laughing – I mean, fair do's, what a way to be woken up!

It took us quite some time to find and gather in the pound of milk-chocolate-covered raisins – there's a lot in a pound y'know. Upon Scottie's startled awakening he had jerked up into a sort of sitting position, and the MCCRs had found their way into the bed, the duvet was sprinkled with 'em and a few had been squashed into the carpet after we had sprung out of bed. I won't record the dialogue of the next ten minutes. It's private!

I didn't drop anything on Scottie again – well – not for seven weeks I didn't. And then, one night, putting the book I was currently reading back on the aforementioned shelf without looking what I was doing (I was using the well trained snake method again) *my* book caught *his* book and knocked it off the shelf and *his* book fell on his face. Needless to say it woke him up . . . Well it would. It was Tolstoy's *War and Peace*!

Sometimes, now, when I'm reading a big book, like, let us say, Antonia Fraser's *Mary, Queen of Scots* I sleep in the guest room!

Well, you can't blame him for making a little request like that, can you?

I'm not going to tell you that once we were in Scarborough and I moved the reading lamp from the bedside table on my side of the bed, and balanced it on the rather wide mahogany bed-head so that it was between us and we could both read. It fell. Not on me . . . On Scottie . . . But I'm not going to tell you that!

My brother Neville . . . 'Our Nev' . . . 'The Admiral', died in May 1975. A piece of the happy and loving pattern of my life snapped off and was lost forever.

Nev died on a Saturday, and I was opening in a new play, at Brighton, on the following Monday, the dress rehearsal for the show was on the Sunday evening, the play was a comedy. I'm grateful it was. I'm not a stupid woman but as I stood in my dressing room putting my make-up on, I felt . . . somehow . . . I could imagine Nev saying, 'I'm sorry this has happened just before your first night our kid!' For the very first time during all the many plays I have appeared in, I was 'off', so that I could travel to Morecambe in Lancashire to the cremation. My capable understudy took over.

It was a beautiful sunny day, as the sad cortége made its slow way to the crematorium, men who had worked with and had been friends of Nev, respectfully walked on each side of the hearse. I found myself thinking '... they've all put their best suits on and a clean white shirt and a black tie!' It's ridiculous to say that a dark suit, a clean white shirt and a black tie looks sad because I don't suppose it really does ... but ... well ... I thought even their well polished shoes looked sad. The amount of people that had congregated at the crematorium denoted that many, many others had respected and loved Nev.

When we were kids, there was a joke that many comedians used, it went something like this: 'I was having a bit of a walk round the cemetery the other day, I'd gone to collect a few jam jars because my mother was going to make some jam!' That's *it*! I mean, that's the joke ... and it always seemed to get a big laugh. When Nev and I were young there weren't any granite or marble vases on graves, the popular receptacle for flowers was an empty jam jar ... usually pressed well into the soil of the grave top so that the wind wouldn't blow it over! The aforementioned 'joke' was usually performed by Neville if, when we were children, we ever walked past a cemetery. Do you know? That old gag came into my head as we got out of the car at the crematorium ... right in the midst of my numb grief. I wondered for a moment, if Nev had made me think of it! *I* think he had.

The service was over. As we got back into the car a tall, distinguished looking man took my hand and gave it a gentle understanding squeeze, his eyes were full of sadness and they looked straight into mine. We didn't speak. The car moved off and had only gone a little way when I realized who he was . . . 'ELOPYAM!', our Nev's best friend when they were lads! Reg . . . who used to work at the MAYPOLE . . . hence his nickname. I hadn't seen him for thirty years. There were neighbours there 'from our Cheapside days' who had attended out of love and respect. Yes . . . they were all there . . .

50

'All down for the finale – please!'

It's over twenty years ago that I spoke at a luncheon at the Piccadilly Hotel for some charity or other, and the gentleman who was sitting on my left was in quite a comfortable position on *The Empire News*. Don't you love that expression, 'in quite a comfortable position!'? Well, never mind whether you do or do not, he turned to me and without any preliminaries, stated, 'Thora – you should write a book!' Please note, I have just mentioned a bit of history. I don't mean the chap who was telling me I should write a book – I mean mentioning *The Empire News*. There's no *Empire News*, full of juicy bits of news of the empire, any more – dead as a dodo – just as there is no *Sunday Chronicle* – which my father swore by! Now there's another marvellous expression, 'swore by!' Swore what by? The times I have heard friends and neighbours in the north use that expression when they have been giving someone a cure for a complaint. They would always end up by saying, 'Well, you just try that love – it'll do the trick, my mother swears by it!' Actually in that last statement you've got 'two expressions for the price of one', because 'do the trick' is another one often used, meaning 'to cure', 'do the job', or 'fix it'.

Any road up, let's get back to the fellow in the *Empire News* who was in quite a comfortable position. He wasn't the first person to have *told* me I should write a book. There had been quite a little band of folks who had *told* me I should. *Asked* me, 'why don't you?' or *enquired*, 'have you ever thought of?' Well, I had 'thought of' – quite a few times, but then I always thought just as quickly, 'who'd want to read it?' Anyway, by the time I had decided to have a go I was always too busy, which stresses once more (with feeling) how very lucky I have been and am, to be employed so much in the kind of work I enjoy.

All right then, about ten years ago I started to make a list of incidents to do with my childhood, but quite honestly, that was about as far as I got! Once again my work, especially on television, really *did* occupy every moment of my time. Rehearsals, learning the words, dress fittings, opening a fête here and a bazaar there. Add to that the fact that I am a housewife as well – and it doesn't leave more time to try and write a book does it?

The bit of paper with the list of childhood incidents written on it got pushed to the back of a drawer.

Six years ago, our daughter Jan gave birth to a baby girl, Daisy Ann Tormé – a golden-cum-marigold-cum-carroty-haired little smasher! You would, of course, expect me, like any other red-blooded grandmother in the world, to rave about her, to tell you how very clever she is, and that her IQ is far and away beyond the average. You would also expect me to say that she can execute a little number like, 'Don't jump off the roof, Dad, you'll make a hole in the yard!' with professional expertise. You would agree, I think, that as a loving grandmother I have a right to think and say, 'She's wonderful!' Well, you would wouldn't you? And you'd be right! I *am* saying and thinking and raving because – well – she's our grand-daughter, isn't she? Bless her little heart! 'Nuff said, Thor – do shut up! The dictionary (my constant companion) says, *'Grandmother, a father or mother's mother,'* and the next word is *'Grandmotherly, like a grandmother, over anxious, fussy!'* Need I say more?

Two years ago, our grandson, James Scott Tormé, practically marched into the world to the swirl of bagpipes! He's a real handsome lad, and no mistake, but don't worry, I'm not going to start on about him. One thing I will say, if you'll allow me, he's the spittin' image of my husband. (That's another of those expressions I heard so often during my childhood. According to the dictionary it means, 'an exact replica, the exact likeness of, as like him as if he had spit out of his mouth.' Well perhaps the expression isn't too savoury but it's descriptive enough. He's named after my husband, James Scott – or to put it more correctly: 'whose namesake he is!' Isn't nature wonderful? Especially the hereditary bit? Young James has the same sort of ears as Scottie, same sort of nose, same sort of little cleft in his chin and the same sort of expressive eyes as his mummy and Scottie. It's fantastic isn't it?

Any road, there's your hereditary bit for yer! James Scott Tormé, the spittin' image of Scottie, his grandfather: Daisy Ann, the spittin' image of her daddy, Mel Tormé; Jan, our daughter, the spittin' image of her daddy, my husband; but – hold on, nobody, but nobody, is the spittin' image of yours truly, me (and you can't blame 'em!), except the thousand women who all claimed they were the spittin' image of me when I was doing the *Meet the Wife* and *The First Lady* series! But of course, they weren't relatives and could afford to risk what folks might say.

So, patient readers, after various anecdotes and going off the subject and back on to it many times, here I am, telling you that it is for our two grandchildren that I have recorded some of the events of my wonderfully blessed happy and loving life – up to now! You see, because Jan and Mel and the grandchildren are domiciled in Beverly Hills, USA, and although we nip over there as often as possible, it isn't as if they lived in the next street. (And with inflation as it is at the moment, who the 'ell would *want* them to live in the next street?)

What I mean is, Scottie and I can't take Daisy and James out for tea or take them into a toy shop or into the park each week, thereby being able to bore 'em stiff with the remark, 'When I was a little girl . . .' (Of course, Scottie wouldn't say 'girl' – well, it's to be hoped he wouldn't.) I was only kidding about the 'bore 'em stiff' bit, because we all know kids love stories about yesteryear, hence the popularity of fairy stories. Not that I'm suggesting that our three front steps in Cheapside were ever likely to turn into a golden coach! But just a minute – did they? That's quite debatable really, when I consider what a happy life I lead.

It dawned on me that my young grandchildren would never *really* know me, I mean the *real* me. All right, they know *me* well enough as Ganny from

England where the Red Buses come from and as the Ganny they come to see in London because it's great fun and there's a musical toilet roll in the 'loo'! Even so, I wanted them to know I wasn't always a 'star' of the theatre and television. (Excuse me using that four letter word, but it was unavoidable in that context.) And it was with that thought in mind that I rescued my list of childhood incidents from the back of the drawer.

I would try and write a book – not for publication – but for James Scott and Daisy Ann.

I want them to know how much I enjoyed my childhood and to let them know I wasn't always a grown up Ganny – like I am now. I want them to know that my childhood with 'our Nev' was really no different from theirs as far as happiness and love and the feelings of joy and sorrow are concerned. I want them to know that although I scrubbed and yellow-stoned 'our front steps' and blackleaded our coal hole and grates when I was only a little girl, it wasn't because I was badly done by or that I had cruel parents. It was to make me capable of running a home and to give me a sense of responsibility when I became a housewife (always providing that some day someone would pop the question!).

I want them to realize that 6, Cheapside, was more than just part of a street, and hecky plonk, were we proud of it. We didn't have electric light (although we all wanted it and eventually had it installed), the houses had gas brackets and gas mantles and we all rather tried to outdo each other with our glass shades that surrounded the gas mantles. I want them to realize that, although we were doing our homework by gaslight and there was no magic tap which when turned produced hot water, we weren't living in the squalor of the Dickensian period and I wasn't going to school in a crinoline. In fact, I would *like* them to know that my knicker legs – with the needlework trimming and either blue or pink baby ribbon threaded through – were the shortest knicker legs in our school! Which goes to show I measured 'em during needle work class with my linen tape measure against some of my school pals' knicker legs! Proof positive that I was blessed with a mother who was a good thirty or forty years ahead of her time.

It will be nice for them to learn how much happiness and love their own mother had given and does give to Scottie and me. They will be wise to listen to their Sunday School teacher, who also happens to be their loving Mummy, and not only listen, but digest. By the time they are old enough to read and understand this book I feel almost sure they will have been taught by their parents that, although a lot of the best things in life are free, there are lot of things that are not – therefore, anything they want badly enough is worth working, saving and waiting for!

I want them to know how much I enjoy, early morning on a beautiful summer's day . . . flowers, wild or cultivated . . . the smell of newly cut grass . . . arriving home after a walk on a frosty autumn afternoon just in time for toasted brown bread and honey, and freshly brewed tea . . . and the scent of chrysanthemums around. I want them to know how much I have always detested hypocrisy, dishonesty, cruelty in any form; liver, kidney, sweetbreads or offal of any description.

I'd like them to believe that if they cast their bread on the waters it invariably comes back buttered. I want them to know how dearly they are loved by their mummy and daddy and that the 'bonus in the love stakes' is because, added to the joy of their existence, they are part of their Mummy, who in turn, is part of us. I want them to know that I am called Ganny because on the first little card Daisy sent to us, announcing her arrival when she was about one hour old, was written 'To my Ganny and Popa'. (Extremely *well* written, I thought for an hour-old child!) I don't really want them to know that their dear mother had missed the 'R' out of 'Granny'. And who could blame her? When only one hour before she'd given birth to, quite probably, the first Lady President of the USA! So Ganny I've remained. There's nothing the matter with a moniker like that is there? Well *I* like it!

Before long, Scottie and I will be with them once again, staying in the lovely little cottage which Jan and Mel gave to us, and which is in the grounds of their house. I won't bother them with any of the details of this effort of mine because we shall be too busy listening to the description of all the things that have happened since our last visit, three months ago. Daisy will fill us in with all her school news, and tell us how many more widths of the pool she can swim. Young James Scott will be looking forward to another birthday, to the accompaniment *not* of one of his daddy's brilliant arrangements, but of his four proud grandparents 'ooooing' and 'Ahhhing'. Mel's parents will be proclaiming 'Oh, Gees, – he's the greatest!' and 'Oh, Gard – look at him'. Equally proud and just as barmy or daft, will be Scottie and me exuding (I think that word's wrong) praise – 'He's really very intelligent!' 'Oh – look!', 'Oh, isn't he bonny?' and 'Bluddy marvellous!' 'Twas ever thus! All these things have the importance of the moment and make anything I have to tell them unimportant until they are old enough to read and understand what I have written with truth and affection.

In any case, on the next trip, Daisy and I will be preparing yet another big production – an extravaganza starring: 'Your own, your very own, Miss Daisy Ann Tormé, who will now sing for you, "Your baby has gorn dahn the plug-ole!"'

I shall buy a copy of the book and send it to them. (My brave publishers who have faith in me needn't worry unduly – because I know somebody else who is going to buy a copy as well – so that's *two* for starters!)

There are many more happy, comic, sad and illuminating moments of my life up to now that I haven't recorded in the book – whether I have chosen what I *have* recorded wisely or not – I don't really know. I hope I have.

Please believe me that, as I write this, the church bells are ringing. It must be practice night for the bellringers. Any road up, they are ringing – like mad!

And that's how it all began.

IS IT THORA?

To my dear and loving daughter Jan
– how clever we were to make a daughter like you.

Contents

Let me explain!

When Thora Hird first appeared on stage in 1911, she did so because the company at the Royalty Theatre, Morecambe, needed a prop doll. In the play a young village maiden is 'done wrong' by the squire's son. Since Thora's mother was playing the village maiden, her father James Hird was the director, and their baby was the requisite few months old, it was handy and convenient for 'our Thora' to be cast in the production as 'the Unfortunate Result'. The Director said to the Actress 'Take *her* on' – and Thora's career was launched.

James Hird was also manager of the Royalty Theatre, and with this job came a house adjoining the backstage portion of the theatre. One part of young Thora's bedroom floor was actually over the backstage wall, and she would lie in bed at night, listening to the actors' dialogue and the audience's response as play after play floated up to her small back room. As she and her older brother, Neville, were growing up the empty stage and property room were their 'playground'.

These were the days of personal advertisements in *The Stage*, frequently including the fact that the person available 'dresses well, on and off'. And the Hirds did.

James Hird had an astrakhan collar to his coat, pale grey spats with pearl buttons and a silver top to his cane, while Mary Jane Hird always wore jewellery bought with savings – because it was easy to pawn. King George V and Queen Mary had just begun their reign, and the Hird family were proud to be members of the 'Theatrical Profession'.

When she was old enough Thora became a member of the repertory company, although, with northern prudence, she kept her day job at the Co-op. Even so, by the time she was 'discovered' by George Formby and signed a film contract with Ealing Film Studios she already had five hundred plays under her belt. She liked to say that she could bring a tray on stage fifty different ways, she'd done *Enter – a maid* so often. With the exception of finding out that on film she couldn't put 'make-up tramlines' all over her face and play characters forty years older than herself, the transition from Morecambe Rep to film parts was a smooth one.

By the late 1940s Thora and her recently demobbed husband Jimmy Scott, whom she nicknamed 'Scottie', had moved permanently down to London, selling Prompt Corner, their first small house in Morecambe, and bringing their daughter Janette down with them to the South. It was a big move, but the right one. As a working mother, and by now the main breadwinner of the household, it was agreed that the focus should be on Thora's career, and that Scottie should do the majority of parenting for Jan – a role he fulfilled admirably. Thora gave constant and unqualified love while at home, and sent daily letters, cards and stories by post when on film location or touring in the theatre. Meanwhile Scottie taught, disciplined and generally devoted a large slice of his life to child-rearing.

This arrangement became more and more necessary as a J. Arthur Rank film contract and some successful plays in smaller London theatres were all adding up to establish Thora Hird as one of that famous band of British character actors admired throughout the world, in what had come to be known as 'Show Business'.

Thora's career progressed. She played broad farce with co-stars like Arthur Askey and Freddie Frinton, but also heartbreaking drama in London's West End theatres; Blackpool Summer seasons alternated with Shakespeare on television; roles in films starring Dirk Bogarde, Marlon Brando and Sir Laurence Olivier contrasted with comedies with Norman Wisdom and Will Hay.

And the broadening and developing has gone on. In the last twenty years her association with some of television's leading comedy directors, and with the playwright Alan Bennett, has made her one of television's most respected performers, while her involvement with *Praise Be!* became a cornerstone of the BBC's religious broadcasting. She has also entered the world of books. The first part of her autobiography, *Scene and Hird*, was published in 1976, followed by numerous smaller books full of homespun thoughts of wit and wisdom, many as a spin-off from *Praise Be!* There have also been books especially commissioned for organisations such as Saga and Help the Aged.

During this astonishing career, and helped continuously by her husband and personal manager Scottie,

Thora glided apparently effortlessly from one medium to the next in a world that had changed beyond all recognition from the one her parents knew. Thora adapted her acting techniques to fit the multi-media world now calling itself the 'Entertainment Industry'.

As the years galloped by, there was one subject that Thora and Scottie never mentioned if it could be avoided, the possible death of one of them. They were such a great team, and worked so well together in their private as well as their public life, that it was impossible to think about one continuing without the other. Thora had been suffering from arthritis for many years, having both hips replaced three times since 1980, and more recently having a heart by-pass, so it was tacitly assumed that she would 'go first' and Scottie would retire to the country, to be close to their daughter Jan. Planning for future retirement for herself has never been on the cards for Thora. Her career was their 'family business', and one does not 'shut up shop' and go away while loyal customers still want what you have to offer.

On 30 October, 1994, Scottie died. He was eighty-eight years old. Thora was about to enter the most difficult period of her life.

As with the majority of women of her generation, Thora had lived in her family home until her wedding day. That day she moved out of her father's house and away from his strong – one might say domineering – influence, into the home and under the influence of Jimmy Scott. I don't think it would need a psychologist to see the similarities between the two men, both strong-willed with a stubborn streak, both loving but leaving no doubt as to who was boss, and both unwilling or unable to give words of praise. Thora had spent her entire life trying to please and impress first her father, then her husband. Now, suddenly, aged eighty-three, she was living alone and had no one to whom she could turn to seek approval, no anchor. Her most loving helper and strongest critic was gone.

Even though an incredible closeness had been maintained throughout the years with her daughter, it was Scottie who had always organised her life for her, read all scripts with her, listened to her words ... no major (or even minor) decision had been made without consulting him. He was her cog and wheels. He had seen to all their business affairs – 'did the books', as Thora called it. He had also cooked and shopped, driven her to rehearsals, helped her to dress when arthritis stiffened her joints, and even put her earrings in for her when her own fingers wouldn't work first thing in the morning. He had been the most nurturing of men, and had done these things to allow her the freedom to do what she did best: being 'Thora Hird' – actress, entertainer, raconteur and communicator.

Unlike most widows, the place Thora felt most on firm ground now was not at home, but back at work. So at eighty-four she continues to work and copes with her loneliness in this way. She is happiest on a stage or in a television studio and, most importantly, giving and getting love from the public, who have always recognised her as one of their own.

If there is a secret to Thora's success it is surely this, that every family has a mother, grandmother, sister, cousin or auntie who reminds them of Thora. Yet behind the very loving and human woman, with ordinary weaknesses and frailties, is an extraordinary woman with a giant wit and a formidable artistic and creative talent. In this book she is doing what is closest to her heart – sharing her life with those she loves.

'And so, Ladies and Gentlemen, it's Showtime! Turn on the spot-light. Roll cameras. It is an honour, a pleasure and a privilege for me to present to you the star of our show, your favourite and mine, the one, the only, Dame Thora Hird!'

– Good luck, Mum!

Janette Scott Rademaekers
February 1996

Introduction

I don't know of many people who are asked to write their autobiography ... *twice!* We only live once, so when I wrote my autobiography *Scene and Hird* when I was sixty-five (published in 1976), I thought that that would be that. I had written it mainly for my grandchildren, Daisy and James, who were still very young then, and living in America. I wanted them to have something so that when they grew up they would be able to read it and learn about me ... from *me*.

But nearly twenty years have gone by since then – in a flash. And how many people do you know who have had the busiest, most productive time of their lives ... between the ages of sixty-five and eighty-five? But think of this: when the last volume was published I was still to meet and work with Alan Bennett; I was still to begin seventeen years of presenting *Praise Be!*; still to do *Hallelujah!*, *In Loving Memory*, *Flesh and Blood*, *Last of the Summer Wine* ... and – well, as much work, if not more, than I'd done in the preceding twenty years. So many lovable, comical, interesting things have happened since I wrote *Scene and Hird*, and still keep on happening ... you'll think I'm being immodest if I tell you how many publishers have asked me to write another volume ... but they have ... so I have. First of all, let me explain the title, *Is it Thora?*:

When you appear regularly on television you become what is called 'a household name'. A nicer way of saying that is that people think of you as part of their family. I was already 'a household name' in the 1970s when I wrote *Scene and Hird*, because as well as my films and theatre work I'd made appearances in television series such as *Dixon of Dock Green* and *Z Cars*, and starred in two long-lasting and – I'm thankful to say – very popular television series, *Meet the Wife* and *First Lady*. When I was doing *Meet the Wife* so many people thought my co-star, Freddie Frinton, really was my husband, that if they saw me out with my real husband – Scottie – they'd say things like 'Never mind, Thora! You deserve your fun! We won't tell Fred!'

But if ever I thought I was 'a household name' before, it was as nothing to what was to happen after 1977, once I started presenting on BBC, on Sunday evenings, the popular hymn request programme *Praise Be!* One of the main things that happened was that everywhere I went strangers would greet me – not because they recognised me as someone from television, but really as though they knew me – as if I were an old friend or a member of their family. And this is where 'Is it ... *Thora*?' comes in.

Whenever Scottie and I had any shopping to do in Oxford Street, which was pretty often, we nearly always went early in the morning to be there when the shops opened – half past nine, ten o'clock. One day, after I'd been doing *Praise Be!* for a few years, we were going into Marks and Spencers for something. The doors had just opened as we got there and there was a smattering of people inside. We walked in, and coming towards us was quite a tall, rather genteel lady, with her daughter. Now this lady was what, in a repertory company, you'd cast as 'the Vicar's Wife'. I mean that very flatteringly – vicars' wives don't all look like that, but that's what you would have cast her as, in a play.

She came out with something that always makes me laugh: 'Oh! Is it ... *Thora*?' Not 'Are you Thora?' They always say 'Is it Thora?' I've had that said to me so often ... and I bet you never thought I was going to finish the explanation I started pages ago, did you?

Well, on this day I had said yes, it was ... *I* was, and – really to my surprise – she burst out crying. And just for a second I felt a bit embarrassed so I said to her, 'Oh dear! I'm not that ugly, am I?' And she looked at me and said, 'No! It's because we love you such a lot!'

Then she started to tell me that her daughter, who was with her – that's when I found out that it was her daughter – had had four miscarriages and was pregnant again. I said, 'Well I'm sure this time God will let the baby be born. I'll be putting her in my prayers tonight.'

Now this lady had got both her arms stretched out to hold me just underneath my shoulders, if you can just visualise the position, rather like a bridge. And at a counter near us – for vests – there was a little lady, no more than four feet nine, very blonde hair cut quite short – I'm sure that if she could have had a cigarette in Marks and Spencers, she would have had one in her mouth. Anyhow, there's the Vicar's Wife, the tall lady, hands just underneath my shoulders, looking at me and talking earnestly, and Little Thing at the vests counter turns round, sees what's going on, rushes over, ducks under the Vicar's Wife's arms, puts her little face up under my chin and says 'Who's bluddy luvely ...? *You* are!' And went! Disappeared! But what I think is so funny is that the lady, the Vicar's Wife, never even noticed anybody had popped up underneath. Anyhow, I said how nice it had been to meet her, and Scottie and I went out of Marks. We never even got what we'd gone there for – and I'm a shareholder!

We got back into Oxford Street, crossed the road and were going down on the other side of the road, when we heard somebody running. Now just because I hear somebody running, I'm not conceited enough to think they are running after me, but there was somebody pelting along behind us at such a pitch, and when they arrived it was a little man about as tall as the lady from the vests counter, and he looked up at Scottie and said, 'Can I kiss 'er?' Scottie didn't have time to say 'With pleasure!' or 'Do you mind?' before the fellow bobs up, kisses me on my chin, and then continues running down Oxford Street ... Scottie looked at me and sighed, 'Shall we go home, love?' I said, 'I think we'd better! I think we've had our Cabaret for today!'

There's another reason I've called it *Is It Thora?*, I mean apart from it being something people say that makes me laugh. It is because I do sometimes wonder to myself, when I sit and think about all the things that have happened to me – *is* it Thora? People seem to see me differently, somehow, from how I see myself.

Have all these things, like getting the OBE and being made a Dame, really happened to the little girl from Cheapside, Morecambe who used to scrub her mother's steps ... and didn't know what the word 'arse' meant?

Well, I try to live up to it, and what helps me most is all the love I get from people. In the first part of my autobiography I wrote a lot about Cheapside, where I spent my very happy childhood with my loving, wonderful mother, father and brother, and although *Is It Thora?* is a continuation from where I left off in 1977, I've included some more stories about the old days too. So many things that happen to me in the present seem funnier or stranger because of the way things were in the past, so I'm not likely ever to forget.

I'm grateful for all the love that I have been blessed with all my life. I sometimes think that I've had more than my fair share of love. No woman could have had a more loving husband than Scottie, or loved their husband more, during the fifty-eight years of marriage we were blessed with. I honestly believe that it is *because* I loved him so much, and still do love him, that I've been able to keep going and keep cheerful since October 1994, when he died. I have so many wonderfully happy memories, and writing this book has helped to bring them all back to me.

Anyway, here goes. *Is* it Thora?

Yes – it – is!

1
On the strait and narrow

I didn't write anything much about my religion in the first part of my autobiography. It wasn't that I wasn't religious then – as I've said many times when being interviewed, there was never a moment in my life when I could say 'Oh, I've found God!' because God has always been *there*, part of my life.

I've always talked to God – sometimes I think I'm inclined to ask him to help me a bit too much. I always seem to be saying 'It's me again ...' In a television studio there's always a floor manager, who is the contact between the artist or artists in the studio, and the producer and director upstairs in the control room, which is called the Gallery. I am convinced that I ask for so many things from God that sometimes he says to his floor manager 'Who is it?' and if the reply comes 'It's Thora' he sometimes has to say 'Oh, tell her I'm out!'

I've always had my own picture of Jesus. I've often spoken about having four uncles who were all Morecambe fishermen, but I must get that in again because Morecambe shrimps are the best in the world. (Her Majesty the Queen has Morecambe shrimps.)

My Uncle Robert had what I've got – in those days it wasn't called arthritis like now. It *was* arthritis like now, but you didn't call it that. You called it rheumatism. Anyhow, my Uncle Robert had had to stop trawling because he couldn't move about. One day he was sitting in our kitchen, his hands on his stick, and even now, eighty years later, I can see those hands, with the bones twisted. All my uncles had beards and black hair like retriever dogs, all curls. (Why are men given curly hair? My brother had all the curls, while I have the straightest hair in the world – *in the world*, not just England.)

Our house was always one for 'Rat-a-tat-tat ... Are you there, Mrs Hird?' And it was usually to borrow something. I say that with great love. Vinegar, two candles, a cupful of sugar, or my favourite one: 'Mrs Hird, my mother says have you got a piece of brown paper and some string, because she wants to send a parcel.' I can see my mother, folding up the brown paper whenever it came round a parcel.

(I do that myself. Not out of any meanness – if it's a lovely sheet of brown paper I could no more put it in the bin than I could put myself in the bin. I fold it up. I've also got a box in the kitchen painted red with 'string' on it, for all the little bits of string.)

However, there's my uncle Robert sitting, hands on his stick, and there's a rat-a-tat-tat and a neighbour comes in, because our door was always open. 'Oh, Mrs Hird, my mother says could you lend her an egg-cupful of vinegar?' Then she says 'Hallo' to my uncle, because everybody knew everybody in Morecambe, and when my mother gives her the egg-cup of vinegar she thanks her and is about to go out – and you don't wonder that in some of the parts I play I remember these ladies, because the things they did quite naturally were more comic than anything anyone could do who was trying to be funny – and she says 'Ee, Robert, tha does look like Jesus!'

I was five. I looked at him and I thought, 'He does! He looks like Jesus. He looks like the little tracts they give us at Sunday School.' But from then on I always pictured Jesus wearing a blue 'ganzie' – our name for the blue Guernsey sweater that fishermen wear, with buttons up one side of the neck – and with a cap over his thick black curls.

When I got to about ten I had a serious phase. I was saying my prayers one night, and I'd been wondering for a while if Jesus really *did* look like my Uncle Robert, when I had another thought – that he *didn't* look like my Uncle Robert, and I shouldn't *think* that he looked like him. It was wicked. My mother, as always, was sitting on the bed, and I was kneeling beside it, and I looked up and said, 'Jesus doesn't really look like Uncle Robert, does he?' My mother took my face in her hands, kissed me on the forehead and said, 'Who says he doesn't?'

And now, aged eighty-four, because I had such a wonderful, understanding mother, I still sometimes think that Jesus looks like my Uncle Robert!

I must admit, religion isn't an easy subject to write about in an autobiography. You can't very well put 'I am very religious ...' But I'd like to say something about it, because, of course, since I wrote the first part, as well as continuing with my acting career I have done seventeen years of presenting – with great love and pleasure – a religious programme on the BBC, *Praise Be!*

All the time I was presenting *Praise Be!* I would get people 'telling me off' in the street! I could go down one of the main streets in London and some lovely old lady – I say 'old lady', how dare I? I'm an old lady myself! – would stop me. I don't mean rudely, just *slightly* aggressively, and she would say, 'Hey! You never played that hymn I asked for! I sent for that hymn because my sister Connie loved it. And you never played it ... you never read her name out.' Then I had all the explanation of 'Well you see, we had sacks of requests, and I'm very sorry ...' As often as not, it would turn out that I *had* played her favourite hymn, and that what she was upset about was that I hadn't read out her sister Connie's name. Anyway, we would always finish up friends, but I might get ten yards further on and somebody would say, 'Oh Thora! D'you mind if I just requested a hymn?'

When I first started presenting the programme, in 1977, we were in 'Green', one of the studios at the BBC Television Centre, big enough for an audience of 350 if we'd wanted one, and in this huge space there was just a chair, a monitor (that's like a television set) and me. I must say, I looked very lonely sitting there on a little platform on my own.

They would put the hymns we were playing on the monitor, because, as some of you know, the hymns were all taken from *Songs of Praise* – in fact, for the first couple of years my series was called *Your Songs of Praise Choice* – but that was a bit of a mouthful, and I'm glad they changed it. I would watch each hymn being sung on my monitor, and then I would turn to one of the three cameras that was bearing down on me, to do what was known as 'Thora's Link'.

In about the fourth programme a hymn on the monitor was being sung by a choir of little boys. There they were, aged about six or seven, little pale blue jumpers on, little pale blue ties, and they were singing 'All things bright and beautiful', and it was lovely. And all of a sudden one little fair-haired lad in the middle of the front row turned to his friend to smile, and all down the side of his face was a birth mark, I think you call it a 'strawberry mark'. And I don't know ... it just upset me so much. The hymn finished and I was cued in to say the next link, but I couldn't because I was crying. The producer and director and the technicians were all upstairs in the Gallery – and I said, 'Someone in the Gallery could have warned me about that!'

The floor manager came over and said, 'They are very sorry. They didn't mean you to be upset.' I said, 'Well, in the future, if ever there's anything like that and I have to speak immediately after it, will you warn me in some way?' So they had to play the hymn through again, and cue me again, and this time I was all right.

About three programmes later there was another row of children, only this time they were all either on crutches or in wheelchairs, all brave, all smiling and singing beautifully. Before they came on the floor manager came over to me and said, 'The director says I have to tell you it's "One of Those".'

In those days I used to wear semi-evening dress, with a rose in my cleavage. I don't know, it seemed a different programme then, a bit more formal. One man wrote and said, 'I've noticed, Thora, that at the end of every programme you say "God bless ... I'll be back next Sunday." But how do you know you'll be back next Sunday? You should say "God willing (or DV – Deo Volente), I'll be back next Sunday."' Another one wrote to say 'I love your programmes and I've watched every one. I love the hymns, I love the way you do it, I love the way you dress, I love the way you speak ... but I don't like your pink nail varnish!'

I took all these checks very lovingly. I never wore pink nail varnish again on that programme, and I always remembered to say 'I'll be back next Sunday – *DV!*'

We moved to a smaller studio for the next couple of years, into what is known as the Presentation Studios, where they do things like the weather. In those days Barry Took was presenting *Points of View* in Presentation Studio A while I was doing *Your Songs of Praise Choice* in Presentation Studio B. (And may I interject at this point that I was one of many thousands of viewers and fellow-artists who were all very upset when Barry was unceremoniously removed from presenting *Points of View*, which he used to do so brilliantly.) Many's the time Barry and I have sat side by side, sharing the minute dressing room, having our noses powdered together!

The smaller studio made it more homely, and we began to have more homely sets, too, with lamps and plants and a comfortable sofa, making it look as though I was doing the programme from my own living room, and I'm sure that that's what many viewers thought it was. A year or two after that, and for many years to come, we really did make the programmes from my home – or rather my daughter Jan's home – but I'll come to that in another chapter.

From the very first series the viewers' letters arrived in sacks. Bill Cotton Junior was then in charge at the BBC, and Dr Colin Morris, a Methodist like myself, was head of religious programmes, and when they were asked how long they thought *Praise Be!* would last they said, 'Until Thora falls off the edge of the pier!'

It changed my life in some ways. For one thing, I've so many friends now who wear dog-collars. And they are all great chaps, I can tell you. Roger Royle, who was doing *Songs of Praise* and *Good Morning Sunday* on Radio 2 for most of the time I was doing *Praise Be!*, often pops in for a cup of tea and a chat; John Tudor, Rob Marshall, Rob Garrod, Colin Morris ... all my friends, and all dog-collars! And I've met as many Bishops as any actress could ever hope for!

I see Colin Morris every year at Wesley's Chapel in the City of London, where we are both invited for their annual 'Carolthon'. I remember one year, standing in the very pulpit John Wesley himself used to preach from, and I noticed from the Order of Service that after I'd stopped speaking the next carol would be 'While Shepherds Watched'. The organist sits just underneath the great pulpit, so I leaned over and said, 'Is that to the usual tune?' and he nodded, and I said, 'Oh, I wish one year we could sing it to Lyngham! It really goes so well to that. That's the tune the Salvation Army Band always used to play when they came down Cheapside on Christmas morning, when I was a child.'

Anyway, we sang it to the normal tune that time, but the following year they invited me again, and I noticed that once again the carol following my little bit was 'While Shepherds Watched', so when I came to the end I leaned over and asked the organist 'What tune?' and he smiled and said, 'Lyngham!' and I said, 'Oh, thank you! That's the best Christmas present you could have given me.' And Paul Hulme, the minister, said, 'We've gone one better than that, Thora. Look up in the gallery.' And I looked, and a Salvation Army Band were standing up in the gallery above me! They'd come along especially for me, to play Lyngham.

So you see, for me, religion isn't just about keeping on the 'strait and narrow' – it's much more about kind hearts, laughter, and loving, joyous moments like that.

2

In Loving Memory

In April 1978 Ronnie Baxter, the director, and Dick Sharples, the writer, came to London to give me the script of a new series, called *In Loving Memory*. They wanted me to play Ivy Unsworth, the wife of Unsworth the Undertaker, played by Freddie Jones. In the first episode Unsworth dies and Ivy becomes the undertaker herself, with the help of her hapless nephew, Billy, brilliantly played by Chris Beeney.

I said to them, 'Well, I won't read it while you're here' – because I never do that – 'but will you tell me, before I read it, is there the slightest chance that I could ever hurt anybody that had been bereaved?' To which Dick Sharples said, 'Do you think we would have brought it to you if there was?'

I suppose I enjoyed doing *In Loving Memory* as much as any series I've ever done. Ronnie Baxter is a great director, one of the best comedy directors in the business, and Dick Sharples is a very clever writer. Chris Beeney was a pleasure and a joy to work with, Avis Bunnage, God rest her soul – what a good actress, and what a good friend – played the next-door neighbour, Joan Sims was in it for several episodes, another very professional, excellent actress who always makes me laugh, and a lot of other very big names would be in it for a day.

And we didn't hurt anybody. At the read-through on the first day of rehearsing an episode, if there was ever the slightest likelihood that there was anything that might pain anybody, then out it would come. I can recall one occasion there was a quotation from the Bible. With *In Loving Memory*, eight times out of ten it opened with me on the telephone. I'd put on my 'posh' voice and say 'Unsworth's the Undertakers ...' – until I knew it was only a neighbour or someone who knew me, when I'd change to speaking normally. This time it began with someone ringing up to ask for a stone, and I had to get out the book of suitable quotations for putting on headstones – 'Rest in Peace' and things like that. The words that Dick had written for me to suggest for this headstone were from the Bible: 'The Lord giveth – the Lord taketh away ... Blessed be the name of the Lord.'

Now, in the early days of the BBC you couldn't say 'My God!', you had to say 'My goodness.' In fact there was a green book of things you couldn't say and do. A lot of jokes are made about it now, things like how if an actor was doing a scene when he was in bed with an actress, he always had to keep one foot touching the floor.

But it wasn't because of the green book that I didn't want to say this line of Dick's. I didn't want to say a quotation from the Bible, or the Prayer Book, to make it sound like a funny line – in fact I definitely wasn't going to. I am experienced enough to know it would be bound to offend somebody somewhere.

I said at the read-through 'We can't say this – it's from the Bible' but just for once Dick did not agree with me. I admire Dick Sharples immensely, and will enjoy acting his words as long as I live, but on this occasion he wasn't very pleased. He said, 'Well it won't matter!' I said, 'Well, it will matter to me.' He said, 'You mean you're not going to say it?' I said, 'No Dick, I'm not ... this will hurt somebody.'

I was adamant, and in the end Dick said, 'Well, I'll write you something else, but it won't be *"comic"* enough for you.' He was really mad. He used to go downstairs to write any new bits. He came back up into the rehearsal room about a quarter of an hour later and skimmed a piece of paper across the table at me, saying 'There you are. See if you can make anything of that.'

He hadn't rewritten the whole scene, just the words I was supposedly reading out of Ivy's book of suitable engravings for headstones. Instead of the Bible quotation, he had written: 'Ta-ra, Grand-dad! All the best. The North lost a good'un when you went west!' Brilliant! I said to Ronnie, 'They'll be able to do a row of knitting during this laugh.' Which was right. By heavens, when we were doing it in front of a live audience, the howl of laughter we got on that line.

Comedy isn't just about learning the words. Well, of course you all know that. You know that this thing called 'timing' is important, which means getting the rhythm of comedy, getting a laugh just by the way you hang a coat on a nail, having the courage to pause just that split second longer than the audience can bear, until everyone is on the edge of their seats with wondering what you are going to say ... and then coming out with it.

There's another thing in comedy. When you have a

comic reply to something somebody has said, if there is a word too many the music of it goes. What I mean is, comedy questions and answers are really music. And one morning in *In Loving Memory* I thought, 'I'm not going to get as big a laugh on this line as I could do if there was a word less.'

I'll put it in 'ta-ra-ras' in this book, so please read it as I put it. If someone says to you 'Ta-ra-ra-ra-ra-ra-*ra*' you've got to, in comedy, answer 'Ta-ra-ra-ra-ra-ra-*ra*' to get the laugh. Do you see? With real words, I mean. But if there is a word too many and you have to answer 'Ta-ra-ra-ra-ra-ra-ra-*ra*-ra' it doesn't work. It sounds silly, but this is really very important in comedy.

One morning I happened to say to Ronnie Baxter, 'I shan't get the laugh I'm hoping to on this, because there's a word too many – the music is wrong.' And he hugged me and said, 'I didn't think anybody ever said that but me!'

Ronnie and I had such an understanding about comedy. Brilliant man, he was, a brilliant man. He's not directing any more; what a loss to television.

Sometimes real life is funnier than fiction. I remember a letter from a girl who wrote 'This really happened. My uncle George died last week, and for years he has told my auntie "I want cremating" and my auntie has always said to him "No, no. You're going to be buried."' – Well, of course it's very difficult, when you're dead, to stick up for what you want. Anyway, this girl said she and her auntie were travelling along in the funeral cortège, and suddenly out of the back of the hearse she saw smoke, and she said to her auntie,

'There's smoke coming out of the hearse!' and eventually the hearse stopped, and they pulled up behind it, just outside Marks and Spencers, in the high street. The driver of the hearse came and said, 'We're going to have to leave you here just for ten minutes, because we're going to get another hearse.' They took the coffin out and put it on the pavement, guarded by two of the bearers who were going to carry it when they got to church.

People were coming in and out of Marks and Spencers, practically having to step over the coffin, while she and her auntie waited in the car. Two ladies came out and one said to the other, 'Well fancy leaving a coffin outside on the pavement like that!' and the other one said, 'Oh, it's Thora, look, it'll be Thora's show, *In Loving Memory*, because there she is in that car!' It wasn't me at all, it was 'auntie'! The girl wrote that she was sure that the smoke was a message from her uncle to her auntie, saying 'I want cremating, remember!'

Such a lot of funny things happened when I was doing *In Loving Memory*, but I think the thing I remember most was the Great Train Journey of 1979. I went up to Leeds from King's Cross every Thursday at lunchtime – I've done that journey so many times over the past twenty years – camera rehearsal on Thursday night, put it into the can on Friday, in front of an audience of about 350, and an early train back on the Saturday morning to be back in London by half past ten or eleven o'clock and have the rest of the day to spend with Scottie at home.

One week, during the winter when we had the very

heavy snows, Avis Bunnage, Joan Sims and I all got on the 12.25 train together, from King's Cross to Leeds. I've always loved Joan Sims. She really does make me laugh. We would often travel back together as well, on the breakfast train the morning after a recording. They'd put the breakfast in front of you, and in those days – I don't know if they do now, because you've got to be very wealthy to afford a breakfast on the train these days – but then there was bacon, egg, sausage, tomato, black pudding, fried potato and a piece of fried bread. And as soon as they'd put it in front of us, before we'd even picked up our knives and forks, Joan would say 'Are you going to eat that sausage?'

But on this occasion we were going up *to* Leeds. Avis was sitting opposite me, next to the window on the corridor, and Joan was next to her. Next to me was a man from an oil rig, his shirt open down to his navel. We're cold, we're freezing, but he isn't. He takes a packet of cigarettes out and pushes them at me and says, 'Do you want a fag, flower?' In one corner is a lady who's going to Leeds to set up a stall with perfumes and wonderful beauty creams at an exhibition. She never gets there, I'll tell you now. In the other corner is a man with a very expensive briefcase, who has got to be at a meeting at half past seven. He won't get there either, I'll tell you for nothing. The corridor is full of businessmen, all standing and pressing against the door. So you've got the picture.

The train sets off and we've been going about twenty minutes when Joan says, 'Er ... Have you brought any sandwiches, Avis?' And Avis says rather sharply 'Yes!' with clearly no intention of opening them *yet* – because there wasn't always a buffet on the train. Meanwhile the train is travelling slower and slower because of all the snow on the line ...

Eventually we get to Doncaster, and out we spew, only to find that five trains before us had done the same thing – there was not an inch on that platform. Joan steps off the train into snow so deep it goes over the top of her boots. We manage to fight our way into the waiting room and find seats while we wait for the next train to take us on to Leeds.

Now, we are due to do a camera rehearsal that afternoon, for a show that we are going to record the following day, and it's a bit important that we let them know that we're not going to be there – because we're not, the way things are looking.

Avis Bunnage was a very able person – I think she must have been a Leader in the Guides – and she knows that, to find someone who works on the railway you have to look for someone with a uniform on that doesn't fit them. So Avis sees a man wearing a coat with sleeves hanging down over his fingertips, and he even has a clipboard and pen, so she says, 'Excuse me, could I trouble you for a moment?' and makes him follow her into the waiting room, where we all are. Avis is very business-like and polite. She says to him, 'I want you to ring up Leeds television studios. This is the number.' He says, 'Oh yes?' She makes him write down the number on his clipboard, and then says, 'Ask for Floor Four.' By which time, he's hypnotised is this man. 'Floor Four?'

'Yes, and then ask for Mr Baxter. Mr Ronnie Baxter. Have you got that down? Let me look. Yes, that's the number. That's the floor. Now, what you say to Mr Baxter is ...' At which point he says,

'Here! Hold on a minute, missis ...'

'Listen! This is very important. Tell Mr Baxter we are marooned on Doncaster Station – as you can see we are – and it is possible that we won't be there in time for the camera rehearsal. What are you going to say?'

And like a child at school, he says, 'Tell Mr Baxter you're marooned on Doncaster Station, and you can't get there for the – what rehearsal?'

'Camera rehearsal.'

Strange to say, I have to tell you now, he did exactly that!

However, we're still sitting there. We've eaten the beetroot and tongue sandwiches. Joan's had two of the eggs, and Avis and I have shared the other egg. Avis goes to her bag, to put the pen back that she'd got out for the man, although he didn't need it, and a Mars bar shows itself. 'Oo! There's a Mars bar there!' says Joan. So, Avis cuts it in three with her nail file, and we have a third each.

Eventually a train comes in. Well, of course, there is not a hope of getting on it, with all these people. We wait a bit longer. Another train comes in. Not a hope. We finally get on the third one, and the man from the oil rig gets on with us. He says it is taking him longer to get from London to Leeds than it had taken him to come from Kuwait, or wherever it was he was working on the oil rig. Meanwhile Avis has found a cellophane bag of mints in her bag and, seeing a lot of businessmen who look as though they haven't eaten for a year, she goes along the coach, saying 'Would you care for a mint?' and everybody takes one. (I'm telling you all this so you'll understand what very glamorous lives we actresses do lead!)

We got to Leeds after nine, very worried that they would have missed us. They hadn't really. Ronnie and Dick came into my room at the hotel and told us that they'd received our telephone message and had had a very good camera rehearsal without us – Ronnie Baxter had played me, Dick Sharples had played Avis and I forget who had played Joan.

Then the three of us had to go down for dinner, because Joan was nearly dying of hunger.

In Loving Memory ran for many years, but people always remember the first one, where the coffin fell out of the hearse, careered down the hill, turned the corner, and shot into the canal. They always remember that. And how we had to throw the wreaths down from the bridge, like a sea burial.

As I say, we had to be so careful about hurting people with a comedy about funerals, but I had many appreciative letters from people who had just lost someone, saying that the series had cheered and consoled them. Because we weren't making fun of bereavement – what we were making a little gentle fun of was pretentiousness, and the way that so many of us, let's face it, know very little about religious rituals. And yet we all have to undergo this very serious ceremony when saying goodbye to our much loved friends and relations. And because it so often happens when we are trying to be at our most solemn and dignified, all dressed up in our best clothes, that something very comical happens ... and we want to laugh, and we *know* the person we are saying goodbye to would have laughed, but because of the solemnity of the occasion, we feel we mustn't.

I always hoped that *In Loving Memory* might help people to stop worrying or feeling guilty about having wanted to laugh at the funeral of somebody dear – by showing them that laughter and loving memories go very well together.

3
Praise Be!

During the seventeen years I was presenting *Praise Be!*, for many people, especially lonely people, I think I almost became like one of the family. So many of the letters started in almost exactly the same way:

> *Dear Thora,*
> *I hope you don't mind my calling you Thora, but I feel I know you. It's like having a friend coming into my living room for a chat on a Sunday evening when you are presenting the hymns on Praise Be! ...*

You cannot know what pleasure those letters gave me. But some of them were very sad, and many of them really made me weep.

I recall a letter from Northern Ireland. It said,

> *Dear Thora Hird, I have a little boy who is maladjusted. He is ten years old. He has never really spoken, but when you come on the screen in* Praise Be! *he puts his hand out and says "Thora!" Please don't answer this letter, because I am the only Protestant in this street.*

A letter from another lady said,

My husband doesn't really know what's on television, but he watches it because it occupies him. But when you come on, I can tell by his face ...

Well, then it makes it worth while being an artist, or being whatever I am. I used to laugh sometimes, when people would write to say 'I don't know what it's called, the hymn, but this is a line in it ...' Well, there are a lot of hymns in a lot of hymn books to look through to find a line!

I could fill a book with the things that happened to me when I was doing *Praise Be!* – and come to think of it, I have written several books about it already! I always enjoy telling the story of one day when I was making *In Loving Memory*. We had a shot that was quite long – if I said to anybody in our business 'It was four pages of script', they'd say 'Well, that's a pretty long shot'. We had just over eighty extras for this shot, because the scene was the funeral of Billy, my nephew, who wasn't dead really, of course, because it was a comedy, but I thought he was dead ... So his best friend, Ernie, was driving the hearse, and Ronnie Baxter, who is such a splendid comedy director, went round to every one of the extras saying things like 'You take your handkerchief out and wipe your eyes. Sir, will you please raise your hat as the cortège passes. You, lady in maroon – just break into tears ...' And he really gave them each an acting part to do.

Right, so it's a long take. Eighty extras all standing ready. Ronnie Baxter has set up a camera some distance away to get a picture of the whole scene. We wait for the light to come just right – a golden evening light that you get over these pretty Yorkshire towns that are on steep hills. The very end of the shot was of me getting out of the car behind the hearse, and saying 'Ernie! What d'you think you're doing?' because he'd stopped the hearse.

As I got out of the car to say my line a lady in a red trouser suit, cigarette in the middle of her mouth, walked into our scene from the side of the road, where she'd been sitting on a wall watching. She came right up to me and said, ''Ere! you never played that 'ymn I asked yer to play, and it was my favourite, and it was me mother's favourite!'

I said, 'I'm very sorry'. The cameras all stopped rolling the moment they saw her. I said, 'But you see, it's very ...' and I got so far, and Ronnie Baxter came up and said, 'Excuse me, Madam! We are filming.'

'*Are* yer?' she said. 'Where? Why? Where is there anything?' meaning cameras. He pointed to where they were and said, really very politely, 'And if you wouldn't mind just clearing the shot, you can speak to Thora when we've done it.' So off she goes, back on the wall, and we have to do it all again, from the top, the women blowing their noses, the men raising their hats and all the rest of it. I get down out of the car and say 'Ernie! What do you think you're doing?'

'Cut' says Ronnie, and *immediately* on comes the red trouser suit again. Another cigarette. 'No, I mean, it's like I said – you never played that 'ymn that I sent for, and you see it was me mother's favourite ...'

I said, 'Well, er, I'm awfully sorry, Madam, I wish I could please everybody, and I do try to. As a matter of fact the hymns are chosen usually by the most requests there are for them. So in that way we do please most people.'

She said, 'Well it wasn't mine you played.'

'No, well I'm very sorry. Which hymn was it?'

And she looked at me, with the cigarette stuck right in the middle of her mouth and she hesitated – 'The, er ... With, er ... Well! I can't remember which 'ymn it was *now*. But it was me mother's favourite and you never played it!'

One Saturday morning I went with my sister-in-law, Rita, to the market at Crowborough, where they have a regular car-boot sale. Rita, Scottie's sister, is a retired Headmistress, so we're all very proud of her. I always call her Miss Brain of Britain. She is a kind, loving auntie to Jan, and after she retired she came to live not far away in Sussex, which meant a lot to Scottie, who was always very close to her.

The first stall we looked at was full of wonderful old postcards, the kind of postcards that you bought when I was a kid – all new, they were not written on or anything – so I bought some of those, then strolled along looking at bits of things. On one stall there was a little jug, bronze coloured, and it really was nice. I picked it up and I said to Rita, 'Isn't this nice? Couldn't you see that full of marigolds?'

I said to the man, who looked like a farmer, with his big red face and rolled-up sleeves, 'Excuse me, how much is this, please?' He said, 'Is it for you, Thora? Have it for nothing.' I laughed and said, 'Well, you're not going to retire very quickly at that rate, giving all your stuff away!' But he said, 'No. I'd like you to have it. My wife ... thought there was nobody like you.' And he burst into tears. It's heartbreaking, to see a man cry. It is really very upsetting. I said to him, 'Oh dear. What's the matter?' And he said, 'She died last week.' And I could see this man fighting his grief, this big farmer, with his shirt sleeves rolled up, standing there ... I said to him, 'Is the pain like a brick in your chest?' And he said, 'Yes. Yes. I'll never get over it.' And I said, 'I know what it is. God gives you that brick. He gives one to everyone who has loved someone very much. And you carry it round in your chest, and it hurts so much, but only because you loved them so much. And God will take all the points off that brick gradually – not that you will love your wife any less ... but this he does. He takes the pain away. He's not going to let you grieve for ever.'

He blew his nose, and I said, 'One day you'll wake up and think, "Eh, that brick's gone." You won't notice it going, but it really does go.'

I have always treasured that little jug, which he insisted I accept as a gift. A few weeks later I was presenting *Praise Be!* from Jan's house in the country, and I was reading out someone's name who had requested a hymn, and as I did so – I was in the kitchen and to the right of me I noticed the little bronze jug, full of bluebells – it looked like a painting. I said, 'Oh, just a minute, doesn't this look nice?' The camera took a shot of the flowers in the jug, and I told everyone the story of the farmer who had given it to me, and when I'd finished even the camera crew were moved. And afterwards I got so many letters from viewers saying 'That's it, Thora. It is just like a brick.'

You can't really put a price on moments like that, and so many happened during the seventeen years I was presenting *Praise Be!* It isn't that *Praise Be!* made me more religious, but it made me more aware of religion. The letters came in *sacks*, and you've no idea what was in some of those letters – the stories of troubles and loneliness and worry. They altered me as a person.

I'd receive letters from many an old lady, seventy-something, eighty-something, saying 'I lost my husband two years ago. Life is very lonely without him ... Sometimes your face on television is the only friendly face I see all week ...' Do you wonder they often made me cry? I can remember one time I was reading the letters after Jimmy had gone to bed, and as usual some of them were bringing on the tears. And he came in, in his pyjamas, and he said, 'Are you coming to be ... What are you doing? Oh! I'll tell you, darling, if you are going to upset yourself like this, I'm going to have to ask you to stop doing the programme.' And when he said that, I thought, 'Oh no. I couldn't stop doing the programme.'

Of course I did eventually. But it taught me a great deal, *Praise Be!*, about the troubles people have, the thousands of lonely people there are, and the great faith so many people have to help them bear and overcome their sorrows. And it's made me realise, more than ever, how very lucky I am.

4
I'm not Beryl

I grew quite used, on *Praise Be!*, to receiving letters to 'Dear Flora', 'Dear Dora', and 'Dear Nora'. I didn't mind too much being confused with Dame Flora Robson, Dora Bryan or – I suppose – Nora Batty! My name is rather unusual, because it comes from a mournful Victorian ballad my mother used to sing called 'Speak to me, Thora!' sung over someone's grave!

Scottie and I, when we had an afternoon free, were very fond of getting on a boat at Westminster Bridge and sailing as far as Greenwich. It was a lovely sail, and I especially liked the man who did the patter, when he said '... and on the left is *Cleera-patra's* Needle.' He always pronounced it like that – and we used to enjoy it so much on a sunny afternoon.

One day we had some friends over from Stockport, Bill and Anne Price, very dear friends of ours. We'd been out to lunch in town and it was a beautiful day, so we decided to take them on the river trip to Greenwich.

Well, there are several shops when you land, and as we passed one shop there were several of those dolls that laugh. I don't know how to describe them if you haven't seen them – there's just this 'ha-ha-ha!' going on. I thought, 'Now that would be a bit of fun, to buy one of those and put it in the toilet.' Because the one I saw rather looked like a box you would press for some perfume to spray over you. But if you pressed this one, all you'd get was 'Ha! ha! ha!' So all four of us went in the shop and we were looking round, and there were jokes and all sorts of things. A very well-dressed lady came in, looked gratified to see me, came over smiling and said 'Hallo ... Beryl.'

And I thought, now I must be careful, so I said 'Hallo' because it seemed the polite thing to do.

'Now when are you going to be on television again?'

I said, 'I think perhaps you think that I'm Beryl Reid?' and she said very challengingly 'Yes!' So I said, 'Well, I'm awfully sorry, I'm not Beryl Reid.' And she said very firmly, *'YOU ARE!'* so I said, 'Well, do forgive me, but I do know who I am – and I'm not Beryl Reid.'

She said, 'You are – and I'll tell you something else – the public are your living. It's your place to be polite to people who watch you on television.'

'Well, I'm quite sure you're right. But I can't pretend to be Miss Reid when I'm not. I do know her very well, and I'm fond of her, so do please excuse me.'

And with that she huffed herself out of the shop, talking to herself, quite convinced that I really was Beryl Reid pretending not to be. And that was that. So we bought the little thing for the loo – and on the pavement is the same lady, with three friends. And they whisper something, and she marches up to me – I can't say she strolls up to me – and says, 'You are *NOT*

Beryl Reid.' So I said, 'No. I know I'm not. I told you I wasn't.'

'You didn't!'

'I did. You said "Hallo Beryl" and I said, "I think you think I'm Beryl Reid and I'm not"...'

'Well just you remember – the public are ...'

'Yes, thank you, I know. The public are my living. And I try not to be rude, and I hope I'm not being rude now, and I'm very sorry I'm not Beryl.'

'Well, remember that. You are *not* Beryl Reid!' and she walked off.

So I'm just telling any of you who are reading this, in case there's any confusion in your minds – this book is *not* by Beryl Reid, and it's not by Nora, Dora or Flora – it's Thora!

5
Meet the family

Families are such precious things. Even now, in my prayers at night I always say to God, 'Thank you for my mother and father and brother, and thank you for the way they wrapped me in love until I was old enough to meet Scottie, who wrapped me in another sort of love.'

On 3 May, 1987, Scottie and I celebrated our fiftieth wedding anniversary. I knew there was a lot of skulduggery going on that we weren't supposed to know about, but we did know that Jan and her husband William were arranging a luncheon for us. The first surprise was that it was on a barge, on the Regent's Canal. They secretly invited people we had known and loved for ever, and there were speeches and lovely food and lots of laughter as we sailed round the Regent's Canal on a beautiful morning and afternoon. It really was marvellous.

But that was only the first part of the surprise. Jan had told us to pack our bags, and bring our passports, and that she and William would be going with us. I had honestly no idea where we were going, and when we got to the airport we still didn't know where we were going. But the man driving the little motor car that took us to the Departure Lounge said to me, 'Do you like Sicily, Miss Hird?' and I said, 'Yes – is that where I'm going?' So that's when we knew. (I *had* been wondering why we needed our passports for a journey round the Regent's Canal!)

Jan was born on 14 December. And, if I may digress for a minute, something that was very different in those days was how you were treated after childbirth. I mean, today, if you'd had your baby on 14 December you'd be up and about finishing your Christmas shopping, dusting the house and so on by 15 December, wouldn't you? But in those days mothers had a long period of 'lying in', when they weren't supposed to do anything at all and just stayed put in bed for two weeks, with the District Nurse calling round every day to make sure you did so. I remember the Christmas Eve, ten days after Jan had been born, all the family were round and they'd all looked in on me and Jan upstairs in the bedroom, wished us Happy Christmas, cooed over her ... and then they had gone downstairs. I could hear them all talking and laughing and having a good time, and I got a bit fed up of being on my own upstairs, so I picked Jan up out of her cot and started to walk down the stairs with her to give them a surprise ... Well! Consternation! Even Scottie – who was the mildest man you could ever meet – shouted at me, 'What do you think you are doing with that baby!?' You really would have thought they had caught me trying to murder her!

What can I say about Jan? Words can't describe how I feel about her. She's been the most loving daughter any parents could wish for, and a tower of strength to me since Scottie died. She gave up filming when her children were born to become a full-time mother, and that's another role she has played to perfection. And I have to say, she still looks like the cover of *Vogue* when she comes out with me for a lunch or something. But you'd expect me to be proud of my own daughter, wouldn't you? So I won't embarrass her any more.

Every parent would like to give their child everything. But they can't, because if they could I would have given Jan the long, happy marriage I have had. On the other hand, if the choice has been unfortunate in a marriage and they haven't found the right one, I'm afraid that I agree very much with them parting. When you discover you've married the wrong one, the misfortune is *there* – in the choice. There's no point in saying it hasn't happened. If there are children they are bound to suffer one way or another. This happened to Jan, but thank the Lord she's very happily married now, to William, and has found all the love and happiness she deserves.

I must give credit where credit's due to our son-in-law, William. He and my Scottie were so close, they became like father and son. He's like Scottie in some ways.

William makes the bread at their house, and it's scrumptious. Every breakfast-time you can partake of William's brown or white new crusty bread. He mixes the flour and stuff the night before, and it mixes and bakes during the night, and hey presto! it's all there and ready for breakfast. (Any of you who owns one of those fantastic Japanese bread-making machines will know how it's done.) Anyway, it's scrumtially-doodillus. Can you just imagine it, with a large cup of beautiful coffee?

Jan has given us two wonderful grandchildren, James and Daisy. I'm so proud of them. My father, my father-in-law and my husband were all called James. And now there's my grandson, James the fourth, six foot one, a handsome lad who looks like Scottie, so there can't be much wrong with that. He's at UCLA (University of California at Los Angeles) at the moment, having been educated in England, at Cumnor House and then at Lancing.

Everybody says Daisy is extremely like me (poor little soul!). Daisy was at Cumnor House and then she went to Benenden. (And if it was good enough for Princess Anne, I reckon it was good enough for my grand-daughter.) Daisy is following in the family tradition of going into the acting and entertainment business. I'm not quite sure about James. We'll have to wait until after he graduates. I must admit, when I saw him play Mozart in *Amadeus* at his school, he was so good ... that I couldn't tell him. This is true. It's a part that shrieks to be overplayed, and he never did. I was very proud of him, but later, when I met him with some of his friends, I couldn't tell him how good he was. I thought they might think, 'Oh, well, it's just his grandmother.' So I wrote to him the next day, and I think he's still got the letter.

When Daisy was a little girl, living in America, on one of my twenty-three visits and Scottie's twenty-six visits – we were always nipping over – Scottie made an egg custard. Now in our part of the country an egg custard is a deep, beautiful pastry crust, and then the egg custard poured in, a little bit of cinnamon on the top, and baked in the oven. It goes to just about the consistency of a blancmange. Ooh, writing about it I could just eat some now!

However, it was the first time Daisy – a little thing, two or three years old – had had one, and her Poppa, Scottie, said 'Eat up your egg custard, Daisy' but she wasn't quite sure about it, and I came in and, really to encourage her, like you do with small children, I said, 'Ooooh! Egg custard!' And all day we had her coming up and saying, 'Ooooh! Egg custard!'

The thing is, it has gone on all through life. I know this sounds rather silly, but we never write to each other without a mention. I usually try to do a little four-line poem about it, but the difficulty is that not a lot of words rhyme with it. There's mustard, flustered and clustered. But not many. In fact I wrote to her the other day, and ended with a little verse – but I had to use flustered again. I put:

So as you read these loving words
I beg you don't get flustered
It's just a letter – nothing else ...
I wish it was egg custard!

It's a lot of nonsense, isn't it? But we do this, and she 'egg custards' me, on the telephone. We'll have a long conversation from America and she won't have said it, and I'll be saying goodbye and saying, 'I love you so much, darling' and she'll say, 'And I love you, Ganny ... Ooh, ooh! And egg custard!'

Daisy plays the piano and sings beautifully – she and James are both musical. They get that from their father, Mel Tormé, but also from Scottie. Daisy has a job in sports promotion, which she took on the understanding that she can have time off for auditions. It's the heartbreaking time, that makes you or breaks you, going along for part after part. I remember it so well, and feel for her so much. I think she'll finish up as an actress. She really is comic, but not in the sort of music hall way that I am.

To be honest, I very rarely see myself in her, but I'll tell you when I do see myself, and that is when she'll be over here in England and it will come the day to fly back, and she will come round to say goodbye, and say in a very small, wobbly voice, 'We're not going to cry ... (sniff) ... are we ...?' And the car will be waiting to take her, and I'll be sobbing and I'll say, 'Don't be like that – it's like me.' And I don't want to be like that either, because I don't want Jan seeing it. Jan has been extremely brave in her life. Her children come and go. They must be as well travelled as anyone of their age.

On 17 January, 1994, Daisy rang Jan from Los Angeles and told her there had been a terrible earthquake half an hour earlier, but that she was all right and that although all the lines were down she was ringing from her car telephone, which was working. It was the early hours of the morning over there, our lunchtime. Daisy told Jan her television had flown through the air and the walls of her condominium (flat) had cracked from side to side, so she was driving to Coldwater Canyon (where her father has a large house built on rock, which would be safer). She had an old school friend from Benenden, Julie, staying with her, and she was all right too.

Jan telephoned from Chichester and reported all this to us, so Jan in Sussex and Scottie and I in London sat anxiously waiting all that day for the next call from America. All day the television was reporting that all the telephone lines were down, the San Diego Freeway, one of LA's main highways, had collapsed, and explosions and floods and mud slides were taking place across Los Angeles, which was in complete darkness.

After about an hour Jan telephoned us again to say that Daisy and Julie had, after a dreadful journey, arrived safely in Coldwater Canyon. Because all the power lines were down and there was no electricity at the house, Daisy had faced her car onto the front and left the headlights on, to light up the inside of the house. Good old Daisy!

We were still worrying about James, who we hadn't yet heard from, until Jan rang to say that she'd heard that he had also managed to reach the Coldwater Canyon house safe and sound. Thank God.

I feel for Jan so much when the children go back to America, but, as she says, it is the best country for them to be in if they really want to make successful careers for themselves in the entertainment business. There's so much more going on there. But I remember how much I hated it during the fifteen years Jan was living in Beverly Hills. When I knew she was unhappy I wrote to her almost every day, even if it was just a note scribbled on the back of a script during a break in rehearsals, to tell her how much we loved her. I see I've written entries in my diaries 'Sent letter number ? to Jan.'

And I know she's the same with her children. Aren't we daft?

6
Listen with Thora

When Daisy was a little girl I'd make up stories for her. Sometimes I'd write them in letters and sometimes I'd tell them to her, whenever we visited them all in Beverly Hills. I remember once I'd bought her a pair of little party shoes in Kensington High Street. I saw them in the window and they were so pretty, in silver brocade with a little golden strap, I couldn't resist them. We were going to America the following week so I took them with me.

I was about to give them to her and then I thought, no, we could have a bit of fun with them. We were all sitting near the bathing pool one morning and I was telling her a story about a little girl who met a fairy, making it up as I went along, and Daisy was sitting there, looking up at me, listening so solemnly with her chin on her hand, and as I got to the end I said, 'So you see, although she hadn't got what all the other little boys and girls had, the fairy said, "We'll give her a little surprise all of her own, something beautiful and fairy-like ... I know, let's hide it in the garden, where she'll find it." And that night the little girl went to sleep, knowing that the following day she was going to hunt all over the garden to find her fairy surprise.'

Daisy said, 'And does the little girl find the surprise

the next day?' And I said, 'Oh! Certainly. Because the fairies promised it!' After she'd gone into the house for her lunch, there I was, scooting round the garden looking for somewhere to hide these shoes. There was an apple tree with a lot of foliage at the bottom, and flowers, so I hid the box among the flowers. After lunch, when Daisy came out again she said, 'So – if the surprise is still there ... could I find it?' And I said, 'Oh, I do hope it *is* there, and I do hope you *do* find it!'

Well, I was so excited, but do you know we were there from two o'clock until nearly twenty to five! She went here, she went there, she looked and she looked, but she never went anywhere near where I had hidden the box. I was beginning to think I'd have to tell her where it was, because I was getting a bit fed up of this by now. I said, 'Oh, Daisy! There was a bit of the story I didn't tell you. There were some beautiful apples near where the fairies lived, and the fairy said to the little girl, "Would you like an apple?" and the little girl said, "Oh, thank you! I would love an apple." The fairy went to the apple tree to fetch her an apple, and as she tried to get it, it fell, because she was only a little fairy. Oh dear me! So the little girl bent down to find the apple, which had fallen down and got hidden among a lot of beautiful flowers. And what do you think she saw? ...'

And she was off! She disappeared – whoosh! In a minute she came back with her parcel, all done up with ribbon. And it was her little face, when she opened up this box and found the silver shoes the fairies had left her. It was worth anything.

I love all children's books and stories. There's never any malice in them. I like to think that one day I might write some children's stories myself. I've read quite a lot of stories for children on radio and television – I love doing it. I was very flattered to be one of the first people to be asked to read the Paddington Bear stories on television, and afterwards Michael Bond gave me a signed copy of the book. I have it at home now, with the yellow pages of script stuck inside it, because on television you have to read a shortened version of the stories. I probably shouldn't be telling you this, but you do, because you have to fit the words to the pictures.

Anyway, I loved reading about Paddington Bear, and of course I always love reading stories for Jackanory. Years ago now I read all the Mrs Pepperpot stories. I think she was my favourite. She had a little striped skirt on, red hair in a little red bun – I used to think she looked a bit like me. Delightful stories. But on one occasion, I remember, we had a few technical hitches, and the producer, Jeremy Swan, had to keep interrupting me. Things went like this:

THORA: 'Hello! I'm going to read to you about Mrs Pepperpot. Now you remember Mrs Pepperpot, don't you? ...'

JEREMY: No ... (hold on!) ... you what? (Sorry, Thor! Just a minute, love) ... Right. Yes. (Sorry – not you, darling.) Right! OK. Cue Thora.

THORA: 'Hallo! I'm going to read to you about Mrs Pepperpot. Now you remember Mrs Pepperpot, don't you? ...'

JEREMY: No! (Sorry, Thor!) Well are you right now? Yes. Good. Yes. Right. (Yes, it's nothing you're doing, Thor! Just some ...) Right. Good. OK. Cue Thora.

THORA: 'Hallo! I'm going to read to you about Mrs Pepperpot. Now you remember Mrs Pepperpot, don't you? ...'

JEREMY: NO! (So sorry, Thora. There's a gremlin somewhere) ... Right? OK. Cue Thora.

THORA: 'Hallo! I'm going to read to you about Mrs Pepperpot. Now you remember Mrs Pepperpot, don't you? ... *Don't* you? Oh well! Sodyer if you don't remember her, because I'm not going to sit here, reading this, if you don't remember her!'

Quite some time later, I was in my dressing room at the Manchester studios, where we were recording *Flesh and Blood* and there was a knock on the door, and there he stood, armful of flowers, and as I opened my mouth to say, 'Hallo, Jeremy!' he was saying, 'Do you remember Mrs Pepperpot? *Don't* you? Well sodyer, if you don't remember her!'

To this day he's never forgotten it!

I was blessed with very good parents. My father – who, by no means could you call a 'religious' man, but I know that he believed in God – he read the Bible *fourteen* times from front to back. Not fifteen, not thirteen, fourteen – and I know, because he told me this so often. He would say to me, 'Read it. Read it often, and understand it. It's the best book you'll ever read.'

After a pilgrimage you see the Bible differently. The

stories come to life. The distances between places are much smaller than I'd ever imagined, and everything becomes so real and vivid.

I was asked recently to read twelve stories from the Old Testament, on cassettes for children. These Bible stories are so interesting when they are told *as stories*. Even in the days when I was doing *Praise Be!*, when I would sometimes be asked to read from the Bible, I tried never to sound like a female vicar. The Bible really is full of wonderful tales of men and women and their adventures, and if you read it as an actress, and not in a special 'churchy' voice, you get more out of it. Well I think so. Reading these Old Testament stories for children this time, when I had just come back from a pilgrimage to the Holy Land, well, I could hardly describe it as a job of work, I enjoyed doing it so much. Later on I did twelve more, from the New Testament. And by the time this book comes out I will have had the joy of recording the whole of *The Life and Death of Jesus* on cassette.

It's when I'm asked to jobs like that that I sit for a bit sometimes and think to myself, 'Are you really good enough for this?'

7
The Olde Lofte

Our home in London is in a Mews and we've lived there ever since Scottie was demobbed after the war.

You have to come in under an archway by a pub and walk down to the bottom of the Mews to find us, walking across cobbles. When we first arrived the cobbling was beautiful, because in the old days they were artistic with the cobbles, every one had to be the same shape. It came up in the centre, like the sun coming up, so the rain could run down the cobbles. And some people still kept hens on the side.

Some time ago now they re-did it, and it's never been the same since. They don't look like anything now. For every five cobbles they took out, they put three back, and instead of packing soil between them, like before, they put concrete. I suppose they made quite a good job of it, but it's never been the same, and they are always having bits up for electricity and such. It took them so long to re-do it, there was one little man who almost became a relative, we saw him so often. We asked him to stay one evening to concrete under our stairs, where we keep the wine, because before that it was just earth. Every morning, going out to rehearsals it would be, 'Good morning, Thora!' all the way up the Mews.

The cobbles in our garage are Staffordshire Blues. If you bought one now it would cost the earth – well, you couldn't get 'em now, anyway. I wouldn't know Staffordshire blue from Coventry pink, but Jimmy knew, because he had spent many years in Staffordshire.

We've given some very good parties in the Mews, especially on New Year's Eves. We've had up to seventy people in the garage – you couldn't get seventy people upstairs in the flat, but the garage could hold five cars – if you packed them like dominoes. We had laid half of it with a wooden floor when we first moved in, because Jan was learning to tap-dance with Jack Billings – a lot of professionals will remember Jack Billings – and we used that as a dance floor, for the parties.

We tried to keep everything as it was. The four horse stalls are still there, although the wooden partitions dividing them have long gone. The Staffordshire blue cobbles still cover the floor. If you look up you can see the squares where the food chutes were, where the hay and oats came down for the horses. There's also a chute where you can put a little lid down, the front has a handle so you can stop it when you've had enough. And if you lift the carpet up in our flat up above, you can see the same squares, only, of course, they've been boarded up now.

In the old tack room at the back of the garage are all the heavy iron hooks for the horse collars, bridles and the rest of the horse trappings. There's a tiny iron fireplace so the coachman or driver could keep warm while he cleaned the harness and horse brasses, and there's an iron sneck (Lancashire for handle) on the door.

Most people have the tack room taken out to make more room in their garage, but we kept ours. I've always loved all these old things. Jimmy had it as a workroom. His drumkit is still in there – two pea-boilers, side drums, bells, cymbals and everything.

Upstairs, between the lounge and the dining room windows, looking out over the Mews, is a hay-gate. There is a door, and if you open the door there's the wooden gate. It's very attractive. I have plant-pots fastened on it, and flowers in front. I keep the door open all day, and hear people coming and going, up and down the Mews ... life going on. I wouldn't be without that gate. I love it. The first thing I do in the morning is open the door to it.

And a loving thing about it was, when I would be coming home from work and the car that brought me back would stop in front of the house, Scottie would hear me and he'd hang over the hay-gate and call down, 'Don't bother getting your keys out, I'll come down!' And I don't have to say that I miss that very much these days.

We call the whole lot The Olde Lofte. It's full of love and memories. Who would want to leave all that? Not me. It's like me – old but well preserved.

8
Handles

Now in this chapter I'm speaking as a lady of eighty-four. Here's me with my arthritis, my stick and all the rest of it. But when I was a little girl, and we lived next door to the Royalty Theatre in Cheapside, in the foyer of the theatre, outside the Dress Circle doors ... I can see it now as I write this – all that red carpet. There were two lots of double doors, and they each had very large brass handles on them, cleaned by a lady with one eye called Mrs Randall. And if I was being comic I would say, 'I do not remember the name of the other eye!' Mrs Randall polished the handles until they shone like gold; when I was little I thought they *were* gold.

Well, as the years rolled by a very sad time came when the Royalty was going to be demolished – which it never should have been, I don't mind adding. And it was a Bradford firm that were demolishing it: I thought, 'It would be a bloomin' *Yorkshire* firm!' Anyhow, they did get on the telephone to me, and said that they understood that it had been such a big part of my life ... and really, it had, when you think how I started in Rep there; I'd played on the stage and under the stage as a child, because we had lived next door for so many years. Yes, I *loved* the Royalty

Theatre. And I don't think that's a misuse of the word.

Anyhow, they asked me was there anything I would like as a souvenir? I thought immediately, 'Yes, please. I would like a set of the Dress Circle door handles.'

They sent them to me, and they now grace the left-hand side of the staircase in my London house. But you see, I didn't think when I was tripping about blithely at the age of four, thinking they were made of gold, that they were going to assist me to go upstairs when I was eighty-four – which they really do. I've got a banister on the other side of the stairs, but those handles help me, and every day I think about the Royalty – up the stairs, down the stairs. And they still shine.

At the bottom of the stairs I have the Exeter Theatre 'pass door' handle. A 'pass door' in a theatre, for anybody who doesn't know – please don't think I think you don't know, but these are terms that, unless you've worked in the theatre you probably wouldn't know – is usually on the left-hand side of the auditorium, and it passes from the stalls to the stage (have a look next time you're in a theatre), and it is private. You have to have permission to use it. It isn't something anybody can just open and go onto the stage. Well, I have the handle of the Exeter Theatre 'pass door' on the bottom door in the Mews. And on the door going into the garage I have the handles from the St James Theatre, in London. So every handle holds a memory, and they all shine so beautifully I'm afraid of finger-marking them sometimes.

I have mentioned many times in articles and things how fond I am of brass. I don't know why I get to like these things that want cleaning – all my life I seem to have been cleaning something. But they look nice, you see, they look so nice as they shine. I'll tell you something else I've got on my staircase – a set of weights, eight pounds, four pounds, two pounds, one pound, half a pound – shining like solid gold. I bought these when I was doing *First Lady*, the drama series where I played a councillor. We used the Barnsley Council Chamber in the Town Hall. There was a councillor there, a real one, a particularly nice lady who invited me to lunch one day, saying she wanted to show me something. Well, she took me into Wonderland! It was a warehouse, imagine this, *full* of scales, like there used to be in shops, that had a marble thing that you put the bacon on, and all these weights. I thought, 'I'll buy two sets of weights, because they'll remind me of when I worked at the Co-op.'

So now, every time I'm going up or down the stairs in my London house I'm reminded both of the Co-op and of the Royalty Theatre, two wonderfully happy and loving periods of my life.

May I say at this point, I don't profess to be the world's greatest authoress, in fact I'm not so much an authoress as much as a person having a little chat with you all. Not that you get the chance to correct me, or answer me back, but most of you who read my efforts *know* me. Well, I mean you know me well enough to understand what I write about, and how I would say things in a chat with you. So let's say I'm like a friend who has nipped into your home for a little chat, and this being a book – you can 'shut me up' whenever you wish!

If you are reading my efforts in bed, you can put

them down at any time, as I haven't written everything chronologically, so 'Goodnight and God bless' to any reader who is just about to snuggle down and drop off!

9
The Mill House, Isfield

Jan met William in America in 1978, at a dinner party in a mutual friend's home. They had both been through broken marriages; William had four children, Jan two. Understandably, neither of them was in a rush to marry again, but as time went by and they saw that all their children mixed in well, they spent a lot of time together and, eventually, in April 1981 they were married in America, in the home of William's best man, the author Barnie Leason.

They married at noon, and then got the six o'clock evening flight back to England, where at long last she was coming home to live. It was joy unbounded for us.

I remember the day, a few months before the wedding, when they came to the Mews and they were so excited, with Polaroid pictures they'd taken of The Mill House, Isfield. It was a lovely old house, big enough for William's four children, who often visited, and Jan's two, to all have a room each. Really, it was a little estate. There were fourteen acres, with a wood and two meadows and a river running into a lake. There were two greenhouses – a big old-fashioned Victorian one that was heated and a modern one with a vine, planted by William, and there was even a dear little cottage, which we eventually moved into ourselves in April 1982, which had originally been a cowshed.

As time went by Scottie and I did the cottage up and furnished it, and we had a conservatory built on the back. We both worked hard on the garden, which really became very pretty, though I say so myself. We had such happy times there, although we couldn't get down there as often as we'd like, because if I was filming or rehearsing early on a Monday morning it was too far to go down there just for two days.

Whenever we were at Isfield I used to love to wake up in the early morning (five-thirty to six o'clock is a magic time) and walk round our garden. As I strolled along, mug of tea in one hand, my faithful stick in the other, the smell of fresh grass, trees, flowers and weeds (and don't forget a weed is only a flower in the wrong place!) permeated the early morning air. The noise of birds getting up – our privet hedges were always packed with nests – was deafening.

The smell of new-mown grass is marvellous in the summer months. Before very long Jan would appear with her dogs, Lucy, Tess and Patch, and they would come up to me and sit looking very pathetic until I reached in the pocket of my duffel coat to give them their first biscuits of the day, four each. Scottie would join us, and those were the magic moments when I was so aware of having *everything* ... everything that matters.

I know a lot of you will be familiar with the Mill House and its beautiful grounds, and the dogs and ducks and geese that lived there, because for many happy years it became the setting for *Praise Be!* Once Jan and Bill had settled in we recorded all the programmes there, and for about ten days each year the BBC would take over the ground floor. They weren't originally supposed to have all that, they were just supposed to be in the living room, but Jan, being such a professional herself, suggested that they use the dining room as a 'producer's gallery' for everyone not needed on 'the set' – i.e. her living room – so they could sit and watch on a monitor, for which they were very grateful. But it didn't end there. Valetta Stallabrass, who was the very good, very dear and loving director of the series for many years, and has become a great family friend, was soon suggesting that we record some of the links by the inglenook fireplace in the study ... and some in the kitchen ... and some in the conservatory. To cut a long story short, by the time the series finished we'd recorded *Praise Be!* links in every downstairs room of the house, and all over the grounds – in the woods, beside the lake, having tea in the rose garden, looking for mallard ducks' nests, gathering daffodils ... you name it, we filmed it. One year, after the director had said, 'Right. That's a wrap!' I said, 'Are you sure? Are you quite sure you don't want to take a shot of me upstairs in the four-poster bed? You've been everywhere else!'

Every year for that week, although the household was disrupted and the hall was full of cables and ground sheets and there was always someone in the downstairs loo, no one minded and we were like one big happy family. For me it was great, because at lunch-time I just had to walk twenty-two steps across to the cottage to have lunch with Scottie, and the make-up girl would come across to help me change and make up for the afternoon show. Or we'd all go out to the local pub, the Laughing Fish. Members of the crew used to put in a special request to the BBC to come back each year, so we usually had the same cameraman and sound man, and even the autocue operator, Jeremy, used to contrive to be back with us every year.

Jan used to arrange the flowers, often having picked them from her own cutting beds, but some were ordered in – and she would often take part in the programmes by doing a reading, or coming in to chat with me on the show, because we got so many requests every year from people who wanted to see her, especially to hear her read, because she does read beautifully. Scottie, Daisy and James, and even William put in appearances over the years, so viewers began to feel they really knew the whole family ... In fact, Daisy can only have been about ten the first year she was on, James two years younger, and as the programme went on for so many years you almost saw them growing up on *Praise Be!*

As for the ducks and the dogs – they were regular scene-stealers. One day we had to pretend I was telling the dogs the story of St Francis of Assisi, and how he loved all God's creatures. The viewers saw me telling the story, and Lucy, Tess and Patch gazing at me in rapt attention, their faces looking for all the world as if they were thinking, 'Oh, St Francis! Oh what a kind man!', the occasional tail thumping. What you couldn't see were three biscuits on the ground in front of them, or Jan, just behind the camera, commanding them to 'Wait! Trust!' As soon as I finished it was 'Good dogs – take!' and three noses plunged forwards to gobble up the biscuits.

The series began one year with me leaning out of the window, and just as I did so a procession of about ten Muscovy ducks waddled by in front of the camera. You couldn't have planned that, or trained them to do it. It was just one of the moments of magic – of which there were many, and I've written about them in my *Praise Be!* books – that all made recording *Praise Be!* at the Mill House such a joyous thing.

The other thing that we all loved about our time at Isfield was our church and our friendship with the wonderful vicar, Roger Dalling, who was like a magician the way he conducted services, and especially the way he told stories to the children, stories which held us all spellbound.

The ancient parish church of Isfield is along a beautifully kept country lane, just opposite the Mill House gates. The river Uck runs close by, and you can still see remains of locks from when it was a busy thoroughfare for barges. You can also see the earthworks of a medieval wooden fortress that guarded a ford in the river. And there was once a Roman road just to the west, running due north all the way from Newhaven to London. So once the little church would have been at the centre of all the main thoroughfares, not hidden away at the end of our little country lane. The great Roman and Victorian empires have grown up – and faded away again – all around that little church. But it's still there, and I'm sure it will be for centuries to come.

10

Hallelujah!

When I was doing the series *Hallelujah!* for Yorkshire television in the early 1980s, written by Dick Sharples, I played Salvation Army Captain Emily Ridley, aged forty-two.

When you are making a programme about something like the Salvation Army, you always take a lot of care not to offend them in any way. Any television company will be careful about that. We had to have a technical adviser from the Salvation Army to let us know whether we were going too far – or not far enough. And I'm happy to tell you, according to the Salvation Army we never went nearly far enough. They said some of the stories they could tell were even funnier than the ones Dick was making up.

That was how I met Rob Garrod of the Salvation Army, who was a captain himself then and their Director of Public Relations – he's something much higher up now. He was our technical adviser and we became good friends, and through him I often became involved with doing things for the Salvation Army proper. Whenever I went to the citadel in Oxford Street to make a personal appearance, on the back wall there would be a big photograph of me, in the uniform and the bonnet, which I was always rather proud of – I quite fancied myself in that bonnet!

I am still invited to many Salvation Army events, including the big 'Carolthon' they hold every year in their citadel in Oxford Street. One year Princess Diana was on the platform as well. Before the show we were all gathered in a room drinking orange juice and cups of tea. It was the first time I'd met her, although I've met her many times since. She's a great giggler, as you probably know, and she was so lovely and natural it was just like talking to ... you! We chatted about one thing or another for a little while, and I was longing to ask her what her favourite hymn was, for *Praise Be!*, but I didn't have the cheek. Then it was time for her to lead us all on to the platform in front of the audience, and as she was going – I don't know whether she'd read my mind, or what – she leaned back and said with one of her giggles, 'By the way, my favourite hymn is "Breathe on me Breath of God" – with the descant.'

When filming out of doors you usually wear a small microphone, concealed somewhere on your person, with leads connecting it to a battery transmitter, which you hide in a pocket or somewhere. The sound assistant will come to clip it on just before 'shooting' starts. For *Hallelujah!* my uniform fitted me like a glove because it had been tailored for me by the Salvation Army's own outfitters, so the transmitter had to be clipped on to the back of my skirt to be hidden from view, and the wires had to come down from the mike, which was pinned on the inside of my blouse, under my skirt, and back up between my legs to connect to the transmitter at the back. Do you follow?

Well, we were filming on an ordinary pavement, just outside Leeds. The mike was already pinned to the inside of my blouse, and the sound assistant came to fix the transmitter to the back of my skirt and connect it up with my mike. Now forgive the way I tell this, because however I tell it, it's going to sound a bit suggestive and I don't intend it to. There was I, in my Salvation Army uniform and bonnet, out on the street with this young fellow kneeling on the pavement and putting his arm up inside my skirt ... reaching up for the wires, you see ...

Just at that moment there were two women passing on the other side of the road, with their shopping baskets full of groceries. One of the women let out such an 'Oh!', and dropped her basket of groceries ... there were apples and potatoes rolling all down the pavement. 'Good God!' the other woman said. 'Just look at that!' In all the commotion I turned to look at them, and the first woman laughed and said, 'Ho! ho! It's only Thora he's doing it to. So that's all right!'

I've often thought – they can send people into space, land on the moon ... you'd think they could invent something a bit cleverer than having to put a hand up your skirt to fix a mike on, wouldn't you?

Captain Emily Ridley was one of those characters that every actress enjoys playing – because although you laughed at her, you also felt sorry for her. The joke was, although she was a Salvation Army captain she should have been much higher ranking by that stage in her career, and really she was a failure and her superiors were a little embarrassed and ashamed of her, because she was terribly accident-prone. In the story, they decide to put her in charge of her own citadel ... but it's a completely run-down citadel. We found a very shabby, derelict building to film in – there was a little sadness about it, but it had the right atmosphere.

It wouldn't have mattered to her if it had been a hen-house, she was so proud to have been put in charge of her own citadel. Helped by the faithful Alice Meredith, delightfully played by Patsy Rowlands, Emily set about, week after week, to go about doing good, and week after week everything always went wrong, in a funny way of course.

There was one thing about her ... she would talk to the Lord, and ask for help or, if she'd done something wrong, to apologise. So many people wrote to me saying, 'I do that! That's exactly how I talk to the Lord ...' And I do too. I don't mean I talk out loud to the Lord in Sainsbury's so people can hear me, but I do talk to him anywhere I am.

I've always loved the Salvation Army and I'm a great admirer of all the wonderful work they do. Every day, all over the world, thousands of people find themselves in too much trouble to be able to help themselves, and the Lord's own Army is always there to lend a hand.

11

A 'first-class' production

Sometimes you know immediately that a play you're in is going to be a *first-class* production.

I felt really honoured to be asked to be in the Screen Two production of Muriel Spark's *Momento Mori*, because you don't say 'Jack Clayton, the director' you say 'Jack Clayton, the genius' if you've any sense. Mr Clayton treats you as a professional, wouldn't take you on unless you *were* a professional and, I'll tell you something for nothing, even if you weren't when you started, by the time you've worked with him for any length of time – you *are* a professional!

In some ways it was a bit like an old school reunion, all the cast having known each other for so many years. It was a joy even to watch the scenes you weren't in, they were all so good. Michael Hordern – oh, what a great man – Maurice Denham, who I've known for a thousand years, Maggie Smith, Cyril Cusack, Zoë Wanamaker, Stephanie Cole – all marvellous artists – and the wonderful Renee Asherson, who I had last worked with in the days before she married Robert Donat; it was really so nice to be with her again. She's such a dainty little soul. I felt very happy to be playing her maid.

We were filming in an ex-naval hospital that had

been shut down for ages, and it was terribly cold. I was playing the servant, the old family retainer, and I had a long scene in bed in the hospital, with John Wood, playing the Detective, at my bedside. I remember I had a line, 'You knew it was her, didn't you?' It was freezing cold, so I was glad to be in the bed. Jack Clayton was there, wearing the biggest muffler you ever saw in your life round his neck, and as he was standing on the set I said, 'Now how would you like this, Mr de Grundfeld?' and he just looked at me, so I said, 'Well, there are five or six ways I can say this. I can say: "You *knew* it was her ..., didn't you?"

or: "You knew it was *her* ..., didn't you?"

or: "*You* knew it was her, didn't you?"

or: "YOU *KNEW* – IT WAS *HER*! – DIDN'T YOU?"

or –'

By this time the crew were all laughing, so I said, 'This is a fact – this is a very important line, and there are many, many ways of saying it.'

But it was something even more than all the above that told me I was in a really 'first-class' production ... Stephanie Cole and I were convulsed by this. The toilet was quite a long way away, along a path outside the hospital, towards the end of a block. The first time I wanted to 'go' was during a coffee break – thank heaven – and I said, 'Excuse me getting out of bed, but I'd like to go to the loo.' 'Right!' said someone, who shot off ahead of me. There were some steps down outside, and I saw there was a car there and a chauffeur who opened the door when he saw me, so I said, 'No! I'm not going home. I'm only going to the toilet.' And he said, 'Yes, I know. I'm taking you.'

And, indeed, that is exactly what he was there for –

a chauffeur to drive us to and from the toilet!

I promise you, that has never happened to me in my life, before or since, and you could tell from that alone it really was going to be a *first-class* production.

12

When I grow up ...

I don't think there is a human being who doesn't have childhood ambitions of some sort. From the time we are able to talk we'll say, 'When I grow up I'm going to ...' And we all know people who have worked hard and sacrificed many things to achieve their ambitions.

When I was about six or seven years old I discovered my first ambition – now do pay attention, because this is a three-act play I'm going to tell you about.

Act One: Every Saturday I went to Dugdale's Pork Butchers ... it was a good'un! Lovely smells of roasting pork, meat pies, butter, black puddings – and 'palony'. (Do you remember palony? It was a sort of pork paste filling in a bright red skin like a very thick salami, sold by weight. I haven't seen any for years. In fact I've never seen any in London. I'm not saying there isn't any in London – I don't want dozens of Londoners writing and telling me off, or where I can get it – I'm simply saying *I* haven't seen any.) Now where was I?

Oh, I remember, I was in Dugdale's Pork Butchers. Every Saturday we had what my mother called 'a *bought* lunch'. I know that sounds as though we never bought any other food, but you understand me, don't you? She meant a 'shop' lunch – no cooking at home. My regular order at Dugdale's was: a quarter of boiled ham, a quarter of tongue and two ounces of corned beef.

Act Two: We would eat it with home-made pickled onions and home-made pickled red cabbage and, instead of home-made bread, I would have been to Dora's – the little confectioner two minutes from our house – for six-penny-worth of 'oven-bottom cakes'. For unbelievers, I will explain that an 'oven-bottom cake' was not a cake at all, but rather like a tea-cake, only slightly thicker and larger, and baked in the oven bottom, seven for sixpence. We'd eat them warm, plastered with creamy farm butter bought from the milkman – Ernie Thornton, in case you want to know his name (and not to be confused with Ernie who drove 'the fastest milk-cart in the west' that the wonderful Benny Hill used to sing about).

Act Three: I would go to Newsome's in Euston Road for two chocolate eclairs, two cream horns and two vanilla slices. When the Four Hirds (Dad, Mam, Nev and I) had had a cake each to finish our meal, the two remaining cakes were cut in two and the four pieces would sit there while we thought which half of which cake we would have. What a meal! Menu: Cold cuts (as they say in America) with home-made pickles. Choice of sweets: pastries various. Milk or Tea. It was the same every Saturday, and it was, excuse my plain English, ruddy lovely.

To return to the ambitions, which is what this chapter is supposed to be about, my greatest ambition at that period was ... to make enough money to be able to have as many vanilla slices as I wanted. I love vanilla slices to this day, and I have got enough money to have them as often as I want – so I suppose you could say I have achieved that ambition.

The second was more serious, and came to me when I was about twelve, when we had 'the City of Pompeii' for History one term. I cannot remember ever being so impressed by any period of history. I thought about it for days – weeks – especially the bit about 'And people are still to be seen, covered in ashes and lapilli, sitting eating their meals.' Covered in lava ... eating their meals ... and dead for years! I nearly drove my brother Nev daft talking about it, asking him questions and badgering him over and over again to explain why the people were sitting eating, and hadn't run away. 'Aw, our kid, do shurrup about bloomin' Pompeii!' he would say, 'It was all so sudden. And they're not still sitting there eating their meals properly now. They're dead. Petrified.' So you can understand, a visit to the city of Pompeii was a 'must' for when I grew up and could see the world.

And yet it was not until 1989 that Scottie and I went to Sorrento, and stayed at the Grand Hotel ExcelsiorVictoria. Scottie had been looking at the diary some time in August and found I had a couple of weeks free the following October. Out came the holiday brochures. 'How about Sorrento? We could stay at the ExcelsiorVictoria – where Jan and I stayed years ago.'

The reason he had stayed there with Jan and without me was because in those days our twelve-year-old daughter was a child film star. (She'll shoot me for saying that, but it's true!) She was in *Helen of Troy* and was filming in Rome for about three months, and of course her father was with her – not in the film, I mean – as chaperone, companion and general looker-after. They suddenly found they had a week or so free, so they decided to spend it in Sorrento, and booked into the Grand Hotel ExcelsiorVictoria (what a mouthful this hotel name is becoming!).

'Of course, it will have altered a lot. But it's a five-star hotel and sounds all right. What do you think?' I was stitching a button on his blazer. 'I think – yes, let's,' I said, as I snipped the cotton after the completion of the button sewing (with shank, kindly note). I was also thinking that Sorrento is very near Pompeii – my childhood ambition was at long last about to be fulfilled. So to Sorrento we went.

As we arrived in our room at the hotel I asked Scottie if he thought it had changed much since his last visit. 'Well, I can't remember every detail after forty odd years,' Scottie said, 'But ... ' at that moment he was interrupted by a waiter gliding into our room with a bottle of very cold champagne and two glasses, who silently opened the bottle, poured out the icy golden liquid and handed us a frosted glass each, and glided out. 'No, it hasn't altered up to now!' said Scottie, as we raised our glasses and wished each other a happy holiday.

Anyway, here I was at last – nearly eighty years old, excited as a child about getting my first glimpse of Pompeii, that long-imagined place – and just a walk away from our hotel.

Oh dear. Everyone, just everyone, advised me against visiting Pompeii, because of my arthritis. The ground is very uneven, and there's a hill to be climbed to get to the entrance. I was determined to go anyway, until I thought of Scottie, who would have to assist me every minute. He said it would be no trouble, but was still afraid it would be too much for me. So, I thought, 'Go on, Thor. Get back in your cheese. I'll keep my own picture of what it all looks like. Sorry Pompeii!'

I'll just write Pompeii on my very small list of things I've always wanted – and never got – and never will.

And why should I? I've had everything that matters – the love of a wonderful husband and family and the love of my friend upstairs, the good Lord. I don't even care about my old wish list any longer, but here it is in its entirety:

1. Eat as many vanilla slices as I want
2. Visit Pompeii
3. Live in a cottage with a thatched roof and inglenook fireplace
4. Play Mrs Pankhurst
5. Own a mink coat and hat

1. Well – of course – I can afford to eat all the vanilla slices I want now, and I still love 'em ... but not being seven or eight years old any longer, I never want more than one.
2. Pompeii. It would have to be from a helicopter for me to see it now ... but I have such a wonderful picture of it in my imagination, I think it might spoil it to see the real thing.
3. I realise a thatched roof is imposs. Dangerous and madly expensive to insure, but I have now got a lovely eighteenth-century cottage with a big stone fireplace,

big enough to display my collection of copper and brass. And in these days of central heating – who could want for more?

4. I'm too old to play Mrs Pankhurst now. And with all the wonderful parts Alan Bennett has written for me over the past twenty years – why do anything less?

5. Mink coat and hat – got 'em! Can't wear 'em (in case somebody chucks an egg at me).

13
'Bluddy Love'

This chapter is all about love – we'll only come to the 'bluddy' bit at the end. Every mother, grandmother, auntie, sister knows that there are so many sorts of love. It's worth your sitting down with a cup of coffee after your lunch and having a think, 'Just a minute ... I'll have a count ... how many sorts of love are there?'

I mean, the love you have for your mother is different from the love you have for your father. The love you have for your brother is different from for your sister or best friends.

I've always thought – and you may agree with this or not, and if you don't agree, it gives you a chance to turn to your friend and say, 'Do you see what she says? That's not right ...' But I think that fathers are inclined to lean to the daughter in the family, and the mother, I am sure, leans to the boy.

I can remember this very vividly. We were an extremely happy household – and you must be fed up of hearing me say that – but my brother Neville was a year and nine months older than I was, and my mother adored him. Bit of a strong word, but my mother loved my brother very much. She loved me too, but I said to her one day, 'You love our Neville more than you love me, don't you?' She looked at me, did my mother, with the actress's face, and she said, 'God forgive you for saying that!' It was as though I'd accused her of murder or something. And she said – I always remember the word she used, because when I was young and I got hold of a new word I didn't understand, the moment I understood it (or thought I understood it) I would use it a lot. She said, 'I don't love Neville one *iota* more than I love you.'

I was using 'iota' in the wrong place for about a month after that, because I liked it. 'She did not leave an iota of food,' and my mother would say, 'Oh no, no, Thora, that's not right!' I remember the word 'adamant'. When I heard the word adamant I thought, 'Oh, that's nice ... No, I'm *adamant*.' Adamant. Iota. There are some lovely words in the language, you know.

But I digress. Love is the word we're talking about. My mother said to me, 'Don't you ever say that again, Thora. I love you both equally.' And of course she did. But I think there is a thing – is 'genetically' the right word? I mean, my father, if I was out a bit late – of course it's so old-fashioned if one talks about it now, 'obedience', but if my parents said to me, 'Right, be in for ten o'clock' I had no reason to think 'Well, five past will do. Six past will do'; I was in for ten o'clock. You were in those days. But I know that if ever I *was* a minute or two late, my mother would be saying 'She's late ...' but my father would say, 'We-ell – she could have been ...' and always make an excuse for me. And my mother, if my brother was ever late, would say, 'Well, Jimmy, he's a lot of friends. They'll be talking politics round the lamp.' That was the lamp in our street. I tell you, this country was run from 'round the lamp' opposite our house. It was an alternative government.

You feel another kind of love for your friends and neighbours. There's even a love you have for an animal, a pet dog or cat. Children love their dolls and soft toys. Then there's the difference between loving somebody, and being 'in love'. There's the times you think you are 'in love', but you're not, like, as in my case, with some of the boys you meet before you get married. Then when you do get married, that's a different love altogether.

When you are a woman and you have your baby, well, that is a love you can't describe. Mother love is a love on its own. I remember when they said to me – 'Here's your baby,' and all in a second thinking a thousand things that every mother thinks, 'Oh, she's mine! Oh, isn't she wonderful?'

I would like to say that I am one of the best mothers in the world. I would *like* to say it, when, forgive me, really I am a bluddy nuisance! This is the truth. There is my daughter, Jan, a grown-up married woman with two children of her own, and they're grown-ups now too. She's a very capable, very loving woman, and I know when I'm ill there's no one I'd rather have around than Jan. But if she's on her own in the house, I'll ring her up about three times that night and I'll make an excuse, although I know she knows perfectly well that I'm really thinking, 'Are you all right?' Of course she's all right! She's much more capable of looking after herself than I am. I'll say to her later, when I see her, 'You must excuse me if I'm a nuisance, but you know it's because I love you.' And she'll give me a lovely look and say, 'I know it's because you love me!' And she laughs.

Sometimes when you love someone, it's hard to say it. Lancashire is a county full of very loving and lovable people. I say that because I know Lancashire and Lancashire people probably better than I know anyone else. And so often they'll say something that sounds *so unkind* – but which is sincerely meant for loving kindness. Here are just two short examples I can think of, just to give you a little laugh before you close the book and go to sleep.

One was when I was in a bad car accident in about 1957, and more or less went through the windscreen. I was in hospital, with my face about a foot wide – blue, yellow, pink – and my mouth was standing up like a figure one, so you might know I really didn't look too pretty! A lady came in, with her niece, who was going into the next bed to have her appendix out. I don't think the girl was nervous, only her auntie kept saying 'There's nothing to worry about, Nellie! Don't be worried.' Well, the girl *wasn't* worried, but after about fifteen times of hearing this, she began to look very worried. Auntie was fussing around and she put five brown fruit bags on the locker between my bed and the girl's and said, 'Now, Nellie, you won't be able to eat these until tomorrow. They'll not let you eat any of these tonight.' Then the nurse came along and said, 'I'm afraid I'll have to ask you to go now, as we've to serve the teas, and it isn't really visiting day.'

(And that's another thing – pardon me just coming off the story for a minute – there used to be 'Visiting Hours: 2 – 3, Wednesday and Saturday'. Nowadays you can visit someone in hospital every day at nine in the morning if you want, and stay all day. Whether that's better or worse, I don't know.)

Anyhow, Auntie started to put on her left glove, getting ready to go. I say this because I want you to visualise this woman with her glove, pulling the fingers on, and as she did so she looked round and noticed me in the next bed. As I say, I was not a pretty sight, and she said, 'Is it ... Thora?' I gave her a sort of nod, and she said, 'Hough! Dear me! What a sight! What a sample!' Then she leaned over me, still pulling her glove on, and the entire ward must have heard her as she whispered very loudly, right in my ear 'What a good job you were never good-looking before!'

Now that sounds cruel, I know, but it isn't. She was meaning to be very kind. And if you work it out – it *was* a good job I wasn't good-looking before!

The other little example I'll tell you about was when I was in Morecambe to play at the theatre in Bank Holiday week. It really was, as we say up there, 'raining stair rods'. I was staying with some friends who had a very nice flat looking out onto the promenade, and on this particular morning I was looking out and there was not a soul to be seen. Just an empty prom, empty beach and driving rain.

Then into view comes a fellow in one of those grey macintoshes that you could roll up and put in an envelope. They were very popular when they first came out. He's got new white plimsolls on – you could tell they were bought for his holiday. An open-necked cricket shirt. And a cap. About two yards behind him trails a little child – I would say two or three years old – in a little red mac and sou'wester. He's got his beach bucket in his hand, and a tin- or iron-ended spade, not a wooden spade, which he's trailing along the ground. The window I was watching them from was open at the top, and I could hear this child's spade scraping along. The man was walking in front, head down, funeral pace, and he suddenly turned round and looked at this kid, trailing along in the pouring rain, and he was fed up, and he said, 'Eeeeee! Come on, bluddy love!'

I thought to myself – the affection in that – 'Come on, bluddy love!' I could just imagine the young mother sitting in the holiday lodgings, with a paperback novel, and the child going mad since breakfast 'Are we going on the sands? Are we going to the sea?' And she must have said, 'Oh, Edwin – take him and let him have a walk along!'

So you see, that's Lancashire folk for you – 'Come on, bluddy love!'

14
Twice nightly

For many years on a summer Sunday evening you had to make up your mind: 'Now shall I watch Thora on the BBC? Or Sir Harry on ITV?' We both had audiences of six or seven or more million viewers – so that wasn't bad going for the 'God slot', was it? Fourteen million or more people between us, watching religious programming.

Harry Secombe and I had first met years ago, even long before we worked together at the London Palladium in 1966 when Harry was presenting a show called *London Laughs*. I had to turn down a part in a West End play to be in it – and thank goodness I did – thirty-two weeks, twice nightly and three shows on a Saturday ... wonderful! At that time I was in a television comedy series with Freddie Frinton, *Meet the Wife*, so Freddie and I acted out an episode from the show on stage.

The second act opened with a big cockney scene. Harry and I rode on stage dressed as a Pearly King and Queen in a lovely little cart, pulled along by a very lovable little donkey who was brought to the side of the stage just a few minutes before he was needed. Of course we all had tit-bits for him before he went on stage. It never went to his head. He was the dearest little thing and – please note, *James Tarbuck!* – I can't remember the donkey *ever* misbehaving on stage! In fact, my greatest wish from then on was to be able to ride in a donkey cart – in real life, not on stage – a wish that was to be granted nearly thirty years later – but that's another story.

Well, years rolled by, and soon after I started presenting *Praise Be!* Harry began presenting *Highway*. So now we were both doing religious programmes, with interviews and hymns, and I'm told that any time they had to stop the filming on *Highway* for a few moments (as you often have to do if an aeroplane goes overhead, drowning out the sound) Harry would unfailingly look up and say, 'There goes Thora Hird in her spy-helicopter again!'

But it was always a friendly rivalry, and eventually the *Highway* team asked me if I would come on Sir Harry's programme, during a time when *Praise Be!* wasn't on the air. I very happily joined him on the sands at Grange, across the bay from Morecambe, where I read 'Footprints' – a beautiful piece about how God carries you through the hardest parts of your life.

It was a beautiful day, and I read it to the best of my ability, and when it got to lunchtime Harry had to be driven off to the airport while I stayed for lunch with the director. As Harry was leaving – I can see him now, hanging out of the window at the back – he shouted out, 'Here! Thora! Don't forget to ask me to be on *Praise Be-e-e!*' And from the busy pavement outside the restaurant I shouted back, 'No! I will! I will! I promise you, Harry, I will!'

And indeed I did. The trouble was, *Highway* was

always on the air during the six weeks in the summer when *Praise Be!* was on. The strange thing was, Liz Barr, who I work with as often as I can when I'm doing my religious programmes and books, was then with the BBC producing *Praise Be!*, and her husband Andrew Barr was with ITV, producing *Highway*. So there was a man and wife, sitting round their kitchen table in their cottage of an evening, working on their scripts, his for Harry and hers for me. Unfortunately even they couldn't get the two companies to agree to let Harry come on my show, because it would have meant that if the audience were watching Harry on *Praise Be!*, they wouldn't be watching him on *Highway*, you see. So that was the reason he never came on. It was a shame, because I would have loved to have had him on my show. He's a very funny, lovable man, with great faith.

So it all goes to show, as someone once wrote in my autograph book when I was a little girl – it was purple kid leather with 'Autographs' in gilt on the front cover – 'The scene is set, the lights are on, the stage is all aglow, but what may happen behind the scenes – only the artists know!'

15
Cream Crackers

In 1987 the BBC presented a series of Alan Bennett's plays under the title *Talking Heads*. Now I've always enjoyed saying Alan's words, but I can remember this time, when I first read *Cream Cracker Under the Settee*, thinking, 'This one is going to be difficult to play without crying.' Among the many things that my father taught me about the business – and, Heaven knows, he taught me all the important things – one was: if you show too much emotion, you won't glean a lot. And it's true is that. Show too many tears and you don't get the people watching you as moved as you will if you fight it a little.

On the first day of rehearsals I got to about page eleven and I could hardly speak it, I was so upset. I apologised through my tears to the director, Stuart Burge. I said, 'I'm awfully sorry. I won't be like this by Friday.' He was blowing his nose, and he said, 'Won't you? I still will!'

It was a forty-four-minute play, or monologue, and Scottie, who was always at the back of me about everything – and I so often wonder what I would have done without him ... well, I know what I would have done without him, probably – nothing ... Anyhow, as it was my habit to get up first in the morning and go straight in the bathroom and turn the taps on, Scottie said to me, 'When you get up in the morning, don't turn your bathwater on. Let's get on the book.' (Meaning – study the words.) Which is what we did.

I said to Scottie on the second morning, 'Would you like a bit of a bet, for fun?' And he said, 'A bet? What about?' And I said, 'That I'll know it in six mornings.' To which that lovely face looked at me and he said, 'Well, of course you'll know it! That's what they're paying you for, to know it!'

Anyhow, little did I think it was going to do all for me that it did. It's a wonderful play to do, a wonderful part for any actress.

But here is an interesting thing: *Cream Cracker* was a play – it was *a play* – about an elderly citizen who doesn't want to be made to go into a home for old people. But it must have seemed very real to a lot of people – I had hundreds of letters afterwards, and amongst them there were at least three I will never forget. One of them, I can see the paper now – avocado, deckle-edged, expensive, *beautiful* notepaper – it said, 'Dear Thora Hird, It is three o'clock in the morning and I haven't been to sleep yet. I saw you last night in *Cream Cracker Under the Settee*, and I *beseech* you, now that our children are all married and gone away, *please* come and live with us! We have a large house in the country. We live very nicely. You are so welcome!'

And I thought, 'A woman like this must *know* – it is a play.' Anyhow, I got through about another fifty letters, and I opened one, and this was on lined pad paper. It said, 'Dear Thora Hird, We only have a little house, but we have a spare bedroom. Don't you go into that Stafford House.' And there was another very nice one and it said, 'I couldn't go to sleep and my husband said, "Are you still awake? What's the matter?" and I said, "Oh, I do hope in the morning they notice she hasn't taken the milk in!"' I'm not making fun – it's a compliment really, that they think you're so good you must be for real. Or, at any rate, they think you are for real, whether they think you're good or not.

The play opens with my character, Doris, getting up off the floor to sit in a chair because she has fallen off the buffet she had climbed on to get down a wedding picture of herself and her husband Wilfred, to dust it, because she has a council cleaning lady, Zulema, who she doesn't think dusts properly. She says: 'Zulema doesn't dust. She half-dusts. I know when a place isn't clean.' Later, when she's down on the floor again, she sees a cream cracker under the settee, where Zulema has also failed to clean properly. And by the end of the evening, she dies.

Mr Bennett knows how to write that sort of thing. You saw the shadow of a policeman through the glass on the front door, and he calls out:

'Hello. Hello. Are you all right?' And she says, 'No. I'm all right.'
'Are you sure?'
'Yes.'
'Your light was off.'
'I was having a nap.'
'Sorry. Take care.'
'Thank you.' She calls again. 'Thank you.' Long pause.
'You've done it now, Doris. Done it now, Wilfred.'

I couldn't get into a taxi-cab, I couldn't anything without somebody mentioning *Cream Cracker*. People stopped me in the street and said, 'Why didn't you call back to him? Why didn't you tell him you were on the floor?' And it was no good my saying to people, 'I didn't say it like that because it wasn't in the play.'

But it did so much for me, that play. However old I was, however long I'd been in the business, it did me so much good and, of course, it got me a BAFTA.

The BAFTA ceremony is like all those things you see on television, where they read out three or four names in each of the different categories: 'And they are: Dee, dee, dee and dee ... and the winner is: ...'

I was invited to the dinner, but I'd been invited many times before and never won anything. On this occasion I was a long way from the stage at Grosvenor House, at a table with Jan and Scottie. Young David Dimbleby made a speech, requesting that when they received their award people shouldn't make a speech thanking their uncles and their cousins and everybody for helping them to act.

So there we are, having our dinner, and it comes to the Drama award and, after they'd shown little bits of the various *Talking Heads* plays, I sat there, being quite used to other years never getting any BAFTA award, and then Peter Davidson from *All Creatures Great and Small* said, 'And the winner is ... Thora Hird in *Cream Cracker Under the Settee*.'

Well! I'll never forget that moment – they gave me a standing ovation. It was probably because I was a lot older than the other actresses, but everyone stood up and cheered and whistled, and it made me feel marvellous.

Getting to that platform to receive it, however, is even more difficult than winning the BAFTA in the first place. The chairs are so close together round the tables, and you're going 'Excuse me', 'Do you mind?', 'Could I get through?' And it seemed to take me a year to get there. However, eventually I got to the stage and remembered what Mr Dimbleby had said, so when young Davidson handed me the BAFTA – they're very heavy, by the way – I was going to leg it, but he sort of kissed me, near me ear. Well, that's what I thought, anyway, that he was kissing me near my ear. Really, he was whispering 'They would like you to say a few words.' So I handed him the BAFTA back, because it was really too heavy for me to hold, and I said a few words, covering a lot of track with it. I told them about my very first stage appearance, when I was eight weeks old, being carried on by my mother. And I could truthfully say that that was the only part I ever got due to influence! I thanked Stuart Burge, and Alan Bennett, of course, who got a big cheer and a round of applause. And I staggered back to my seat with my first BAFTA, a very proud and happy woman.

When I was very young in the business, as long as people were saying, 'Thank you very much' and 'That was very good' I felt that was reward enough, and I certainly never thought I would come to this time of my life and start receiving awards like the BAFTA for drama, the Pye award for Comedy, the Royal Variety Club award for my contribution to the world of entertainment, another special silver BAFTA – just for being Thora Hird I think that was – and become the first woman member of the Royal Television Society's Hall of Fame – elected on 15 May, 1993 ... and several other things, like the Help the Aged and Tunstall Golden Award, and a Woman of the Year award – but they're not really for acting. Of course I'm proud of them. I'm not one of those actors who uses them for a door stop or hides them away in a cupboard and pretends they mean nothing – I polish them lovingly and keep them on the sideboard.

That reminds me, I have an old pot hot-water bottle from when I was a child, and an old flat iron, and I noticed the other night that Jan has put a pot hot-water bottle as one door stop, and a flat iron as another, so those are two ideas I'm going to pinch. But I can assure you that no BAFTA of mine is going to end up a door stop!

16
Alan Bennett

So many people ask me, 'What's Alan Bennett like?' It's very difficult, really, to describe Alan. He talks to me as though I was his grandmother, but I wouldn't say I knew him very well personally, only through acting what he writes. Even then you don't always know whether he loves or hates the character he's written for you to play.

Of course, he is a very funny man. He sent me a postcard one day, from Yorkshire, where he lives when he's not in London. It said, 'Just come back for the day to put a new lavatory seat on. Love, Alan.' That's Alan, you see. I had another postcard, also from Yorkshire, and it was just like a postcard you'd get from anyone, and I read it and thought, 'There's nothing funny on this postcard. It's not like Alan, this.' And then I turned the postcard over, and it was a beautiful picture of the Yorkshire moors, and in the corner it said, 'Soldier's Bottom'. So then I knew why he'd sent it.

There was one morning at rehearsal. He arrived. His clothes are very good but I can't say he's the smartest man I've ever seen in my life. He nearly always wears a good suit – but often with a pair of shabby grey cricket boots. He says, 'Well, they're comfortable.' This day he had on a rather beautiful overcoat – a very good coat, although I did notice the sleeves went down to his fingertips. When we were going home he was putting it on and I said to him, 'That's a nice coat, Alan. Is it new?' He said proudly, 'I've just bought it. Do you like it?' I said, 'Well, I do ... I'd like it even better on somebody a bit bigger than you.' He said, 'It was in a sale.' He was so proud of it because he'd bought it in a sale, and he thought that that excused everything, whether it fitted him or not. And I thought, 'Aren't you lovely! You can afford fifty overcoats like that, to fit you. But because this was in a sale ...' I'm a bit like this myself. Of course, he's a northerner too, and we're all a bit careful.

He really makes me laugh, especially when he's telling stories about when he was a little boy, with his mother and father and aunties. He told me a story about being on top of a bus with his auntie and, as they passed the gasworks in Leeds, she said to him, 'Alan – that is the biggest gasworks in England.' And he said to me, 'Well, you know, Thora, when you're about ten you're not that interested in the gasworks, whether it is the biggest one or not,' so he just glanced at it but didn't say anything, and after about another minute or two his auntie sort of straightened herself up and said, 'And *I* – know – the manager!'

In one of the plays I did for him I had one of the funniest lines – as far as I am concerned – that I have ever had to say. It was a play called *Me, I'm Afraid of Virginia Woolf*. In it I have a son, Trevor, at the Polytechnic. We're in the cafeteria at the Poly, having a cup of tea, and I'm beseeching him to say that he is at 'College'. You know the sort of woman.

'Well, you could *say* you were at College.'

'I can't, Mother. I'm at the Polytechnic.'

'Well, it's the same thing.'

'No it isn't.'

In the conversation, in the play, he happens to mention the word 'lesbian' and you know by my face that my character does not know what a lesbian is. And she keeps asking him, 'But what is a lesbian?' and he doesn't answer, but eventually he gets so fed up he says to her, 'Oh, mother! They are women who sleep together.' She looks him straight in the face, and says

'Well, that's nothing! I slept with your Auntie Phyllis all during the air-raids!'

That's the line. I really do think it's funny. Alan can write four words and link them together and they can be funny, or they can be very sad. I remember a speech I had to make about losing a baby in *Cream Cracker Under the Settee*:

'I wanted to call it John. But the nurse said it wasn't worth calling anything, and had we any newspaper.'

The sadness in that. Telling you what happened in so few words, without ever mentioning the word 'miscarriage'. And later in the same speech she says, 'And Wilfred said, "Oh yes, she saves newspapers. She saves shoe boxes as well."' (He means for a coffin, you see. You know at once.) She goes on, 'I don't think Wilfred cared very much about losing the baby, because it was then he talked about us getting a dog ...'

You can see the fellow, can't you? It was at that point, at rehearsals, that I said to Stuart Burge, 'I hate bloody Wilfred! I don't know what I married him for!'

I think perhaps the reason I've enjoyed working

with Alan so much is because, in my own small way, I do the same as him. Behind his work are all the characters he's been listening to and conversations he's overheard, and behind my acting are the people I grew up with, who came round to our house and who came in the shop when I was working in the Co-op. That was when I saw and overheard so many funny things that people did, and where I learned many little 'bits of business', little things you can do that say almost more than a page of words about what the character is like.

Alan has a brilliant ear for how people say things, especially north country people. Now, we're all guilty sometimes of not sticking exactly to a script, especially when it comes to little words like the conjunctions. Every actor and actress has at some time altered the words a tiny bit to make them easier to say. But if Alan has put 'but' you say 'but', you don't say 'and' or 'if'. He'll say immediately 'That's a "but".' He's never unpleasant about it. He'll just be walking about with his hands in his pockets at the far end of the studio, and he'll say quietly, 'that's a "but".' He knows what he's written, what he wants you to say, and it's so good you want to say it right.

If anybody thinks I've said all this because I'm hoping that he'll ask me to work with him again ... they'd be quite right.

17

Russell Harty

Television critics were never fair to him. They could never understand his popularity, but as far as the public were concerned he was one of the most entertaining chat-show hosts in the business, mainly because he had the cheek of the devil and didn't mind asking anybody anything. I went on his show three or four times and he always used to say, 'I'm going to ask you about that time when you were in hospital after the car accident,' and I always said, 'Oh no, I told that last time I was on, Russell!' And he always said, 'Never mind, it's worth telling again!' So I did! And now I've told you about it again in this book, haven't I?

Things never went quite right when Russell was around. I don't mean he was accident-prone, or anything, but things always seemed to go a bit askew. He was a very good friend of Alan Bennett's – they had met at university, I believe, and stayed friends ever since. While we were doing Alan's play *Me, I'm Afraid of Virginia Woolf* in Yorkshire, Russell was there watching – and when we were doing the scene I've told you about, in the Polytechnic cafeteria, Russell was sitting at the far end, and when I said my line 'That's nothing ... I slept with your Auntie Phyllis all during the air-raids,' he laughed so much the director had to ask him to leave.

Russell was driving back to London the next day by car, and Alan said to me, 'Why don't you go back with Russell? You'll be company for each other ...' So I gave my train ticket to the stage manager (she said she would find somebody who would use it) and I set off with Russell in the car.

We were going along and he said to me, 'We'll stop at –' do you know, I just can't think of the place where it was – 'because, there is a very good restaurant called The Vineyard.' I said, 'Oh, great.' And we arrived at – you see, I'm no good with maps and so on, so I still don't know where it was – but we arrived in the high street of the town where this restaurant was, and there was a man coming along with a dog and Russell said, 'Ask this fellow if he knows where it is.' So I put the window down and said, 'Excuse me, sir, could you direct us to a restaurant called The Vineyard?' and I notice out of the corner of my eye while I'm saying this that Russell is rooting around for something on the floor of the car, his side, so his face isn't showing. I thought, 'Oh yes? *Oh* yes!' So I said to the gentleman with the dog, 'Only Mr – *Russell Harty* – and I are going there for lunch.' And the man said, 'Well, no, I don't know where it is' and went on. Then I saw a girl coming towards us with a perambulator – Russell is still craning his head round so no one will recognise him. I put down the window again and asked her if she knew where it was. 'Oh, is that Russell Harty?' she said immediately. She didn't know where the restaurant was either, but there was another lady coming along, extremely well dressed, and I leant out and said, 'Excuse me, madam, could you direct me to a restaurant called The Vineyard!' and she said, 'Oh! Thora Hird! Oh what a pleasure to meet you!' and I said, 'Thank you ... and could you tell us ...?' and she said, 'And is that Mr Harty? Oh, fancy meeting two of you at the same time ... Oh, this is such a surprise. Are you visiting the town for long? Are you making a programme here?'

'No. Yes. Thank you. We're just passing through. But have you any idea where the restaurant is?'

'Yes' she said, 'You're right outside it!' And we were! We had been parked right outside this bloomin' restaurant the whole time. Somehow that was typical of how things happened when you were with Russell.

God rest him, he was a good friend and a very lovable man.

18
The Queen and I

On 29 November, 1990, I took a lot of care getting ready. I wasn't really nervous – anxious, yes – excited? Yes. I hired a dignified car and chauffeur in matching grey (well, the car was, and his uniform was). I arrived at her house exactly on time – to the minute. There were only eight of us for lunch, six guests, our hostess and her sister:

Her Majesty the Queen, and Her Royal Highness Princess Margaret.

A lot of funny things happen to me, I'm very happy to say, and I know a lot of funny people. And like everybody else that's human, I'm wrong as often as I'm right. But this is an occasion when I was wrong ... or right ... but read on and take your choice!

I had come home one afternoon in October. Scottie was just about to lay the telephone on its cradle and he said, 'Oh, just a minute, she's here,' and held the telephone up again. As I went over to him I mouthed, 'Who is it?' and he shook his head to say that he didn't know.

Now at this point I need to interject something. You all know Michael Jayston, the very clever actor? Some years previously we had both been together on location filming for a BBC drama series, *Flesh and Blood*, in which he played one of my grandsons and I was the eighty-year-old matriarch of a cement family. I came down to the hotel dining room one morning and there was a letter for me from some retired Major or Colonel, asking me to come out with him for a drink. He'd fallen on hard times since leaving the army, otherwise he'd have asked me out to dinner. I thought, 'What a shame!' I wasn't going to go or anything, but I thought, 'How sad.' So I was telling Michael about this letter, over breakfast, and I was saying 'Isn't it sad? When they've done so much for their country, you know ...' And I saw his face twitch, just the slightest in the world. I said, 'It's a proper letter, isn't it?' He said, 'Oh, it's sure to be! You will go, won't you?' So then I knew ... he'd written it. Because Michael is a great man for playing practical jokes on people, but they never hurt anybody.

So back to the morning of the telephone call. When this modulated voice said, 'Miss Hird? This is the Controller of the Queen's Household' I thought, 'Oh yes, I bet it is! Michael Jayston! Ha-ha!' But instead of saying, 'Come off it, Michael' I thought, 'I'll enjoy this performance for a bit,' and then this *beautifully* modulated voice, far too good to be anyone's but an actor's, told me that Her Majesty was desirous of me going to have lunch with her ... I thought, 'Come off it' – I'm sure you'd have thought the same. Then when he said, 'And we realise what a busy lady you are, so there are three possible dates ...' Well, I could just hear the Queen saying, 'Tell Thora, I'm ironing on Tuesday, and I've a bit of baking to do on Wednesday, but any Thursday ...' And I thought, 'All right,

Michael. But go on ...' So I kept up with it and I said, 'Well it's only Thursday, really, that I'm free.' To which the gentleman thanked me very much and said that I would be further advised later on. So as I hung the telephone up Scottie said, 'Who was it?' and I said, 'It was Michael bloomin' Jayston ... The Queen wants me to have lunch with her ... I don't think!' I added, 'He is a scream, isn't he?'

In the middle of the following week a very large gilt-edged invitation card arrived which informed me that Her Majesty the Queen was desirous of me having lunch with her on Thursday, two weeks ahead of when the card arrived. Well I really was, I think the expression at the moment is 'gob-smacked.' I wrote back immediately.

At the big gates of Buckingham Palace, as you are all aware, there is often a uniformed policeman at each side. I'd heard on the early morning news that the Ambassador of Turkey was to be received by the Queen – that day. When I'd heard it I'd thought, 'Hold on! Jayston hasn't gone to the expense of having a *card* printed as well, has he? Because if she's receiving the Ambassador of Turkey ...' As we got near, we saw the procession leaving the palace – we'd already been in a back street, killing seven minutes because we were early – and as we arrived at the gates one of the policemen put his hand on top of the car, looked in and said,

'Oh! Hallo, Thora. Go right in.'

This is the truth! I couldn't believe it! At Buckingham Palace ... 'Hallo, Thora ... Go right in ...' The chauffeur said to him, 'How about the parking?' And he said, 'It's all right. There's only six people today.' And all the time I'm saying to myself, 'Hallo, Thora ... Go right in ...'

Anyway, the gentleman with the beautifully modulated voice who I had spoken to on the telephone, who was *not* Michael Jayston, of course, was about four steps down on a side entrance, and in I went. There were two people already there. One was professor Sir Magdi Yacoub, the great man who does the heart transplants, and the other was the man who was for so many years the voice of tennis, Dan Maskell. I was taken over to Dan Maskell, who I already knew, but I hadn't before met the Doctor, so I was very pleased and proud to meet him. The next person to arrive was a Dame, not of the theatre, of industry, and still to arrive was a Romanian author (who *nobody* knew, so we all made a bit of a fuss of him), and the head of the Baltic Exchange.

So it was all very pleasant, the footmen wandering about offering everybody cigarettes, which nobody took. We had a nice sherry, and all had little bits of chat with one another. And suddenly the Master of Ceremonies announced that he did wish to apologise for Her Majesty being a moment or two late, but she had been receiving the Turkish Ambassador. At that point four little corgis ran in, and I thought, 'She'll be here in a minute.' And she was.

She was very kind to us all. We'd formed a row, without being told, out of respect, because we felt that was what we ought to do. She asked me what I was doing at the moment, and I said, 'Well, Your Majesty, we've finished another batch of *Last of the Summer Wine* last night, and put the Christmas one "in the can".' And she smiled and said, 'Oh, when does it come out? My mother never misses one.' So that was nice, wasn't it?

Princess Margaret joined us for lunch. It was all very beautiful – a wonderful experience. The Baltic Exchange asked me how my beautiful daughter was, and said, 'I was so in love with her when I was fifteen!' You like to hear these things, you know, when you're a mother. The whole thing was like going to have lunch with a relative you were very fond of. And of course – the grub was good.

When you hear me say so often how proud I am of being a Lancastrian, you've to excuse me, because I am, and of course the Queen herself is Duke of Lancaster. That sounds wrong, but it's right.

We were in America some years ago, Scottie and I, and Jan was giving a formal dinner party in a restaurant. There were nine tables of people, including quite a few English friends who were staying, and the British Ambassador, who Jan knew very well, a charming man; his wife was a Lancastrian so Jan put me at one table, the Ambassador's wife at another, herself at another, and so on, so that there was at least one Lancastrian at each table. When it was time for the Loyal Toast, the British Ambassador stood up and said, 'I would ask you to be upstanding to drink the health of Her Majesty, Queen Elizabeth the Second ...' and as we all pushed back our chairs and stood up, he went on 'Duke of Lancaster'. So we all drank the toast and then sat down. Opposite me was sitting the lady who owned the Beverly Hills Hotel, and she said, 'Thora, who is the Dook of Lancaster?' On my left was Elm Williams, head of Twentieth-Century Fox at that time, and he said, 'Who's the Dook of Lancaster, Thora?' I wasn't going to say, straight off, because I thought it would be more fun to keep them guessing. And all round the room you could hear this buzz going round all the tables – 'Who's the Dook of Lancaster?' Some clever dick at another table said, 'It's Philip.' So I said, 'Oh no it isn't.' But I still wouldn't say, and Group Captain Leonard Cheshire, who founded the Cheshire Homes, was on my right, falling about as everyone was arguing about 'Who's the Dook of Lancaster?' Eventually we told them that the Queen herself is the Duke of Lancaster, because whoever is on the throne of England, whoever they are, even if they are a dog or a cat, they are also the Duke of Lancaster. I'll never forget that night – the wonder and laughter about this Duke of Lancaster – I think it made them think that the British are completely mad.

The day after we got back to London, shortly after that night, was the day that Prince Charles and Diana announced their engagement. There was a Lancastrian occasion in one of the City Halls, and the Queen came and we gave her the usual big sheaf of red roses, the red rose of Lancashire. As she stopped to speak to me along the line, I said I had just returned from America and that we had offered the Loyal Toast while we were there, and she looked at me so nicely and said, 'I should think they find that rather peculiar, don't they?' And I said, 'Not half so peculiar as you being the Dook of Lancaster!' and she nearly dropped her sheaf of roses she laughed so much!

19
D. Litt.

I couldn't get the velvet cap on right – none of us could ... Oh well. I was a bit disappointed that I hadn't had a little more time to fiddle with it, but we were all being bustled along at such a rate into the procession. Mind you, the Chancellor had got her velvet cap on beautifully – but then, she also had a beautiful face to go under the beautifully put-on cap. I said to her later, at the lunch, 'Look how your cap looks! How beautiful! I hadn't time to put mine on properly. But you would know exactly how to put yours on – this was the wonderful thing about your mother, she was everybody's idea of a princess and she always wore her hats so beautifully!'

Yes! I was talking to our lovely Princess Alexandra. Do you remember her mother, the Duchess of Kent, and how beautifully she wore those brimmed hats? Oh, I do.

Never mind the cap ... off we go. There must have been more than a thousand students seated in the hall as we proceeded to the platform.

We hadn't been settled for very long before a very brilliant gentleman stood up and read pages and pages – all about me! I didn't realise there was so much of interest to tell about me. Then I was called to approach Princess Alexandra and (I was going to say 'before you could say Jack Robinson' but it was rather longer than that) ... anyway, by the time I sat down again I was a D. Litt. or, to put it in full, a Doctor of Letters of the University of Lancaster. Never mind my velvet cap being askew – no woman who had left school at fourteen without an any-level to her name could have been prouder.

Earlier that morning, when I was being driven to the Graduation Hall in Lancaster to receive my honorary degree accompanied by Scottie and Jan, we passed a building that made me go 'Heee-aaah!' (If you want to make that noise – just take a long intake of breath expressing surprise, shock, delight and a flood of memories!). We had just passed the Ashton Hall, Lancaster ... where the Lancaster District Co-op, where I worked as a cashier for ten years, held their annual Dinner and Dance ... tickets half a crown.

I had gone one year with my best friend Peggy wearing a new ball gown (made for me by Doris Brown from further down our street) in eau-de-nil satin, low-waisted, a skirt with four handkerchief points and about a ten-inch deep piece of georgette round the bottom. I can see it now. I do hope you can visualise it. Sounds 'orrible, doesn't it? Really it was quite pretty, and it was my first proper ball gown and I thought it was beautiful. I wore real silk stockings and brocade evening shoes in pale pink and green ... *eau-de-nil*, white gloves, and a little evening bag with a lace-edged hanky in it, a mirror, lipstick, my half-crown ticket and another half-a-crown in case I needed any money apart from my bus fare – sixpence to go and sixpence to return home.

When Peg and I arrived people were already being seated for the dinner. A band was playing a chart-topper of those days – 'Horsey, keep your tail up'. We were very excited as we took our places, looking forward to an evening of dancing and a delicious dinner.

I will now tell you exactly what did happen. The soup (cream of mushroom) was being served. There was a lot of laughter and jolly chat, and as the waiter started to put a plate of soup in front of me, he caught his elbow on the chair-back of the person next to me and ... he tipped the entire portion of soup straight into my lap. It went right through the dress and real silk stockings, and it was very hot. I let out a yell, jumped up, and Peg rushed after me into the Ladies' Room.

Now there's something that isn't as good as it was in 'the good old days' – because it's better – and that's the Ladies' Room. I mean, in those days there were no little piles of hand towels, no machines blowing out hot air, no boxes of paper tissues, nor even soft lavatory paper. All there was was a 'roller-towel' behind the door, already damp with finger marks and so high up we could only reach the bottom two inches, both being little 'uns. And as for drying my dress with it ... impossible.

I had to take the dress off to rinse the soup off the front, disarranging my hair, which was in fashionable 'earphones' – plaits wound round like saucers. I had to get soup off me, as well as the dress, and by now the tears were very near, my cheeks bright red, and the front of my dress dripping wet. We did the best we could with our two little lace-edged hankies, tidied my hair and bravely went back to our dinner places. You will appreciate that by now dinner was nearly over.

Soon the dancing started, and a young fellow came up and asked if he could 'have the pleasure' of this dance. I said, 'I can't dance with a wet frock.' As sharp as a knife he answered, 'I'm not a wet frock!' He said that if we were dancing the wet patch wouldn't show ... and, of course, it didn't. It didn't dry completely, but it did begin to dry and I danced every dance – not always with my new comedian friend, although we danced together quite a lot. By the time the band played 'God Save the King' both Peg and I agreed that we had had a really good half-a-crown's worth.

As I drove by this same Ashton Hall on 5 December, 1990, over fifty years later, with my husband and daughter in a chauffeur-driven limousine ... to be made a Doctor of Literature for Services to Lancashire ... I thought – well, this sort of evens things up, somehow.

So when I stood up at the graduation ceremony to give the reply on behalf of myself and the four other honorary graduates to Princess Alexandra and all the students in the hall who had spent the last three years studying so hard for their degrees – I told them the story of the Lancaster and District Co-operative Annual Dinner and Dance because, in a way, that was how I earned my degree, wasn't it?

20

Morecambe revisited

In 1993 I was awarded the accolade 'Local hero for outstanding achievement as a citizen of Morecambe and Heysham, presented by the *Morecambe Visitor*.' That's the local paper. I'm a 'hero', kindly note, not heroine. I seem to have changed sex.

The pier at Morecambe was a great big chunk of my life, a happy chunk, a marvellous chunk, and talking about it and revisiting it has been part of my life, and also of several television programmes I've made.

One of Russell Harty's shows took me back first. We visited Prompt Corner, Scottie's and my first home together – that's still there. And the clock tower. Now the clock tower at Morecambe, on the promenade, was where we always used to make for to play after school. Your parents would say, 'All right, but be home by five o'clock for your tea.' And you'd have no excuse to be late, you see.

Russell and I were filming near the clock tower, on the Promenade, and believe you me, this was about March, there wasn't a soul, there wasn't even a seagull walking about. There was just us and the film crew.

I said, 'Russell, I used to play round this clock tower

after school.' And I can see Russell now, in his duffel coat, hands in the pockets, looking across at the Central Pier saying, 'That's not the pier that you're always on about, is it?'

Now I have always been so full of pride about the Central Pier, where my father was manager. I promise you the white flagpoles were painted every three months. The flags that fluttered from them, of all nations, were washed and cleaned. It was threepence for a deck chair, and my Dad would say, 'Don't put that one out, it's dirty. No one wants to pay threepence to get their summer dress dirty.' There's a lot of thought in that.

But now, on this dark wet morning, it looked so sad and neglected. Which it was – it was sad and neglected. I said, 'Yes. And if my father could see that now, he'd turn over in his grave, because the pier was ...' and Russell said, 'Well it doesn't look anything now.' I said, 'I'm not asking you to say it looks anything now. I'm asking you to try and imagine – flower boxes all along the edges of the deck, beautiful forms all painted white ...' and I'm standing in the rain, selling him the pier, and he will keep saying 'Yeah, well, it doesn't look like it now.' And in the end I was so cross I said, 'Oh well, you – you've no imagination!' I expected everyone to know the pier as I had known it.

In 1939 the Pavilion on the Pier at Morecambe burned down, and as I've described in the first part of my autobiography, I saw that. There were three domes. They called it the Northern Taj Mahal, because it was the loveliest pavilion of any pier in England. And forgive me telling it again, but round one of the small domes my brother had doves, and round the other dome we grew mustard and cress – a packet of seeds over a damp blanket and it would come up in two days. The day I saw those domes burn down, I stood on the Promenade with hundreds of other people and I thought, 'There's the dovecote gone' – I don't mean the doves were still there – they'd left when my father did, long before. And as the fire crept across, I thought, 'And that's the mustard and cress' – and this was *years* before when we'd done this, when we were kids, but it was all so vivid to me. And the big dome ... but that's all being sad, and this isn't a sad book. But that pier meant so much to me for such a long time. As children we practically lived on it, you see.

In March 1981 the television cameras came back to Morecambe with me for a special *Songs of Praise* in Green Street Methodist Chapel, where year after year my mother had sung the solo 'I Know that My Redeemer Liveth' from Handel's *Messiah*.

It was great to be back. Every time we started filming the introduction in the town, another old friend would come over, saying 'Ee! *Thora?* Is it you?' We'd have a lovely chat, but then we'd have to start the filming all over again from the beginning.

The hymns were accompanied by the local Salvation Army band, the successors of the band I had stood and sang with so often as a child on a Saturday evening, a sixpenny bag of tea-cakes in my hand from Dora's. After tea on a Saturday my mother used to say, 'Go down to Dora's, will you, and get us seven tea-cakes for tomorrow, four currant, three plain – and don't stay too long singing with the Salvation Army.' Because they were always outside Dora's shop on a Saturday, when she did her second baking at six, so you could have your tea-cakes still fresh for Sunday. And Happy Jack, one of the Morecambe fishermen, would be there in his little hat and blue ganzie, his voice so loud they could hear him in Barrow-in-Furness – you could have heard him across the Bay at Grange when he sang 'Onward Christian Soldiers'. That's when that hymn first impressed me so much. He was always called 'Happy Jack', and I don't wonder.

Anyway, for *Songs of Praise* the Salvation Army Band were there, and of course they had their own conductor. But there was another conductor in the pulpit for those of us singing in the congregation. So there were two conductors, do you follow? We all stood up to sing a hymn that is another of my great favourites because it reminds me of my uncles, who were all Morecambe fishermen: 'Will Your Anchor Hold?' 'Our' conductor raised his baton, the Salvation Army band conductor raised his baton ... and suddenly the band was away like an express train: 'Terra-rum-pum-pum-terra-rum-pum-pum ...' and arrived at the end of the first verse and chorus in about twenty seconds flat!

'Our' conductor, the one in the pulpit conducting the congregation, his baton still poised in the air, turned very slowly round and just *looked* at the Salvation Army Band conductor, who, still conducting, turned round too, looking very surprised to see that we hadn't even *started* singing yet! It was quite a comedy routine, and part of a very loving evening of happy memories, laughter and hymn-singing.

I went back quite recently with Melvyn Bragg for *The South Bank Show*, directed by Bryan Izzard, in 1993. But sadly the pier wasn't there by then. When I got back to Morecambe the first thing I did was visit the Promenade, and as I looked I thought, 'Oh! It's gone!' The pier, the piles – everything.

It had looked for years as though it was going to fall down or be washed away. In fact, I remember saying to somebody when I'd been up for a dinner, 'What's going to happen to the pier?' and they had said, 'I think it's been sold to America.' Well, I mean, if you want a joke without a laugh, that's it. So I had said, 'Well, I suggest that they put all the councillors on it, cut it off at this end and let it float to America ... and let it take them with it!' I was always so upset about the pier being neglected, you see, having known what it had been and could be.

So when I was doing *The South Bank Show*, Bryan Izzard filmed me standing on the forebay – all that now remains of the pier – with Scottie, and I chatted to Scottie about when I'd been late for work in my Dad's office, running all the way along the pier. Or, as I used to say, 'up the pier'. My headmistress used to stick her hand up in the air, pointing to the sky and saying 'Thora, the pier does not go up. You either go *on* the pier, or you come *off* the pier.' But I still always said 'up' the pier and 'down' the pier.

I don't know if I ever did a sadder interview, telling Scottie all about it. Saying 'There used to be the ice cream stall ... That's where there used to be the weighing machine, with all the brass polish ... called jockey scales, so you were like half a pound of sausage, you were put on and weighed properly, with weights. And all the lovely automatic machines. Over there was the book kiosk. There was a toffee kiosk. There was Mr Anthony with his little penny cornets. Mr Bradley taking your photograph – a very wet photograph he pinned on your summer dress. Many of those I had taken, for a penny. When I got home there was never anybody on the photograph – it was a grey nothing.'

So that pier, wherever it is, God rest it. It'll be ashes now. It never went to America for its holidays.

Also on *The South Bank Show* we visited the Morecambe Winter Gardens, which at least they are now trying to save – another beautiful place that's been left to fall into disrepair. When I was a kid I used to say to people, because I was a bit of a clever head – 'Did you know that the aerial span of this theatre is bigger than Drury Lane?' I didn't really know what 'aerial span' meant, but I thought it sounded good ... and it was true. It was a wonderful theatre.

For *The South Bank Show* they asked me to stand where the fourth row of the stalls had been. There were little bits of iron, where the seats had been fastened to the floor, and I stood on the fourth row next to the aisle, where I had sat so many years ago the night the Winter Gardens was reopened – beautiful new velvet curtains, everything that could be gilded re-gilded ... but none of that impressed me as much as the drummer in the new sixteen-piece orchestra that had been taken on for the variety shows. I looked at that young drummer and I thought, 'Well, he's not going to get away if I've anything to do with it!' It was Scottie. I stood with him there again, on *The South Bank Show*, and they had put a drumkit in the orchestra pit, where he used to sit. It was a bit sad, in its way.

I'm happy to say that now the Japanese, I think it is, have taken an interest in the Winter Gardens. It's such a beautiful building, and it's just empty, and it really looks so sad. When I was there this last time I was looking at the dress circle and I suddenly remembered the dress circle barmaid, who was always so smart, dressed in black sateen with a corsage on. Barmaids always used to wear a corsage in those days. And all the people who had been top of the bill: Leyton and Johnson, George Formby, Florrie Ford ... great names. I remember Florrie Ford singing 'Has Anybody Here Seen Kelly?' then go off the stage and it was 'three choruses for change' – in theatrical jargon that means that the band played the chorus through three times, and then she came back on in pink sequins, as opposed to blue ones. And a big hat with feathers. Oh, the acts were so beautifully presented.

I know I lived at the right time. I lived at the right time for me, because I have so enjoyed all these things.

21

Postman's Knock

It was in the Winter Gardens' ballroom that my best friend Peg and I had been to a late dance on a Wednesday. It cost a shilling to go, and was open until one o'clock in the morning. We used to buy ten cigarettes – we'd smoke two each on a Wednesday night, and three each on Saturday nights. I say 'we'd smoke' – but really you just sat with your cup of coffee, in the 'fauteuils', a cigarette in your left hand ... we thought it made us look grown up. They were sixpence for ten, and we paid threepence each for a packet a week.

It was coming to the end of this Wednesday night dance; the variety show had been over for two or three hours before that. Peg and I were standing watching the dancing when two gentlemen came and stood near us, and I found I was standing next to Scottie ... I can see him now, in a long black evening overcoat, wearing a white evening scarf with the fringe very near his chin, the other end nearly on the floor, and a black, snap-brimmed trilby. The first thing I thought, when I saw the scarf on lop-sided like that, was 'He's had a drink!' The second thing I thought was, 'What a leading man!' He was medium height, brown hair, very twinkling blue eyes, good cheek bones and he had a dimple in his chin. They started to chat to us, and you could do that in those days, without any fear. Then they offered to see us home, but with such pride I said, 'We have a car.'

We have a car! It was a boy called Edwin Sybil's Austin 7, about as big as a chocolate box, that we used to get about seven of us in. Edwin and his friend, Tollo Bullock, would run us all home. We hadn't spent the evening with them, but we were all part of the same friendly gang. But that evening, as Peg and I went out of the Winter Gardens, down the side steps that lead onto the promenade – we were just in time to see the Austin 7 going whizzing past ... they'd left us behind!

It wasn't far to where I lived, so we started to walk home, and when we were about halfway there, these two 'gentlemen of the orchestra', Scottie and Bill Glover, overtook us and said, 'Have you been stood up?' They walked us home, and that's how I got to know Scottie ... it was really my friend Peg he was interested in, because she was very beautiful.

There were fourteen of us – and when I say 'in a gang', don't misunderstand me. Fourteen of us who were all good friends is what I mean, who visited each other, all our parents knew each other, and each mother would put up once every fourteen weeks with you having all your friends round, and make the sandwiches and whatever else you were having, and we called it a party. I don't suppose the sophisticated young people of today would call it a party – but it was a party.

Well, it was Dorothy Spencer's turn on 14 December, and she had her party, and we were all there, and I went with a boy ... it's awful, but I can't remember who it was. But Peg, my friend, took

Scottie. We had met him and Bill at the dance in about September, and this was a few months later on. It was near enough Christmas to make it a Christmas Party, and all the decorations were up. You used to make your own in those days, with loops of coloured paper.

One of the games we used to play was Postman's Knock – somebody went out of the room, knocked on the door and said 'Post!' and opened the door, and he said who the letter was for, a girl, and she would then go outside with him, the door was shut, he kissed her, then he came back in, and she knocked on the door, called 'Post!' and called a boy out. Very sophisticated, I don't think. But very enjoyable, you see.

On this occasion Peg called Scottie out, and then, really to my surprise, but I suppose it was because I was the only other person he knew there – I can't think of any other reason – Scottie called me out.

And the end of this story is ... we never went back in!

22

A finger of rings

While we were still out of the room for Postman's Knock, Scottie asked me to go with him to the pictures the following night. We went to the Whitehall, and the film had Ronald Coleman and a German actress – I wish I could remember what it was called. And Scottie bought me a box of *Terry's All Gold*. He was to buy me *Terry's All Gold* all my married life – so that's a free advertisement.

Anyone who lives in Morecambe will tell you that when winter gets going there's usually a force-ten gale along the promenade, and there was that night. Opposite the Whitehall was the shelter, for visitors in the summer to sit in, and we just paused in this shelter for me to put my head-scarf on out of the wind. Very politely Scottie said, 'Excuse me, but are you going out with anybody regular?' Lovely expression that, isn't it? I said, 'Well, I've a lot of friends ... but no. Why?' and he said, 'Because if you are, I won't see you again.' What a gent! Anyhow, having said no I wasn't, I saw him every night for four years.

When I say, if I'm giving a talk or anything, that Scottie and I 'were courtin' for three years – sometimes, nowadays someone will come up to me afterwards and say, 'What was that word you said, that you and Scottie were?' The first time I didn't know what they were after. I said to this very nice young girl, 'That we were ... very happy?' She said, 'No, it was more like something you did.' She meant 'courting'. She didn't know what courting meant! There are a lot of things, you know, that are going out of the language. I bet half of you reading this book couldn't describe a gas mantle if I asked you ... could you? I think that – not in my lifetime – but by the end of the next century people won't know what all sorts of things were – chimneys, for instance. Do you think young kids will know what chimneys were in fifty years' time?

But back to courting. Now, there were stages of courtship. If you said, 'He's doing a bit of courting' you meant he had his eye on a girl and might be going to ask her out, or might even have taken her out a few times. But if you said, 'He's courting' you meant it was serious – there'd be an engagement ring in about a year.

We got engaged after three years. I've said Scottie was an attractive man, and he was, very good-looking and very charming, and he had been engaged twice before. I never bothered to ask him who broke it off ... the girl or himself.

Anyway, we got engaged, and it was lovely because – I always say 'our' grocer, 'our' greengrocer, they weren't open just for us, but you always called it that – well 'our' jeweller was Jim Hargreaves, whose shop in Euston Road backed on to Cheapside, where we lived, and so of course we went to him for the engagement ring. A lot of time was spent looking at rings on black velvet fingers.

I couldn't decide which one I liked best and, knowing us very well, Jim said, 'Take this finger of rings home with you, Thora, and bring it back in the morning.'

He gave us a piece of black velvet with about ten rings on, and we took them home. My mother's face was a study when she saw us put them on the living room table. 'Good gracious!' she said.

'Mr Hargreaves says that Scottie and I can look at them and take our time to decide which one.'

My mother's face! She said, 'You are *not* leaving those here over night.' Now who was going to rob us? I don't know. Number 6 Cheapside, Morecambe, in a street house – we hadn't anything for them to rob. But my mother went to sleep that night with all the rings, on the piece of black velvet, under her pillow. They'd have had to knock her head in to get them!

There was one ring, an African white diamond, not very big, but also not the smallest I've ever seen, I have to say. And each side of it there were three, two and one – tiny, tiny diamonds. The ring was platinum – very modern for those days! It was very pretty, and much the most expensive – about three pounds more than any of the others. I said to Scottie, 'Did either of your other engagements have a bigger ring than that?' and he said, 'No'. So I said, 'Well, I'll have that one then.'

I've still got it, and I always wear it every year on our anniversary, 3 May. I love it. I also had a white gold wedding ring, even though there were certain ladies who said, 'They're not like a *proper* wedding ring, are they?' So I was glad when 'Quackie' Mortimer, a good friend of mine who was getting married at the same time, also chose to have a white gold wedding ring.

I've always loved and treasured both of these rings but, as for many people who marry young, fortunes change and over the years I've been given one or two rather more expensive pieces of jewellery that I'm also fond of, including some rings.

Not so long ago I had a part as an old country woman in an episode of *All Creatures Great and Small* – which I undertook with great joy, may I say. I was up in Yorkshire for the filming, and just as I was coming out of a florist's one morning – because I'd been out to dinner the night before and wanted to send some flowers to my hostess – I came face-to-face with a lady carrying two full plastic bags from the supermarket; these bags were pulling her arms out as she trotted along. She gasped, put down her bags and said, 'Is it Thora?' I said it was, and she said, 'Oh! We always watch you on the telly. We wouldn't miss you for ...' she stopped. She was staring at my hand holding the pot plant I had just bought. '... Where is it?' she demanded. (That was exactly what she said: 'We wouldn't miss you for ...' (pause, change of tone) 'Where is it?')

'Where is what?'

'Your ring! That lovely diamond ring you always wear – like a stamp.'

'Oh, well, I don't always wear it when I come up to film.'

'Oh' she said, 'Don't you? What a shame. I love that ring. I watch you on telly just to look at that ring. Well, ta-ra then.'

And she picked up her two plastic bags and marched off, leaving me standing there feeling quite embarrassed, as if I'd been caught on camera not acting but going 'Have a look at this ring! Eat your hearts out!'

(And may I say to any burglars who may be reading this – it may look like a stamp, but it's nothing like the size of a stamp, it's quite small really, and it was a present from my beloved Scottie and means a lot to me, so please don't steal it!)

23
Scottie and me

Scottie and I were married for fifty-eight wonderfully happy years, and I know just how lucky I've been. It was a marriage, a love affair, a friendship and a partnership. He was better educated than me, and whenever I came across a new word, new to me that is, in a book or newspaper I was reading I would ask him what it meant and how to pronounce it. Then I'd use it as often as I could, bringing it into all our conversations. He was very good, but many's the time he'd say to me, 'Would you like to find another new word to use? You've been using that last one in all the wrong places for a fortnight, and I'm getting a bit tired of it now!'

When I first started jotting down little thoughts into an exercise book, ideas of things to put in this book, Scottie was with me, and I'd like to include some of them in this chapter, just as I originally wrote them when he was pottering around in the garden outside, or sitting in his favourite armchair next to me. I hope it will give you something of the flavour of our everyday life together, Scottie and me.

DECEMBER 1993

It's amazing the things you can put into books these days, that you couldn't at one time. I mean, I don't mind telling you now that I was a virgin when I got married. I'm not swanking about it – I was. I must admit that sometimes when Scottie and I are having a laugh – and, bear in mind, my husband is a good-looking man who always has a twinkle in his eye for a pretty girl, and the thing is most women have a twinkle in their eye for him, too! – I say to him, just for fun, 'You know, if I had my life over again, I wouldn't be a virgin when I got married.'

And he'll say, 'Oh yes you would!'

'Oh no I wouldn't! ... I think probably, I would have liked to have had the experience of ten men ...'

'Don't be daft!'

'All right ... twelve men, then!'

It was a different world when we were young, and I married him in white. There was a character, Bella, I played many times in the forties and fifties in productions of *Saturday Night at the Crown*, the play that Walter Greenwood wrote especially for me. Old Bella has a few stouts inside her, and she says to the two men at the next table in the pub, talking about a girl who's just left, 'And I'll tell you something else – thems falsies she's wearing ... Talks about getting married in white? God forgive her!'

It used to bring the house down. I suppose there

are young people today who wouldn't even know what that line meant, would they?

January 1994

Scottie was up at 4.30 this morning, and I joined him for a cuppa in the lounge at 5.30. We love the first few hours that start our day. Not that we're always drinking tea at 5.30 am – but I would say that eight mornings out of ten we are. Breakfast is always the same – lovely hot buttered wholemeal toast, spread with Marmite for me and home-made marmalade for Scottie.

We always – well, nearly always – watch the six o'clock news in the mornings. Of course I often have to be up at that hour anyway, because a car will be coming to pick me up at 6.15 to take me off to work, when I'm filming out of London. I've often been swept off at 5.30 if the filming is quite a distance away. I love a busy life!

15 February, 1994: Pancake Tuesday

Full marks! Well done! Credit where it's due ... and all that jazz. It is a well-known fact – or should be – that Scottie makes pancakes better than anyone in the world. I mean it! They're splendiferous ... and I've just eaten *five* ... so I should know! Hot and sizzling from the pan, with fine sugar sprinkled on them and fresh lemon juice squeezed over the sugar. Ooh, blimey! Even writing about it makes my mouth water – I wonder if there are any more? Excuse me a moment.

Do you know, he's made pancakes on Shrove

Tuesday every year of our marriage apart from the six years during the War when he was in the airforce? Honestly, he seems to improve yearly. It's been a wonderful week for grub. On Monday we had every sort of vegetable nearly, diced into small cubes – onions, celery, carrots, turnips, peas, corn and potatoes mixed with cubes of shin beef all in gravy.

Thursday 17 March, 1994: St Patrick's Day

It's amazing how many people ask me, 'Do you enjoy your work?'

I can honestly answer 'Yes I do,' but what I'm going to say now is not about enjoying 'the acting bit', it's about duties – yes, duties – that I enjoy when playing my housewife character – I mean, that is, being me, myself, at home with Scottie.

I'm sure a lot of you will agree that there are a lot of household tasks you simply hate doing, whilst there are others you enjoy. I know someone who enjoys making beds; I have another friend who would happily spend her life cleaning and dusting. I even know someone who likes ironing! Everyone's different, aren't they?

Well me, meself, personally (as my old dresser used to say), I dislike ironing and making beds (so I'm glad I'm not a chambermaid!). However, I like the effect of these jobs, so I always make my bed as soon as I get up and before I go to the bathroom, so that when I return from my ablutions I gaze on a neatly made bed, with my lovely white tri-pillows sitting at the top.

In case you are just about dropping off at this point, I shall now tell you all about one job I *love* ... when I'm at home at that time of day, that is ... here it comes: making our tea! Now then, isn't that exciting? Wasn't that worth staying awake for?

I love the two of us being in the kitchen together, the smell of tea being brewed, of wholemeal bread being toasted and buttered, making the sandwiches, perhaps with tuna emptied into a bowl with some finely chopped onion, a dessert-spoon of tomato puree, a dessertspoon of salad cream or mayonnaise, a suggestion of salt and pepper, a splash of vinegar ... mix all together then, using a spatula, spread it over the buttered bread. Should you also want a slice of lettuce or some watercress, lightly salted, in the sandwich – add it! Scrumptious.

Hold on, though, here's another tasty little offering coming up. We always have a jar of sliced onion in vinegar in our sauce cupboard. Do you? Did you notice that bit? Sauce Cupboard? Ahem! Well, we need one, don't we? For all the sauces, spices and herbs we use. For this next little item, toast some bread lightly under the grill, take it out and spread the untoasted side with butter or marge or whatever you use, then carefully arrange some sliced onion on each piece and cover that with slithers of cheese (preferably strong, crumbly Lancashire farmhouse, if you can get it). Pop it all back under the grill until the cheese is melted and golden. Sprinkle a little Worcester sauce on it before eating – or, and this is me, soy sauce. I cannot describe the sensation of the first mouthful – except to say that it is bloomin' splendiferous.

I know this isn't a cookery book, but I'll just add another sandwich filling, which is one of our own originals: you need a tin of corned beef, an onion, three fresh tomatoes, salt and pepper. Pour boiling water over the tomatoes and leave for one minute, then you can easily remove the skins. Put all the ingredients through the mincer until it's like a paste. Result? Indescribably tasty sandwich spread. It is, honestly ... do try it. We always have dishes of sandwiches with this filling when we give parties, and they always go first, there is never one left, and everybody asks how to make the filling.

If – and I do mean *if* – you are still hungry after that, have a portion of pears (Conference), lightly stewed in water with a dash of brandy, cloves and brown sugar. All prepared by Chef Scottie the day before. Ooh, mate! Finish up with two or three cups of Earl Grey tea in your favourite armchair.

And I hereby declare that our 'tea-time revels', either in London or in our country kitchen, are the favourite 'part' of my life.

Of course, I don't know if I'd enjoy it so much if it wasn't Scottie who was the other character in these particular performances!

Looking back at these diaries has a bit of sadness about it, now that these things can only be memories. But no one who has been loved as much as I was for as long as I was – fifty-eight wonderfully happy years – has any right to feel sorry for themselves. So I won't be. I'll just say 'Thank you, Scottie – I loved every minute of it.'

24
Shhh – Can you keep a secret?

I don't want to boast about doing things well, but I will boast about one thing, and that is, I can keep a secret. I can keep a secret *very* well ... An example of just how good I am, just to show you, goes back to when I was at school. One day one of my friends, Connie, said to me, 'Can you keep a secret?' and I said, 'Oh yes!' and we locked little fingers on it. (People of my age reading this book might know that locking your little fingers, that means 'I Promise.') Connie told me something which I never told anyone – nothing would have dragged it out of me.

I ran into her again – oh, *years* later, I suppose we would both have been in our fifties by then – and I said, 'You know that secret you told me while we were at school? I've never told *anybody!*' And she said, 'What secret?' And I said to her, 'Oh, Connie! You remember! One afternoon you told me such a secret, and we locked little fingers on it, and you said, "You won't tell anybody, will you?" And I said, "No I won't" and I can tell you now, I never have told a soul.'

She started laughing and said, 'Well can you tell *me*? I've forgotten what it was!' And I said, 'Your periods had started! You said, "Promise me you won't tell anybody" and honestly, I never have!' And she said, 'Well, you can now – I've just gone through the change!'

So now I've told you – but believe me, you would never have heard it from my lips before now!

25

Let's have the Irish jig!

Prior to having a heart by-pass operation in 1992 I had a ... I wish I could remember the long word for what they were going to do, but any of you who have experienced it will know that they put wires along your veins, with a little sort of balloon thing on the top, and if the balloon blows up, that vein's all right. That's as near as I can tell you.

There was a little room with six little beds in it, and there were four gentlemen and a lady and myself all waiting for ... whatever this examination was. When it was my turn I was called through into the little operating theatre, and there were three or four nurses standing there, and the first thing they said when I went in was, 'Do you like Ella Fitzgerald, Mrs Scott?'

I must admit I thought, 'What a peculiar thing to ask me,' but I said, 'Oh, yes ... yes. She's very clever.' I suppose I must have had rather a strange expression, and one of the nurses said, 'Only, you see, we've only got three tapes, and Doctor – WhateverHisNameWas – likes to do this to music.'

So I said, 'I see. Well – what are the other two?' She looked and said, 'Well, er, this one's an Irish jig ...' I said, 'That'll do! Let's have the Irish jig.'

So I lay there, with these wires being pushed

through, to the strains of this Irish jig 'De, la de li da de do da, blero, dub dub dub ...' because I'm a great admirer of Irish dancing and the tunes. And the doctor carried on with his work, very seriously ...

I went back into the other room and in about five minutes the doctor came through and said, 'I think an operation, don't you?' And I said, 'Well, I don't know. You're here to tell me that.' And he said, 'Yes. We'll say the 26th of January.'

There's nothing funny about the operation, when it's open-heart surgery. In fact the only thing to smile about is I've felt so much better since. It was such a success, I might even be able to manage a bit of an Irish jig myself!

26
Incredible illucinations

Have you ever experienced an hallucination? Because if you haven't ... don't bother. In fact, a lot of what I'm going to tell you isn't very nice, so if you're easily upset, miss out this chapter.

Just after my open-heart surgery, while still at St Mary's Hospital, I suffered from hallucinations – and I'm here to tell you, they were not at all funny.

I said to Jan, 'What are all those little chickens with red caps on doing under that sink?' And she said, 'What chickens? Which sink?' There were *thousands* of them. Tiny little chickens, red combs. In the end, Jan couldn't convince me, so she said, 'I'll go and pick some up and bring them for you.' She came back and said, 'There's nothing there, Mummy.' I said, 'Well, there's some pigeons there, with cooks' hats on.'

Then I thought the room was a foot deep in flour. I said to Scottie, 'Oh look! It's all over the knees of your suit and everything!' He said, 'What is?' I said, 'This flour.' He said, 'Which flour?' I said, 'All over the floor!' He said, 'There isn't any flour!'

I said, 'What? You're going to tell me in a minute there aren't two miniature polo bears standing up there!' He said, 'Well, there aren't.' I said, 'There *are* – they're only as big as guinea pigs.'

I was in Liberty's in Regent Street, two o'clock in the morning, everything was pink, the counters and everything. Jan was with me, covered in a pink sheet. I went out into Regent Street. There was a clock. A quarter to two, it said. Nobody there, and I came back and said to her, 'There's nobody in Regent Street.' She said, 'No, there won't be ... What are you doing?' And I said, 'I've lost my See-No Net.'

That was after the heart by-pass. Then with the last operation that I had, in 1994, on my leg, I was out for four hours. And Jan *told* the surgeons, in front of me, 'I don't know whether there are new drugs these days, but two years ago my mother nearly drove this hospital mad with hallucinations.' They said, 'Oh, she'll have a few.' I did as well. It's the anaesthetic.

Thank God Jan was always there the following morning, because I had terrible dreams. She slept in a chair by my bed. Every morning I would say 'Did I?' or 'Didn't I?' or 'Did we or did we not?' I said to her one day, 'Did we sleep on the stage of the Grand Theatre in Blackpool last night?' and she said, 'No, Mummy, of course we didn't.' I said, 'Oh, come off it! There was a three-piece suite that was used in the play, and I got in one of the chairs, and didn't a woman of the streets come up and give me two tablets in a glass? And I wouldn't take them?' She said, 'No. *No*. Oh dear, here we go again!'

There were lots of mornings like that. Then there was a lady doctor, who came and took my blood-pressure, and as she went away I noticed that on the floor she'd dropped a half-hoop of five-pound notes, sprayed out evenly, and three twenty-pound notes folded up. So I waited until another doctor, a young man, came into the room, and I said, 'Oh, do excuse me, you know the doctor that just went out? She's just dropped those on the floor.' And he said, 'Dropped what?' I said, 'The five-pound notes – there, on the floor.' He said, 'I can't see any five-pound notes.' I said, 'Oh come along! Don't be stupid! There's a whole arc of five-pound notes, and three twenty-pound notes ... I'm looking at them now – folded ... and that lady has just been in, because these two gentlemen ...' and I turned round and the two men who were sitting there had no heads ... and the doctor said, 'Well, Mrs Scott, it's all right, but there aren't any five-pound notes.'

The thing that gives me the most horrible feeling of fear is that there will be a black beetle or a cockroach. I've never been able to stand them. So when they moved me to a room further along the corridor, I sat in a chair, looked down, and there were four beetles. I called for the nurse. I said, 'I'm so sorry to trouble you, but I can't stick beetles, and look, there's four there ...' And she said, 'Where?' 'There ...' She said, 'I can't see any beetles.' I said, 'Oh look, they're *moving*. Of course you can!' So she went and got a mop out of a wet mop bucket, slopped it on them, and went off. And I sat there. I cannot explain how I feel when I see a beetle. And I saw three more, in front of me. So I called her again. She said, 'What is it now?' I said, 'There's three more beetles – there ... there.' She said, '*Where?*' I said, '*There, look!* Walking on the floor.' So she goes for the mop again. Slops it.

I'm sitting in this chair, not knowing what to do in case I see another beetle, and a girl who must have been Flower Power, covered in flowers and everything, was asleep on my right, with a very well-dressed man with her. And I said, 'Did you see those beetles?' And he shook his head, and I thought, 'I'm not sticking this! I'm not sitting here in this chair in this dark room with beetles crawling all over!' And I went outside and got in a car. I said, 'Would you take me home, please?' And a friend took me home to where I was born, in Cheapside.

The following morning I said to Jan, 'I must set about ordering a 'phone for my mother.' And she said, 'Why, Mummy?' And I said, 'Because I noticed, when I went home last night, she'd wondered where I'd been, and she's not on the 'phone.' Jan had quite a bit of trouble persuading me that my mother had been dead for years.

Apparently I was in the same room all the time, from going in to coming out. I was never taken to another room. I thought there was another bed next to mine with a white-haired, very nice old gentleman in it, and a lady of about seventy with a nice perm. There was a television at the bottom of their bed, and when it got to one o'clock I said to the nurse, 'Would they mind if I had the news on?' So whether she asked them or not I don't know. Anyhow, later on in the afternoon Jan arrived, and the television was on the floor on its side. I said, 'Did somebody knock that television over or something?' And the nurse said, 'Which television?' I said, 'That one, at the bottom of their be ...' And there was no bed! Nobody in it. And I said, 'Just excuse me, will you? There was an old lady and gentleman in a bed here this morning, wasn't there?' She said, 'No. There's only been your bed in here.' And I said to Jan, 'Take no notice!

There was a man and a woman in bed here, with a television ...'

Jan said the best one was when the surgeons came in one day, and they said, 'How are you, Mrs Scott?' Jan herself had been out of the room going to the loo or something, and they'd walked in with her and they'd been talking, and I said, 'Very well thank you.' And Jan said, 'Well, I'm afraid Mummy's had a few hallucinations.' And I said, 'Nothing that matters, you know.' And they went out, and I said to Jan, 'You can tell those people to come out from behind the television now!'

I think I was quite a disruption to the life of the hospital, but Jan says I wasn't, because there was only her with me all the time.

Now, what is there prettier and nicer to talk about ...?

27

A hen called 'Thora'

I went to the Chelsea Flower Show in 1988, and as I approached the Rosemary Roses stand the press cameras were clicking away. Rosemary Roses had written to me the year before to ask if they could 'bred' – which is the funny word they use – and name a rose after me, and of course I had said they could – who wouldn't be proud and honoured to have a rose named after them? All the roses on the stand were breathtaking, and there in the middle was a very large display of the palest of pink roses, almost white, with hair-fine lines of deep pink and the most wonderful perfume. I felt like crying ... the name-ticket on them said 'Thora Hird'.

It's a floribunda rose or, as Jan always calls it, a 'Thorabunda' ... to think that years after I've gone to live in 'the great entertainment world in the sky' such a beautiful rose with my name will still be growing in people's gardens and giving pleasure.

Actually, I've got quite a collection of living things named after me now.

Many of them have come as a direct result of working on *Praise Be!* Liz Barr, the original producer of *Praise Be!*, still went on writing the *Praise Be!* scripts with me after she left the BBC, and if ever you saw me visiting a place to interview someone where there would be animals in the picture, you can be sure it was at Liz's suggestion, because she is someone who, like my daughter Jan, is daft about animals.

For instance, in 1993 I went to talk to Paul Heiney on his traditional Suffolk farm. Oh – magic is the only word for it. He had all the old farming equipment, shire horses to do the ploughing, and a shepherd's hut on wheels to take into the fields during lambing, and a farmyard full of hens, sheep and pigs – all just as I remember farms from when I was a child. It was like travelling back to another age. I'll never forget sitting with Paul on a hay bale in the evening sun, surounded by the sounds and smells of the farm, talking about faith. And after my visit, when his big black sow Alice had a litter, he wrote in his column in *The Times* – I've still got the cutting – that because he'd so enjoyed my visit, and because he was sure I wouldn't mind, he was naming one of the piglets 'Thora' in my honour. Well, I thought it was indeed an honour!

Another year I visited the Donkey Sanctuary in Sidmouth, in Devon, to interview the founder Elizabeth Svendsen, MBE. Dr Svendsen founded the Sanctuary to take in unwanted and ill-treated donkeys and give them a home for life. Today there are over six thousand donkeys living there, and the Sanctuary needs a computer to keep all the details. But every single donkey is treated as an individual. Some of them go on to earn their keep once they are well and strong enough, by giving rides to little disabled children. For these children, making friends with such gentle, friendly creatures, and riding on them, gives them self-confidence in all sorts of ways, and it can be an important part of their development.

I've always loved donkeys. Donkey rides were part of the seaside holiday for both children and grown-ups when I was growing up in Morecambe ... All these years later I can still recall the sound of the donkeys going home each summer evening after their hard day's work on the sands – the harness, with its bells on the brow-bands, jingling as their big heads nodded up and down, their little hooves tapping along the sea-washed stones of the ramparts. We children would run along beside them for a few yards, patting their hindquarters, and as we called out 'Goodnight, Neddy!' they would blink their heavy-lashed eyelids, as much as to say 'Goodnight, children, we'll be back tomorrow.'

All my life I have wanted to ride through the countryside – not on the stage, I mean, like at the London Palladium, but properly, along country lanes – in a little donkey-cart. And I did it there, at the Donkey Sanctuary, in my 79th year – and I have to tell you, I enjoyed it more than if they'd given me a mink coat or a cottage with a thatched roof! It was another dream come true.

The other thing that was lovely was that one of the donkeys in the Sanctuary had been expecting a foal the night before I arrived, and they said, 'If it's a girl, we'll call it Thora, because she's coming tomorrow.' Well, it wasn't, it was a boy, so they called it Thor, which is just as flattering, because all my closest friends call me Thor.

But I've another one! I had the joy of visiting a convent, All Hallows, Ditchingham, in Norfolk. Now

I don't know, why do we always think that a Mother Superior will be an elderly nun with a kindly round face and called Martha? The Mother Superior at All Hallows is called Sister Pamela. You wouldn't think of a Mother Superior as 'Pamela', would you? Well I wouldn't, although I don't know why, really.

I don't know how to describe her. She is the most wonderful person, attractive, clever and kind, the most loving, dear person that I'll ever meet.

I had a happy day filming there – animals everywhere, and such a warm, loving atmosphere, I wish I could describe it better. In the kitchen, where they were washing up, there was a cat sitting on the windowsill, watching them.

It's where Sister Maud lived, who, between the ages of eighty and ninety, wrote a collection of little poems called 'Tailwags'. The sisters collected them together in a little book, and before I ever went to the convent I had been quoting Sister Maud on *Praise Be!* Here's an example:

'Only the tail-end of life is left,' I said,
And into my head
A thought came out of the blue,
A thought from you:
'But that is the cheery end,' you said,
'So see
That you use it for me.'
And I said 'Amen' and raised my head.
'I will glorify God with a wag,' I said!

While I was there it was time to feed the hens. And there was one sister, a girl of about twenty-three, plump, beautiful, smiling face, black waist apron on. She took me to see the hens being fed, and on the way she said, 'By the way, you'll see a hen in a minute that lays blue eggs!' Well, you're not going to say 'Are you telling the truth?' to a nun, so I said, 'Does it?' And she said, 'Yes, and not the blue of a thrush's egg. Bluer than that!'

And there, indeed, were four beautiful *blue* eggs. It was a black hen. She said, 'We thought we'd like to call it Thora ... Would you be offended?' Offended? It was the proudest day of my life!

At the end of that day's filming at Ditchingham something quite strange happened. Not that what happened at the end of the day was strange, I don't mean that, but just listen. Or 'read on', I should say.

We were travelling in a large hired car, and as we were leaving I got in the front and Chris Mann, the very clever director of *Praise Be!* that year, got in the back, leaned over and slammed my front door shut – just as Sister Pamela leaned in to kiss me goodbye ... and these dear little fingers on this dear little hand were caught ... Oh, I *felt* it. I was so upset. And I looked at her, and I knew she was fighting for the tears not to come, and she said, 'Oh, I ... ah ... I ...' I was out of that car quicker than I've told you, and I put my arms round her and said, 'Oh! Your little hands!' She said, 'I'll go and put them under water.' Which she did, and we had to leave her and drive off. I hated that journey, thinking about her ... and I didn't speak to poor Chris the whole way back! I know he didn't mean it, but it really had upset me.

That night the whole crew of us stayed at a motel. I've never been as cold in my life! I'll tell you, I woke up in the middle of the night, opened my case and put on three cardigans, wrapping one round my legs – you should have seen me! Well, you shouldn't have seen me. Thank goodness you didn't see me.

This was, I'd say, about three o'clock, half past three in the morning, because I looked at my watch and I thought, 'Good gracious me, I've got to freeze for another five hours!' And then I wakened again at half past six, still very cold. But when I wakened both times, my first thought was for these little fingers, and each time I said a little prayer for her. I said, 'Dear God, please don't let her hands be injured or maimed.'

During the following day I tried to get her twice on the telephone. Both times they were at prayer, so I didn't worry again. But the following day I got her on the telephone, and I said, 'I'm just ringing up to see about your poor fingers,' and she laughed and said, 'We-ell! My nails are going a little bit purple and blue, but they are all right and I'm not in pain. By the way ...' she said, 'Did you say prayers for me that night?' And I said, 'Yes, I did.' She said, 'Yes, I knew. What time? Was it about half past three?' I said, 'Well, round about then! And then again ...' and we both said together, '... at about half past six.'

I said to her, 'Well, how would you know?' She said, 'I didn't know for sure, but I did feel you were praying for me.'

We've kept in touch by letter ever since. She always ends her letters with a P.S. 'Love from the hen!' They're having a new bit built on to the side of the convent, where you can go if you've been ill, and I've said that whatever else I'm doing, I'll be along to open that. I had a letter from Pamela the other day, while I was writing this chapter. She wrote:

> *A few weeks ago I had a lovely, restful holiday with some friends who live on a farm near Kingston. They keep Welsh black cattle. While I was there a lot of lovely little calves were born, and I told my friends about Thora the Hen, so now there is also a delightful frisky Welsh black calf called Thora!'*

So you see, that's a rose, a pig, a donkey, a hen that lays blue eggs, and now a Welsh black calf – all called Thora! And it's not bad going, is it? You'd have to go more than a day's march, wouldn't you, to meet somebody else who had all that?

28

All things bright and beautiful

My mother loved the simple flowers that grow on the railway side, marguerites, dog daisies, foxgloves and – I think above all – cowslips. I was speaking at a lunch, and amongst the gentlemen of the press there was Keith Waterhouse, a clever writer, a northerner, and we were chatting and I said, 'I can remember something you wrote – eight or nine years ago. I remember it vividly' and he said, 'Gracious! Was it so inspiring?' I said, 'Well, it was because you mentioned cowslips. You said there aren't as many cowslips these days. And I remember turning to Scottie and saying, "He's right!"'

He *was* right. When I was a child, if you went along any railway side, or in my case along the canal bank, you could always pick a bunch of cowslips. I thought about Keith Waterhouse's article so much, and the next time I was in a garden centre I was roaming through and I saw there were some cowslips, so I bought a pot, thinking I would give them love and care as never. And you think I'm going to say, 'And now there's a huge bed of cowslips', don't you? But there isn't. I could do nothing with them. I used to talk to them and say, 'Aren't you feeling so well, loves? Shall I take you indoors?' But they did nothing.

Nothing. Which is rare for me, because I'm not clever but there isn't much that doesn't come up once I've planted it.

I've got those books of gardening by the Old Wives, which say things like, 'If you're going to cut down an elm tree, don't do it until the third Thursday in the month, and face the south.' They may be right! One thing they say that I have proved does work very well: 'If your roses are covered with green fly, get a piece of garlic and plant a small bulb underneath each rose bush.' I can't stand garlic in food, it always upsets me, but we grow lots of roses, so I tried this. With a dibber I put a little bulb of garlic underneath each rose bush. And you're going to say, 'And the roses were still all covered in green fly ...' Well, they weren't. We didn't have a green fly all summer on the roses. Apparently they are like me – garlic upsets them.

I can be absolutely mesmerised when I'm gardening. Take Gypsophilia seed – it's like powder. Whenever I'm planting seeds I'm thinking, 'This little bit of dust is going to turn into a bush full of little white flowers ...'

Scottie so often used to find me standing transfixed in the garden, staring at seeds in my hand, and he'd say, 'Oh, hallo! Are we off again – meditating?' and I'd say, 'Yes, we are, because I cannot believe that this little, tiny, mite of thing is going to be a bed of snapdragons!'

Autumn and winter can be breathtaking too, can't they? The changing colours of the leaves on the trees, spiders' webs along the hedges, silver with dew, and the aroma of garden rubbish being burned on bonfires.

Oh, I love that! And the end of the year, with the sparkling frost outlining every leaf and branch and blade of grass, until we reach that magic moment when the year turns, and the first dear little snowdrop pushes its way into view.

I've always admitted we're a bit daft in our family – regarding certain things, that is. And snowdrops – or at least the arrival of same – has always meant a great deal to us. When Jan lived in Beverly Hills I would always keep my eyes open in January for the first bunch of snowdrops to appear in London on the barrows. I would buy a bunch and put them in a certain china vase that had belonged to Jan and which she had loved when she was a little girl. Then I'd ring Beverly Hills, whatever time of day it was, and say 'Hey, Jan! I've just put some snowdrops in your little vase.' It always delighted her. Not exactly an earth-shaking event, I know, but the sort of thing our family's life has been full of and blessed by.

Of course, now that Jan and William live in Sussex they have patches of snowdrops all over their garden each year, and I have some in my cottage garden, too. And do you know – yes, of course you do – if I am in London when the first little white treasure pops through, Jan will ring up and say 'Guess what!' and I will say, 'A snowdrop is out!' Not very sophisticated, are we?

I think I told you all this about the snowdrops in my last book – so if I did, I apologise that you've had to pay twice to read the same thing.

This is only a 'little' story, but it is so full of love that I want to tell it to you. It holds love, sadness and great joy ... that's why I'm telling you. I would like to begin 'Once upon a time ...' but that would be silly, and this is not a fairy story, but a true one.

You remember I've told you about the mallard ducks in Jan's garden at Isfield? Well, one year, when Mother Mallard's twelve little ducklings were just old enough to go on the lake in the Millhouse grounds, we all watched them swimming about with as much admiration and oohing and ahing as though no ducklings had ever swum on a lake before. When Mother Mallard came off the water and waddled off, the dutiful babies followed her in a fluffy yellow line ... beautiful ... But suddenly Jan said, 'Hey! Hold on a minute. There's one missing ...' Needless to say, we all started counting aloud 'One, two, three ...' but at eleven we each stopped. We all started to search among the reeds and plants growing around the lake, but no luck. Isn't it amazing how quickly joy can turn to sorrow? Only a few minutes before we had been enthusing about the little duck family swimming about, and now suddenly ... misery and anxiety. Mother Mallard sat down after shaking her feathers, and her family pecked at the grass and quite honestly showed not the slightest concern that one of them was missing.

Oh, hecky plonk! It was going to be a very upsetting evening for Scottie, William, Jan and me. The dogs had been with us when we were watching the display on the lake, but then had wandered off somewhere. Just as we were giving up searching for the missing duckling, Jan saw Patch trotting towards us from the far end of the lawn. Jan gave a little gasp, and then gently said, 'Come here, Patch.' As Patch approached we all saw the head of the tiny mallard duckling hanging out of her mouth. That was all. Just the head. 'Patch, come here' Jan said again. She was kneeling down. Patch approached and sat down in front of her. Jan put her hand out palm upwards, and Patch dropped the baby duckling onto Jan's hand. We held our breaths. The duckling stood up. Shook itself. Hopped off Jan's hand, down onto the grass, and joined its brothers and sisters! There was nothing wrong with it!

Patch, bless her, had realised the little thing had wandered away from the rest of the family, picked it up in her soft 'gun-dog' mouth, and returned the happy wanderer to Jan. Praises, pats, biscuits were showered on 'You wonderful dog! Who's a good girl, then?' and Patch just sat there, laughing, because dogs do laugh you know. Her face seemed to be saying, 'I bet you dozy lot thought I'd eaten that duckling, didn't you?' Well, let's be honest, we dozy lot *had* thought that!

You've heard of the 'happy hour' haven't you? It's usually in a pub, when the drinks are cheaper for an hour, but I'm not referring to that kind of 'happy hour' – I'm referring to a *very* happy hour I have just experienced.

I needed some eggs, and Jan said she would run me down the lane to Boathouse Farm. I said, 'Give me ten minutes to get myself ready.'

'You don't need to bother too much,' she said, 'You'll only be meeting cows and sheep!'

She was right ... but not quite. We *did* see cows and sheep at Boathouse Farm, but we saw something else – dozens of 'em, all beautiful – lambs and calves. I'm not exaggerating, honestly, I have never ever seen such wonderful offspring, and some of the lambs had been born only the previous night, and some that very morning. They were all frisking about, and a tiny, dark grey, black-legged one ran straight up to me. I picked it up and stroked its tiny nose with my little finger. It put its little mouth round my finger and started to suck like mad. I apologised to it, and told it the Milk Bar wasn't open. I looked down and there was Mum, who had walked over and was baaing something, perhaps it was, 'Now I've told you not to talk to strangers!'

Jan was cuddling a dear little white lamb, quite content to snuggle against Jan's warm heart. The farmer's wife, Mrs Martin, is such a kind person, and she amazed me by telling me something about every individual sheep and lamb, things like, 'That lamb won't feed off its mother, so we're bottle feeding it' or, 'You see that mother over there? She had triplets ...' and so on. Not only did the mother sheep all look exactly alike to me, so did the lambs, apart from being black or white. But to Mrs Martin they were all unique individuals.

There was a little grey-and-black lamb in a pen on its own, and Mrs Martin said, 'That one's an orphan.' Now until she said the word 'orphan' I had been thinking how happy and contented it looked. But an orphan! I suddenly felt very sad and the tears started to well up. But Mrs Martin said very cheerfully, 'It'll be all right. One of the girls from the village is coming for it, and she'll hand-rear it.'

We moved into the cowsheds, where there were dozens of very large cows, all lying down, chewing the cud. The building smelled of fresh hay, and I've never experienced such serenity except in a convent or church. The animals looked so content, and a few had little calves cuddled up beside them. One calf was just a few hours old, and looked at Jan and me with its sweet little face on one side, as much as to say, 'So this is the great big world, is it?'

Oh, I did enjoy that afternoon. I was sad to leave them all.

All the way home I was singing the words of one of my favourite hymns, 'All Things Bright and Beautiful', and especially the chorus:

All things bright and beautiful
all creatures great and small
all things wise and wonderful
– the Lord God made them all.

29
Nothing like a Dame

Of course, in all our lives we have exciting moments. I had an extra-wonderful moment when a letter arrived from Downing Street to say I was to be awarded the OBE. I had to watch it, because you can lose your OBE if you tell anybody. You can! You can lose that OBE by going into your grocer's next day and saying, 'Hey! Do you know, I'm getting the OBE!' Until the official announcement it is strictly private.

Nobody was more surprised than I was when I got it, although at first I supposed that OBE must mean Outside Broadcasting Expert! You are always given the full title if you are speaking at a nice luncheon, when they'll say, 'And our speaker is Miss Thora Hird, Most Excellent Order of the British Empire', that's what it is, and it sounds even better.

You see, I think I get so much more pleasure out of achievements like this, because I wasn't always *it*, if you know what I mean. Thora Hird, OBE ... scrubbed her mother's steps ... didn't know what the word 'arse' meant!

In September 1992 we'd been on a cruise, Scottie and I, and when we got back, as always, we couldn't open the front door for the mail. We had a routine: put them in piles: Thora Hird, Mr James Scott, T. and J. Scott Ltd, and then we opened them accordingly. One Thora Hird envelope looked a bit important so I opened it, to read a very nice letter informing me that I was to be made a Dame of the Most Excellent Order of the British Empire.

Well you can imagine how I felt, can't you? Here it was, in print, on 10 Downing Street notepaper. As before, when the recipient receives the news, they are requested, nay, ordered (politely) to tell NO ONE. It can be very difficult, let me tell you. For one thing, my husband was reading my letter over my shoulder. But I can swear on my life that we told no one, not even Jan.

People don't seem to think of me the same way as I think of myself. Even after I'd got the OBE people would still say to me, 'Why haven't you been made a Dame?!' and even, '*When* are they going to make you a Dame?' It's not that I want to swank about this, but it's just that I find it so moving, and so strange – there was even one man in Brighton who wrote every week of his life, until I got it. They must have said in the end, 'Oh, it's that man again! Give it 'er! Give it 'er, because we're getting fed up of all this!'

When I telephoned Downing Street – to make sure it was right, because, as I told them, 'I've already got the OBE' – they said it was right.

In June 1993 I was making a series of programmes for the BBC, produced and directed by Bryan Izzard, called *Thora on the Broad and Narrow* at Pinewood Studios. I couldn't tell you how many films I made at Pinewood for Rank Films before the war. I don't mean I starred in any of them – they were mostly one-day, two-day character parts. But it was like a homecoming, and when I was back there doing *Thora on the Broad and Narrow*, almost every day there would be rat-a-tat on my dressing room door and someone would stick their face round and say 'Hallo, Thora, do you remember me?'

On the day the Honours list was announced – 11 June, 1993 – I was sitting in my dressing room at lunchtime, not aware that at that very moment the list was being read out on the one o'clock news. I had had an early call that morning and hadn't seen the papers or spoken to anybody, and I honestly didn't remember that that was the day the list was to be published.

There was a knock on my door and a very happy looking floor manager came in saying, 'Who keeps things very quiet, Thora?' I answered 'Who ... what? What are you talking about?' He then said, 'Will you please come on the set – *Dame* Thora.'

I went along with him, and as I entered the set the music of 'There is nothing like a Dame ...' was playing, and the champagne corks started popping. Everyone was very kind, bless 'em, and it was lovely that it happened when I was there, at Pinewood, a place so full of memories for me.

When I returned to my dressing room at the end of the day's work the notice on my door had been changed to Dame Thora Hird, all done out in beautiful letters.

Jan could hardly speak when she telephoned me that evening. Our grandchildren were both at UCLA (University of California at Los Angeles), and she immediately wanted to set wheels in motion to bring them over for the investiture. When I said the expense was to be thought about, she said – and this is typical of her – 'How many chances will they get to see their grandmother standing with the Queen of England inside Buckingham Palace – and get to be inside Buckingham Palace, too?' I gave in.

On the morning I was to go to Buckingham Palace to receive my insignia from the Queen, Jan, Daisy, James and I travelled together in the car. Scottie had forfeited his seat, because you are only allowed three people, and he said it was more important for the grandchildren, and anyway he'd been along to see me receive my OBE. So there we were. I had to go in one door, and they had to go in another one. It all takes place in the Ballroom, if you've visited Buckingham Palace, and there is a large orchestra at one end, playing all the time. Everything runs very smoothly and is rehearsed to the second.

I found out when I got there that I was 'first on'. Now in the theatrical world the first on the bill are called 'curtain-raisers', it's never a star act, and I said to the gentleman, 'Oh, good gracious! That doesn't sound very good. Am I to be the curtain-raiser?' and he said, 'Well, whatever a curtain-raiser is, you aren't that, because you are the only one to be made a Dame here today.'

Anyhow, then I got a little bit nervous about making my curtsey to the Queen. I wanted to do it, but having arthritis so badly I was afraid of falling. So when they pinned the little hook on my coat, which they do so she can just hang the thing on, I told them I was getting anxious, so they brought me a page to escort me the whole time, even when I did my walk up and turn to be presented to the Queen. So I managed my curtsey all right. She has four Beefeaters with her, standing ready in case you're going to attack her!

There are two pieces of insignia when you're a Dame, and when the Queen was pinning on the lower one she looked up at me and smiled so beautifully and said, 'This gives me great pleasure.' At the end, when she was leaving, Jan and James and Daisy were sitting in the front row and Daisy gave the Queen a big smile – she has a lovely smile, Daisy – and the Queen gave her a really big smile back. Daisy thought that alone was worth flying over from America for – and I'm sure it was.

Perhaps I should give Daisy the last word in this chapter. While we were having our lunch, after the investiture and before the celebration party we gave for friends in the evening, she wrote this little rhyme, which she read out at the party:

The papers wrote, the word was out
The truth by all was seen –
Dame Thora was in London
And chatting to the Queen!

She looked a real beauty
Her suit and hat were blue
And Jan was there, and so was James
And even Daisy, too.

At 'curtain up' she came on
The Queen pinned on the treasure
She smiled and said, 'Dear Thora,
This is giving me great pleasure!'

Nothing like a Dame

Dame Thora got her Dameship
Or is she called a Knight?
And then, our tummies growling,
We went to get a bite.

The Ritz was just ... too *Ritzy!*
So where do you think we choose?
Cheese and onion sandwiches
With Poppa, in the Mews!

And now it's back to LA –
Oh, Ganny, I'm so flustered –
You know *I can't round off this rhyme*
Without the words 'Egg custard'!

30
Summer Wine

In 1979 I was filming the BBC drama series *Flesh and Blood*. I was playing the eighty-four-year-old matriarch of a family cement firm.

Among all the appointments I had for it – going for shoes, going for coats and all this – I see in my diary 'Appointment with Joyce – make-up'. Joyce was a wonderful artist. She took so much pains with my wig, dressing it so carefully – because in those days I was in my sixties, playing a lady of eighty-four, and I had to wear a wig. These days I am eighty-four, often playing a lady in her sixties, and I'm happy to report – I don't need a wig!

In the latest batch of *Last of the Summer Wine*, recorded in 1995, Joyce was back with me again for the first time since *Flesh and Blood*. We were both overjoyed to see one another again. It's one of the lovely things of our business, making friends with people you work with, and then years later working together again.

I suppose Edie, the character I play in *Last of the Summer Wine*, is supposed to be in her late sixties, so I've done a complete reversal in fifteen years. Joyce said, 'They've made you up a wig, just in case you'd like to try ...' Well, I did try it on to please her, but I didn't wear it. I don't know why, but for all my complaints about my hair being too fine and too straight, it has done me one good turn by never going grey. It's still my own colour, for what colour it is, although I don't think I would have minded if it had gone pure white – I think white hair is very beautiful.

Incidentally, any minute now *Flesh and Blood* is going to be shown again on television, and I'm very interested to see my younger self playing eighty-four ... now that I actually *am* eighty-four.

The little village of Holmfirth, in the Yorkshire Dales, has become quite a tourist attraction, with posters at railway stations saying 'Visit *Summer Wine* country'. There's a pretty little tea-shop called The Wrinkled Stocking, and in the middle of the village there's a pair of stone wellingtons with a little slot at the top where you can put money in for the hospital – that's Compo's wellies. And there are many things that have come about as a result of the television series that I would say have made Holmfirth into a very thriving, prosperous little place.

Of all the people who have stopped me in the past eleven years or so to make any remark about *Last of the Summer Wine*, only one person, a lady I met on a train, has ever in any way shape or form run it down – and that was because she lived in Holmfirth, and seemed to hold me personally responsible for spoiling her peace and quiet on a Sunday! I suppose you can't blame her, really, if she'd moved there hoping to get away from it all.

Everyone else I've ever spoken to has always said how much they enjoy it, and how they only wish it was on every week. So I reckon that Compo, Clegg,

Foggy and company will go on a bit longer yet. There can't be much wrong with a series that has been so popular for twenty-five years.

I've had some good directors in television – a joy to work with, so many of them – and I've got to say about Alan Bell, who directs *Last of the Summer Wine*, that he's Dr Barnardo to me, and to us all. He never loses his temper ... he just quietly goes on. And another thing, which is a bit technical, but I'm going to say it: someone who is an editor and cutter is always a very clever man or woman. And if you get a director on a film who has been an editor and cutter before, you're always pleased because you know that they can see in advance the shape of the scene you're doing, and where it will begin and end in the final cut. So there's never any flim-flam about doing everything seventy different ways before they finally make up their mind which one they want.

When I'd been working for six months with Alan Bell on *Summer Wine*, I said to him one day, 'Excuse me asking, Alan, but were you an editor and a cutter ever?' And he said, 'Yes, for years. Why?' And I said, 'Because it shows, in your directing.' Any artist will tell you that to work for a director who has had experience as an editor and cutter is a joy.

When Alan first asked me to play a cameo role in an episode of *Last of the Summer Wine*, I was very pleased – but I can honestly say that I thought that was all I would do. Little did I think that I would still be part of the 'ensemble' eleven years later. It isn't difficult to explain how enjoyable it is. We all have so many laughs about old times, because we're all professionals who have known one another for ever – I mean to say, all of us are over twenty-one, and many of us have played together in different things over the years, going way back. Even the smaller parts are real old pros, like Danny O'Dea playing the man with thick glasses who bumbles about raising his hat to lamp-posts and generally mistaking everything he doesn't see. He usually only has one line per episode – but he always gets a good laugh on it because he's a wonderful comic, one of the best.

The thing people nearly always comment on to me is the business I do with putting down newspaper underneath my husband's anatomy wherever he walks, stands, sits or leans. It seems to strike a chord! To be honest, I have so few lines in each episode I'm glad to have a bit of business that I can have some fun with. With the newspapers, I can make it funny by managing to shove one under his hand or his elbow or any other part of his anatomy he's just about to put down – without even looking at him. I enjoy that, and the coffee scenes, when we all lift our cups at the exact same moment. These things get a good laugh, if you get the timing right to the split second, because they're funny when they happen in life. That's what it's all about, really.

It's a joy to share a caravan with two old friends, Kathy Staff and Jane Freeman. The three of us 'run the country' very successfully from our little dressing room on the moor! There's a lot of laughing, a lot of serious talk, and a lot of affection in our little caravan ... which also has a 'little' lavatory – none of us can get into it, especially not Kathy when she's wearing her 'Nora Batty' padding!

I do hereby declare that if it happens to be a cold day on the edge of the Yorkshire Moors, and my arthritis is being a bit more painful than usual, the kindness of Kathy and Jane is such that, well, they couldn't be kinder, that's all ... There is kindness and there is great kindness, but their kind of great kindness is of the super-kind kind.

But, like I said, it's a comedy about old people, and none of us in it has still got our twenty-first birthday to look forward to. Next to my bed at home I have a little framed saying, the first thing I see every morning, and it says

'Don't stop doing things because you're growing old – you only grow old if you stop doing things.'

I think it's so *true*. The one thing that has helped me most is the fact that I have been able to keep on working, because for me that is the thing I am most afraid of, not being able to work. I have had arthritis for a long time, and anyone who has got it knows the sort of pain that is. I always say to the Lord, 'I won't complain about any of the pain I get when I'm not working, if you take it away when I do.' And he does. As soon as I start working – whatever it is, the pain disappears. So I try very hard to keep my side of the bargain.

For a short while last Spring, though, I thought that my working days might be over. It was in April 1995, and I was down in the country where I have a cottage, and all of a sudden when I put my foot on the floor – whoohoosh! – I've never known such pain in my life.

I really have not. Fortunately Jan was there. She said, 'What's the matter?' And I said, 'I can't get up.'

She rang my doctor in London, then she packed my house up, put all the food in the car (it's a two-hour drive) and we got there for seven o'clock. The doctor examined me and said, 'This is a hospital job' I said, 'When? Tomorrow?' And he said, 'Tonight. I'm sending for the ambulance.' So I went straight to hospital.

I had had both hips replaced in 1980, and I'd had my right hip replaced a second time, which is as much as any surgeon wants to do, but this time it wasn't the hip, it was the bone from the knee to the hip, the femur, that was not holding the replacement hip as it should. So I've got a longer metal piece there now, but I can't tell.

Surgeons are brilliant people, and are always accorded a lot of respect. When they come round to your bed – and anybody reading this knows what it's like, if you've been in hospital – it's a royal visitation. Mine said, 'You see, Mrs Scott, it isn't usual for us to cure a lady of eighty-three ...' and here he paused dramatically '... to go back to work!'

I didn't like that, but I didn't say anything. And about two mornings afterwards he came round again, with another surgeon, and he asked me, had I any pain? and I said, 'Well, it's a little bit painful, but ... no, no, I'm really doing marvellously.' And he said (again), 'I should think you are! You see, we aren't used to curing people of eighty-three ...' (dramatic pause for effect) '... so that they can go back to work!' I didn't say anything, because I wouldn't be rude to this brilliant man, with the other surgeon and all the nurses fluttering round him. But the third time he came round he had a set of students, and he was telling them all about what I'd had done, and then he turned to me and he said, 'You see, Mrs Scott ...'

– and I held up my hand and said, 'Don't say it! Please!'

'Say what?'

'That you are not used to curing people of eighty-three ... to go back to work!'

And he laughed, I will say. I didn't mean to be rude, but I thought, 'If he says that every time he comes round ...' Because I had every intention of going back to work, you see. It was what was keeping me going.

Acting happens to be the kind of job you can go on doing long after normal retirement age – if anyone will have you! I mean to say, plays are about people, and all people grow old, so old people can have parts.

I had my operation in April 1995, and was due to be rehearsing for the new series of *Summer Wine* in June, and I had one fear – Alan Bell is such a considerate, good man, and I thought if ever he said to me, 'Thora, could you just ...?' and I had to say to him, 'I cannot do that, Alan' I would be broken-hearted.

So I thought it was better to be very brave, and say that I didn't think that I would be able to do the next series. And it took a lot for me to say that. But when I started to say it, Alan said, 'Well, wait a minute ... I've seen all ten scripts.' I said, 'Oh yes. And supposing that there's something that you ask me to do and ...' He held up his hand, 'Hold on! You can drink a cup of coffee, can't you?' I said, 'Yes.' He said, 'Well, you've the coffee morning in all ten. Every one. You can get in the car, can't you?' I said, 'Well, just between the wheel and the seat ...' And he said, 'Yes, well, you won't have any problems with that, because we are building a false front. And the car will be on a low loader, so there's no effort getting in. There is nothing in all the ten scripts that a dog or cat couldn't do – well, if they were clever.'

Even as I'm writing this chapter, I'm just about to go off next week and film the next ten episodes, and an extra one for Christmas. They've even organised a little golf buggy to take me from place to place when I'm there, and I know that I will be given every consideration, and I can only say that I am proud and grateful to belong to such a good-hearted, talented group of people.

31
'In the mood'

As I've said many times, if I couldn't be acting I would have to be doing something – or I wouldn't be happy. And although I'm in my eighties now, that's not really that old, when you look at the Queen Mother – on the fiftieth anniversary of VE Day, for instance, standing outside Buckingham Palace, aged ninety-five, joining in all the words of the songs, did you notice? I kept thinking, 'Oh, I wish somebody would come out and give her a chair!' I know how difficult it is to stand. (That's one thing I cannot do. I could not stand in a crowd watching anything for any length of time. Even in my back kitchen in the Mews I have little stools under the table, because sometimes, if I'm drying the pots after washing up, I have to sit down to dry them.)

Watching the Queen Mother that day, I suddenly vividly remembered the year Jan was about four. I rang up Vera, her nanny, to bring her down from Morecambe to London for VE Day. Jan had a little cardboard hat on, like a Union Jack, and it had across the front of it 'Well done, boys!' She fell asleep on her nanny's knee in my dressing room, and the little hat fell forward a bit: 'Well done, boys!' I can remember that so vividly.

One of the places I love to visit, and do quite regularly, is the Royal Star and Garter home, a retirement home for 'our boys', disabled sailors, seamen and soldiers. Four of them living there fought in the First World War. One is over a hundred years old. They help make poppies for selling on Remembrance Day. I first went there when I was eighty-one, to do an interview for *Praise Be!* There was an old boy there, Jimmy, ninety-nine, a real cheeky devil. He said, 'I fancy you, you know.' I said, 'Oh, do you?' He said, 'Yes. How old are you?' I said, 'I'm eighty-one.' He said, 'Oh! Go away! Come back when you're a bit older!'

Something they all remember, because it was very popular during the war years, is the 'thé dansant', a dance held in the afternoon, where tea was served. It was regarded as a safe, respectable venue for nice young men and women to meet one another, and in particular for servicemen on leave to meet girlfriends. Many a person of my generation remembers a courtship that began at a thé dansant. So it is only fitting that Age Concern, a charity I try to support as much as I can, should hold a thé dansant every year at the Kensington Town Hall.

Lady Mountevans, a dear lady about as high as a grasshopper, always telephones me to remind me to come: 'Dearest Thora! I don't know, I really do not know what we'd do without you! Because, you see – they expect you there. You follow me, don't you? They expect you there!'

There's a procession in, the Lord Mayor of Kensington and his wife, two or three VIPs, the Metropolitan Police Commissioner, Lady Mountevans and me. And everyone cheers – 'Hurray!' You never heard such a noise in your life. All the tables are full. They've a number on their tickets, with some wonderful prizes, Thorntons chocolates, wine, that sort of thing. One year there were three bottles of champagne, better than Dom Perignon, and I said to Lady Mountevans, 'Hey, these are a bit good, aren't they?' and she said, 'Shhh! I got them out of my husband's cellar before I came out!'

There will be the police band playing 'In the Mood', and a couple of thousand old folk, who will all have brought along their bed-slippers to dance. One year, the girl sitting next to me was very – how can I describe her? – tall, good tweed suit, non-stop smoking – and it was the actual woman that *Prime Suspect* was written about – the police woman detective. While we were chatting she noticed a small old woman dancing all by herself on the dance floor – the police band playing 'In the Mood' – this is perfectly true – twirdle-der, twirdle-der – she's got the bed-slippers on, with turned-over tops and pom-poms – twirdle-de, twirdle-do – all on her own – twirdle-de, twirdle-de – white hair, ever so thin, all her little pink scalp showing through – and 'Prime Suspect' said to me, 'Oh, look at that poor old soul! I'll put my fag out and dance with her.' I said, 'Hold on! Do you know these people?' She said, 'No' and I said, 'Well, I know 'em. Have a care!' She says, 'Ah no! I can't watch her dancing on her own.' So I said, 'Go on then.' I watched. She put her fag out, went onto the floor and said to the little old lady, 'Do you want a dance, love?' But she twirdles off on her own, saying 'Gerr'off! Whey up! I'm enjoying meself!'

She was laughing all the way back, and she said, 'You were right!'

Now, I've never wished that I could be anybody else – but there are quite a few people I greatly admire. I could mention fifty, but that isn't what this book is about; so I'll just tell you about three extremely dedicated, capable women who are also my dear friends.

Sandy Chalmers is Judith Chalmers' sister, and for many years was at the BBC but now works full-time for Help the Aged – and believe me, they are so lucky to have her and her colleague Pat Banon. Dorothy Crisp is the Welfare Officer at the Star and Garter Home, looking after the old boys there with great love and care; and Monica Hart works for the Stroke Association.

They work like wallop for their different charities, and what always impresses me is how clever, conscientious and reliable they are – if they say they'll do something, it's done. If I was half as good as any of them, I'd be proud of myself. So I would like to put on record, in this book, what a pleasure and an honour it has been to get to know them and to call them my friends.

32

The new girls

People are always saying to me 'You do enjoy your work, don't you?' and I do, because it brings me into contact with such a lot of nice and clever people. I could sit for hours talking about 'old pros' and the stars that people of my age know about, but one of the great advantages of television has been that I also meet and work with some of the new very clever people, like Victoria Wood and Julie Walters. I've only been in one thing with Victoria, a play she'd written herself called *Pat and Margaret*. What a clever woman she is. She does everything so well – stand-up comedy, writing and performing comic sketches, singing and acting ... we had to do all that in the old days of Variety, but not many artists who have grown up with 'the box' have such a big range.

I've been in three plays for television with Julie Walters, two by Alan Bennett. A play I did most recently with Julie was called *Wide-eyed and Legless* ... Please don't ask me why it was called that ... I do know that it is a wonderful play, based on real characters and a true story. It was also an extremely sad play – which was strange, considering the three main parts were played by Julie Walters, Jim Broadbent and myself – none of us exactly known as tragedians. Julie played a woman with that terrible illness they can't seem to get at the bottom of, ME, Jim Broadbent was her husband, and I was his mother, getting the first signs of Alzheimer's, but not so bad she has to be put away. I had some very comic lines, but everything had a sadness about it. It was beautifully written by Deric Longden, the man whose true-life story it was – the man Jim Broadbent was playing – and adapted for television by Jack Rosenthal. Deric was kind enough to say to me afterwards that I '*was*' his mother – I'd portrayed her exactly how she had been. So that was nice.

I always enjoy working with the 'new' talents like Victoria and Julie – well, they're young compared with me. They are brilliant and they are assured. Their approach to the work is different from the way I was brought up. I can see that, although I find it difficult to explain. I'm not criticising, but it is different. I am sometimes a bit surprised, I will say, how even very young artists these days – and, I mean, sometimes it's children I've acted with – will talk back to the director, and argue with him or her. I would never ever have done that when I was starting out, and it's rare for me to do it even now.

If I were to pass on any advice to a young person thinking of coming new into our business today, I would say two things are most important: first of all – be on time. My father taught me that, and it is really so important. I'll never forget the time I was in a play he was directing, and one morning I arrived for rehearsals out of breath from running and one minute late. He said, 'You're late' and I said, 'Well, only a minute ...' and he said, 'There are sixty people in this room, Thora, waiting to begin this rehearsal, and I'm here, that's sixty-one, and with you it's sixty-two. So you have wasted not one minute but sixty-two minutes of people's time. Don't be late again, and please apologise now to everyone you have kept waiting.' I went round the room apologising to all the actors and extras – the play was *The Desert Song*, so there were dozens of them – and I never was, and never have been late again. Early? Often. It is true, what my Dad said, that if you begin the day by keeping everybody waiting, it will get the whole cast, not just you, off to a bad start.

The second thing I would say is most important is to do your homework. I mean by that, don't wait until you arrive for the first read-through before you begin to study your part. Read the whole play and then your own part several times before you arrive for the first rehearsal. This, too, is out of respect for your fellow-artists. Some actors will turn up to the first read-through without even having looked at their script beforehand, and won't put any expression into their reading. I think this is depressing for everyone.

I would say that if you've got any talent, and you keep to these two rules – being on time and doing your homework – you won't go far wrong.

Well, I think that's about enough from Mrs Perfect for this chapter, don't you?

33
Monologues

In the Victorian period 'The Monologue' was the great thing, a recitation with music at the back. Even if you couldn't sing, you could always do a monologue. We had a big trunk at home, with music in, pictures of artists like Little Titch on the front, and lots of monologues – heartbreaking some of them were! I wish I still had that trunk and its contents today.

You need a pianist who can play you perhaps a dozen chords. Seven chords will go to any monologue, if the meter is da-da-da-de, da-da-da-de, da-da-da-da-da-da-da-de. A good pianist will put a few twiddles in as well.

When I was doing a Sunday morning job recently in Chichester Cathedral, with Don Maclean, they sent me a script – and I could not believe it. It said 'Thora recites "The Lion and Albert"'. And I said, 'But it's a religious programme!' And they said, 'Oh, well! We'd like you to do it anyway.' I'll never know why. But I loved doing it. You can tell a professional comic has written it. My favourite two lines are:

'It just goes to show', said Mother, 'that the future is never revealed –
If I'd known we were going to lose him – I'd have not had his boots soled and heeled!'

I used to perform a lot of monologues in the old days. I even wrote one once. It's a bit risqué, but you'll forgive me, because I was much younger then! There was a disaster many years ago, in the 1950s, at Lynmouth in Devon, when the River Lyn flooded and swept away homes and everything in its path, and many lost their lives. Morecambe, my home town, were giving a big charity concert to raise money for the relief fund, and they asked me if I would go back and appear in it, because I was at that time appearing in the West End. I said of course I would go, which I did, early on the Sunday morning.

It wasn't until I got on the train that I thought, 'But what am I going to do? I can't just walk on and say – this is Thora ...'

In those days – it may be the same now, I don't know – *The Observer*, the Sunday paper, had quite a wide border round the edges. I had a pen, so I thought I'd try to write myself a monologue on the border of the paper. So I wrote it on the train, and was able to perform it that night. It went something like this:

Now I'll tell you a tale that will make you turn pale
It's a tale full of pathos and strife,
It's the tale of an actress who tried to get on
Well, in short, it's the tale of me life.

Now my parents were clever – well, of course, they were
'pros'
And the theatre was well in me blood.
My father, an actor, was top of the bill and he worked
... When he could ... If he would.

As a child my ambition had only one trend –
To appear at Dru-ary Lane
And to hear cries of 'Thora!' each night without end
And take curtains again and again.

At a quite tender age I appeared on the stage
As 'Willie' what died in East Lyn.
How was I to know that by being in that show
I'd embarked on a life steeped in sin?

Well, to panto I strayed and a big hit I made
– I used to take bow after bow –
The producer was rude and exceedingly crude
'Cos he cast me to type – as 'the Cow'!

When the pantomime's run – of a fortnight – was done
All the rounds of the Agents I went.
I was in great demand – you can quite understand –
I soon found a job – in the Big Tent!

As I entered the ring in a pink-sequinned thing
'The show must go on!' I'd repeat.
I was no common flop, for I'd got to the Top ...
I was getting twelve bob, and me keep.

I met a knife-thrower – a nice kind of chap
Who said that he'd had seven wives.

Is It Thora?

Though he'd treated 'em well, he'd a sad tale to tell –
How he'd lost them through chucking his knives.

Then one day along came the Ringmaster's son –
He was tall, he was dark ... he was bad
And he told me of things that I knew nowt about
And of pleasures that I'd never had.

So I met him that night by the old rustic bridge
And I knew there was something astir.
Perhaps it was fate – but I found out too late –
I was tripped, and I slipped ... What a cur!

At this time of my life I became lady wife
Of Lord Cheetham of Rogham – pronounced Dan
With his gifts and his smiles and his saloon bar whiles –
Well, he won me ... the dirty old man!

We'd a cat-and-dog life, and I knew, as his wife,
My career would soon go to the wall.
My ambition! My art! Oh! Dru-ary Lane ...
How could I give the works to them all?

So a friend of mine got me a small billiard ball
Which I ground to powder, fine, white
I could easily slip it in his cup
– 'Cos he always had Horlicks at night.

When he came home that night I could see he was tight,
'Cos he kissed me and started to wink.
'I'm not thirsty,' he said, 'I'll go straight to bed ...
Don't bother to get me a drink.'

Then I noticed the cat lick its lips – and fall flat
So I rushed out to 'phone for the vet
When I called again later he sounded quite stunned –
She gave birth to a small snooker set!

Well I stayed on with Dan, and I'm happy to say
That now I'm at Dru-ary Lane.
It took a long time, and it's been a hard climb,
But I knew that I'd get there some day.

I take the full stage, and I'm called, like I said,
And there's no one gives back-chat to me.
I'm adored by the men ... each morn, eight to ten,
I'm the star bluddy cleaner *– that's me!*

34
'Kipyrairon'

'Kipyrairon'? No, that's not Cypriot or Greek – it's English for Keep Your Hair On! When we were kids we were always using the expression KYHO – meaning don't lose your temper. However, I don't mean it in quite the same way in this story – well, it's not worth calling a story, it's more an observation: men have a lot of natural advantages over women. I've always thought that. I'm not jealous of 'em, or anything – in fact I'm jolly grateful that I was born a female. Oh yes! They're welcome to being men as far as I'm concerned!

But just think – they don't have to bother to wear make-up; they can wear the same suit for months; they can wash their hair in two minutes, run a comb through it and immediately look smashing, sexy and sinful; they don't suffer the worry of periods, or the absence of periods; and, of course, their biggest advantage of all comes when they go to the toilet to spend a penny.

Anyone like me, who wears slacks most of the time, will be familiar with the drill: unzip slacks, slacks down, roll-on down, tights down, panties down ... and then the return journey, or second house or however you wish to describe it. I don't wish my scribblings to cause any offence ... but this is true, isn't it? A fellow just stands there, for no time at all, unzips or unbuttons, performs, zips or buttons, takes his bow and walks away, while we ladies are still only halfway through Act One, Scene One ...

Men do have one great disadvantage, though – so many of them go bald. And by 1993 Scottie had gone a bit thinner on top – well, quite a lot thinner on top, to tell the truth.

Now, I had never thought, in all the years we were married, of enquiring about where he went to be 'tidied up' or how much it cost. He told me often enough about when he was a little lad, and how his Auntie Emma used to send him to the local blacksmiths for a haircut. His mother had died when he was seven years old, and in the village where he used to stay with his Auntie the blacksmith didn't only shoe the horses, he cut hair as well. Little lads like Scottie acquired his services for three ha'pence – a penny halfpenny! And I can remember my brother Neville, who had dark curly hair like a retriever dog, having his hair cut by Mr Hodgeson the barber – for threepence.

Well, by 1993 Scottie was no longer a little lad, but he had a lot less hair than when he was, so when he said one day, 'Shan't be long, love. Just going to have my hair cut,' I thought nothing of it. When he returned I couldn't see much difference, to tell the truth, but I made no remark until we were having a cuppa about half an hour later, when I said, 'He hasn't taken much off, has he?'

'No ... but it feels tidier.'

'How much does he charge, as a matter of interest?'

I asked as I started to pour him a second cup of Earl Grey.

'Five pounds fifty.'

'!!! *How* much?' I asked, nearly dropping the teapot.

'Five pounds fifty. It was six pounds fifty where I used to go.'

Now I was not a wife who ever grumbled about what Scottie spent. We had one purse between us, and one never questioned the other ... But *five pounds fifty pence!* Just to clip off a few hairs!

A few minutes later a friend of ours, Edgar, dropped by, and bearing in mind we knew him very well, when I was pouring him a cup of tea I said, 'Hey, Edgar ... how much does it cost you to have your hair cut?' and I started laughing, not to be rude, but he's very nearly bald. 'Six pounds fifty' he said. Honestly! I nearly had to have a tablet. After that I kept bringing the subject up, with all my female friends, and they'd say things like: 'Oh ... ten pounds?' or 'I think he pays about twelve pounds. Of course he has a manicure as well' or 'I think it's about eight pounds, ten pounds fifty with a singe ...' I still can't get over it – but they never batted an eyelid! It's *me,* you see! I'm still thinking of three ha'pence at the blacksmith's, or threepence at Hodgeson's, and the days when I had a shampoo and 'marcelle' wave with tongs – for a shilling! I must remind myself that I'm in my eighties now – and try to 'keep my hair on'! It would be cheaper, wouldn't it? Five pounds fifty! They must have been charging him a search fee!

I've gifts and cards from Jan from when she was a little girl, and I still get lots of pleasure from looking at them now and again. I look at sweet little floral cards that cost about threepence (old money), and you can sometimes still see the rubbed-out pencil mark of the price on the back of larger, beautiful cards, that cost about half a crown (old money), and like anyone else in my age group, I'm always thinking 'Blimey! I paid £1.80 (new money) for a card just like this yesterday!' It's not that I begrudge a penny of it, but it's very relieving to be able to say 'Would you just look how much this card costs!'

It's all part of life's rich pageant, isn't it? On a par with six spring onions in a bunch, 75p (new money). Whenever I remark on the price of spring onions, which I did when I bought some just yesterday, Jan always says sensible things like, 'But you see, Mother, it's not the six onions that cost 75p. It's all the work of cleaning and preparing them, and packing them up for sale in bags.' I suppose she's right. But I mean – did you *ever* think a large loaf of bread would cost 85p? Good gracious! A two-pound loaf used to cost fourpence halfpenny (old money) when I was a child. Oh well, Thora! KYHO!

35

Things ain't what they used to be – or are they?

When you get to my age (that means old – but I don't feel it), you hear a lot of your contemporaries saying things like, 'We-ell, things aren't as good as when I was young' and 'I don't know what the world's coming to!' I know I'm getting just as bad about thinking that many things aren't as good as they were in the old days ... artists who think nothing of turning up late for rehearsals, for instance – but we won't go into that again. And I also know that sometimes things aren't 'as good as' – they're 'a lot better than'!

A case in point was on 13 July, 1994. We were down at the cottage, and Felix, my agent, rang me up to say that a certain firm wanted me to do a fifty-second 'voice-over'. Now, for the sake of people who don't understand what a voice-over is, and I don't know why everybody should, it's a voice saying nice things about the product in an advertisement, only the owner of the voice is never seen – only heard.

I've known artists who say 'Oh no! I wouldn't ever do adverts.' I do them. I'm quite happy to earn my living doing them, providing they go with the sort of person I am. And I've never been asked to do any that wouldn't.

It is amazing, when you go for the filming, to

discover that you are not the most important person, however big a star is doing the advertisement – the *commodity* is the important bit. I remember years ago doing the advert for a Dutch soap powder. The box was designed obliquely, half in silver and half in green, and I just reached out to move it and they cried out 'No! No! Don't touch it! You might fingermark it.' And anytime I went near it, they warded me off. Eventually I was frightened of this box!

When I did *Cup a Soup*, which I did for two years on and off, they had to film me drinking it when there was steam coming off the cup ... never mind that it would scald me! I only minded because I rather like it – it's very nourishing is *Cup a Soup* ... or it is when it's not scalding hot.

Years ago – some of you may remember – I was the voice-over for *Mother's Pride* bread. I used to say: 'I'm the Mother in *Mother's Pride*, you know! They named it after me.' I became very well known for that. I was doing a Blackpool show, and when I walked on with a loaf of *Mother's Pride*, we *both* got a round of applause!

But I digress. On 13 July, 1994, Scottie and I had only just arrived at the cottage for a week's break when Felix telephoned about my doing this voice-over, so I said, 'No thanks, Felix, because we're only just down and Scottie and I want to spend some time together.' An hour later the telephone rang again, and it was Felix to say the client had been on again, offering twice the money. And I said, 'It's still "no" Felix, because I want to stay down at the cottage with Scottie.'

The following day Felix rang up again: 'How does

this grab you? They'll send a chauffeur and a car to your cottage, take you and Scottie into London, you'll do the recording, the car will wait and take you both back?' Our cottage is two hours from London, so that would be four hours' driving for a fifty-*second* voice-over. (And you're wondering about how far away I've got from 'things aren't as good as they used to be', aren't you? Go on – admit it!)

Well, I first came to London at the end of 1938 on a film contract with Ealing Studios, and by 1940 and for the next two or three years I was doing quite a few voice-overs. In those 'good old' days nearly all the filming for cinema adverts was done in underground cellars in and around Wardour Street. You would go through an ordinary street door and then down a lot of stone steps, dank and dark, into musty cellars that must have been under the London streets in Dickens' day, and looked it, and felt like it ... it was for the simple reason that the thick stone walls shut out all the sound of the London traffic and street noises, so they were the quietest places to do this sort of work. Safe from bombs, too, I imagine.

In those days, with a bit of luck, after you'd been working for an hour and a half someone might say 'Wanta cuppa, darlin'?' (You can probably imagine what an important person I was in those days – just down from Morecambe!) The tea would have been brewed about three hours before, because in war-time nobody ever threw old tea away – they just added more hot water. The only *good* thing you could say about the tea they gave you then was that it was wet ...

So that was in 'the good old days'. Now we come

back to 13 July, 1994. The chauffeur collected Jimmy and me from the cottage and drove us to London, stopping at the entrance to a little cul-de-sac, at the far end of which was a very grand main entrance, surrounded with nearly a foot of brass. Inside was a lift to take us *up* – not *down*. Just as the lift doors opened to let us out on the second floor, a smooth young gentleman stepped forward to greet us saying 'Tea ... coffee, Dame Thora? Or would you like breakfast?'

Now that's the first thing he said, I swear to you: 'Tea ... coffee, Dame Thora? Or would you like breakfast?' We went into a beautiful place, with a three-piece suite in flaming red ... I don't mean *flamin' red*, I mean flame-coloured upholstery. Every glossy magazine and newspaper were laid out on the sofa table, with plants and vases of flowers on every polished surface. A young fellow was half hidden by the flowers on the reception desk, where the telephone never stopped ringing, and he never stopped asking us if we'd like some fresh coffee. Eventually I went into the studio.

It took no more than thirty minutes to record the voice-over, and then we came out. The car was waiting to drive us back to the cottage, and all the way home I was thinking 'Why would people say things aren't as good? Things are flippin' well a *lot* better than I remember 'em!'

Another thing – when I first started in the business, because I played so many bit parts I always had to be at the studios at 6.30 in the morning for make-up, because the small parts had to be in first, so the stars could come in later. Then the Actor's

Union, Equity, made it a rule that nobody had to be in earlier than 7.15. So that's something else that's much better now.

Never mind 'It's the best thing since sliced bread' – there's been lots of better things since sliced bread. You are reading the words of someone who was here before the birth of *Zebo*. When I was a girl, before black-leading the grate, I had to mix the black stuff up in a saucer, and it was awful if you got it on your hands, because there were no rubber gloves ... rubber gloves! That's something else, you see. And now, you don't need to black lead the grate anyway, with the invention of electric fires, and central heating. You don't have to clear out the ashes first thing in the morning, going out in the icy cold in your pyjamas ...

Then there are the toiletry things you get now ... with wings. Nearly every advertisement on the box is a young woman saying 'I don't know I'm wearing one' or 'I feel so assured ...' (I'm sure you know what I'm on about.) Then there's men's aftershave, as long as they don't wear more than just a dab ... and clean men! After all these years men can come into a room and you don't know if it's a man or a woman. A man always had a leathery smell. It wasn't at all bad, actually, I didn't think, but you certainly knew they were there.

And if anyone is still not convinced by this little tale that some things *are* better now than they were then, I'll say six words to you:

'Duvets – washing machines – *Marks and Spencers*!'

36
High days and holidays

In my job I've always been able to get out of London quite a lot. For instance, on *Praise Be!* I journeyed all over Britain to interview people, and on *Last of the Summer Wine* we do the filming in Yorkshire. Every time that I'm driven along the edge of those beautiful Yorkshire moors it strikes me how lucky I am to work among such beautiful natural scenery, the miles and miles of white and purple heather.

I've been travelling to and from Yorkshire regularly over the past twenty years, because so many of the series I've been in have been made there: *Flesh and Blood, Hallelujah!, In Loving Memory, Last of the Summer Wine* ... as well as roles I've had in *All Creatures Great and Small, Heartbeat* and many others; even some of the Alan Bennett plays have been made up there. So let's put it this way, I've always had less chance than Scottie of being bored. He stayed at home seeing to everything – VAT, book-keeping, future work, cooking, shopping ... everything. He never moaned – well, hardly ever. And so it was only fair that he should be the one to choose where we should go on holiday when the diary said we could. And I'm here to tell you, Scottie became a World Expert at finding interesting places for us to visit.

When one thinks of the sad situation in the former Yugoslavia, the dreadful killings and people driven from their homes, I find it difficult to believe that in the 1970s Brian Rawlinson, the actor, who is a very dear friend of ours, and his friend Billy, and Scottie and I all went there for a holiday together, and there was more laughing in that fortnight than a lot of people have in their lives.

When Brian comes round to see me, which he often does, to this day we still talk about it. The whole holiday became like a spy romance that we all took part in, and all because Brian had just bought a beautiful white Burberry coat. When he came up to us at Gatwick, where we were all assembled because it was a package holiday Scottie had booked us on, he was wearing this new white trench-coat and a pair of dark glasses and Scottie said, 'My God! You look like James Bond!' And Brian said, 'Hush up! Tell no one. I am.'

I was reading a romantic novel by Mary Stewart, which tickled Brian because he's a bit of a clever head, and when we got to the hotel we were all trying to describe everything we saw as though in a Mary Stewart romance: 'The sunlight glinted on the fine gold hairs of his hand ... she waved at the figure on the hill with her chiffon handkerchief ...' and the holiday rapidly developed into a Mills and Boon/spy story.

We went by coach to Split, where Diocletian, or one of those Roman Emperors, had built this enormous palace – so enormous that after the Empire fell the people just filled in the spaces with houses and shops, so you actually go into Split through the gates of a palace. Of course now the town has spread all round outside the palace walls as well.

From Split we got on a boat and cruised among the Dalmatian islands, and ended up in Dubrovnik. We sailed among 'a thousand islands', I think they said, on an old British steamship, and in the dining room the columns were square with a mirror on each side, bevelled mirrors, and all the trimmings were oxidised brass. A real old British steam yacht, with tremendous atmosphere.

We started to pass notes. I gave Brian a letter 'from the War Office', saying 'You know exactly why we've sent you ...' On one of the islands we sailed past there was an old wartime defence block thing, and on it there was an upside-down anchor. I was leaning over the rails, clutching Brian's arm and saying out of the corner of my mouth – by this time we were saying nearly everything out of the corners of our mouths – 'Do you see the anchor?' as though it were a coded message!

As I turned away I looked up and saw a lady with long black hair tied back, and I hissed 'Don't turn round!' Of course Brian did turn round, and said, 'It is! It's her! It's Sonia! She *knows*.'

This woman was really from the cover of *Vogue* – rock pink trouser suit, turban to match, straight black hair tied back in a bun, and Brian said, 'Oh, she's a spy. She's Sonia, a well-known spy.' And whenever she appeared after that we'd be saying things like, 'Don't look now ... your six o'clock. She's here ...'

Scottie came out of our bedroom one morning, on the ship, and kicked over a wine bottle. He picked it up, and there was a note in the top, and I heard him laughing and he came back in and said, 'Hey, look at this.' It said, 'You will get your final instructions when

...' and then 'bullet holes' had been burned into it with a cigarette. And the signature started, then slid downwards ...

We went all the way up to Montenegro and the palace of King Og. The road there really climbed, hairpin bends all the way up to the high plateau. I hate heights, so I had to get down on the floor of the coach.

It's all limestone, that's why it's so beautiful, and the rock goes right down into the sea – there are no beaches in Yugoslavia, just little concrete platforms that you sit on. All the places had an atmosphere. That whole coast. We sat on the concrete beach. Every time anybody passed, Brian would look at me significantly ...

Years later, when the troubles started and they were bombing Dubrovnik, Brian rang me up and said, 'Oh, do you remember, darling, we sat under the stars there every night?'

We did. We went to a concert in the old Venetian palace. And it was there, in the garden, under the walls of the old Venetian palace, that we spent our last evening ... We were sitting outside and we had just got to the coffee and petits fours, and it went quiet and Milan, our tour guide, leant forward and said in a strange, very deliberate tone, 'The stars are very bright tonight.' It was the way he said it – very softly and deliberately ... like another coded message!

Brian leapt on the chair and said, 'It's him!' Then he pulled out a toy gun he'd bought that afternoon as a present to take home to a nephew, and went 'pank! pank! pank!' with the caps.

You wouldn't do that today in Yugoslavia ... Scottie was saying, 'You daft bugger. Get down! You'll have us all arrested!' What was so funny was that there were all these rather solemn ... Serbs? – I suppose they would be, wouldn't they, in Dubrovnik? – and they just sat there. Nobody turned round. Nobody asked 'What are they doing?' Nobody anythinged. They didn't look up from their dinner.

When Brian got home I sent him a letter 'from the Foreign Office', posting him to some terrible outpost of the Empire ... And eventually he got the sack ... Well, we had to end it somehow.

Please believe me, our holidays are usually more sane than that. Of recent years Scottie and I, often accompanied by Jan and William, have been on several hugely enjoyable cruises organised by SAGA. They are holidays especially designed for retired people, and suit us down to the ground. Jan and William can always get off and explore wherever we land at the different ports. Scottie sometimes would go with them, and sometimes stayed on the ship with me, but I always stayed on board and usually wrote my diary. Here is a diary entry from the last one we all went on together:

23 March, 1993

Believe it or not, I am sitting in the middle of the Bay of Biscay ... in a comfy chair in the aerobics room of the *Black Prince*, cruising into Madeira! Jan is in an aerobics class, and I've just had a massage on my back and legs to give my poor old arthritic joints a holiday treat. There is scarcely any motion as the ship sails along I-i-in the-he-Ba-ay-of-Bi-is-ca-ayo. The four of us, William, Jan, Scottie and I are enjoying a little cruise, calling in at most of the islands of Tenerife. The food is splendiferous and I'm having a lovely rest. I shall be free for a couple of days after we return home – just enough time to unpack, chuck the dirty laundry into the washing machine – before I begin the next series of *Praise Be!*

As I've told you, Scottie and I moved into a cottage next door to Jan and William's home in Sussex. This next extract from my diary is about a 'day trip' we made, and goes to show what a happy time can be had without ever leaving our own shores. If you haven't ever been to Bosham (pronounced Bossam), promise yourself you'll go someday.

TUESDAY 5 APRIL, 1994

Last night my bloomin' old arthritis was such a nuisance after I went to bed that by 3.45 in the morning I had never shut my eyes. Now I have no intention of being a moaning Minnie, but when I got up this morning I was so tired and felt so rotten that I could scarcely walk from one room to another. Jan was to call round at 9.30 because Scottie and I wanted to do some shopping, and she was going to put my wheelchair in the back of the car and drive us.

(From now on I shall refer to my wheelchair as my WC if you don't mind – no offence.)

When Jan arrived I asked her and Scottie to excuse me going with them. I will admit that after they had gone I felt a bit sorry for myself, and lonely. Silly cat. And after another cup of tea and a look at the paper, I was thinking, 'I'll do a spot of watering ... no, I won't, I'll clean that copper kettle and get it brighter ... no, I won't, I'll clean the front door knocker and letter box ... no, I won't ...'

By the time I had finally got my cleaning equipment out and started work on the door brasses, Jan and Scottie were back, packing items in the freezer and fridge.

Then Jan suggested I got my hat and coat on and we all drive to Bosham. Scottie suggested we lunch there. I suggested I got myself ready pronto.

The sun was shining on the sea of Chichester harbour as we drove past, and everything looked so clean and bright, with glorious boats bobbing about.

The houses at Bosham are all beautiful and the gardens cared for. The ancient church is embroidered on the Bayeux Tapestry in France, or at least a part of it is. Scottie and I had visited Normandy with Brian and Billy in 1966, and we'd seen the Bayeux tapestry. Bosham was where Harold had his fort. He had sailed from Bosham when he was captured by William of Normandy, William the Conqueror, and was made to swear that William could be the next king of the English after Edward the Confessor died – which is all shown on the tapestry. I said to Jan how peculiar it was that we should have seen the church on the tapestry in France before we ever saw it here, in our own country.

After lunch we walked – well, I didn't, I was pushed in my WC – along the sands and all around Bosham. We arrived back at Jasmine Cottage in time for tea, but Jan excused herself as she wanted to take her dogs out for a walk. What a lovely, unexpected trip ... and what a daughter!

37
Jasmine Cottage

In 1993 Jan and William sold the Mill House set in its lovely grounds at Isfield. It was a hard decision, but their children have all grown up now and are away studying or working and they visit at different times, so no longer need to each have a room of their own. Jan and William decided to look for a smaller place with less land to look after. This of course meant that the cottage that Scottie and I had enjoyed staying in for eleven years was sold along with the estate. We had enjoyed every minute of our time there, so we couldn't grumble, and didn't. I was very busy, as usual, so hadn't much time to feel sad about missing our lovely country weekends. One day the furniture van arrived at our London address and neatly deposited all our cottage furniture and belongings in the garage, which, as I've described in an earlier chapter, is a big one. (But no more parties in the garage for the time being.)

Jan and Bill chose a house on the outskirts of Chichester, and Jan says she has at last found her 'dream' home. She has always wanted to live in a real period Queen Anne house, and now she does, and she is delighted. I couldn't get to see it until a few weeks after they moved in, but it is gorgeous. No, that's the wrong adjective – it's beautiful – dignified – refined. That describes it better. It's smaller than the Mill House, and the grounds are less extensive, but that was part of the reason for moving – to find somewhere smaller. But the best was yet to come! Here is the entry from my diary:

9 July, 1994

> We've all used expressions like 'Ooh, how lovely!' 'Oh, what a surprise!' or 'Oh, I can't believe it!' haven't we? I said all that as we arrived at Jasmine Cottage for the fourth time, and saw the front garden.
>
> Our first view of it was at Christmas 1993, when we stayed with Jan and William in their beautiful new home and discovered that the cottage next door to them was *for sale!* The owners, who were exceptionally nice people, never advertised their 1780 period cottage ... they simply told Jan and William in October that they were moving, and Jan was on the telephone to us three seconds later!

In 1993 Scottie and I had joined them for Christmas, as always, and the first thing we did was take a peek at what was to be our new cottage over the handsome flint wall.

There wasn't much of anything showing in the garden then. Our second view was on 13 January, 1994, after we had bought it. Chichester was flooded and there were little boats sailing up and down the lane outside – but neither Jan's house nor Jasmine Cottage got wet or even damp. The cottage garden was a carpet of crocus and snowdrops, and I mean *a carpet!* It was breathtaking.

28 February, 1994:
10.30 pm

> The big day has arrived! The furniture van is here outside our London abode and we are getting all packed into the pantechnicon for the cottage. It's the usual cantata – hot tea for the men on the team, and after that it's all go ...
> The van is now all packed up and our London garage looks a bit twelve-o'clock-lonely.

So it was a case of hey up! Jasmine Cottage, here we come, and on 1 March we moved in. It was our third visit, and the primroses and aconite had taken over, daffodils were in bud; later narcissi and tulips were pushing their way through.

I'd always hoped to be able to leave Scottie with what my mother called 'an easy going on'. I mean I'd always hoped to leave things arranged so that Scottie – or I – wouldn't be a nuisance to Jan and William, or anyone else come to that, after the dear Lord called one of us home. Now we wouldn't be 'next door' to them like in a town street – their garden and the high, flint wall separates the two houses – but I was thinking that Jan could be round at the door of Jasmine Cottage in two minutes if her Daddy was living there on his own. There would be no need for her to catch a train or drive two hours to London to see if he was all right. I know our daughter very well, she's like most daughters, extremely fond of her father – and me

– and for quite a few years I'd thought about this situation. Somehow I'd always imagined that Scottie would be the one left on his own ...

1 April, 1994

My dear mother's birthday, God rest her. Our first Easter at Jasmine Cottage. I am sitting comfortably in my dear little study penning a few lines. It is Good Friday, and as I look out of the window I can see masses of primroses, tulips, daffodils, anemones, all a wonderful mass of colour. I am also trying to get my study ship-shape, so I can put my hands on anything without having to search. Most of my stuff arrived in large cardboard boxes unopened from our last cottage, and as I didn't pack them myself I'm having to unpack each one to discover what's in it.

Before lunch I spent over an hour looking at old Mothering Sunday cards, Father's Day cards, birthday cards, wedding anniversary cards from Jan and the grandchildren. I've packed them all away again carefully in yet another box, because they are too lovely to throw away and have been chosen with such loving care by our dear daughter, son-in-law and grandchildren. What a hoarder I am ...

Saturday 2 April, 1994

After a very windy and wild night I'm sitting in the study and the sun is pouring in through the window. One of the fences has been damaged by the storm during the night, and Scottie is out there – I can see him – well wrapped up, repairing the damage with William's help.

9 JULY, 1994

And now in July, this – a blaze of colour. All along each side of the straight, forty-eight-foot long path from the front gate to the front door are beds of deep red rose bushes, dozens of them. William clipped them all to about four inches high in February, and now we are gazing open-mouthed at a sea of deep red blooms each side of the garden path. It seems like fate that the great red rose of Lancashire borders each side of our garden path, doesn't it? Along the outer walls of the garden the herbaceous borders are packed with every kind, colour and shape of bush and plants, and the walls smothered in climbing roses, clematis, and summer and winter jasmine, of course.

As I write this Jan has just popped in with a huge bunch of sweet peas. I don't mean just *sweet peas*. These are *specials!* Each stalk boasts about nine or ten blooms. And the colours! And the perfume! Oh, mate! She's also put some of their home-grown potatoes and beetroot in the kitchen.

I've just cleaned the brass Georgian door knocker, the door knob, letter box and key-hole on the very clean white front door, and while I was doing it I noticed a bush of the deepest purple lavender and some big bushes of pinks. Every time I put my nose out of doors I notice another plant. Some alyssum is pushing its way through the York stone path, but it looks so cheeky and pretty

I shan't dig it out or let 'the gardener' dig it out. Oh yes! We have a gardener now. Jan has finally persuaded Scottie to take on a lad for a few hours a week, and he looks more like a leading man than a gardener. But at eighty-seven it's time Scottie took things more easily.

As I sit here at my desk, in my little gem of a study, swanking about the house and garden, I must ask you to try and excuse me. In our three previous country cottages we have always had to prepare and make a garden ourselves – which we've loved doing – but here the garden was all ready for us, and just the size we can enjoy at our age.

The back door opens out not into a back garden, but onto a patio, so no digging for Scottie, just watering the plants in several very large earthenware urns – and there's even a tiny fountain. Yes, I know how lucky we are.

We've never wanted to be a trouble to Jan and William. She always says 'Well, you wouldn't be!' But we would be. But now we won't be – will we?

That summer's day in July, after I had written the above, Scottie and I sat together on a little bench, like a love seat, under the eaves, to drink our morning coffee and admire the front garden. Scottie said to me, 'Aren't those roses beautiful?' And I said, 'Aren't they lovely!' and he said, 'And aren't we bluddy lucky to have all this?'

It was our last summer together.

38
To be a pilgrim

In May 1994 I celebrated my eighty-third birthday on the Sea of Galilee, and what better place to be wished a 'Happy Birthday' by my darling Scottie than where Jesus must have so often celebrated his? You can't ask for better than that, can you?

We had arrived at the hotel late the night before, and as we are both early risers we were awake to sit on our balcony and watch the sunrise over the Sea of Galilee early the next morning. The boats they take you out in – 'dhows' are they called? – look just as they would have in Jesus' time, and even the boatmen were wearing New Testament costume, and you really feel that nothing but time separates you from Jesus and his first disciples.

I have started leading pilgrimages in my eighties – and it sounds so important that, but let me tell you here and now, the importance isn't so much as the love about it, and by the time you are reading this book I will have just come back from my third, God willing. It all came about because on one of my *Praise Be!* programmes a few years ago I had one of my little filmed chats – you would never have really called them 'interviews', it was always much less formal than that – with the Bishop of London, Rt Rev. David Hope, who is now Archbishop of York. I'd never met him before, and Valetta had decided to film me walking along a London street with my *A to Z* in hand, looking for the Bishop's Palace and knocking on the door of a little house to ask, and the Bishop *answering* the door himself, which – of course – is most unlikely. We only did all these things to impress you. And he did live in a little house, not a palace.

Well, I have to say this, and I'm sure many people have said it about David Hope – who's a northerner, by the way – he is such a *handsome* man! Oh dearie me! If you got a few of those American film directors over, they'd all be saying 'Well, we'll find a story about a Bishop, just so we can use you!'

We hit it off straight away, and had a lovely chat over a cup of tea that he had made himself in his little kitchen, and there too I met his chaplain, Rob Marshall. That was the beginning of a great friendship between our family and Rob Marshall, and it was with Rob that a few years later, in 1994, I headed my first pilgrimage to the Holy Land. Scottie and Jan came with me. We didn't know it at the time, but it was to be Scottie's and my last holiday together.

To say anything about that pilgrimage is never going to be good enough. It was marvellous. It was ... well, *marvellous* ... going to the places that you knew Jesus had been to. When I was first asked to *head* a pilgrimage to the Holy Land, I did say, 'I'm really not good enough to head a pilgrimage to the Holy Land. Why would you ask me?' To which they answered, with no sense at all, 'Because we think you are!' So that must have meant 'good enough'. But the thing was, I knew that I didn't really know enough about everything in the Bible to tell other people, so I was learning new things all the time as we went along, and I wasn't afraid to ask.

In the middle of the Sea of Galilee the captain turned off the boat's engines, and the sense of tranquillity you get at the moment when the boat is at rest – well, as Scottie said, it can't really be described in words. It was so still, you couldn't even hear water lapping against the side of the boat.

The only English people on the boat were Jan, Scottie and myself. Everybody else was German, and I don't speak a word of German.

We sailed across to a beach, not a sandy beach, just a gravel beach, with plants and things, and I cannot describe the tranquillity when we stopped. I wouldn't know what words to use, only to say that we had landed on the spot where the miracle of the two fishes and five loaves happened, where Jesus and his disciples fed five thousand people, a story I often read on *Praise Be!* The Minister with the German people stood up and went into the bow of the boat and read what I *knew* was the story of the loaves and the fishes. I don't know any German, but I knew that that was what he was reading.

When he'd finished reading he came and sat in the seat in front of me and turned round, put his elbow on the back of the seat and said to me in English, 'Do you believe in the Lord God?' And I said to him, just as simply, 'I'd be a very unhappy woman if I didn't.' And he stood up, started to conduct, and all the

Germans sang 'Happy birthday to you!' in perfect English. I found myself crying.

Anyhow, we set sail again, and – they are business-people, as anybody else is, over there – when we got off the boat there was a large, round, modern building, coffee coloured. As we walked over, the owner was speaking to Rob Marshall and a little boy came up and said something, and the fellow said something back and then clipped him hard over the ear. I thought, 'What a shame!', and the little lad ran off. In five minutes he was back, with the most beautiful brooch made of the tiniest conch shells you ever saw, all coloured differently, from the bottom of the lake of Galilee, and he said, "Appy Birthday to You!' I've still got it – the most wonderful present I've ever been given.

Scottie and I had been to the Holy Land once before, about ten years previously, and I had visited the cave where Jesus was born. There is a silver star set in the ground in the stable, which over the years has been enlarged, and you go through it into what is almost a little Cathedral. Any mother reading this will understand when I say the happiness was almost entire but for one thing – I wished Jan was with me. I remember there was a little nun there all the time, the first time I went, and I knelt there, saying a little prayer and thinking 'Oh! I do wish Jan was with me!'

Well, of course, when we went back there this time, Jan *was* with me. She was just as inspired as I was, and wished her children could have been with her. Not everyone believes that it really is the place where Jesus was born, because of course no one can prove it, but I think it was.

When we went through into the little Cathedral place Rob Marshall said, 'I think we'll have a hymn while we're here, and I think we'll have Thora's favourite.' So somebody just gave us a note 'Doh' and we all started 'Onward, Christian Soldiers, marching as to war ...' I'll never forget it.

Cana is not far from Nazareth. I remember thinking 'I'm glad Mary and Jesus didn't have too far to walk for the wedding.' It was about eight minutes by bus. We walked down a little alley to a tiny church, which was all stone, and as you went in there were a lot of huge water jars, like the jars you see in the pantomime of Aladdin.

In Jesus' time, at a meal or a wedding banquet the best wine was always served first ... well, it still is, isn't it? If you've guests coming for dinner, you get out your best bottle of wine, and you only get the plonk out later, when they've drunk all the good stuff. Without trying to be comical, the Miracle at Cana must have been performed while everyone could still realise it was a good wine, instead of waiting until they'd had so much they didn't know what they were drinking.

I stood in front of this church, with Scottie, and I thought 'It's so small. Mary could have stood just here, where we're standing, before they went into the church for the wedding.' At the wedding banquet Mary told Jesus, 'They've run out of wine.' And Jesus had answered, not in these words, but according to the people who know more about this than me, to the effect 'Well, what do you expect me to do about it?' And then he had said, 'Are those jars full of water?' And they said, 'Yes, they are.' And he said, 'Well, tell them to drink that.' And they did, and of course, what was poured out was the best wine anyone had ever tasted.

Needless to say, opposite the church – there is a little store selling wine! They don't try and kid you it was a drop that was in the original stone jars or anything like that, but they do give you some in a very tiny little wooden cup. And nearly everybody bought a bottle of wine as a souvenir, because it was so impressive, the church at Cana.

I'll never forget it. As I'm writing this now, this minute, I could be there. It wasn't cold, it was just a cool, stone, square entrance to a church. Jimmy and I had been married for fifty-eight years, and there in the little church we renewed our marriage vows together, and I've got a wedding certificate from Cana in Galilee to prove it!

I didn't know enough – in fact, let me be honest and say I knew very little about the Transfiguration. So before we went, because I knew we were going to the place where it might have happened, I said to Rob Marshall, 'Tell me about it, will you? Tell me like you'd tell a child at school.' And he did. I couldn't wait to go to see the place where it happened.

For the people who don't know this, and I didn't, it is up a very, very steep mountain, Mount Tabor, and Jesus and three of his disciples walked up all the way. We went in a black Mercedes taxi. I felt very guilty, going in a Mercedes, knowing that he'd trudged up all this way – well, we all did – but I could visualise Jesus with Peter, James and John plodding up this mountain. You can see for miles up there.

There is a community of Franciscan friars who live at the top, and, like in all these places, there were souvenirs for sale. I saw a little carved cross, not too big for a gold chain I have, and I thought 'I'll have that, if it's only to know I bought it here.' And I had the cross in my hand when one of the Franciscans, called Andrew, walked across to me and put both his hands round both my hands that were holding the cross, and he said, 'Thora Hird! Oh, I saw you in a lot of black-and-white films!' And I said, 'Half a mo! I wasn't in *that* many! I'm not *that* old!' We laughed, and then for half an hour Brother Andrew talked to me and it didn't matter what kind of simple things I asked him, it was as though he'd expected me to ask these things. Actually, he did most of the talking, and for once, even though I'm an actress, I was happy to let him and just listen, because he knew so much. And he said, 'Before you go, tell me, is there anything that you've thought very deeply to yourself, since coming here?' I said, 'Well, I've thought about it all very deeply, but what I'm going to say sounds a bit silly. As I put my own sandalled foot down, I've looked at the ground each time and wondered if Jesus put his sandalled foot there, where I've put mine.'

All the while we were talking he'd taken the cross out of my hand, and with his thumb was blessing it, moving his thumb to make the sign of the cross over and over again. And he said, 'Thora, if you put your foot there, you can be sure that Jesus put his foot there!'

The guide suddenly says, 'And that's where Jesus baptised so and so ...' and you look and you see and you think 'It's still the same. Everything else has altered, but that pool hasn't altered.' And when we went near to the road where he – you can easily get upset as well, if you're daft like me – where he was dragging the cross to Calvary, I really could see him, with this cross, dragging it, dragging it. I wish I could tell these things with the worthiness they deserve.

Because, of course, all of us who are Christians, it's like those of us who are Royalists – you see the Queen, don't you, and you think 'Oh! I actually was where she was standing!' And you see, I was. I was at the garden of Gethsemane ...

I can remember sitting on a form outside the Garden of Gethsemane, I suppose for not longer than ten minutes, which can seem a long time if you're on your own. Nobody passed. There was no one about but me. And I sat there and I thought of Jesus and the Garden. I always feel that that was the one place where I knew, for certain, that Christ had been there.

I led another pilgrimage early in 1995, to biblical sites in Jordan, and by the time you read this I will have been on yet another one, in early 1996. If you went a dozen times, you wouldn't have seen everything.

Now if I told you properly about Petra, one of the places we visited in Jordan, you would turn to whoever was in the room – and if there was nobody in the room you would turn to the wall – and say, 'She's exaggerating.' Because Petra is the most breathtaking place I've ever been to in my whole life. You're in the desert and you see these mountains the colour of Blackpool or Morecambe Rock – pale pink. The story – and I love to believe anything that is so beautifully told as this – goes like this:

Five thousand years ago there was a Bedouin alone, on his horse, and he was approaching these rock pink mountains and noticed that one looked as though there was a split from the top of it to the bottom. (Please read this with care, because it's difficult to describe it to you without taking you there to show you the spot.) And as he got nearer to this thin split in the mountain he realised it was just wide enough for him to go through on his horse. He went through, and to his amazement there he saw before him a city. Not a sophisticated city – you can still see the caves in the mountains where the inhabitants lived. And as he turned round to leave, he was stopped and he was told – now this is five thousand years ago, so I can't prove it, but this is what they say – he was told that if he told anybody about this place, he and his family would be hounded down and killed. So as far as we know, he didn't tell anybody ... but I don't know how anybody knows that that's what happened if he *didn't* tell anybody ... but I still think he didn't. (Are you still with me?)

Now then, we get to the Roman period, and a lot of Romans were riding about on horses, and they, too, found this place, and took it over.

But in all this time, the place hasn't altered. You still have to go to it either on horseback, which Jan did, or in a Roman chariot just like in the Hollywood film of *Ben Hur*, with horses pulling it and a man standing up in front. Well, Rob Marshall and I got in a chariot, and

I swear to you that this one was so old it was not refused by Charlton Heston – it was refused by Ramon Novarro! It was falling to bits. But we got in, and even the poor horse dragging us along was falling to bits. However, off the people on horseback went, and we went in the chariot. Rob put his foot down, and if he reads this he'll remember that I'm telling you the truth, and it went through the floor of the chariot!

Anyway, we eventually went through the opening in the mountains, and there were all the usual little boys selling snuff boxes, beads, all sorts of things. And on the right there was a large cave, and you know how the top of a cave is often very rough and uneven? Well, they'd touched up all the uneven bits with yellow, blue and red. It looked like a stage set for Aladdin. And all round the walls of this cave were necklaces and jewellery, and one thing and another – and all absolutely caked with sand and dirt. Because the fellow can't shut his shop up at night – it's just a cave.

We went in, and Rob saw a coffee pot that looked – well it looked from the Bible, it was so old – and he bought that. I saw they were building a little fire in the middle of the floor. I thought, 'Well, perhaps that's something they do, just build little fires to sit round,' so I didn't say anything, I just sat round it with them, the man who owned the shop and four other men, who all looked like brigands to me, drinking mint tea.

You know the head-dresses they wear? You've seen them, the striped head-dresses in black and white, or red and white, that they wrap round their hats and over their mouths to keep out the sand – like big tea towels. I bet you didn't know that the red-and-white ones are that colour because of the white and red roses of York and Lancaster at the Wars of the Roses ... Come on, be honest, you didn't know that, did you? Our Jordanian guide told us, and he didn't know we were from Lancashire, so it must be true ... I think.

I had already bought myself one of these – how could I resist? – and I had bought one for Jan, and she was very glad of it, because she had wrapped it over her nose and mouth, for galloping along on this horse. And as she passed the cave ... you've seen a horse rear up? Jan's horse reared up on its hind legs just outside the cave entrance, because of Jan stopping it suddenly, not able to believe her eyes at the sight of me, crouching round a little fire, drinking mint tea with five brigands, thoroughly enjoying myself!

There were some rather lovely voile shawls, big enough to use for a tablecloth for afternoon tea, and I asked how much they were, and when he told me a lady near by said, 'How much is that in English money?' and he said, 'Eight pounds.' So I said, 'Oh! Do you take English money?' He's got the full garb on, flowing robes, tea-towel round the head, because that's how he *lives*, behind this crack in the pink mountains, and he looks at me with this toothless grin and says, 'Do I take English money? How else did I go to England eight times ... and marry a girl from Hull?' I couldn't believe it, but it's true. So I paid him eight pounds, and I've got my shawl to prove it.

I do so hope that you can go to the Holy Land some day, if you haven't already, to look around and stop and think. Part of it is no different from walking down Oxford Street, but the parts where the gospel stories happened seem unchanged since Jesus walked there.

happened seem unchanged since Jesus walked there. It makes the Bible come to life in such a vivid way. They say that every actor should do a season at Blackpool, and I say that every Christian should spend at least a week in the Holy Land!

39

'Just a tick, Jan!'

Early in February 1994 Jan said, 'Before all your furniture is moved out of the Mews garage and taken down to the cottage, do throw away or give away anything you've finished with and don't really need any more. I'll come up for a couple of days and help you, because knowing you, Mother, I know what it'll be – and you're nearly as bad, Father ... hoarding things.'

I am. I am a terrible hoarder. This is true. I look at a saucer that was probably part of a tea-set my husband bought me when we were courting, or one my mother left me, and all that's left is a saucer, and I think, 'Oh, well, I can't throw that away. No, I'll put a plant pot on it.' And as a result – a lot of rubbish I've got – rubbish, rubbish, that nobody else would keep!

Jan will come to London sometimes, and look at my desk. Now I must admit – my desk – I sometimes don't know whether to declare it open or set fire to it. There's fan mail, there's letters asking me to open this and open that. And she'll say, 'Have you gone through that pile?'

'No.'

'Right!' And she'll go through it, and I'll see her throwing stuff away. She'll say, 'Well, it's just stuff.

You don't want to know about somebody who are the best carpet cleaners round Bayswater. No, this is rubbish! You don't want this.'

I wish I could be like that, but I bet there's a lot of you reading this who are like me and keep stuff, don't you? I look in my drawers sometimes and I'll think, 'Oh! I'll have a real chuck out here.' And I find by the time the drawer goes back there's as much stuff in it as when I took it out, and all I've done is revive a lot of memories. But that's how I am, you see.

Well ... we started. There were many, many tea-chests, all full of stuff, such as piles of plates – none of them matching but each holding a memory. Cups, jugs, small glass dishes, etc. You know the sort of things I mean.

It was like a comedy play: As Jan put a pile of plates in a box ready for the thrift shop, I would be pleading, 'Just a tick, Jan ...' and pick up a chipped saucer – the only remaining bit of a tea service we bought before we were married. 'We can't give this away! I'll use it for a plant or something. Your Daddy bought me this before ...'

Pyoo – in a black bag it went, for the dustbin. Because Jan is a great chucker-awayer, do you see. And she'd say, 'You don't want this, do you?'

'Well, what is it?'

'Just another odd cup – you don't want it.'

'Well, let me look, if it was ...'

'Yes you *can* throw it away, Mummy' Jan would say, taking it off me again. 'You'll never use it, and you've three lovely tea-sets complete. And you won't use these ... or these ... or these' she would go on, putting more odd cups and saucers in with the plates.

'Oh! Do you remember when we bought those, Scottie? One Saturday morning when we were ...'

'Give them here' interrupted Jan, and two more coffee saucers and three mugs sailed into the thrift box.

For the next three hours the script never varied. 'You don't want these ... you'll never use that ... I *know* I bought it for you – thirty years ago – but it's no use now.'

I was using beseeching remarks like, 'I *will* use it, I'll use it for a plant ...' or 'My mother gave me that ...' or 'You made that for me when you were at school ...' It was ridiculous. Jan was quite right, and I really knew it. And even now, as I'm telling you about it, I can't even remember what half the stuff was.

When we got to the clothes department, she turned out piles of good sweaters, woollen cardigans ... dozens of things that were too small for me. Twenty shirts of Scottie's, all laundered, but too big at the neck because he'd lost so much weight...

'Oh good!' said Jan, 'These can go to the Salvation Army. They're always grateful for good clothes.' I started my usual protests, but she took no notice of me and off sailed hundreds of garments I'd enjoyed wearing – but, as she rightly pointed out, could no longer wear.

At this point Scottie suggested, 'We could do your shoe cupboard out next ...' but we decided to leave that for another day. I'll have to let you know how I get on in another book!

But do you know, when I went upstairs again to make us all a cup of coffee, I had such a feeling of satisfaction – yes, pure satisfaction. It wasn't rubbish we were getting rid of (not in my mind, anyway) but things that would be welcomed by people down on their luck. So it wasn't a case of 'Goodbye, old friends' but a case of passing on a lot of things that might benefit someone else.

Actually, Jan said something that was so true, and although it upset me a little at the time, or rather it moved me, it was so sensible that I'll finish this little chapter off with her words. She said,

'You see, we had to do this now. One day I'll be standing here on my own. Something will have happened to you and Daddy – it's going to, one day – and I shall be so dreadfully unhappy. So everything that we pass on to charity today, is going to be one less thing for me to look at and feel sad about when that day comes.'

40

'Well done, Scottie!'

In, I think it must have been March or April 1994, we went to a big concert on a Sunday night, in Drury Lane, where I was to receive a special Silver BAFTA award. As we went into Drury Lane, standing in front of the theatre there was an arc of photographers, and in their usual friendly way it was, 'Look this way, Thor!' 'Give us a grin, Thor!' and so on. Well, Scottie was with me, and my manager, Felix de Wolfe and Brenda, his wife. I turned to bring Scottie up beside me for the picture, only to notice he wasn't there ... he was flat on his face on the floor.

Everybody thought he'd tripped on the edge of the carpet, and they got him quickly on a chair, and a girl in a beautiful evening dress came up and said, 'Take no notice of this ...' meaning her dress, because Scottie's nose was bleeding ... 'I'm a nurse.' And eventually he was all right.

I collected my award, but I asked to be excused from the dinner afterwards, because I was very worried about Scottie. I wanted him to go to see the doctor the next day, but he said he felt fine and there was no need. In fact, he couldn't even remember what had happened. But now, I think I know what it was.

A few weeks later, one morning when Scottie came

home from shopping in Queensway he said, 'I'm so glad to be home. I was afraid I was going to faint for a minute while I was out.' I started to be a little anxious, then, about him going out on his own.

It's a funny thing to say to people in a book, is this. Well, not funny – I don't mean F.U.N.N.Y., I mean *strange*: I didn't know what a stroke was. At least, I knew what a stroke *was*, but what I mean to say is I wouldn't have known if I'd seen anybody having a stroke.

I was combing my hair in my room one morning – as you know, ours is quite a small Mews house – and Scottie had gone through into the bathroom to shave. And while I was combing my hair I heard a crash on the floor, like one of my big copper pans falling off the wall. And I called out, 'Is that one of the pans that's fallen off the wall?' He didn't answer, so I put my comb down and went to look in the kitchen. But there was no pan on the floor. I went into the bathroom and there was Scottie, fallen backwards into the bath, as if in a faint. His legs were over the side of the bath from the knee – do you follow what I mean? His knees and feet were over the side. And it sounds such a terrible thing to say, but it's true, I thought, 'Oh, doesn't he always have such clean shoes?' They were so polished, you know, his shoes. And at the same time I said to him, 'What is it, darling? Did you go dizzy or something?' And he didn't answer me, but he sort of put one arm out a little bit, so I got hold of it but soon realised that, from the position he was in, there was no way I could pull him out. There was no water in the bath or anything, but he had broken the tray that had all the sponges and soap, and it's a wonder it hadn't cut his neck open, but he was spared that.

I ran to the telephone. I'm blessed with good neighbours, and I called Gail, who is a dear friend, and said, 'Gail, Scottie has slipped and fallen. Is Bob there?' Because I knew her husband was a big strong fellow. And she said, 'Oh Thora, he's out, but hold on ...' and she hung up. So I went back into the bathroom, and Jimmy was still there, not saying anything. As a matter of fact he never said anything again. Ever. But at that point I wasn't to know that.

Suddenly Gail rushed in with a gentleman I'd never seen in my life before – well, nobody in the Mews had, he'd just bought a Mews house the week before, and as she'd come out of her door – she's an American – she'd called to him, 'Hey, Neighbour, we're needed. Come on!' So he'd followed her! Well, none of us could move Jimmy, and Gail said, 'I've rung for an ambulance.'

I have to give the ambulance service full marks – they were no time at all. And two ambulance men came upstairs, and one said, 'Go downstairs, Thora. We know exactly how to pick your husband up.' Gail and I went to the hospital with him.

I'm sure now that on that evening at Drury Lane, when Scottie fell down, he was having his first stroke, just a minor one. But this was a massive stroke from which he never recovered. There are more people than you'd ever realise die *in a day* in the world, with a stroke. Somebody dies every five minutes.

We always sat with him, Jan and I, in the hospital, in case he was awake, and yet I knew he wasn't awake. I don't think he ever really knew any of us were there.

No, that's not quite right. Our grand-daughter Daisy flew over from America, and our grandson, and Daisy was so upset because she loved him so dearly. She'd say, 'Poppa? It's Daisy ... Squeeze my hand if you know it's me.' And he did squeeze her hand. So perhaps he did know a little.

After three weeks they made a hole in his stomach and put a tube in to feed him, because he was rejecting food all the time. Before this they had twice told us to prepare for him dying that tea-time ... which he didn't. I went home that Saturday tea-time, after they'd put the tube in.

When I got home I went into my bedroom and I sat down on the edge of my bed and I said, 'Please, God ... Would you take Scottie, in his sleep?' Because I could see this dear man, who had been so alive, so full of life before his stroke, just lying there, responding to nothing. Well, that was seven o'clock. Seven hours later, at two in the morning, the telephone rang. Jan was staying in the next room, so she answered it, and she came in and she said, 'Mummy ... Daddy's free.'

I don't want you to think that because I asked for him to die, God took him. I am quite convinced that God would have taken him whether I'd said that or not, because God knows when he wants you to go. It just happened to coincide that it happened after I'd said 'Please take him in his sleep.' And it's just that I'm so grateful. I know it sounds funny to say that.

We went straight to the hospital, at two in the morning, with dear John Tudor, our minister, coming in from the country – I don't know how he got there as soon as we did. Scottie was on his side, just as I'd left him that tea-time, *just* as I'd left him, and I thought

'Thank you, God.' And I mean, for a woman who loved her husband as much as I loved mine ... and I didn't cry. I looked at him, lying there so peacefully, just as though he were asleep.

We didn't have a funeral for Scottie, we had a Service of Thanksgiving taken by our dear friend John Tudor at Westminster Central Hall Chapel. We had his favourite hymn, 'Oh Happy Day', but really you should have been at our house the night before, when the organist telephoned me and said, 'Is this the right tune for "Oh Happy Day"?' He played it to me, down the telephone, and I said, 'No! No! Oh – no! Hold on. We'll sing it for you.' And there was Jan and me, each on a different telephone extension, going 'O happy day, O happy day when Jesus washed my sins away ...'

'OK, I've got that' he says, so he played it, and we carried on: 'He taught me how to watch and pray, and grow more loving every day ...' we got to about there, and he said, 'All right, I've got it now.' But the next day he said to me, 'Oh, I don't know ... I'm that nervous.' And to be honest, it didn't go quite right. Jan managed to keep going, but there seemed to be more words than tune, if you know what I mean, so some of us kept getting lost ... which was a shame, but there you are.

Everything else was great. We even had some of the jazz music that Scottie used to play when he was a drummer with the band; John Tudor gave a loving talk, then Scottie's best friend, Bill Price, and Daisy, and James, all stood up in turn and said how great Scottie had been and different things about him. There were many dear friends there – some had travelled from Scotland and Europe and even America – and I realised how loved he had been by so many people. And it sounds funny to say this, but it really was a joyous occasion, and at the end, when the coffin was leaving, it seemed just right when Jan shouted out, 'Well done, Dad!'

There were hundreds of letters of condolence, and they all said what a kind man he was. One man wrote who breeds carnations and said he had 'bredded' this beautiful carnation in maroon with a yellow edge, and could he have my permission to call it 'Thora's Scottie'? Of course I said he could. A little later on he sent me a picture of it, and then a little later after that I got whatever it is you get when a new 'breed' is accepted by the Horticultural Society. What a lovely thing to do.

The Ancient Order of Foresters, who had made Scottie and me life members, said that they had built a new summerhouse at one of their old people's homes, and wanted to call it 'James Scott's Summerhouse' and I thought – how he must have been loved.

In the spring of 1995 they were opening new Stroke Association offices in Staffordshire, and they asked me to go and open them, and I was so happy to do it. Scottie and his family spent a long time in Staffordshire when he was young, and his father was MD at the Majestic, and they were known in the Potteries.

There was a church service at which I spoke from my wheelchair, because I had only come out of hospital from having the operation on my leg two days before. They all showed me so much kindness, and they had put a big plaque on the wall, in slate, and it said, 'In memory of Jimmy Scott, husband of Dame Thora Hird.' Jan and I unveiled it, in Staffordshire, and we thought how nice it was that it should be there, where he had spent so many years of his youth.

Do you remember how I told you about the summer before, when Scottie and I were sitting outside Jasmine Cottage having a cup of coffee, and he said, 'Aren't those roses beautiful?' and I said, 'Aren't they lovely!' and he said, 'And aren't we bluddy lucky to have all this?'

The following summer John Tudor, who had just retired from being Minister of the Methodist Central Hall, Westminster, and who has been such a good and dear friend of both Scottie's and mine, and Cynthia, his wife, came down to the cottage one weekend. It was a beautiful day.

William and Jan had dug long narrow trenches all along the front of each of the forty-eight-foot rose beds, edging the path from the front door to the gate. They scattered Scottie's ashes all along each bed, and then covered them. So that's where his ashes are. It's nice they are resting there. John stood between the two beds and spoke about this wonderful man. Then he said, 'Your ashes are going here, Jimmy, because you loved these rose trees so much.' And we said prayers. Just Jan and William, and Rita, Jimmy's sister, were there, and John and Cynthia. I sat in my wheelchair. It was gloriously sunny, and now, every time I go down the path I say, 'Good Morning, luv!'

41

An easy going on

Jan has been a pillar of strength. She comes up on the train from Chichester to see me, and if I can get away for the weekend she'll drive me down to the country in Scottie's car, which is now my car. For a few days I will stay in my little cottage next door to her and William, and we'll visit some of their very dear new neighbours or invite them round for drinks at Jan and William's. We'll all have a lovely, happy time, and then Jan will drive me back to London and return to Chichester by train.

It's when she leaves our house in London to go back to Victoria Station for her train that the stupid ache starts. As she goes out of the door I'll lean out over the hay gate and watch her walk away, up the Mews. She seems to turn back into that little girl who used to walk up the Mews to school. And I can't stop crying. Aren't I daft? Or selfish ... or ungrateful ... or what? I know we shall be on the telephone in a few hours, saying 'Goodnight and God bless' so why the heck do I feel so miserable? However, it has now dawned on me that the reason I dare to feel miserable on such occasions is because I'm *selfish*. I mean that. Just plain, bluddy selfish. Let's have a show of hands on that ... I see. Just as I thought – carried unanimously!

Jan knows that I don't like being on my own. That's why I very rarely am. There's always someone dropping in. But she herself quite enjoys being on her own. I think that's the great difference between us. When Bill's away I'll telephone to say, 'Are you all right?' and she'll say, 'I'm loving it!' Jan likes to have a lot of 'space', as people say these days, but I don't think I really want there to be any space at all.

I'm not a bit fond of my own company. I wish I could be fonder of it sometimes, but no, I don't like Thora Hird very much to be on my own with. I can't think of any time when I've been on my own when I've thought, 'This is it. This is how to be.' I'm always so glad if there's somebody coming in for a coffee or something.

It isn't that I hate myself, and I can't blame Jimmy for this, but you see there has always been somebody there, all my married life. I'm so used to saying, 'Oh, I'll just put the kettle on.' Why do I need someone to tell that to? I don't know why it bothers me so much. I just don't like being on my own. And there's nothing I can add to that, only I shall perhaps underline it in this book: *I do not like being on my own!*

Scottie died just before our fifty-ninth wedding anniversary. I've been a very lucky lady to have had a happy and blissful marriage that lasted so long. I had no intention of pouring my sorrow onto anybody, particularly not onto Jan, because I knew how brave she was being for my sake. Nobody could have loved her father more than Jan loved her Daddy. I do sometimes feel depressed, but then I'll look at her, standing there, and she'll suddenly look just like a school mistress.

She can be quite bossy, my daughter! She'll say to me, 'Shoulders back! Come on! Shoulders back!' when I'm only walking from the dining room to the kitchen to wash up or something. 'Don't be bending down like that!' 'No, Mother. Don't use your stick like that – do it like this.' I said to her the other day, 'Oh, please, do let me do something right just for once ...' and she said, 'And don't be sorry for yourself!' So you see I can't win.

Only I do know that she loves me ... As I sit here writing this I can see her coming up the garden path, and this will be to *command* me to stop working for a few minutes and come and have a coffee. Which I shall obey with pleasure.

The strange thing about love is – it goes on. It doesn't die. It is a fact, you know, that my love for my husband has helped me over losing him. I love him no less, although he isn't actually with me, and I think of Jimmy's love for me so often. Wherever I've got to in life, wherever that may be, I wouldn't have got there without the love of my husband. He was always just that little supporting bit at my shoulder, and he still is now. I don't mean I see him – but I feel him there. I have photographs of him all round the house, where he is looking straight into camera and laughing – he had a good laugh – and it always looks as though he's laughing at me, and believe you me, he's with me *so much*. I just know he's there. I say 'Morning, Scottie!' to his photograph every day, and I always say 'Goodnight, God bless, Scottie.' And if that's my way of easing the pain a little – well, it's a very good way.

As I've already described, early in 1995, a few months after Scottie died, I went with Jan on pilgrimage to Biblical sites in Jordan. We'd arranged it long before, and Scottie should have come with us. One day we were standing at the top of Mount Nebo, where Moses stood and looked out over the Promised Land for the first time. We could see Galilee. There was a little Byzantine church which tradition says is built over Moses' tomb. It was like those very old cottages, wattle-and-daub, and inside there weren't any pews, just long forms, with leather tops. No backs. As I went in, I said to Jan, 'This is the sort of church your Daddy would have liked. He would have said, "Now this is a *real* church."' There was nothing, really, about it at all, only, I don't know, a feeling of love in it.

I sat down and – like many of us who've lost the ones we love – you sometimes can't cry until a few weeks after. I didn't with my mother. Sitting in this little church I suddenly thought, 'Oh, I'm going to cry.' I said to Jan, 'I'm going to cry' and she said, 'Well cry, Mummy,' and put her arms round my shoulders.

But, as I've told you, when I was doing the programme *Praise Be!* I got so many sad letters, and I really mean heartbreaking, and I'd read them, and cry, and Scottie would come in the room and he would say, 'Now, come on.' That's three words: now, come, on – which meant – 'We don't want any crying.' I sat on this form in this little wattle-and-daub church, and I felt the tears starting at the base of my stomach and coming up – the heartbreak I felt in my body – and just about a foot in front of me, I don't mean I saw anything, there was nothing to see, but as clearly as I'm saying this to you, I heard him say, 'Now come on.' And I stopped. I didn't cry.

Jan said to me when we got outside, 'Maybe a good cry would have done you good.' I said, 'No, your father told me not to.'

This book should be coming out in about June 1996, and I'll just have had my eighty-fifth birthday – DV! Because I hope I don't have to tell you – I'm not ready to go just yet! I still love life, and love my work, and as long as I can go on working and giving people a bit of pleasure either by acting or, if the day comes when I'm not asked to play any more parts, by writing, then that's what I shall be doing. My prayer is the same as the one written on the tomb of Winifred Holtby, the Christian novelist who died in 1935:

> *God give me work till my life shall end –*
> *And life till my work is done.*

Amen to that, say I.

Meanwhile, now I've finished this book and am about to send it off to my publishers, I'm off on a Christmas cruise with my daughter, and in the Spring we'll be off again together, leading another pilgrimage to the Holy Land, along with Rob Marshall. And, do you know, there's still as much acting work as ever in the pipeline? Never a dull moment, eh?

I have so often been asked by journalists who are interviewing me for newspaper or magazine articles, 'Would you have rather been where you are now when you were young, or how you were then – now?' Well, I'll tell you what I tell them. If my life was to start all over again, *I wouldn't alter a thing*.

Appendix

The Highlights of Thora's Life and Career

1911 Born on Sunday 28 May
Debut stage appearance at six weeks old at the Royalty Theatre, Morecambe

1921 Becomes Morecambe's May Queen

1926 First paid summer job at Morecambe's Central Pier Music Shop

1927 Works in her father's office, Central Pier, Morecambe

1928 Sales assistant/model to hair accessories company for Winter Gardens Trade Fair
Cashier at Co-Operative, Lancaster

1931 Joins Morecambe Repertory Company at the Royalty Theatre

1933 Meets future husband, James 'Scottie' Scott, drummer with the Winter Gardens Orchestra

1937 Scottie and Thora are married on 3 May
'Discovered' as a film actress by George Formby

1939 Film debut in Ealing Studios' *The Black Sheep of Whitehall* starring Will Hay
The Big Blockade, film starring Michael Redgrave and Frank Cellier
Careless Talk Costs Lives, Ealing Studios' war-time information film

1944 West-End debut in *No Medals*, Vaudeville Theatre, followed by film version of the play *The Weaker Sex*

1948 *Flowers for Living*, New Lindsay Theatre, London. First major role, playing Mrs Holmes

1949 *Fools Rush In*, film co-starring Sally Ann Howes

1950 *The Queen Came Riding By*, Duke of York's Theatre, London. Thora plays Emmie Slee

1951 *The Happy Family*, in Festival of Britain Year, co-starring with Henry Kendall, Duchess Theatre, London

1954 Meets Sir Charlie Chaplin, and has tea at the Savoy Hotel

1955 *The Queen Came Riding By*, BBC television version of the play in which Thora plays Emmie Slee and daughter Janette plays Kitty Tape.
Saturday Night at the Crown, Oldham Repertory Theatre and National Tour
The Love Match, Rank Films, co-starring Arthur Askey

1956 *The Love Match* tour, summer season at Grand Theatre Blackpool and transfer to Palace Theatre, London, then on to Victoria Palace, London

	Tiger on the Tail, film, Ealing Studios *One Good Turn*, film co-starring Norman Wisdom
1957	West-End run of *Saturday Night at the Crown*, Garrick Theatre, London Seriously injured in car accident
1958	*The Love Match*, film version of the play *For Better, for Worse*, film
1960	*Saturday Night at the Crown*, Scarborough season
1961	*Happy Days*, twenty-two weeks, twice nightly, Grand Theatre, Blackpool
1962	Scottie writes *The Best Laid Schemes*, which Thora stars in for the Blackpool season at the Grand Theatre *A Kind of Loving*, film directed by John Schlesinger and co-starring Alan Bates
1963	*The Best Laid Schemes* transfers to Torquay for summer season *The Bed*, a pilot series that eventually became the highly popular *Meet the Wife* Thora's *This Is Your Life* with Eamonn Andrews *All Things Bright and Beautiful* national tour *The Best Laid Schemes* transfers to Bournemouth for summer season
1966	Stars alongside Harry Secombe, Jimmy Tarbuck and Russ Conway in *London Laughs* at the London Palladium in a thirty-two week season of twice-nightly shows. *One Born Every Minute*, BBC 13-part radio series

Call My Bluff, BBC television series
Dixon of Dock Green with Jack Warner, BBC television series
The Good Old Days, BBC television series
Jackanory, BBC television series
Late-Night Line Up, BBC television series
Television advert for Biotex, ATV

1967 Plays the Nurse in *Romeo and Juliet* in the BBC's Play of the Month series
First Lady, BBC television drama series filmed on location in Barnsley

1970 *No, No Nanette*, Theatre Royal, Drury Lane, playing Pauline

1972 *The Nightcomers*, film directed by Michael Winner

1976 First part of autobiography, *Scene and Hird*, published

1977 Begins *Praise Be*, BBC television series that ran for seventeen years

1978 Plays Ivy Unsworth for *In Loving Memory*, ITV television series co-starring Chris Beeney, Avis Bunnage and Joan Sims

1979 *Flesh and Blood*, BBC television drama series

1980 Starts filming *Last of the Summer Wine*
Has both hips replaced at the age of 69

1982 *Hallelujah*, Yorkshire Television comedy series based on the Salvation Army

1985 Awarded OBE on 1 November

1986 Stars in Alan Bennett's *Afternoon Off* and *Me, I'm Afraid of Virginia Woolf*

1987 Thora and Scottie celebrate their Golden Wedding Anniversary on 3 May
Stars in Alan Bennett's *Cream Cracker under the Settee,* part of the *Talking Heads* BBC television series

1987 Wins Best Actress at the BAFTA awards for *Cream Cracker under the Settee*

1988 New breed of rose named in Thora's honour at the Chelsea Flower Show

1990 Lunch with the Queen at Buckingham Palace

1992 Becomes Dame of the Most Excellent Order of the British Empire
Heart bypass operation at the age of 81

1993 Becomes first woman member of the Royal Television Society's Hall of Fame
Receives 'Local Hero' award in her home town, Morecambe.
South Bank Show celebration of Thora's life, presented by Melvyn Bragg
Thora on the Broad and Narrow, BBC television series filmed at Pinewood studios

1994 Celebrates 83rd Birthday by the sea of Galilee
Scottie dies at 88 years of age

1995 Femur surgically reinforced with iron rod at 83 years of age
Voice-over for cuppa-soup advert on ITV that runs for several years

1996 Second half of autobiography, *Is It Thora?*, published

1997 *Thora's Book of Bygones* published

1998 *Lost for Words*, Yorkshire Television, co-starring Pete Postlewaite
Dinner Ladies with Victoria Wood and Pozzitive Productions for BBC Television

Numerous other Appearances include:

Film
Tobacco Road, 1941
Maytime in Mayfair, 1949
The Great Game, 1953
Over the Odds, 1960
Term of Trial, 1962
Rattle of a Simple Man, 1964
Some Will, Some Won't, 1970
The Entertainer, 1975
Consuming Passions, 1988
The Tailor of Gloucester, 1989
Little Pig Robinson, 1992
The Good Guys, 1993
The Wedding Gift, 1993

Television
Momento Mori, BBC

All Creatures Great and Small, BBC
Pat and Margaret, BBC
The Queen's Nose, BBC
Wide Eyed and Legless, BBC
Heartbeat, ITV
Intensive Care, ITV
Perfect Scoundrels, TVS

Awards include:

BAFTA Award for Best Actress for Alan Bennett's *Cream Cracker under the Settee*
The Pye Award for Comedy
The Royal Variety Club award for contribution to the world of entertainment
Special Silver BAFTA Award for services to the entertainment industry
Help The Aged Award for services to charity
Tunstall Golden Award for services to charity
Woman of the Year Award for services to charity
Doctor of Letters at Lancaster University

We want to hear from you. Please send your comments about this book to us in care of the address below. Thank you.

GRAND RAPIDS, MICHIGAN 49530 USA

WWW.ZONDERVAN.COM